The Brilliance
of Swedish Glass,
1918–1939

The Brilliance of
Swedish Glass,
1918–1939
An Alliance
of Art and
Industry

Anne-Marie Ericsson
Märta Holkers
Gunnel Holmér
Maths Isacson
Lars Magnusson
Derek E. Ostergard
Clarence Burton Sheffield, Jr.
Nina Stritzler-Levine
Elsebeth Welander-Berggren
Nina Weibull

Derek E. Ostergard and Nina Stritzler-Levine, *Editors*

Published for The Bard Graduate Center for Studies in the Decorative Arts, New York,
by Yale University Press, New Haven and London

This catalogue is published in conjunction with the exhibition
"The Brilliance of Swedish Glass, 1918-1939:
An Alliance of Art and Industry"
held at the Bard Graduate Center
for Studies in the Decorative Arts
from November 21, 1996
to March 2, 1997

Exhibition curators:
Gunnel Holmér, Derek E. Ostergard, and Nina Stritzler-Levine

Project directors:
Derek E. Ostergard and Nina Stritzler-Levine

Project assistants: Lisa Arcomano and Vincent Plescia

Catalogue production:
Martina D'Alton, Roberta Fineman, Alice Hopkins, and Michael Shroyer, New York;
Sally Salvesen, London

Translations:
Charles S. Fineman

Composition by U.S. Lithograph typographers, New York

Typeface and jacket image selected by Derek E. Ostergard

Printed in Italy

Library of Congress Catalog number: 96-078504

ISBN: 0-300-07005-5 (cloth); 0-300-07044-6 (paper)

On the cover:
Footed covered urn (detail of cat. no. 70), designed by Edward Askenberg, 1929; Johansfors
Glassworks. (Länsförsäkring Kronoberg, Växjö, Sweden)

Frontispiece:
Footed covered urn (cat. no. 70), designed by Edward Askenberg, 1929; Johansfors glassworks. (Länsförsäkring Kronoberg, Växjö, Sweden)

Endpapers:
Details from an urn with underplate designed by Simon Gate, 1920; engraved by Gustaf
Abels. (Mrs. Agnes Heller Collection, Kungstenen Foundation, Stockholm University)

Funding for
"The Brilliance of Swedish Glass, 1918–1939:
An Alliance of Art and Industry"
has been generously provided
by the following:

Orrefors/Kosta Boda

Skandinaviska Enskilda Banken

The American Scandinavian Foundation

The Consulate General of Sweden, New York City

The Swedish Institute

Scandinavian Airlines

An anonymous donor

Contents

Foreword

In the long history of glassmaking, few passages have equaled the magnificent glass that was produced in Sweden in the early part of the twentieth century. Glass is a fascinating material, beginning with its dramatic creation in the fire of the furnace. It can be delicate or monumental, ethereal or earthy, both beautiful and functional. Between 1918 and 1939, Swedish glassmakers forged an alliance with their nation's leading artists and explored the full range of artistic and functional possibilities in the medium. In the process, Swedish glass grew to international prominence, becoming one of the most important representations of modernism in the decorative arts.

"The Brilliance of Swedish Glass, 1918–1939: An Alliance of Art and Industry" presents some of the finest examples of Sweden's extraordinary achievements in glass and serves as a starting point for an in-depth examination of an exciting chapter in the history of twentieth-century design. This subject is especially appropriate to The Bard Graduate Center. Many aesthetic and technical issues that came to define modernism during the period between the world wars are evident in Swedish glass production at that time. Their study requires an interdisciplinary approach that encompasses political history, economic and social history, and many aspects of the history of twentieth-century art and design. The collaboration between Swedish artists and manufacturers, the persistent role of craftsmanship in Swedish design, the theoretical underpinnings of Swedish design, and the relationship between traditionalism and modernism are explored through a series of essays as well as detailed catalogue texts for the objects in the exhibition. A primary focus is the work emanating from Orrefors Glassworks, the leading manufacturer of art glass from 1918 to 1939.

A project of this scope and ambition demands the collaboration of numerous individuals. Foremost I would like to acknowledge the generous support of the exhibition donors: Orrefors Kosta Boda; Skandinaviska Enskilda Banken; Scandinavian Airlines; the Consulate General of Sweden, New York City; The American Scandinavian Foundation; The Swedish Institute; and an anonymous donor.

Three curators have worked together to bring this project to fruition. The idea of presenting an exhibition of Swedish glass was originally proposed in 1992 by Nina Stritzler-Levine before the inauguration of The Bard Graduate Center. The exhibition itself was shaped in its final form by Derek E. Ostergard, associate director of The Bard Graduate Center, who brought connoisseurship and a knowledge of glass history to the project. Gunnel Holmér, curator of glass at the Smålands Museum, Swedish Glass Museum, Växjö, Sweden, joined the curatorial effort. I am especially grateful to Ms. Holmér, who has been an incomparable partner in this endeavor, sharing her extensive knowledge, and providing ready assistance with many details. Karl Johan Krantz, director, the Smålands Museum, supported the project from the beginning.

"The Brilliance of Swedish Glass" includes a remarkable selection of loan objects, including many works never before shown in a public exhibition. I am tremendously thankful for the generosity of the institutions and private collectors in Scandinavia, Europe, and the United States: Ms. Birgitta Crafoord; Mrs. Brita Hellner Kjellberg; the Collection Görander; Länsförsäkring Kronoberg, Växjö, Sweden; Bo Knutsson Art and Antiques, Sweden; the Orrefors and Kosta Museums; The Smålands Museum, Swedish Glass Museum, Växjö, Sweden; Mrs. Agnes Hellner Collection, Kungstenen Foundation, Stockholm University; Nationalmuseum, Stockholm; The Oslo Museum of Applied Art; Musée d'Art Moderne de la Ville de Paris; The Royal Ontario Museum; The Cleveland Museum of Art; The Detroit Institute of Arts; The Metropolitan Museum of Art; The Newark Museum; and The Museum of Art, Rhode Island School of Design.

My thanks go to the authors who have contributed a high level of scholarship to this catalogue: Lars Magnusson, Maths Isacson, Clarence Burton Sheffield, Jr., Anne-Marie Ericsson, Nina Weibull, Gunnel Holmér, Elsebeth Welander-Berggren, Märta Holkers, and Derek E. Ostergard. The very difficult task of translating the Swedish manuscripts and critical research materials was undertaken by Charles S. Fineman, Robert Dunlop, and Miranda Mirchanek.

The Bard Graduate Center has brought together a talented and committed production staff: Martina D'Alton, Michael Shroyer, Gloria Dougherty, Roberta Fineman, Alice Hopkins, and U.S. Lithography, typogra-

Introduction

Since the end of the First World War, Swedish glass has been synonymous with excellence in design and craftsmanship. It has become the most highly acclaimed product of the Swedish applied arts industries in the international marketplace, equaling the work of the finest glassmakers elsewhere. Its emergence in the period between the two world wars also had profound repercussions beyond the applied arts. Through exports and exhibitions Sweden's glassworks helped to spread the doctrine of Swedish sensibility and design, and by mid-century "Swedish Modern" was at the forefront of international design, representing a progressive approach to living as much as to design.

At the beginning of the twentieth century, however, Sweden and its glass industry still lagged behind the rest of Europe in terms of industrial growth, and the country was without an international presence in applied arts. Although there were many flourishing glassworks, their products were largely derivative and sometimes poorly made. The first stirrings of change came after the 1914 Baltic Exhibition in Malmö. This exposition may not have been truly international in scope, but it offered an opportunity for Swedish applied arts to establish a place in the wider design community of the region. Instead, Swedish work, including its glassware, was sharply criticized for the conservative, outdated aesthetic that it represented. The most outspoken critics were members of Svenska Slöjdföreningen (The Swedish Society of Craft and Industrial Design). They called for a concerted effort to elevate Swedish design by forging an alliance between art and industry. Through the society's intercession, artists and manufacturers united to produce "more beautiful things for for everyday use." Art had come to the factory.

The Swedish glassworks were the first to recognize the benefit that would derive from working directly with artists. Soon after the Baltic Exhibition, Orrefors hired two promising painters—Simon Gate and Edward Hald—the first in a line of talented innovators. The success of this and other collaborations between the glassworks and artists may be attributed in part to the nature of the glassmaking process in Sweden's glassworks. Although often quite large in scale, most glass factories straddled the line between serial and handmade production. The industry continued to extol the individual craftsman, and artists were respected and nurtured in a collaborative environment.

This evolution of Sweden's glass industry and its embrace of modernism parallel the transformation of Sweden from an isolated, agrarian society to a modern industrial nation. The glassworks reflected pronounced shifts in the socioeconomic and political life of the nation, and their fortunes would have a reciprocal effect on the nation. As part of a thriving economy they had an impact on the labor markets and the structure of rural Swedish society and contributed to the gross national product.

Sweden's neutrality spared it the most devastating consequences of the First World War. Not only had the conflict redrawn the map of Europe and altered the hierarchy of social classes, but it also reshaped attitudes toward art and society. In the aftermath, changes in the ideological and aesthetic framework of the European design community were carefully observed by Swedish artists, designers, and craftspeople working in the glassworks. Initially borrowing aesthetic elements from the elitist modernism of the French, the Swedes produced a unique brand of modernism. It was as appropriate for one-of-a-kind luxury pieces as it was for mass-produced objects, but glass was its first and foremost expression.

By the late 1920s glass had become the barometer of Swedish modernist design, helping to define the wide parameters of the Swedish response to modernism. By that time the Swedish design community had begun to pursue a more egalitarian approach to design. Well-made functional objects, devoid of the ornament that had made Swedish glass so popular in the 1920s, expanded the base of Swedish modernism in the 1930s while still embracing the more elitist work. Orrefors contributed considerably to these developments and was rapidly becoming the leading Swedish glassworks. A relatively young factory, it was unhampered by tradition, administered by enlightened management, and fortunate in its choice of artists. Many of the technical advances and the governing aesthetics in art glass originated in the Orrefors factory. Other Swedish glassworks followed their lead, and some, such as Kosta, an older factory, made significant contributions of their own. In the process the glassworks began to assume individual identities that became stronger internationally than the notion of a general, cohesive Swedish design movement.

The stunning ascendancy of Swedish glass during the interwar years can be traced through contemporary design journals, the many international exhibitions of applied arts, and the commercial success of Swedish glass in the international marketplace. While in Sweden itself there was almost a symbiotic relationship between the glass industry and the nation, in the international applied arts arena Swedish glass was considered a separate entity, judged on its own merits and not because of its national identity. Wherever it was shown, Swedish glass received critical acclaim and conferred great prestige on the nation.

Although the growth of Sweden's glass industry diminished during the Second World War, Swedish design regained its position of international prominence in the postwar period. As the twentieth century draws to a close, Swedish glass continues to represent a most remarkable union of art and industry. The artistic and technical complexities of the medium and the broader implications of its development in Sweden are examined in depth in "The Brilliance of Swedish Glass, 1918–1939: An Alliance of Art and Industry."

Many individuals have been responsible for bringing this project to fruition. Gunnel Holmér, curator at the Glass Museum of Sweden in Växjö, has been a partner in all aspects of the project. She assumed a wide array of responsibilities, from object selection to catalogue preparation and shipping arrangements. Gunnel's kindness and willingness to participate in all decisions has helped to refine this project in the course of its long preparation.

At The Bard Graduate Center the greatest support was given by Lisa Arcomano and Vincent Plescia. They displayed an unparalleled dedication to the project and consummate professionalism. Lisa's experience with catalogue preparation and the assembly of exhibitions has been invaluable. She handled critical negotiations with great finesse. The project benefited greatly from Vincent's extensive knowledge of the decorative arts and his rigorous methodology.

In January 1996 Elsebeth Welander-Berggren joined the project as curatorial associate in Stockholm. She provided enormous help with the final revisions of the object list while establishing contact with principal lenders in Sweden. At Orrefors Mona Engström, company archivist, and Per Larsson, the company's photographer contributed greatly to the final stages of the project, confirming many important details. Per met the challenge of photographing that most difficult of all medium, glass, and set a standard for photographic work in this catalogue. At Stockholm University, Nina Weilbull was indispensable on many fronts. She provided us with the opportunity to examine the Hellner Collection, the source of many important loans. Per Bergström, the university's photographer, also produced exceptional illustrations in a timely fashion. Mikael Ernstell, curator of decorative arts at the Nationalmuseum, supported this exhibition and secured significant loans. Barbro Houstadius was also very helpful. At the Museum of Applied Arts in Oslo, Anniken Thue, director, Widar Halen, associate director, and Randi Gaustad, curator of glass, provided essential documentation and loaned two of the earliest pieces of Orrefors glass to enter a public collection. In Lund, Sweden, Birgitta Crafoord made her collection available to study important issues of connoisseurship. Loans from her collection form the core of the latter part of the exhibition. In Sweden we received considerable support from the following individuals, who generously loaned works from their collections: Mr. and Mrs. Lennart Görander, Dick Söderlund, Brita Hellner Kjellberg, and Bo Knutsson.

The catalogue brings together a fine group of scholars who have made significant contributions: Lars Magnusson, Maths Isacson, Gunnel Holmér, Märta Holkers, Clarence Burton Sheffield, Jr., Nina Weilbull, Johan Mårtelius, and Elsebeth Welander-Berggren.

In the United States and Canada, colleagues at several institutions were generous with research information, time, and loans: Ian Wardropper, Ghenete Zelleke, and Nora Buriks at The Art Institute of Chicago; Henry Hawley and Carol Chula at The Cleveland Museum of Art; Stephen van Dyk at the Cooper Hewitt Museum, New York; Mary Ann Wilkinson at The Detroit Institute of Arts; Sophie Krebs and Suzanne Pagé at the Musée d'Art Moderne de la Ville de Paris; Ulysses Dietz and William Peniston at The Newark Museum; Martha Deitz, Jane Adlin, and Jared Goss at The Metropolitan Museum of Art; Thomas Michie and Jayne Stokes at the Museum of Art, Rhode Island School of Design; and Peter Kaellgren, Brian Musselwhite, and Howard Collinson at The Royal Ontario Museum. Additional assistance was provided by Gregory M. Wittkopp and Ryan Wieber at Cranbrook Art Museum; Betsy Baldwin and Barbara File, archives, and Mary Doherty, photography department, at The Metropolitan Museum of Art; Marianne Aav at the Museum of Applied Arts, Helsinki, Finland; Davira Targin at The Toledo Museum of Art; and Marianne Lamonica and Pedro Figuerdo at the Wolfsonian Foundation.

The project would not have been realized without the generosity and support of many individuals. Dag S. Ahlander, consul general, and Görel Bogarde, deputy consul general, at the Swedish Consulate in New York, provided enthusiasm, funding, and important contacts in Sweden and the United States. Orrefors Kosta Boda served as a principal sponsor and lender; Gören Bernhoff, managing director, Anders Björck, director of product development, and Oyvind Saetre, president, Orrefors North America, gave their time, support, and enthusiasm, Margareta Artéus, manager of public relations at Orrefors, was also very helpful. Jan Forbes at the Orrefors Kosta Boda Gallery in New York and Richard Kaplan, former president of Orrefors, North America, provided assistance. Karl Johann Krantz, director of the Glass Museum of Sweden was an early and enthusiastic supporter of this project.

Others who provided considerable support include: Birgitta Lönnell, Christina Hamacher, Catharina Mannheimer, and Harriet Lindh at The Swedish Institute; Kerstin Wickman and Anita Christiansen at Form Magazine in Sweden; Helena Smedberg at Bukowski Auktioner; Helen Aravantinos at the Leeman Agency; Jennifer Opie and Reino Liefkas at the Victoria and Albert Museum, London; and Anders Reihnér, Gunilla von Arbin, and Lynn Springer Roberts. We are indebted to the research and scholarship of Helmut Ricke, whose numerous publications on Swedish glass were invaluable.

Other individuals at The Bard Graduate Center helped to complete the project: Lisa Podos, director of public programs; Linda Hartley, director of development; Tim Mulligan, director of communications; Bobbie Xeureb, chief librarian; Jim Finch, director of finance; Steve Waterman, chief preparator, and the entire installation crew; Peter Gammie, Eileen McDonagh, Doru Padure, Jill Gustafson, Susan Wall, Donika Volkert, Marcial Lavina, Greg Negron, Kelly Moody, Carolee Goldstein, Miao Chen, Orlando Diaz, Jorge San Pablo, Terence Lyons, Chandler Small, Kenneth Talley, Melissa Post, and Ronald Labaco.

Production of the catalogue was the work of Martina D'Alton, Michael Shroyer, Stephanie Salomon, Alice Hopkins, Roberta Fineman, Glorieaux Dougherty, and U.S. Lithograph, typographers. We are grateful to Charles S. Fineman, Robert Dunlop, and Miranda Mirchanek for their translations of Swedish texts.

Finally, our thanks to Susan Weber Soros who made the first trip to Sweden in December 1992 to determine the feasibility of this project and whose enthusiasm for Swedish glass has been considerable.

Derek E. Ostergard
Nina Stritzler-Levine

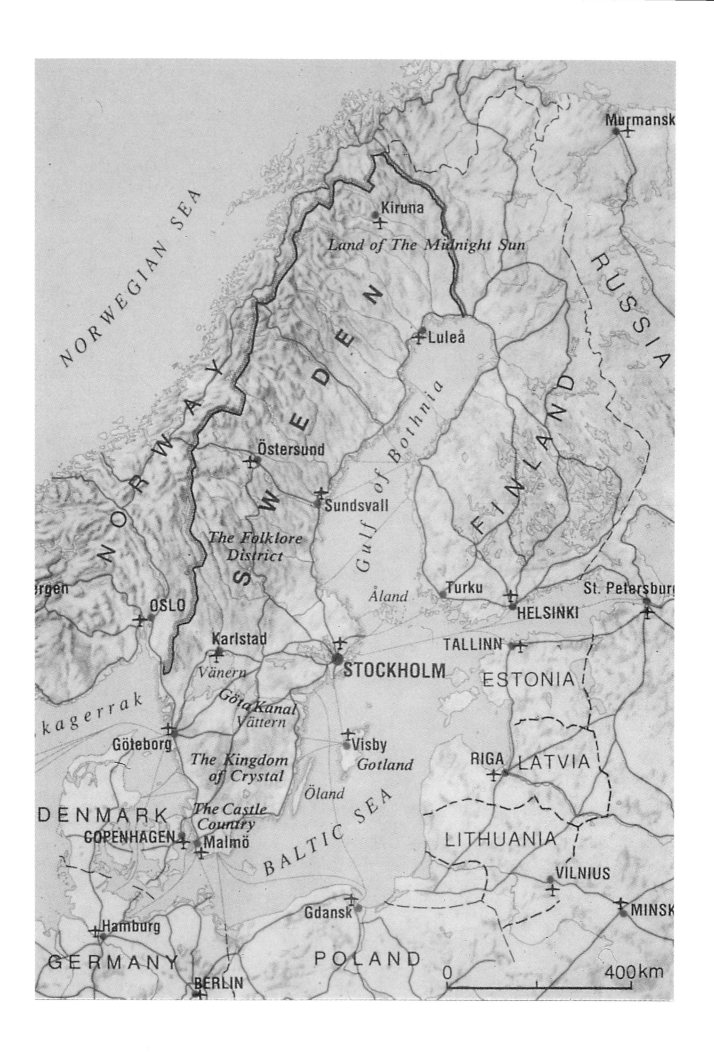

CHAPTER ONE

Sweden and the Swedish Model, 1900–1950

Lars Magnusson

Despite periods of rapid change and cautious adaptation to the political and economic realities of the outside world, Swedish society since the end of the nineteenth century has been structured and characterized by continuity and compromise. Swedish culture, marked by a high degree of homogeneity, allows Swedes to enjoy considerable solidarity with one another and with their history. Their shared agrarian background seems as close as the next summer, when most urban Swedes flee to country homes to be reborn as farmers and tillers of the soil. Many of the old traditions thus live on, evolving with the times.

The Swedish Model

Sweden's special character has been described as "the Swedish model," a phenomenon based on a society built in progressive steps through compromise and founded on the principles of a collective democracy. The Swedish model fuses pragmatism with the security of a social welfare state, creating an environment that has been called "the people's home." Sweden is also known as the "land of the middle way" and the incarnation of the welfare state.[1] Not surprisingly, Sweden has been studied as a model for advanced welfare policy in the Western world, especially in the areas of social policy and full employment.[2]

In many ways, however, the concept of a Swedish model is difficult to define. A somewhat narrow interpretation centers on the specific relationship between the employers' and workers' organizations in the labor market following the Second World War. This relationship was characterized by a relative absence of conflict between the various groups. Another view interprets the Swedish model as the social welfare policy that was formulated in the 1930s and affected the populace as a whole.[3]

Underlying both interpretations, and underpinning not only the peaceful relationships in the labor movement but the structure of Swedish welfare as well, is a spirit of compromise between social classes. This has been integral to Sweden's policies and economy in the twentieth century and has historical roots that go back several centuries. "State" and "society" are synonymous concepts, the state being an indispensable part of Sweden's social structure. Medieval Sweden lacked a powerful class of feudal nobility, and most peasants remained independent, although they did not enjoy complete equality. Despite differences in income and property, however, an egalitarian and homogeneous spirit was generally in clear evidence[4] and remained unshaken by the onset of the Industrial Revolution, which occurred at the end of the nineteenth century in Sweden. The relatively swift pace of industrialization, especially after 1870, actually served to strengthen this homogeneous national character. This was the case with the glassworks, as well as with industry as a whole. As elsewhere a broad proletariat was created, and an exodus from agriculture occurred. While the top of the social pyramid was very small, the base was broad and relatively homogeneous.[5]

Another part of the equation that makes up the Swedish model is the role of the Swedish state. Since the sixteenth century, the power and influence of the state has steadily increased. In particular, state- and town-administered welfare programs, which became cornerstones in the Swedish model, are based on a general trust in the state's ability to govern the country fairly and successfully. The state's growing authoritarianism, however, only partly explains the distinctive nature of Sweden's society. State control has been tempered by a relatively high level of democracy in Swedish society. In contrast to many other West European countries, Sweden's constitutional monarchy is based on a longstanding democratic-popular tradition. This has helped to stimulate consensus and to nurture the ability to make decisions and compromises between the various groups in the country. Swedish democracy has a collective bias, in contrast to, for example, the United States or Great Britain, where democracy of a more individualist stance dominates. This creates a great deal of maneuvering room for various organized interests in Sweden and makes corporatism a major component of the Swedish model.

The Trade Union Movement

Sweden is also the promised land of popular movements, especially the trade and temperance unions and, even earlier, the nonconformist Free Church movement.[6] The establishment of popular movements hastened the development of organized interests that demanded reforms in social policy. Social action became a natural part of the collective democracy—with corporative strands—that emerged. The popular movements had other important functions. Free Churches and temperance lodges nurtured democracy by teaching techniques for conducting meetings and for organizing votes. Operating on the principle of "one man, one vote," they also taught how compromise

could achieve more than confrontation. In the "historic compromise" between capital and labor and in the creation of welfare in the twentieth century, these popular movements undoubtedly played a major role.

Thus Swedish society was better prepared for the turbulent social changes brought about by the Industrial Revolution. A series of moves and countermoves occurred between workers and business: when workers found the wage structure to be much too "open," they readily organized into trade unions; to counter the unions as well as to regulate competitive conditions on markets, owners organized into special interest groups; and to protect itself against these special interests, the state in turn chose to regulate competitive conditions, guaranteeing an open agreement through legislation. Similarly the state found that unimpeded competition within the export trade often led to unwanted consequences. To support "its" industry, the state introduced protectionist customs taxes. The period from the 1890s onward became one of protectionism, and economic policy became aggressively nationalistic.

Industrialization and the concentration of capital increased, and there emerged a kind of "organized capitalism"[7] not just in Sweden, where it was especially powerful, but elsewhere in the Western world. There are several explanations for its strength in Sweden where industrial capitalism was always based on a small number of rapidly growing businesses, especially in mechanical engineering, the lumber industry, steel, and paper and pulp. The middle class, which included most business owners, constituted only a fraction of the population. Furthermore, as industrialization occurred rapidly, society's infrastructure became outdated and required a radical new construction; this increased the demand for regulation and intervention in the name of the public good.

Until 1870 Sweden had, to an overwhelming extent, been an agrarian society with all the problems that this implies, especially among the landless rural population. As the country rapidly shifted to industrialization, new social challenges came to the forefront. Fast-growing industries and towns, for example, created sanitation and public health problems that were often difficult to solve. The new factories required a permanent workforce, unlike earlier times when industrial labor had often been seasonal in nature. Full-time workers and their families became completely dependent on the workplace for their livelihood and welfare. During economic depressions or when modern industry consolidated and reorganized, workers could not fall back on agriculture—even if it had provided a meager living at best. After 1900 conditions were considered so abysmal that the principal secretary on the Emigration Committee, Gustav Sundbärg, warned that more and more people would be forced to emigrate. "What is needed is a general economic shake-up among our people," he said.[8]

It was in this environment that the trade union movement found ready support. Yet the organization of the workers was not as simple as trade union leader Sigfrid Hansson argued in his seminal study of Swedish trade unions when he wrote, "Industrialism and the trade union movement are practically associated with one another."[9] In fact workers in the heavy industries such as lumber, iron, or steel were rarely leaders in establishing trade unions. Rather it was those elite, skilled workers in trades such as printing, metalworking, and carpentry, and in the machine shops, who first organized in the 1890s with a view toward drawing up collective agreements with employers. The glassworkers achieved a nationwide federation of workers in 1898, building on a number of small local unions. Many of the early trade unions established by typographers, carpenters, and metalworkers originated in liberal worker federations and similar organizations.[10]

The characteristic division among these traditional crafts left a mark on the organizational structure of the trade union movement in its early stages: trade unions were initially organized according to specialization as the earlier federations had been. It was not until the second and third decades of the twentieth century that the so-called industry principle triumphed, whereby membership in a trade union was based on one's place of work, not the specific trade. This reflected the ascendancy of new groups within the trade union movement who came from the heavy industry of the twentieth century.

The modern trade union in Sweden has been compared to an open cartel whose primary mission is to limit competition for labor and regulate pay scales. In the early stage of the movement, however, goals also included principles of social reform. From this, a powerful symbiosis developed between the trade unions and policy branches of the government that has been characteristic of Sweden's labor relations. In order to strengthen the socialist component and coordinate demands for collective bargaining and general wage demands, Svenska Landsorganisationen (LO; The Swedish Trade Union Confederation) was founded as the Swedish trade union movement's central organization in 1898. In response, owners and employers organized into special interest groups that were initially local or industry specific. The most powerful of these was the Verkstadsföreningen (Machine Shop Federation) founded in 1902. But as the trade union movement grew stronger and more centralized, employers felt the need for a corresponding central organization, and in 1902 the Svenska Arbetsgivareföreningen (SAF; Swedish Employers Association) was founded.

The first demand that the trade unions initiated was for generating collective agreements. Starting with the first central Machine Shop Agreement in 1905, collective bargains were drawn up between employers and trade unions in most branches of industry. At the national level as well there were negotiations between the LO and the SAF. In the so-called December Compromise of 1906 employers recognized workers' rights to join trade unions in exchange for the recognition by workers of employers' right "to manage and distribute work." In succession these organized interests built up institutions for negotiations and compromises and created a set of regulations with several fixed rules and standards. Where the trade union movement was concerned, the collective agreement meant that their interests had been recognized. But employers also needed SAF as their central organization; for them a more regulated labor market would counteract reckless competition for labor and in the long run would create a more stable environment. The existence of the trade unions and employer organizations helped thwart spontaneous strikes and other problems of an unregulated labor market.

A New Role for the State

Industrialization and economic change also contributed to creating a new role for the state and its institutions. Heavy industry required better railways and roads and new housing for its workers. It demanded that competitive restrictions and trade agreements be respected to prevent destructive competition and assure respect for trademarks, patent regulations, and so on. Now that new products depended on industrial labor performed by workers in cities and towns, new demands were made on the way the society in general was organized. Furthermore, the successive dissolution of the traditional social security system for families and local communities created the need for new social programs, especially to protect children, the elderly, the sick, and the unemployed.

In Sweden in the second half of the nineteenth century the functions of state and local agencies began to change. Railroads and postal systems, prerequisites for economic expansion, were already being run by the state. A modern educational system was established and public welfare was reorganized. Unsanitary conditions and their effects in densely populated towns were identified, prompting measures to cure them.[11] In the 1880s, in particular, a policy debate raged over society's responsibility for the welfare of its fellow citizens. A central issue was the open market capitalism that was then being pursued. Social liberals such as Adolf Hedin, S. A. Hedlund, and Fridjuv Berg championed workers' protection and offered legislation that would solve the "social question." In an 1884 parliamentary bill, Hedin, as the leader of the social liberal camp in the Riksdag (Parliament), called for improved worker protection and proclaimed laissez-faire Manchester liberalism a "false" and "immoral doctrine." "Worker solidarity for the maintenance of the way the state is currently organized" requires social reforms, he asserted. In late-nineteenth-century Germany, however, these welfare institutions came to have starkly authoritarian and patriarchal traits. They served as weapons in the fight against democracy, socialism, and trade unions. In Sweden, adapted by the political left, these institutions came to have a more local, democratic, and general shape.[12]

The result of Hedin's bill was the creation of the Arbetarförsäkringskommitté (Worker Insurance Committee). Its work then formed the basis for, among others, a 1889 law on "protection against trade danger" which also stipulated the introduction of workplace inspection. And there followed an 1891 health insurance fund law which required the state to provide funds for private health insurance. At the same time restrictions on women and child labor were introduced (1881, 1900, and 1909), and in 1913 a pension law was passed, forming the basis for a modern pension system. The money expended in pensions and insurance payments may have been modest at first, but it represented the beginning of reforms that laid the groundwork for the welfare society to come.

Liberals with social commitment were the primary early promoters of reform policies. After the turn of the century, however, Social Democrats won greater representation in Parliament and the demands for social reforms strengthened. The Socialdemokratiska Partiet (SAP; Social Democratic Party), which was inaugurated in 1886, had another view of how reforms should be shaped. They emphasized changes that primarily benefited workers collectively, while both liberals and conservatives emphasized that reforms should promote self-help and the individual's own assumption of responsibility. Within the Centralorgisationen för Socialt Arbete (CSA; Central Organization for Social Work) in particular, these demands for individual responsibilities, moral reform, and temperance in the face of increasing excesses found their most prominent forum. Even certain Social Democrats took part in the CSA's work in the 1920s. Leading liberals and Social Democrats created a broad political coalition which emphasized social reforms and suffrage.

Social Democrats and the Saltsjöbad Agreement

The 1920s began with a deep economic depression that threw hundreds of thousands of workers out of work. During the period that followed a dramatic societal revolution occurred. In the export industry in particular, which was at a low ebb, a painful process of enforcing greater efficiency and mechanization was implemented. However, this also occurred in many industries relying on the domestic market, for example the glass industry, which experienced increased mechanization during the late 1920s.[13] Agriculture met with sharp competition from abroad and had to be reduced. Sweden was also one of the West European countries that was most plagued by strikes and conflicts. But gradually the confrontational mood abated. In the late 1920s, responding to an initiative by the state, various factions of the labor movement convened to discuss solutions to labor's problems. At the 1928 labor conference a Labor Peace Delegation was established to promote mutual understanding between labor and management, but the result was negligible.

The international crisis, which is symbolized so dramatically by the 1929 crash of the American stock market, affected Sweden as well. Antagonisms between labor and management again intensified, and conflicts or confrontations rose sharply. Beginning in 1930 unemployment was high, and in 1933 the so-called Kreuger crash occurred, the Swedish equivalent of the 1929 Wall Street crash.[14] After this, starting in 1934, economic conditions improved noticeably. Unemployment dropped and production increased. The upturn was especially significant for domestic industry, but the export industry slowly recovered as well. In the wake of the 1932 Riksdag elections power was assumed by the Social Democratic Party under the leadership of Per Albin Hansson.

By means of the so-called cow trade with the Bondeförbundet (the peasant party),[15] Hansson was able to create political stability for his government. Ernst Wigfors, a Social Democrat and the Minister of Finance, tried to implement a cautiously expansionistic economic policy, but this played only a small role in the economic reorganization that got under way after 1933. Furthermore it would be a mistake to associate the Wigfors policy directly with the program of state-induced increases in consumer demand as devised by John Maynard Keynes. In the United States Franklin D. Roosevelt had similarly launched his expansionist New Deal without knowledge of Keynes. Swedish economists Gunnar Myrdal and Bertil Ohlin had also developed ideas similar to those of Keynes despite starting with different theoretical assumptions. All emphasized that the major problem was faltering demand. To remedy this, the state had to increase its expenditures and run a budgetary deficit in times of economic depression. Of greater importance in this context was the increased competitiveness that had been produced by the structural change and increased industrial productivity of the 1920s together with the devaluation of the Swedish krona in 1931. Thus, as isolated events, neither the expansionist policies nor the "cow trade" with the Bondeförbundet were particularly important in solving the economic crisis. In a broader context, however, they were part of a complicated sequence of political and social events whose effects would have far-reaching consequences for the way Swedish society and its economy developed.

With the 1932 elections, the Social Democratic Party began its forty-four-year-long control of government, which only ended in 1976. The 1930s were also a time of historic compromise between labor and capital which established the unusually peaceful conditions that have existed in Swedish labor relations ever since. This compromise, culminating in the Saltsjöbad Agreement (1938), led to long-term Social Democratic hegemony and created the foundation for the overall welfare policy, characterized by the strong collective traits that distinguish Swedish society.

In 1938 the Saltsjöbad Agreement was signed in the Grand Hotel in Saltsjöbaden, after two years of negotiations. This agreement between the LO and the SAF was precipitated by government's threat to prepare legislation to secure labor peace. Hansson's Social Democratic government viewed labor peace and stability as an important prerequisite for their own program. Many of the conflicts in the labor market initially had a tendency to affect third parties. In the uneasy political environment that characterized the 1930s, it was feared that such conflicts would mean that the middle class would opt for authoritarian political solutions. To prevent such an occurrence, the government invited labor and management to negotiate. But both the LO and SAF were opposed to government intervention and feared legislation. After much political maneuvering, the parties chose to act without government involvement and to work together to achieve a voluntary agreement. In fact both the LO and the SAF were tired of conflict after a decade of labor strife that had netted little gain for any of those involved. There was every reason to try something new, and the Saltsjöbad Agreement was the result. Its main points outlined regulations for negotiating solutions to labor conflicts. These, together with the 1928 collective agreement law, made it much more difficult than before to initiate strikes and lockouts. Labor peace seemed secured, and the threat to third parties reduced. But the concept of the Saltsjöbad Agreement also often refers to something else. After 1938 several follow-up agreements were signed, and a dialogue on mutual understanding between the parties was initiated. In this way, after 1938, a negotiating structure was established that could be used to settle the hard issues that had once served to sour relations between the parties.

On the whole the Saltsjöbad Agreement fostered a climate in Sweden that was conducive to growth and efficiency. Organized labor recognized the need for profits in industry, structural efficiency, and regional change. There existed a spirit of compromise based on ideas of collective welfare, equal distribution, growth, and economic efficiency.[16] However, by fostering efficiency and structural change within industry, the Saltsjöbad spirit also caused many small, less efficient plants to close. Thus after 1938 the Swedish model was responsible for the rapid restructuring of many industries, including the glass industry.[17]

Welfare became both an end and a means. Besides promoting a higher standard of living for all, welfare policy also attempted to create increased economic efficiency and growth. Instead of giving cash unemployment benefits or some other form of direct payment, retraining of the unemployed and active labor market measures were initiated. For this purpose a powerful agency, Arbetsmarknadsstyrelsen (AMS; Labor Market Administration) was established in 1947. Even the wage policy of the trade union movement (known as the solidarity wages policy) had been established to create growth. Leading trade unionists believed that higher wages ultimately resulted in growth in the economy. At the same time, however, the trade unions had to accommodate profits for the owners, incorporate efficiency measures, and even engage in a painfully difficult restructuring of industry. Full recognition of these realities did not occur until after the Second World War.

The Saltsjöbad Agreement also confirmed the trade union leaders' belief that the only way to advance was through strong professional organizations representing both workers and owners or employers. The agreements, negotiating structure, and conversations between the parties gave professional organizations greater "power" in relation both to the opposition and to their own members.

Swedish Corporatism

Various factors—including the Saltsjöbad Agreement and its aftermath, the long duration of the Social Democratic Party's control of government, the powerful impact of the "people's home" ideology, and an economic policy tinged by Keynesianism—formed the basis of a decision-making model that has sometimes been labeled "corporatist." *Corporatism* is usually defined as a power structure in which different interest organizations either cooperate with the state (the liberal variant) or are incorporated under it (the totalitarian variant). From the beginning Swedish interest organizations followed the liberal variant of corporatism. Administrative government agencies, in particular the civil service, have long had great autonomy, which survived the institution of parliamentary government in the early nineteenth century. As that century progressed the state bureaucracy became increasingly dominated by professional civil servants. After 1900 organized interests came to acquire a great deal of influence in state affairs, just as earlier the Riksdag and government had joined together to implement specific policy. In the twentieth century, however, the involvement of the citizenry was ensured through these interest organizations. Sweden thus came to have strong traits of collective democracy.[18]

Interest organizations were drawn into the machinery of state mainly through civil service management boards and major parliamentary committees. The first corporate institutions in which the parties to the labor market were represented emerged immediately after the turn of the century. For example, on a worker's insurance council that was established in 1902 there were five employer and five worker representatives. And in 1912 when the National Board of Health and Welfare was established, both management and labor were represented in force on its board. This model then established patterns. At the local level as well, starting in 1903, the parties were represented in, for example, the administrations of public employment offices. Thus the corporate model had already been well tested in Sweden, but in the early 1930s it expanded even more, and through civil service boards, state committees, and so on, the parties took the good of the state into consideration while championing their own demands. They gained much experience in cooperation and negotiation, which would continue to bear fruit in the postwar era.

The People's Home

The "Saltsjöbad spirit" between labor and management was not the only result of the compromises of the 1930s. Both sides recognized the importance of economic growth in and of itself, and this formed the basis for welfare policy that began in the 1930s. Toward the end of the decade the leading ideologues within the SAP and the trade union movement agreed that an equitable income distribution policy could only be brought about through rapid economic growth. In an authoritative 1941 program report the LO emphasized that "the trade union movement must work to strengthen and develop the business community because only with a strong business community can the working class hope to achieve better economic and social conditions."[19]

During the 1930s the redistribution policy that promoted growth gave the Social Democratic Party an ideological focus it had lost to a great extent in the 1920s when it had abandoned the notion of a rapid socialist transformation of society. In 1928 the SAP ideologue Nils Karleby, in his book entitled *Socialismen inför verkligheten* (Socialism faces reality), formulated the new direction for Social Democrats.[20] Rather than nationalization of business and industry as a goal in itself, equal rights for workers and a role for them in society and social planning became the aim. Karleby also defined the Social Democratic Party as more than a purely class party, but as one encompassing ordinary citizens as well. This view was strengthened by the Social Democrats' showdown with Bondeförbundet in 1933. Per Albin Hansson's "people's home . . . whose foundation is community and common feeling" became a metaphor for these new cooperative efforts.[21]

The Social Democratic Party and the worker movement added a new weapon to their arsenal with the "people's home" ideology. The concept spurred on the formulation of social policy that followed in the wake of the Social Democratic Party's takeover of power in 1932. The notion of a "people's home" encouraged the building of a society that eliminated social need. "In a good home equality, consideration, cooperation, and helpfulness prevail," Hansson asserted in his groundbreaking "people's home" speech.[22] During the 1930s Gustav Möller, the Minister of Social Affairs, initiated many of the reforms that ultimately transformed Sweden into a welfare country. Möller reasoned that the social reforms he introduced in the 1930s—unemployment insurance, prenatal care clinics, state employment offices, housing for large families, and a one-week vacation—should be national in scope. This aim of "solidarity" became the Swedish—and later the Scandinavian—model's most distinctive feature.[23] Reforms were to be shaped as laws which in theory would apply to all citizens. Möller was also the architect of the 1946 national pension plan whereby equal tax-free payments, regardless of income and property, were to be made. This was followed by the introduction of tax deductions for children and of a free school-meal plan.

In contrast to Möller's view of welfare as a right of citizenship, economist Gunnar Myrdal and sociologist Alva Myrdal represented a more selective approach to welfare policy, especially presented in their famous book *Kris i befolkningsfrågan* (The crisis of population; 1934).[24] According to the Myrdals, the disturbing issue of a declining birth rate in Sweden in the 1930s had to be addressed through improved social services such as the establishment of day-care centers. Women had to be included in the "people's home" concept as full and productive members of Swedish society. Overall the Myrdals advocated a social policy that was implemented along strict rationalistic lines, one that established science, order, and planning as its lodestars.

The Myrdals also seemed to endorse functionalism as an ideal modern architectural and artistic aesthetic to be applied to home construction, interior design, and societal planning. The philosophic core of modern society was reason and rationality, and planning referred to everything from domestic interiors to the way society in its broadest sense should be organized. What was reasonable was also attractive. Functionalism in this form, especially when applied to housing and interior decoration, made its appearance at the 1930

Stockholm Exhibition. At the same time functionalism's advocates attributed heroic traits to mass consumption. In the politically correct society that the social engineers envisioned, the department store operated as the perfect combination of consumption, democracy, and rationality. The functionalists also often focused on women's issues to win support for an ideology of mass consumption. It was thought that with modern appliances in kitchens and a streamlined approach to shopping, women would be freer and better able to expand their role in society.[25] After the 1930s the fate of many consumer industries including the glass industry was influenced by this emphasis on mass consumption, modernism, and functionalism. The Swedish model also promoted efficiency, which forced the closing of many small plants and businesses and sometimes of whole segments of industrial branches that were less competitive internationally. Paradoxically, this has also assured the survival of a modern Swedish glass industry reliant on modernist and functional design combined with high technical quality.

The Swedish model continued to be refined and developed in the postwar years, reaching a high point in the 1970s. By the 1990s, however, many facets of Swedish life based on this model have come into question. Welfare, for example, is considered to be too costly to maintain, and fairly extensive cuts to programs have had to be made. At the same time many of the strict economic regulations have been abolished, and superficially at least Sweden is beginning to place a greater emphasis on free market and private solutions. How much of this transformation will become permanent remains to be seen. Without question the historic legacy on which the notion of the "people's home" was formulated is still vigorous. Ultimately Sweden is a society containing strong elements of a compromise philosophy and collective democracy that builds structures as tenacious as its culture, national identity, and historic legacy.

1. For early discussion of the Swedish model, see Marquis Childs, *Sweden, the Middle Way* (New Haven: Yale University Press, 1936).

2. For general background on Sweden, see Lars Magnusson, *Sveriges ekonomiska historia* (Stockholm: Tiden Förlag, 1996).

3. Anders L. Johansson, *Tillväxt och klassamarbete: en studie av den svenska modellens uppkomst* (Stockholm: Tiden Förlag, 1989).

4. See Magnusson, *Sveriges ekonomiska historia*, chaps. 2 and 3.

5. See Lars Magnusson, "Den svenska modellen," in *Äventyret Sverige: en ekonomisk och social historia* (Stockholm: Utbildningsradlon, 1993).

6. The "Free Church" movement is defined as the group of nonconformist churches which proliferated in the late nineteenth century and were in opposition to the Lutheran state religion.

7. Svenbjörn Kilander, *Den gamla staten och den nya* (Uppsala: Acta universitatis upsaliensis, 1991).

8. Quoted in Magnusson, "Den svenska modellen," p. 294.

9. Sigfrid Hansson, *Den svenska fackföreningrörelsen* (Stockholm: Tiden Förlag, 1938), p. 7.

10. For further discussion of Swedish trade unions and the glass industry, see chap. 2 in this volume.

11. Torsten Gårdlund, *Industrialismens samhällë* (Stockholm: Tiden Förlag, 1942).

12. S. E. Olsson, *Social Policy and Welfare State in Sweden* (Lund, Sweden: Arkiv Förlag, 1990), p. 125.

13. See chap. 2 in this volume.

14. The Kreuger crash refers to the downfall of the Swedish financier Ivar Kreuger (1880–1932). When his international financial empire collapsed Kreuger committed suicide in Paris on March 12, 1932. See Lars-Erik Thunholm, *Ivar Kreuger* (Stockholm: Fischer, 1995).

15. The "cow trade" refers to the agreement between SAP and Bondeförbundet by which the Bondeförbundet gained protectionist duties upon corn, meat, and so on in exchange for its support of an SAP government.

16. Johansson, *Tillväxt och klassamarbete,* chap. 4.

17. See chap. 2 in this volume.

18. Compare B. Rothstein, *Den korporative staten* (Stockholm: Norstedts, 1992). Rothstein isolates a "formative moment" in the 1930s (chap. 6).

19. *Landsorganisationens 15-mannakommitté, Fackföreningsrörelsen och näringslivet* (Stockholm: LO, 1941), p. 4.

20. Nils Karleby, *Socialismen inför verkligheten* (Stockholm: Tiden Förlag, 1928).

21. Quoted in Magnusson, "Den svenska modellen," p. 304.

22. Ibid.

23. Gosta Esping-Andersen, *Politics Against Markets: The Social Democratic Road to Power* (Princeton: Princeton University Press, 1985), pp. 145 ff.

24. Alva Myrdal and Gunnar Myrdal, *Kris i befolkningsfrågan* (Stockholm: Tiden Förlag, 1934).

25. See, for example, Yvonne Hirdman, *Att lägga livet tillrätta* (Stockholm: Liber Förlag, 1990).

CHAPTER TWO

Swedish Industrialization and the Glassworks

Maths Isacson

Maths Isacson

Fig. 2-1. Workers at the Kosta Glassworks, 1900. (Småland museums arkiv)

The Swedish glass industry's rise to international acclaim began in the difficult years just after the First World War. Although Sweden had remained neutral during the war, the country felt the repercussions of the profound ongoing international economic crisis in the early 1920s. Businesses that had done well during the war years collapsed, and workers were laid off or saw their wages greatly reduced. The work day was limited by law to eight hours, causing further labor conflicts, and there were repeated strikes and lockouts. Poverty and insufficient housing were widespread, especially in the rapidly developing industrial towns.[1]

In both economic and political terms, a demonstration of strength was required to overcome these economic setbacks. It came in the form of industrial modernization, a détente between labor and management, and innovative approaches to government by those in power. By the end of the 1930s a foundation had been laid for the exceptional Swedish welfare system that flourished in the postwar period,[2] and Sweden's glass industry had become a world leader.

Early Industrialization, Regionalism, and Reform

For most of the nineteenth century Sweden remained an agrarian society . Agriculture and cattle farming still employed three-fourths of the population at mid-century.[3] The slow pace of industrialization was partly due to the strict regulations imposed on the economy by the Riksdag (Parliament) in the early 1800s.[4] Beginning in the second quarter of the nineteenth century Sweden embarked on a long, gradual reform of business, industry, and society in general, which stimulated growth and economic reorganization. In 1848 a corporation law made it easier to create capital with broader ownership, resulting in more opportunities for large and small investors with little risk of personal bankruptcy. By the 1870s many industrial companies had incorporated,[5] and by the end of the century the state had dissolved compulsory restraints through legislation and new ordinances,[6] creating reliable, risk-free capital, new production technology, and opportunities both for business ownership and for employment in industry and shipping.(fig. 2-1)

During the course of industrialization, differences between regions intensified. Industry and craft production were divided geographically. There were mines, blast furnaces, and ironworks in the mining district of Bergslagen, as well as in Uppland, Småland, and Västra Värmland; textile manufacturers in the towns of Borås and Norrköping; glassworks and cabinetmaking in Småland; and stone quarries and canneries in Bohuslän.[7] Regional specialization also created an expanding domestic market for the iron products, carpentry, textiles, and other products that came from rural areas and towns and were separate from the output of the old craft guilds and state-regulated factories.[8]

These rural areas (fig. 2-2) also offered access to seasonal labor, with workers drawn from the small towns and surrounding farms. The transport of raw materials and finished products required a large workforce as did routine maintenance and the construction of new buildings. Until well into the twentieth century this work was done by peasants and farmers during the slow agricultural season. Furthermore, these industries, including glassworks, consumed large quantities of fuel in the form of timber and charcoal, which required transportation from the forests. Timber was also needed by the sawmills and pulp factories. Before electricity became economically feasible in remote rural areas in the early part of the twentieth century, factories had to be located near brooks, streams, and rivers that provided water power. Such locations were frequently some distance from cities, ports, and workers' housing.[9]

It was partly the predominance of rural locations for Swedish industry that made the industrialization of Sweden less harsh in human terms than it was elsewhere. In England and Germany, for example, the living and working conditions for the population of workers in the rapidly growing industrial cities left much to be desired. The same was true in Sweden's few large cities, where workers were beset with similar problems.[10] The great majority of Swedish industrial workers, however, lived in small factory towns in the countryside where, thanks in part to size and location, higher standards of living were easier to maintain.

By the mid-1890s Sweden's new sawmills, iron and steel works, pulp and paper mills, brickyards, and carpentry shops, among others, employed approximately one-half of the industrial workforce.[11] Most of these businesses had difficulty achieving stability in their workforces, in getting young men to settle down in one place. Companies were consequently forced to invest both in the construction of quality housing and in welfare provisions. In this way many factory owners also hoped they could forestall the trade union movement and socialism.[12]

Industrialization became linked with a regeneration of the countryside, but different regulations, new production technology, and a stable level of foreign demand were needed before real progress could be made. This occurred in four stages. During the first, from 1830 to 1850, as in other industrialized nations such as England, the textile industry took the lead. The second stage occurred in the mid-nineteenth century when the lumber industry became the driving force, gradually giving way to iron and steel works as well as engineering. Beginning in the 1870s, during the third phase, large sums of money were invested in factory buildings, railroads, and roads. Finally, in the 1890s, the wood pulp industry, mining, and the lighter consumer products industry developed, causing an accelerated economic growth.[13]

By around 1900 Swedish industry had reached its "maturation phase," employing close to 300,000 people. The country had a successful export trade and consumer products industry for the expanding urban and industrial population, together with an increasingly advanced manufacturing technology, producing machines and tools for factory use. At this time Swedish contributions and improvements to industrial technology began to achieve commercial success in the international market: the separator, steam turbine, three-phase motor, acetylene gas unit, ball bearing, Primus camping stove, and various precision measuring tools, among others, were Swedish innovations. During the previous century, a number of specialized manufacturing firms had been established which now assumed a prominent place in the Swedish, and later international, business community: ASEA Brown Boveri (power plants), SKF (ball bearings), Ericsson (telephones and communications), Alfa Laval (food processing technology), and others.[14]

The Glassworks and Industrialization

The glass industry had no direct role in Sweden's industrialization. Its product development, however, was informed by changing economic and social condi-

tions. Orders for window glass and domestic glass kept pace with urban development and a burgeoning middle-class market.

The glass industry had become established in the southern part of Sweden,[15] in Kronoberg and Kalmar counties, near the region's large forests and farm populations. A special "glass culture" established roots in these areas, with jobs and skills passed down from generation to generation.[16] The Kosta Glassworks in Småland (fig. 2-3), founded in 1742, was the earliest, and thus became the progenitor of many small glassworks at the end of the nineteenth century, as Kosta workers left to form their own companies.

Slightly more than sixty glassworks were started between 1870 and 1899,[17] and the number of workers rose to just under 6,000 (2 percent of Sweden's industrial workforce). Between 1863 and 1903 glass production increased on average 4.8 percent annually and employment by just under 4 percent. Several years into the new century the growth reached a peak and halted. Employment dropped somewhat but rose again, at least temporarily, between 1915 and 1919, after which there was a significant decline.[18]

Several of the late-nineteenth-century glassworks, such as Orrefors, were started by or associated with an older ironworks. Glass production, like iron smelting, required fuel in significant quantities, and the existing ironworks often had access to this from large forested

Fig. 2-3. The Kosta Glassworks and village, ca. 1940. (Småland museums arkiv)

areas. Extant housing and factory buildings could be converted and used without costly investment. The same crews that worked for the ironworks could be employed by the glass factory and continue to produce food, cut timber, and transport goods to and from the factory and its community.[19] Glassworks thus adopted the ironworks' supply patterns and social systems. Self-sufficiency was important and a factory culture was encouraged. People took pride in their work and looked down on the rural peasantry in the surrounding countryside.

While there was a feeling of solidarity among men from the same glassworks, there was also a clear social stratification, with the owner and director of the glassworks at the top and a few administrative employees immediately under them. They knew their workers well but at the same time were careful to keep a distance. The workers were further divided socially. The professional, skilled glassworkers—glassblowers, cutters, and smiths—made up the upper stratum and had greater advantages than seasonal agricultural workers and day workers. Women and children performed certain simple functions as cutters, etching assistants, glass carriers, packers, and edge cutters.[20]

Toward the end of the nineteenth century, as companies expanded and the trade union movement drew more supporters, it became all the more important for owners of glassworks to maintain the isolation and social independence of the glassworkers. They invested in relatively spacious and attractive worker housing which had large gardens and outbuildings. Companies also looked after workers' welfare, offering education, markets, health care, and leisure activities. All of this challenged the trade union movement at the beginning of the century. Starting with democratic elections in the early 1920s, the government assumed greater responsibility for schools, welfare, job placement, health care, and housing.[21]

Sweden's first glassworks had depended on highly skilled immigrant labor, and even as late as the late nineteenth century many skilled glassworkers were foreign born. Glassblowers and cutters, for example, came from Germany or one of the other Nordic countries, but their importance had diminished significantly relative to earlier times. The increased industrialization and growth of glass manufacturing required wider recruitment. Starting at the end of the nineteenth century, workers at glasshouses were to a great extent hired locally as well as from other factories.[22] Skills were passed down through generations, but new workers also streamed in from the countryside.

Once settled, glassworkers seem to have been less inclined than other industrial workers to move on to other jobs. An 1898 study shows a strong tie to tradition existed among the country's glassworkers.[23] About half of those with the highest qualifications were following

in their father's trade. Three-fourths of all glassworkers had worked at the same company throughout their lives.[24]

The growth of the glass industry at the end of the nineteenth century went hand in hand with an increase in mechanization and specialization of labor. This affected the composition of the labor force. At Kosta, for example, with just over 350 employees in 1900 (see fig. 2-1), the percentage of skilled workers declined in favor of unskilled labor. Furthermore, Kosta later employed a large group of children under the age of eighteen, and in 1905 girls accounted for about 3 percent of the labor force. Initially children worked primarily during periods of expansion at factories that produced glass for windows, containers, and domestic and laboratory use.[25] By the early twentieth century, however, child labor was on the decline at the glassworks as it was in Swedish industry as a whole, thanks to more sophisticated technology and stricter legislation.[26]

Life in the glassworks has been described by Ragnar Bengtsson who in 1916, when he was thirteen years old, was hired at the Kosta Glassworks. He started in his father's workshop, doing menial jobs and working his way up until in 1941 he became a glassmaster.[27] In the glassworks there were two French melting furnaces "with [twelve] big globe crucibles so that practically the entire blowpipe was needed to get near the glass when you worked out of it to the bottom. . . . The men who made cut and embossed glass worked around [a large gas-fired warming] furnace" in the middle of the foundry. The floor "was made up of wide planks, and there were large chinks between them. During the dark months of the year light came from two big gas lanterns hung in the middle of the room. We also had the glow from the hot furnaces."

Water for drinking was brought from an outside pump by young boys. There was a urinal for the workers in the foundry and an outdoor privy. Housing was included in the wages until 1944, along with a small garden, "the chance to have a pig or a chicken," and, until early in the twentieth century, free firewood. The living quarters were often barely adequate, with most workers housed in a dormitory and sharing a kitchen. Married couples were given space in the attics or a single room.

Trade Unions and the Glass Industry

Union organization in Swedish glassworks was partly spurred on by English and Danish examples. The low cost of Swedish glass was pushing prices down in the international market, and when nonunion Swedish workers immigrated to other glass-producing countries they threatened the nascent trade union movement by working outside the union. To combat this threat, at a meeting of the International Glassworkers

Union in London in 1893, organizers allotted £20 for Danish agitation among Swedish and Norwegian glassworkers.[28]

The first trade union within the Swedish glass industry had actually been founded three years earlier, in 1890, by workers at the Arboga Glassworks, a glass bottle manufacturer in central Sweden.[29] In 1893 trade unions were started at the Kosta Glassworks in Småland and the Kungälv Glassworks in west Sweden. They were short-lived, but before the Kosta union closed in 1897, workers at six other Småland glassworks had been inspired to establish their own trade unions. The Kosta union committee had also taken the first step toward organizing a national federation of Swedish glassworkers. With the demise of the Kosta chapter, however, organizing activity ceased. A year later, in 1898, the cause was taken up by workers at the glass bottle plant in Surte who launched a federation for Swedish glassworkers. Unlike many other Swedish manufacturers, management at the glassworks had little opposition to their workers' union organizing.[30]

Trade union organization in the glass industry achieved its goals in the early years of the twentieth century. In 1907, when Glasarbetarförbundet (The Glassworker Federation) merged with Svenska Grov-ochfabriksarbetareförbundet (The Swedish General and Factory Workers Federation), thirty-three glassworker chapters representing 1,280 members, or a quarter of the country's glassworkers, joined the new federation. Membership fell off, however, as it did in other industries, after the trade union movement's defeat in the general strike of 1909.[31]

Tradition and Renewal in the Swedish Glass Industry, 1918–39

By the outbreak of the First World War, Swedish industry had completed the first uncertain phase of industrialization and was on firm ground. Between 1870 and 1913 industrial production had increased an average of 4.4 percent annually, which was a significantly better rate than that of the overall Swedish economy. The number of industrial workers also increased substantially to approximately 370,000,[32] while starting in the 1880s the number of agricultural workers had steadily declined. Although three-quarters of the population still lived in rural communities, barely half of the country's population earned its living from agriculture and forestry. Industry, trade, and the service sector had surged strongly ahead. As early as the turn of the century, the value of industrial production surpassed agriculture, and by the 1930s more Swedes were employed in industry than in agriculture (fig. 2-4).[33]

The First World War temporarily halted rural migration. Swedish industry actually made gains—and big profits—in the 1914–18 period, accompanied by speculative industrial investments. At the same time,

Fig. 2-4. A family of Swedish farm laborers, 1930s. Wages and working conditions of agricultural workers were an important political issue in the 1930s. (Nordiska Museets arkiv, Stockholm)

however, the standard of living of workers and small farmers fell dramatically, creating social unrest and stirring up revolutionary fervor that reached a peak in 1917. The Social Democrats and Liberals formed a government but were unable to avert the economic crisis that loomed in the aftermath of the war. In Sweden unemployment climbed from 5 percent to just over 25 percent in 1920, with some sectors of industry approaching just over 30 percent.[34] It took several years for economic conditions to improve, and as they did Swedish industry gradually recognized the pressing need to reform their production methods. The catchword became "rationalization"—using machines, the workplace, raw materials, and manpower as efficiently as possible. American ideas about scientific management, which had been developed by the efficiency engineer Frederick Winslow Taylor early in the century, slowly began to gain favor in Swedish industry. Large manufacturing and clothing firms were first to adopt efficiency methods successfully.[35]

The glass industry explored alternative avenues of change. Rather than resort to a massive reform of technology and reorganization of labor, many glassworks pursued a close collaboration between industry and

Fig. 2-5. The engraving workshop at Orrefors Glassworks, 1917. (Småland museums arkiv)

artists. Even at the end of the 1930s production remained essentially an industrialized form of handicrafts in which professional glassblowers, cutters, and decorators worked with dynamic artists,[36] and mass production was united with design. Firms, such as Orrefors (fig. 2-5) and Kosta, which manufactured glass for domestic and medical use, also produced household and ornamental glass. And it was here that glass artists and their designs had a major impact and were instrumental in the survival and success of this segment of the glass industry. Companies producing window glass survived by converting to machine-produced glass starting in 1927, leading to a doubling of production per worker, per hour, and a commensurate reduction of costs. A third group of glassworks, those producing both window glass and jars and bottles, found new markets for their products such as the large glass bottles that replaced wooden casks at breweries.[37]

While Swedish glassworks had almost as many employees in 1939 (5,370) as they had in 1919 (5,450), there had been major fluctuations in employment and restructuring within the industry during this period. Some glassworks closed while new ones were established, occasionally by unemployed glassworkers. It was relatively inexpensive to start or renovate a foundry.[38] Around 1920 there had been sixty glassworks, and by 1940 this number had been reduced to fifty. The largest firms, those with more than 200 employees, were fewer in number, while glassworks with between 51 and 100 employees had grown in importance. In 1935 this group, together with businesses that employed between 101 and 200 workers, accounted for 69 percent of the total number of workers in the glass industry. In 1920 that figure had been 48 percent.[39]

Just as in the rest of Swedish industry, the glassworks were hit by the international economic crisis of the early 1920s, and it was not until 1928 that production again reached levels equal to those during the First World War. In the early 1930s Sweden felt the impact of the worldwide economic depression (fig. 2-6), and production levels at the glassworks again dropped, although not as sharply as they had a decade earlier. Recovery also occurred more quickly. For the glass industry as a whole, production volume increased almost 60 percent between 1933 and 1937.[40] Producers of window glass seemed to be hardest hit in the 1930s; their employment figures peaked in the late 1920s. This reduction in employment is partly

Fig. 2-6. An employment office in Stockholm during the economic depression of the 1930s. (Nordiska Museets arkiv, Stockholm)

explained, however, by the introduction of machines that replaced manpower in some factories. Where there had been approximately 600 workers in 1919, twenty years later there were barely 500 despite a strong increase in production. As ten glassworks had become two, namely Orrefors and Kosta, these two had also become significantly larger.

Glassworks that produced windows and bottles also cut their workforces but in this case a long-term decline was responsible. Where there had been 1,140 workers in 1919, in 1939 there were 820, and twelve firms were reduced to five. They used more modern technology and were significantly larger than they had been at the start of the interwar period. During the 1930s these glassworks experienced increased competition from paper companies that produced packaging, but since the market was also growing, employment was affected only marginally.[41]

Factories producing glass for domestic and medical use constituted by far the largest group, both in terms of the number of firms and of employees. The glassworks increased by just two, from thirty-six to thirty-eight, while the workforce, after a decline in the early 1920s, increased throughout the decade. This was not true· industrywide; the domestic and medical glass industry employed approximately 4,000 workers in the beginning of the 1930s, but by 1939 that figure had dropped to 3,670 while sales of household and ornamental glass were strong. Urban renewal and the building of federally funded housing projects (fig. 2-7) that were integral to Sweden's welfare system increased the demand for this type of glass. Swedish firms could hold their own against foreign firms in the domestic market. Swedish export glass also gained during the 1930s.[42]

Despite critical successes, increased sales, and good employment figures, however, the glass industry as a whole was not very profitable. Factories producing glass for domestic and medical uses were often badly managed, resulting in lower production. Even so, new firms were established while companies producing window glass and glass bottles, such as Gullaskrufs Glasbruk AB (in 1926) and AB Flygfors Glasbruk (in 1930), switched over to production of glass for domestic and laboratory use.[43]

During the 1918–39 period producers of household and ornamental glass were not specialized. The participation of artists in the glass industry, beginning at Orrefors just after the First World War and gradually becoming the norm at smaller glassworks, changed this somewhat. Orrefors overtook Kosta, the larger company, as the leader of the glass industry, setting industry standards. Under the motto "more beautiful things for everyday use,"[44] Orrefors and other glassworks transformed glass from luxury objects for the elite into everyday designs for a broad stratum of society. Although in the mid-1920s there was a return to more elegant glassware for special occasions, ordinary household glass was shown beside art glass at international expositions and contributed to the world renown of Swedish glass.

The 1929 appointment of designer Elis Bergh at Kosta also contributed to an exciting renewal of the old glassworks' production.[45] Starting in the early 1930s more and more producers of glass for domestic and medical use invested in design. And in keeping with the functionalism of the time, simple yet attractive everyday glass regained its position. The glassworks began to acquire their own individual characteristics. Within a short time, for example, Eda had successfully found its niche with opalescent glassware. Other firms developed their own signature glass: Strömbergshyttan specialized in a bluish silver glass primarily designed by Gerda Strömberg; Gullaskruf in pressed

Fig. 2-7. Stockholm in the 1930s. The Stadshuset (City Hall; Ragnar Östberg, architect) with its tower is seen in the center, and across Riddarfjärden Bay is the district of Södermalm with its factories and worker housing. (Nordiska Museets arkiv, Stockholm)

glass; Målerås in tableware; Pukeberg in lighting glass; and Skruf and Åfors in robust domestic designs.

Over the course of just two decades the Swedish glass industry had become one of the preeminent makers of quality glass in the world. Its success came from rapidly changing socioeconomic, political, and cultural conditions. While collaboration with artists provided new incentives, other issues, such as the labor movement, an ongoing reliance on traditional craft techniques, new formal concerns, and the development of viable marketing strategies, were equally compelling. Although such tradition and renewal contributed significantly to the advancement of the glass industry, underlying its achievements and assuring its survival has been the loyalty of the Swedish glassworkers to their chosen craft and the very high level of their skill.

1. On Sweden's economy and industry in the interwar period see, among others, Ulf Olsson, "Industrilandet Sverige," in Birgitta Furuhagen, *Äventyret Sverige: en ekonomisk och social historia* (Stockholm: Utbildningsradion/Bokförlaget Bra Böcker, 1993); Lennart Jörberg, *Den svenska ekonomiska utvecklingen 1861–1983* (Lund, Sweden: Meddelande från Ekonomisk-historiska institutionen, 1984); and Erik Dahmén, *Svensk industriell företagarverksamhet: kausalanalys av den industriella utvecklingen, 1919–1939*, vols. 1–2 (Stockholm: Industrins utredningsinstitut, 1950).

On Swedish glass and Sweden's glass industry during the interwar period see Helena Dahlbäck Lutteman, "Storhetstid och världsryckte 1917—andra världskriget," in Märta Stina Danielsson, ed., *Svenskt glas* (Stockholm: Wahlström and Widstrand, 1991) and Jörberg, *Den svenska ekonomiska utvecklingen*.

For urban developments during the period, see chap. 1 in this volume, and Yvonne Hirdman, *Att lägga livet till rätta: Studier i svensk, folkhemspolitik* (Stockholm: Carlssons förlag, 1989), p. 93; and A. Davidson, *Two Models of Welfare: The Origins and Development of the Welfare State in Sweden and New Zealand, 1888–1988*, Publications of the Political Science Association in Uppsala, no. 108, p. 137.

2. See chap. 1 in this volume.

3. Extensive land reclamation, new farming methods, improved animal husbandry, and better technology, together with the beginnings of mechanization, yielded ever greater harvests and more meat and dairy products. Thus despite a rapidly growing population (from 2.35 million in 1800 to 3.5 million in 1850), agriculture kept pace. See Jörberg, *Den svenska ekonomiska utvecklingen*, pp. 19, 28–30; and Maths Isacson and Lars Magnusson, *Proto-industrialisation in Scandinavia: Craft Skills in the Industrial Revolution* (Leamington, England: Berg Publisher, 1987).

4. Industrial growth required not only more relaxed commercial regulations but also new institutions that would simplify and stimulate business; technological development; a flexible and better-educated workforce; and available capital. As early as the 1760s there had been criticism of the Riksdag's restrictive regulatory system (see Staffan Sjöberg, "Sex hundra år av svenska äventyr," in Furuhagen, *Äventyret Sverige*). By the 1840s opposition within Swedish society had united around a series of reforms. In 1842 public school education was mandated. Literacy was necessary if workers were to be able to function within the factory environment and to participate in trade unions, political parties, and other organizations (see Anders Nilsson and Lars Pettersson, "Utbildning, ekonomisk omvandling och tillväxt," in Furuhagen, *Äventyret Sverige*). The democratic process, with its open elections to political assemblies, also required that adults be able to read and write.

In 1846 the guild monopoly was abolished, and crafts began to flourish. Trade was liberalized as, for example, new opportunities opened to women in business and industry. The important iron industry achieved greater freedoms, but it was not until 1859 that centuries-old protectionist regulations were completely abolished. In 1864, further repeals were made (see Sten Carlsson and Jerker Rosén, *Den svenska historien*, vol. 12 [Stockholm: Bonniers lexikon, 1967/1994]; and Artur Montgomery, *Industrialismens genombrott i Sverige* [Stockholm: Almqvist & Wiksell, 1947], pp. 83 *ff.*).

While early nineteenth-century legislation had restricted the mobility of much of the workforce, with fines issued to those who left their employers (or masters), burgeoning industrial capitalism required a mobile workforce, and around mid-century, the Riksdag adopted resolutions to allow workers to change jobs. Overpopulation in rural areas, however, helped to undermine the intent of the law (see Montgomery, *Industrialismens genombrott*, p. 59 *ff.*). Capital was more readily available as the credit market expanded through new savings and business banks. Transportation systems improved, from the construction of canals linking the interior with the coast and east with west to better roads and railways (see Torsten Gårdlund, *Industrialismens samhälle* [Stockholm: Tiden Förlag, 1942], pp. 150 *ff.* and 169 *ff.*).

5. Gårdlund, *Industrialismens samhälle*, pp. 196 *ff.*

6. Lennart Schön, *Industrialismens förutsättningar* (Lund: Liber Förlag, 1983).

7. Other industries developed elsewhere. In Närke, for example, especially in and around the towns of Kumla and Örebro, a major shoe industry emerged; in western Västmanland the roof tile industry grew; and along the coast of Norrland sawmills and pulp factories. See Eva Vikström, *Industrimiljöer på landsbygden. Riksantikvarieämbetet* (Stockholm, 1995), chap. 2; Isacson and Magnusson, *Proto-industrialisation in Scandinavia*, chap 2.

8. For population trends see *Historisk statistik för Sverige*, pt. 1, table 2. On regional specialization see Isacson and Magnusson 1987.

9. There were some exceptions. Late-nineteenth-century machine shops, ready-made clothing industries, bakeries, breweries, cigar factories, and other consumer goods firms were less dependent on hydraulic power and heavy transport. These businesses put their faith in steam power and electricity and were more apt to establish themselves in cities and larger towns where they also found a large and growing number of customers (Gårdlund, *Industrialismens samhälle*, pp. 130–43).

10. For the situation in Sweden see ibid., pp. 358 *ff.*; Bo Gustafsson, *Den norrländska sågverksindustrins arbetare, 1890–1913* (Uppsala: Scandinavian University Books, 1965); and Jörberg 1987. For the English debate on the consequences of industrialization for the living standards of workers see Arthur. J. Taylor, ed., *The Standard of Living in Britain in the Industrial Revolution* (London: Methuen, 1975), pp. 29–32. In a few of the large Swedish cities workers were beset with similar problems as elsewhere. Urban population grew twice as quickly as the overall population; in 1913 slightly more than one-fourth of the population lived in cities and densely populated areas where living conditions (especially in Stockholm and Gothenburg) were substandard. Tuberculosis ended many lives in crowded wooden shacks lacking indoor plumbing or running water, where waste and garbage were emptied into the alleys (see Olsson, "Industrilandet Sverige," pp. 53, 69).

11. Gårdlund, *Industrialismens samhälle*, p. 279; Olsson, "Industrilandet Sverige," p. 68.

12. See Olof Nordström, *Svensk glasindustri, 1550–1960* (Lund, Sweden: Geografiska institutionen vid Lunds Universitet, 1962), chap. 3; Ulf Eriksson, *Gruva och arbete: Kiirunavaara, 1890–1990*, vol. 1, 1890–1920 (Uppsala: Ekonomisk-historiska institutionen, 1991), pp. 190 *ff.*; and Tommy Svensson, "Bruksinstitutioner och folkrörelser i Jonsered," in B. Andersson and Tommy Svensson, eds., *Samhälle och idrott i Jonsered, 1830–1980* (Jonsered: IF, 1985).

13. Olsson, "Industrilandet Sverige," pp. 49–66; and Bo Gustafsson, "The Industrial Revolution in Sweden," manuscript, 1994.

14. Gårdlund, *Industrialismens samhälle*, p. 85; U. Olsson, "Industrilandet Sverige," pp. 65–66.

15. For a history of the glassworks in Sweden, see chap. 6 in this volume.

16. *Hemma på Kosta: I Glasriket, människan-miljön-framtiden* (Växjö: ABF/Svenska Fabriksarbetareförbundet, 1982), pp. 18–20, and Vikström, *Industrimiljöer på landsbygden*, p. 27.

17. Seventeen of these were bankrupt by the turn of the century, but some, such as Åfors, Sandvik, Bergdala, Johansfors, Rosdala, and Orrefors, are still in operation. About ten new firms started during the 1870s and the workforce practically doubled. O. Nordström, "Förteckning över glasbruk och hyttor i Sverige 1150–1990," in Danielsson, ed., *Svenskt glas*, pp. 411–14. Also see chap. 8 in this volume.

18. Gårdlund, *Industrialismens samhälle*, p. 144; Vikström, Industrimiljöer på landsbygden, p. 27; Christina Johansson, *Glasarbetarna 1860–1910. Arbete, levnadsförhållanden och facklig verksamhet vid Kosta och andra glasbruk under

industrialismens genombrottsskede. Meddelande från ekonomisk-historiska institutionen vid Göteborgs universitet, no. 15 (1988), pp. 26–27.

19. O. Nordström, *Svensk glasindustri*; and Vikström, *Industrimiljöer på landsbygden*, p. 27.

20. Johansson, "Glasarbetarna 1860–1910," pp. 96–97.

21. O. Nordström, "Miljön kring glasbruken," in Danielsson, *Svenskt glas*, pp. 405 *ff.*; and Bertil Jakobsson, "Företaget, kommunen och individen," *Uppsala Studies in Economic History* 15 (Uppsala: Uppsala University, 1976).

22. O. Nordström, "Förteckning över glasbruk," pp. 385–86; Johansson, "Glasarbetarna, 1860–1910," pp. 97–98; *Hemma på Kosta*, pp. 16–17; Torbjörn Fogelberg, *Ett sekel ibelysningens tjänst: Rosdala glasbruk 1895–1995* (Växjö, Rosdala glasbruk, 1995), pp. 29–45.

23. K. Key-Åberg, *Arbetsstatistisk studie öfuer glasindustrin* (Stockholm, 1899).

24. Gårdlund, *Industrialismens samhälle*, p. 285.

25. At the turn of the century approximately one-fourth of the workers in Sweden's glassworks were underage. Of these 2 percent were under the age of twelve. For a study of child labor in Sweden see Lars Olsson, *Då barn var lönsomma* (Stockholm: Tiden Förlag, 1980).

26. Johansson, "Glasarbetarna, 1860–1910", pp. 83 *ff.*

27. *Hemma på Kosta*, pp. 23 *ff.*

28. Ibid., p. 77.

29. For information on the trade union movement in Sweden see chap. 1 in this volume.

30. Johansson, "Glasarbetarna, 1860–1910," pp. 177–78, 185; *Hemma på Kosta*, pp. 77 *ff.*

31. Johansson, "Glasarbetarna, 1860–1910" p. 179; Klas Åmark, *Facklig makt och fackligt medlemskap: De svenska fackförbundens medlemsutveckling, 1890–1940* (Lund, Sweden: Arkiv Förlag, 1986), pp. 72 *ff.* The 1909 general strike was the first major conflict in the Swedish labor movement. In it the Swedish National Federation of Trade Unions (Landsorganisationen; LO) opposed the Swedish Employers Association (Arbetsgivariföreningen; SAF). It followed a long period of economic recession climaxing in the summer of 1909 when the SAF called for a lockout. LO responded with a general strike and about 300,000 workers walked away from their jobs. The trade unions lacked the financial wherewithal for a long strike, however, and gradually the workers returned to work. As a result of this defeat, the trade unions saw their membership shrink by more than 50 percent during the next few years (from 240,000 members in 1907 to 118,000 in 1911). See Bernt Schiuller, "Storstrejken 1909: Forhistoria och orsaker," *Studia historica Gothoburgensia* 9 (1967).

32. Åmark, *Facklig makt och fackligt medlemskap*, p. 230.

33. Jörberg, *Den svenska ekonomiska*, p. 13; Mats Larsson, *En svensk ekonomisk historia, 1850–1985* (Stockholm: SNS Förlag, 1991), pp. 15–16, 20; U. Olsson, "Industrilandet Sverige," pp. 61 *ff.* The official figures, however, do not include female agriculture labor.

34. U. Olsson, "Industrilandet Sverige," pp. 74 *ff.*

35. Hans de Geer, *Rationaliseringsrörelsen i Sverige* (Stockholm: SNS Förlag, 1978); see also, among others, Lars Magnusson, *Arbetet vid en svensk verkstad: Munktells, 1900–1920* (Lund: Arkiv Förlag, 1987); and Maths Isacson, *Verkstadsarbete under 1900-talet: Hedemora Verkstäder före 1950* (Lund: Arkiv Förlag, 1987).

36. "Rationaliseringsutredningens betänkande," pt. 2, *Statens offentliga utredningar* (1939) 14, p. 113.

37. Erik Dahmén, *Svensk industriell företagarverksamhet: kausalanalys av den industriella utvecklingen, 1919–1939*, vol. 1 (Stockholm: Industrins utredningsinstitut, 1950), p. 163.

38. O. Nordström, "Förteckning över glasbruk," p. 405.

39. "Rationaliseringsutredningens," part 2, pp. 113–14.

40. *Svenskt Industri* (Stockholm: Industriförbundet, 1948), p. 343.

41. Dahmén, *Svensk industriell företagarverksamhet*, vol. 1, pp. 111, 163; ibid., vol. 2, pp. 56–57.

42. Ibid., vol. 1, pp. 111, 163; ibid., vol. 2, p. 87.

43. Ibid., vol. 1, p. 301.

44. This comes from a seminal book of the same name, Gregor Paulsson, *Vackrare Vardagsvara* (Stockholm: Svenska Slöjdföreningen, 1919).

45. Helena Dahlbäck Lutteman, "Storhetstid och världsryckte 1917—andra världskriget," in Danielsson, ed., *Svenskt glas*, pp. 111–12; Dag Widman, "Jugendepokens konstglas," in ibid., pp. 53–57.

CHAPTER THREE

Social Needs and Aesthetic Demands: Ellen Key, Gregor Paulsson, and Swedish Design, 1899–1939

Clarence Burton
Sheffield, Jr.

Fig. 3-1. Ellen Key at her desk, ca 1899. (From Mia Leche-Löfgren, *Ellen Key-hennes liv och verk* [Stockholm: Nature och Kultur, 1930], pl. 14).

And above all one must not believe that beauty is a good fortune which only a few can obtain.[1]

And the only possibility to obtain anything of beauty which is mass produced, for a reasonable price, is that the factories, especially of furniture, wallpapers, glass, textiles, porcelain and metals unite with the practices of *konstslöjd*, in order that everything from the simplest and smallest object (e.g.—the matchbox) to the largest, yield beautiful forms and appropriate decorations. Only when nothing ugly can be found to be purchased; when the beautiful is just as affordable as the ugly is now, can beauty for all become a certainty.[2]

Ellen Key

With these words from *Skönhet för alla* (Beauty for all; 1899) Ellen Key (fig. 3-1) provided one of the principal ideological grounds for modern Swedish design. A Swedish writer, activist, and educational reformer, Key advocated greater cooperation between industry and handicrafts, and offered practical advice regarding the domestic interior which increased public awareness of its importance. Two decades later art historian Gregor Paulsson continued Key's line of argument in his radical pamphlet, *Vackrare Vardagsvara* (More beautiful things for everyday use) written in 1919. He expanded her basic aesthetic philosophy and promoted its alliance with modern industrial technology in order to realize its broader social aims. The importance of both texts to the development of Scandinavian modernism has long been acknowledged, but their essential arguments have yet to be critically examined, closely compared, or placed within a broader intellectual context.

Key's argument in *Skönhet för alla* acknowledged the uneasy tensions between the city and countryside, the wealthy and poor, the educated elite and common

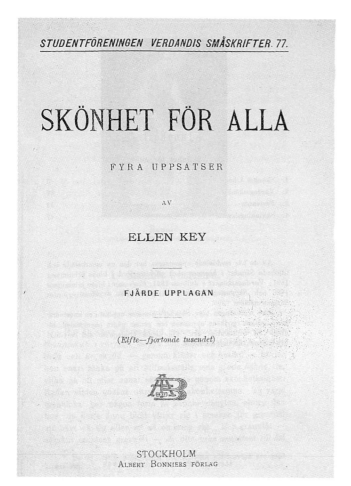

STUDENTFÖRENINGEN VERDANDIS SMÅSKRIFTER. 77.

SKÖNHET FÖR ALLA

FYRA UPPSATSER

AV

ELLEN KEY

FJÄRDE UPPLAGAN

(Elfte—fjortonde tusendet)

STOCKHOLM
ALBERT BONNIERS FÖRLAG

Fig. 3-2. Title page of Skönhet för alla (4th ed., Stockholm: Bonniers, 1908).

laborer. She was keenly aware of the impact of technology, urbanization, and population growth on traditional Swedish society and believed that it could be improved by uniting beauty and utility. Above all she praised the simple interiors of the rural peasantry and their self-sufficient lifestyle. which emphasized the open-air and fresh, natural colors. There is a subtle nationalism in her admiration for the rural and growing mistrust of foreign styles, especially the "vulgar German," which she criticized as dark, heavy, and oppressive.[3]

Ellen Key was careful, however, not to reject her era in favor of a utopian past. In fact she adopted a somewhat ambivalent attitude toward modernity. She recognized that neither the urban nor the rural home lacked its share of beauty. What truly mattered was each person's attitude toward the beautiful—the distinct style, personality, and aesthetic preferences of the individual. The three most important factors in creating a more beautiful home, according to Key, were simplicity, functional efficacy, and individual taste. In *Skönhet för alla*

(fig. 3-2) she described a set of fundamental axioms or rules of thumb that influenced subsequent generations and became synonymous with the international perception of the modern Swedish home.

Overall her book had an optimistic tone. It emphasized social obligation and the egalitarian belief that beauty was potentially accessible to all. She condemned frivolity, imitation, and excess, viewing the domestic interior as a kind of *Gesamtkunstwerk* (total work of art) in which everything had its proper place and reflected the individual occupant's desires and needs. Key equated good taste with "honesty."[4] Things should be logical and straightforward; appearance and reality must be one and the same.

These maxims had a pervasive and profound impact on Swedish society. The popularity of her design reforms was aided no doubt by her friendship with many of the leading intellectuals of her day, as well as by her simple persuasiveness. Her writing style is characterized by a strong cultural idealism combined with a maternal warmth and generosity, which at times approaches naiveté. Key's arguments are often emotionally charged, if not impassioned. Her popular appeal and strength as a speaker color her written work as well. In subsequent decades her aesthetic philosophy inspired the design reforms of Gregor Paulsson, which were closely linked to the emerging liberal social democracy. An understanding of Ellen Key's aesthetic reforms, therefore, is essential to a proper comprehension of the Swedish Modern design that emerged at the end of the 1930s.

Key's aesthetic reforms must be considered within their broader historical context. Her contributions reflect the growing European interest in progressive design, based in a broader movement that sought to elevate the decorative arts, improve public taste, and create a more pleasing interior space. Impulses from England and Germany were closely followed in Scandinavia.[5] Jacob von Falke, later the director of the Österreichisches Museum für Kunst und Industrie in Vienna, wrote extensively on the improvement of artistic handicrafts and the decoration of the home. In 1871 he published *Die Kunst im Hause* (Art in the home), in which he called for a stronger alliance between what is useful and what is artistically beautiful in the home, and he traced the history of interior design.[6] Von Falke greatly admired Scandinavian handicrafts and folk art and visited Sweden in 1870 at the invitation of the king, Karl XV, in order to catalogue his personal collections. Von Falke's ideas, which were closely related to the writings of Gottfried Semper, were widely discussed in Scandinavia and extremely influential.

The design reforms of German architect Hermann Muthesius and the Deutscher Werkbund (established in 1907) were also closely followed in Scandinavia.[7] Muthesius regarded the reformation of the design of the home as one of the most urgent tasks of his time. He advocated improved craftsmanship and a greater emphasis on form, materials, and function as a means by which to achieve this aim. Among his many works that were translated for Scandinavian audiences, *Stilarchitektur und Baukunst* (Style- architecture and building-art; 1902) was one of the most important.[8] In *Das englische Haus* (The English house; 1904-05), he also wrote on the English cottage style which he admired.[9]

Another decisive influence on Scandinavian design at this time was the Austrian architect Adolf Loos who was harshly critical of new ornament, demanding simpler, more functional forms.[10] His conception of beauty as a harmonious arrangement of parts and functional utility seems to reverberate in Ellen Key's desire to combine simple, expressive beauty with practical usefulness. Key was also strongly influenced by the English Arts and Crafts movement, which sought to reinvigorate true craftsmanship in the production of goods and to create a more pleasing interior. The English design magazine, *The Studio* (founded by Charles Holme in 1893), was widely read in Scandinavia and played an important role in disseminating these reform ideas, as well as reporting back on Scandinavian developments to an English audience.[11] English developments were also closely reported in Swedish periodicals such as *Idun* and *Ord och Bild* (Word and image).[12] Key's aesthetic doctrines were certainly influenced by the English reformers John Ruskin and William Morris, whom she frequently acknowledged, but there are also significant differences between their doctrines.[13] She viewed them as "aristocratic dilettantes" with a pessimistic regard for the aesthetic preferences of the collective masses, and she disagreed with their negative assessment of mechanical technology and the role of industry.

Key's intellectual roots and inspirational sources were extremely varied and somewhat idiosyncratic, and ultimately they are hard to pinpoint. Her beliefs and opinions changed over time; they reflected her shifting enthusiasms, continuous doubts, and frequent peregrinations. She always maintained a strong intellectual attachment to the German philosophical tradition, especially the work of Goethe and Nietzsche. She was also something of an anglophile.[14] Elizabeth Barrett Browning, George Eliot, John Ruskin, Walter Pater, Herbert Spencer, and John Stuart Mill, all played important roles in her intellectual development. In her later discussions of art and society she frequently referred to Leo Tolstoy and Baruch Spinoza.[15]

Her discussions of art and material culture, which are deeply insightful, as well as occasionally ingenuous, also contain a certain myopia. There are remarkable, unexpected silences, given her interests, curiosity, and travels. There is no discussion, for example, of

Fig. 3-3. Caricature of Ellen Key by Albert Engström; inscribed, "thanks for bringing to life love's half-forgotten art." (From Dagens Nyheter, July 15, 1906)

the great international expositions, although she traveled to Paris in 1900 and would have also attended the Stockholm Arts and Industrial Exposition of 1897.

Ellen Karolina Sofia Key (1849–1926) was born into the privileged ranks of Swedish society.[16] Her father, Emil Key, was a noted politician and gifted speaker. Her mother was a member of one of Sweden's wealthiest families. As a young woman Ellen Key met many of the leading politicians and intellectuals of her day in a home filled with books and lively debate. She achieved fame and notoriety for her outspoken opinions, especially of love and marriage (fig. 3-3). Her early interest in the *folkhögskola rörelse* (Folk High-School movement), peasant culture, and the rural lifestyle led her to visit the Nobelist Bjørnstjerne Bjørnson in Norway.[17] She also admired the playwright Henrik Ibsen and defended him for his deep insight into domestic life and the relationship between the sexes.

Key's opinions were complex, idiosyncratic, and at times ambiguous. She was a feminist who also recognized a woman's maternal role, a socialist who championed the individual, a liberal defender of "free love" who also believed in the traditional "nuclear family," a member of the urban elite who admired rural society and the common laborer. She studied philosophy and was strongly influenced by Friedrich Nietzsche's ideas regarding the great personality's dominant role, as well as Herbert Spencer's social Darwinism.[18] Her lectures on Swedish cultural history at the Stockholm Workers' Institute from 1883 to 1900 were extremely popular.[19] She also frequently engaged in polemical debate on such topics as nationalism, artistic beauty, sexuality, and the education of children.[20] Her reviews and literary criticism often appeared in *Ord och Bild*. She corresponded with the poets Rainer Maria Rilke and Sigbjørn Obstfelder. Her extensive travels and public lectures throughout Scandinavia and Europe, as well as her prodigious writings, added to her fame.

Ellen Key's social and intellectual circle included artists Richard Bergh, Carl and Karin Larsson, Anders Zorn, Hanna Pauli, and Prince Eugen; art historian Carl G. Laurin, and publishing magnate Karl Bonnier. They considered themselves "enlightened" radicals, calling their group *Sällskapet Juntan* (The Junta Society), and often met for meals and intellectual stimulation (fig. 3-4). Key's home at Strand near Alvastra became a sort of intellectual refuge for her many friends and admirers.[21] She was also a distant relative of Axel Key, professor of pathology at the Karolinska Institute in Uppsala, who was active in the national health reform movement.[22]

Skönhet för alla

Skönhet för alla (Beauty for all) consists of four essays, written between 1870 and 1897 and first published together in 1899.[23] The first essay, "Skönhet i hemmen" (Beauty in the home), states Key's basic conviction that the best objects are simple and affordable and easily satisfy their intended purpose.[24] Above all they should reflect individual taste and human needs. This argument responds to the Swedish philosopher and nobleman Carl August Ehrensvärd, whose ideas regarding taste and beauty she quotes throughout her text.[25] He defined beauty as orderliness, a healthy freedom from imperfection that is attained through clarity, simplicity, and truth.

In this first essay, which is the longest and most significant part of the book, Key posits a number of basic axioms for more tasteful design to serve as standards by which to create a more beautiful home. They follow no specific order or hierarchy and are interspersed throughout the chapter. Her basic recommendations include these convictions:

All of our things should satisfy the purpose for which they were created.[26]

They should fulfill their purpose with simplicity and ease, excellence and fullness of expression; otherwise they fail to achieve beauty, notwithstanding the corresponding demands for use.[27]

Above all, homes must vary; everything must reflect the individual taste and needs of their occupants.[28]

A room first receives its character when its occupants reveal their soul there; when they show us what they recollect and love, how they live and work on a daily basis.[29]

It is the interconnection, and agreement of things which first and foremost produce beautiful rooms.[30]

It is always best to maintain the character of the material itself as much as possible, the natural form and color.[31]

The beauty that is attained by the least possible loss of time and expense is the most meaningful kind of beauty for the simple home.[32]

"Genuine taste" understands how to create an attractive overall impression from the most dissimilar circumstances and the most varied means. It is ultimately the "pure taste" that recognizes that moderation and unity are prerequisites for beauty in the home, as well as in all other artistic creations.[33]

Personal taste best develops when one surrounds oneself with artistic beauty and learns to appreciate it.[34]

To embellish a room Key strongly recommends the use of books and works of art, especially reproductions of famous masterpieces. Museums play an important educational role, according to Key, permitting the study of objects from the past and how they have been collected and preserved. They increase public awareness, stimulate thought and reflection, and help to improve overall public taste. She urges readers to visit the simple and unified domestic interiors at the folk museum at Skansen in Stockholm, while arguing against blindly copying them since it is impossible to truly step from the present back into the past.[35] The present era, of course, has "too many new needs and new means of satisfying them."[36] At best one can only hope to preserve such antiquities, and adapt them to modern life.

She notes that the city dweller has greater access to museums, libraries, and cultural attractions but lacks the independence and vitality of the "country folk" who are able to find beauty in nature and their closest surroundings.[37] She argues that those who live in the country are more self-sufficient than city dwellers, less materialistic, and freer to create their own domestic space without the dictates of others. They find beauty in nature rather than on the walls of the museum. Instead of finding music in a concert hall, they discover melodies in the forests and fields. Instead of relying on thoughts collected in books and libraries, rural society possesses a rich oral tradition which surpasses many novels.

Key did not imply, however, that the modern city dweller is any less capable of experiencing beauty. Both places have their advantages, and "neither the country nor the city is consequently without its share, when it comes to beauty."[38] The most important factor is one's attitude. One must always maintain an open mind, reserve judgment, and constantly seek to challenge one's beliefs. Key advocates a life unfettered by material objects and superficialities, receptive to the depths below the surfaces of appearance, and thereby able to internalize beauty. She calls this attitude "a receptive heart and open soul." Above all she argues that wealth and luxury are not prerequisites for good taste or the appreciation of beauty, especially without a deep "inner sense of joy and beauty."[39] This mystical, quasi-religious attitude was a recurring theme in her writing, intimately connected to her conception of beauty, as well as her belief in a distinctly Swedish national character.

On first impression this rejection of material objects may appear contradictory in a tome devoted to beauty and interior design. Key ultimately argues for an intellectual and psycho-spiritual sense of beauty, which places human beings over material things and implies an *vardagslivets estetik* ("everyday aesthetic"). Her argument acknowledges a fundamental tension between the "wealthy with means who lack taste, and the poor with taste who lack means."[40]

The second essay, "Vardagsskönhet" (Everyday beauty), describes the intrinsic differences among human beings, the fact that no two people ever view any situation or evaluate any one object exactly alike.[41] Like the moral philosopher who must acknowledge the existence of evil, or the psychologist who must admit human dissatisfaction, Key recognizes that some people simply refuse to experience beauty. They are indifferent or disinterested in such things; their feelings for beauty are never aroused. She thereby distinguishes between two types of people. One possesses a special soulful sense of beauty. The other perceives only material superficialities and lacks a deep inner sense of beauty.

In the book's third essay, "Festvanor" (Festival customs and practices), she describes the special role of national holidays, such as Christmas, New Year's Day, and Easter, as well as birthdays and other ritual occasions, for the decoration of the home and our overall sense of beauty.[42] She notes the impact of these occasions on children and cites the mother's role in establishing festive family traditions and assuring their continuity. According to Key, a mother is "an artist of the domestic sphere" who can awaken her child's inner feelings and respect for beauty. This brief chapter encapsulates the broader implications of Key's social

Fig. 3-4. *Vänner* (Friends) by Hanna Pauli, 1900-07; oil on canvas. The Sällskapet Juntan group included Ellen Key (center), Hannah and Georg Pauli, and the Bergh, Bendixon, Fåhreus, and Bonnier families. (Nationalmuseum, Stockholm)

aesthetic for all family members, especially children, and for their education. In fact a subsequent work, her best-known book, *Barnets århundrade* (The century of the child; 1900), dealt specifically with the education of the child.[43] The rights and interests of the child, woman, and worker are the three most common themes throughout her oeuvre.

The final and shortest essay of the book, "Skymningsbrasan" (The twilight hearth),[44] is also the most symbolic, poetic, and nationalistic essay in *Skönhet för alla*. It describes the Scandinavian love of the hearth and the special role of fire in Nordic life and myth. According to Key the rich oral tradition of the north revolves around the hearth. It is the center of the home, where children gather to listen to folktales, heroic legends, and ancient sagas, and where adults can sit cozily with a book. The long, dark Nordic winter only strengthens the importance of the hearth. Fire has many meanings for Key. It becomes a metaphor for creativity: it warms and comforts, it illuminates darkness, it indirectly provides nourishment by warming food and drink. Fire is mysterious and magical, potentially dangerous and unpredictable. It also provides a metaphor for the inner joy and enthusiasm with which we should conduct our lives. She identifies the hearth as the core of the domestic sphere; its dancing flames and glowing embers provide an almost indescribable coziness, intimacy, and warmth.

The Scandinavian Context of Key's Reforms

Like the French philosophers and aestheticians Montesquieu and Taine, Key argued that Swedish geography and climate have an important impact on the aesthetic preferences of the Scandinavian population. She believed that the long, dark winter and the short summers of the midnight sun directly influenced social custom, living patterns, and public taste. Color, lighting, and interior atmosphere had a definite impact on mental health according to her. She described the ". . . power of the soothing, warm, really happy or bright colors, which not only increase the healthy life force, but also have the effect of calming mental illness."[45] In her repeated calls for fresh air, natural light, proximity to nature, and a rural lifestyle, Key shared much with the German *Lebensreform* ("reform of lived experience") movement and anticipated the popular Swedish "hygienic-aesthetic" programs of the first decade of the twentieth century. Key recognized the implications of her aesthetic philosophy for the human body, physical fitness, and mental health.

Key's ideas about beauty and the home are inseparable from her feminism and are closely related to the *hemsljöd* movement. The term *hemsljöd* is a distinctively Scandinavian concept and not easily translated into English.[46] It refers to the growing enthusiasm for artistic handicrafts and folk arts during the nineteenth century, triggered largely by increased nationalist fervor in Scandinavia. The typical forms of *hemsljöd* are textiles and needlework, wood carving (including rosemaling), wrought-iron work, and jewelry making, or in other words, the "domestic arts."

National societies were organized for the purpose of instructing women in the native crafts traditions and helping to preserve them. One of the most important in Sweden was Föreningen Handarbetets Vänner (Association of Friends of Textile-Handicrafts) founded in 1874 under the leadership of Sophie Adlersparre, a prominent feminist organizer. Föreningen för Svensk Hemsljöd (The Society for Swedish Domestic Crafts), founded in 1899 by textile artist Lilli Zuckerman and supported by Prince Eugen, pursued a similar goal.

Key's aesthetic reforms were also motivated by a desire to give women more freedom, better health, a greater sense of contentment, and psychological balance. She recognized the power of women to shape the home, thereby creating a more secure and stable domestic sphere. They were also responsible for establishing customs and preserving family traditions, including the handicrafts implied by the concept of *hemsljöd*.

Key was not the first Swedish woman to articulate a new view of the home. Mathilda Langlet wrote a guide for housewives in 1884 in which she objected to dark, cramped, and cluttered interiors.[47] Langlet, who also wrote children's literature, argued that since the domestic interior was the place where the family gathered, it served a vital role despite its frequent lack of comfortable furnishings.

An important precursor of Key's aesthetic philosophy was the "beauty in the home" movement promoted by Lorentz Dietrichson.[48] A Norwegian, Dietrichson was professor of art history at the University of Stockholm, and beginning in 1870 he sat on the board of directors of Svenska Slöjdföreningen (The Swedish Society of Craft and Industrial Design). He returned to Norway in 1875 to assume the first chair in art history at the University of Oslo. Key most likely had heard his lectures on beauty in Stockholm and was certainly acquainted with his ideas since they belonged to the same social circle. Dietrichson equated beauty with morality and truth; the three were inseparably linked in his philosophical system.[49] He argued that a beautiful home (or private sphere) was necessary in order to have a beautiful, healthy, and moral society (public sphere). Dietrichson recognized that the best way to achieve this was to have greater cooperation between producers and consumers. He believed that those who make handicrafts must refine their sense of beauty since this will also lead to more refined consumers and thereby a more pleasing and harmonious domestic life.[50] Dietrichson also acknowledged the special role played by women in maintaining the home, however,

STUDENTFÖRENINGEN *VERDANDIS* SMÅSKRIFTER. 131.

ETT HEM

DESS BYGGNAD OCH INREDNING

AV

RAGNAR ÖSTBERG,

arkitekt.

TREDJE UPPLAGAN

(*Tionde—trettonde tusendet.*)

STOCKHOLM
ALBERT BONNIERS FÖRLAG

Fig. 3-5. Title page of *Ett hem* (3rd ed., Stockholm: Bonniers, 1908).

and advocated a completely different type of interior space than that defined by Ellen Key. His ideal home was modeled after those of the aristocratic elite, and he had a deep respect for historical tradition, especially the Old Norse or Viking revival style. His home had dark walls with heavy curtains and contained large, imposing furniture. The overall effect was one of solemnity, gravity, and purpose. The lighting was filtered and subdued. Darkened floors were believed to lend stability to the room, whereas white walls and natural light were regarded as disturbing. Dietrichson continued the primitive concept of the safety of the enclosure, whereas Key regarded the interior as a logical extension of the natural exterior.

Many of Key's ideas regarding beauty, the home, and domestic space were closely shared by her Swedish contemporaries. Her books and articles were undoubtedly widely read and discussed throughout Scandinavia and had an enormous impact. Like Key, the art historian Carl G. Laurin lectured at the Stockholm Workers' Institute (1899–1929), where he discussed the role of art in society and the home.[51] He argued that one should strive for light and soothing decorations and avoid too much decoration. It was important to respect older historical styles, according to Laurin, but best primarily to use a newer style that was closer to contemporary tastes.

Another important figure for disseminating Key's ideas was Erik G. Folcker.[52] As secretary of Svenska Slöjdföreningen and a leading theorist of Swedish interior design he had tremendous influence. He focused especially on the design of furniture and the need for simpler more rational forms. Folcker recommended the use of large windows and light curtains in the family gathering room in order to achieve a warm, pleasing overall effect. Alf Wallander, Folcker's close friend and a leading glass and ceramic artist, also stressed the need to create a more beautiful home.[53] Like Ellen Key his conception of beauty emphasized the need for light and pleasant surroundings due to the harsh Nordic climate, and he also decried the demoralizing effect of German imports. He advocated "simple and noble" objects arranged in a harmonious way. Wallander especially admired Key's progressive social engagement and her keen intuition. He too recognized the need to teach beauty in the schools and the importance of greater cooperation between artists and the general public.

Ellen Key's aesthetic reforms also influenced the writer and activist, Louisa Johanna [Elna] Tenow, who used the pseudonym of Elsa Törne. She started the Solidar movement, which advocated more functional and hygienic domestic spaces.[54] She argued that cleanliness and comfort were essential aspects of beauty and that a sanitary, well-designed, and rationally planned household helped to liberate women.

The noted Swedish architect Ragnar Östberg praised Key in a short treatise *Ett hem* (A home; fig. 3-5)—a work whose argument shared many affinities with *Skönhet för alla*.[55] Like Key, Östberg advocated simple, tasteful design that was affordable and comfortable. He recognized the need to create a pleasing overall unity, praising the merits of wood, natural light, and fresh air and offering practical advice on the choice of furniture and other interior details. Östberg stressed the need to satisfy individual desires, practical needs, and personal tastes in the design of the home. His book also contained drawings and floor plans and was as much a practical guide as social propaganda.

Together these individuals and others writing around the same time continued the basic aesthetic reforms articulated by Ellen Key. They advocated a more tasteful, functional, simple, and affordable

Fig. 3-6. The "Green Room," Workers' Institute, Stockholm; designed by Ellen Key with Richard and Gerda Bergh, 1899; furniture by Carl Westman; additional designs by Alf Wallander and Nils Kreuger. (From Ellen Key, "Folket och konsten," *Varia* 1 [1900], p. 33)

domestic space, in short, what came to be regarded as a more "beautiful" home for all the Swedish people.[56]

The aesthetic reform movement also had an impact in Denmark where the crafts tradition was invigorated by the *Skønvirke* ("works of beauty") movement begun in 1907 by the architect-designers Jens Møller-Jensen and P. V. Jensen Klint.[57] The *Skønvirke* movement, which regarded itself as distinctively Danish, advocated simple and harmonious forms, the use of beautiful materials, a strong commitment to the classical tradition, and a deep respect for peasant handicrafts and native color.

Many of Key's aesthetic principles were realized in the rooms she designed during the spring and fall of 1899 for the Workers' Institute in Stockholm. The so-called Blue and Green rooms (fig. 3-6) were created in collaboration with artist Richard Bergh, his wife, Gerda, and architect Carl Westman, together with artists Alf Wallander and Nils Kreuger. They sought to demonstrate how someone of modest income could create a simple and cozy room of beauty. These model rooms thereby effectively mediated the tension between attaining beauty and having only limited economic resources.

For Key, the residence built by artists Carl Larsson and his wife, Karin Bergöö Larsson, was the epitome of her aesthetic ideals (fig. 3-7).[58] A country cottage known as Lilla Hyttnäs, in Sundborn, Dalarna, the house was inherited from Karin's father in 1889. Over subsequent decades it was added to, refined, and

Fig. 3-7. *Pappas rum* (Grandpapa's room) by
Carl Larsson, 1894; watercolor on paper.
This was reproduced as one of the illustra-
tions in Larsson's book, *Ett hem* (Stockholm:
Bonniers, 1899). (Nationalmuseum,
Stockholm)

remodeled. It became a central motif in Carl Larsson's
art and was popularized in a series of illustrated
books, including *Ett hem* (A home; 1899), *Larssons*
(1902), and *Åt solsidan* (On the sunny side; 1910).[59]
The house was regarded as the embodiment of
Swedish coziness and charm, reflecting a unique attitude toward furnishing the home which was a part of a
distinct national character.[60]

Key would most likely have seen Larsson's series of
watercolors of his home, which were first shown at the
Stockholm Exhibition of 1897. The renderings of these
bright interiors, with their simple and tasteful decorations, white walls, natural light, warm colors, book-
shelves, and eclectic blend of traditional and modern
objects, were consistent with Ellen Key's design dictates. Larsson's choice of furniture in particular,
revealed his love of the simple designs of the Swedish
peasantry and the more refined neoclassical styles of
the Gustavian and Empire traditions.[61]

Gregor Paulsson: Beauty for the Masses

Ellen Key's socially oriented aesthetic philosophy
made a deep impression on art historian Gregor
Paulsson (1889–1977; fig. 3-8) who would publish his
own views on design in *Vackrare Vardagsvara* (More
beautiful things for everyday use; 1919).[62] Paulsson
succeeded in uniting Key's ideas with the Deutscher
Werkbund's radical program for architecture, art, craft,
and industry, as well as the emerging progressive
social democracy of modern Sweden. He was closely
associated with Svenska Slöjdföreningen throughout
his career, serving as director and editor of its journal

Fig. 3-8. Gregor Paulsson (1889–1977). (From *Form* 73, no. 2/3 [1977],
p. 36)

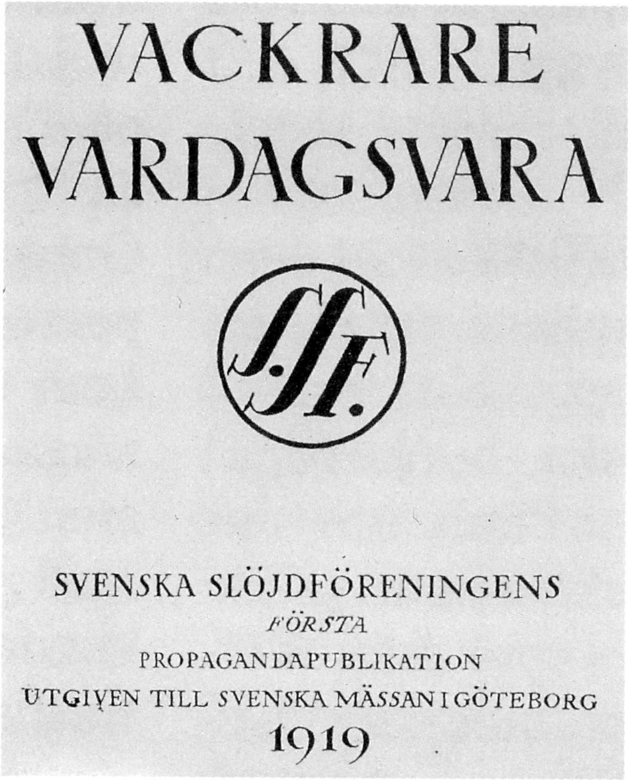

VACKRARE VARDAGSVARA

SVENSKA SLÖJDFÖRENINGENS
FÖRSTA
PROPAGANDAPUBLIKATION
UTGIVEN TILL SVENSKA MÄSSAN I GÖTEBORG
1919

Fig. 3-9. Part-title page of *Vackrare Vardagsvara* (Stockholm: Svenska Slöjdföreningen, 1919).

from 1920 to 1934 and as chairman from 1943 to 1950. Paulsson provided the theoretical justification and ideological foundations for the 1930 Stockholm Exhibition and was a driving force behind the subsequent functionalist manifesto, *acceptera* (To accept; 1931), which was written in collaboration with architects Erik Gunnar Asplund, Sven Markelius, Uno Åhrén, Eskil Sundahl, and Walter Gahn. A basic principle that guided Paulsson's career was the belief that "there exists a necessary connection between [artistic forms] and the political and social character of the period during which they originated."[63] This idea began with the Viennese art historian, Aloïs Riegl, who posited the *Kunstwollen*, an artistic will to form, in order to describe the evolution of a culture's artistic forms.[64] In his autobiography Paulsson described his initial encounter with Riegl's ideas as "my actual birth as an art historian."[65]

Paulsson's ideas also reflect the shifting attitudes resulting from Sweden's emergence in the international arena and increasing prominence in modern design.[66] Erik Wettergren and Paulsson severely criticized the 1914 Baltic Exhibition in Malmö for its excessively expensive objects that showed a one-sided concern for the needs of an elite bourgeoisie.[67] They lamented

the broad popularity of these luxury goods and regarded the Baltic Exhibition as a failure, even though it helped to draw international attention to the Nordic countries. Consequently Wettergren helped to establish a *förmedlingsbyrå* ("contract bureau") in 1914; its goal was to increase cooperation between artists and industry and to help establish a set of strict guidelines that they should follow. Wettergren claimed that Ellen Key's ideas were the inspiration for this project. In 1917 Wettergren and Paulsson's ideas reached fruition in Hemutställningen (The Home Exhibition) sponsored by Svenska Slöjdföreningen at the Liljevalchs art gallery in Stockholm. This exhibition, which featured a number of simple, but tastefully designed rooms containing industrially manufactured objects, as well as a display of art wares and home furnishings (glass, porcelain, rugs, and tiled stoves and heaters), satisfied Ellen Key's earlier demand for affordable products for the low-income worker, an idea that had first been practically realized in the rooms Key designed for the Stockholm Workers' Institute in 1899. The 1917 Home Exhibition was heralded as a decisive breakthrough, a successful new direction for Swedish design.[68]

Vackrare Vardagsvara

Like Ellen Key, Gregor Paulsson sought to unite art and industry in a cooperative enterprise and thereby to create artistic forms which were socially responsible. In 1919 he expressed this desire in his now famous utilitarian credo and the title of his most important and widely influential work: *Vackrare Vardagsvara* (More beautiful things for everyday use). The manifesto built upon the argument first developed in *Den nya arkitekturen* (The new architecture; 1916) and continued many of Key's basic ideas, while advocating a greater role for industry, technology, and mass production in creating a modern aesthetic of beauty.[69] Paulsson intended *Vackrare Vardagsvara* as propaganda, clearly stating this ambition in the subtitle: "The first propaganda publication of the Svenska Slöjdföreningen / Published for the Swedish Exhibition in Gothenburg" (fig. 3-9).

In subsequent decades "More Beautiful Things for Everyday Use" became a slogan for modern Swedish design. The book consists of nine short chapters interspersed with black-and-white illustrations and featuring works of glass by Simon Gate, Edward Hald, and Emil Olsson-Ollers. The book's design and format amplify its message. The first and last chapters conclude with, respectively, a repeat of his credo, "Vackrare Vardagsvaror" and the dictum, "Alla Varor Vackrare!" ("all things beautiful"), both set in bold, uppercase type. The chapters are arranged to proceed almost hierarchically from a general discussion of taste, beauty, and industry to the stages of production and consumption. The argument acknowledges the cooperative roles of the artist-creator, worker-manufacturer, seller, and social consumer in this process. His central conviction is that beauty should have a permanent place in our lives.

In the first chapter, "Är Smaken Olika?" (Are tastes different?), Paulsson addresses the wide disparity in individual taste. He laments the proliferation of cheap, inferior imitations while recognizing the enormous improvements in mechanical technology, as well as better economic, political, and social conditions. He uses Swedish glass to illustrate the way in which individual tastes are relative and dependent on context. He notes that:

> Two persons in the presence of the same object could have completely opposite opinions; a cut crystal vase could be considered by the one to be tremendously beautiful, by the other detestable. Who is correct? Answer: to a certain degree both.[70]

Paulsson argues that judgments of beauty always depend on context and circumstance. Artistic forms are not absolute, nor are they merely a matter of coincidence. He recognizes that Swedish society had largely overcome the class differences of previous centuries, but the so-called "beautiful wares" and decorative objects of the present are little more than cheap and inferior imitations. He speaks of a future "modern beauty," which would build entirely upon technical possibilities. Paulsson believes that, by means of mechanical technology, all members of the society can enjoy beautiful and useful everyday objects. He proposes a new direction in mass production and standardization, and greater cooperation between art and industry. According to Paulsson, by reestablishing uniformity in production, greater unity in overall social taste will be realized. For him unity in taste is equivalent to social unity. This is the far-reaching consequence of his argument and the true meaning of his motto as he notes, "unitary taste also creates a uniformity in all of society's forms . . . this is the deep meaning of the expression, 'more beautiful things for everyday use.'"[71] Paulsson regarded beauty as a spiritual force (akin to Riegl's *Kunstwollen*), which penetrates all things and extends equally from the private to the public spheres. He also regarded beauty as the means by which Swedish design could distinguish itself from the rest of the world and thereby enable Sweden to achieve greater economic strength as well as social harmony.

Chapter two, entitled "Industri och Skönhet" (Industry and beauty), clarifies his attitude toward the machine, modern taste, and the modern conception of beauty. Paulsson argues that art and industry, the traditional craftsman, and factory worker have historically been at odds with one another, and he seeks to recon-

cile this conflict. In order for this to be accomplished we must cease to imitate the old and strive to create new forms by using the new technology of the period. Paulsson regards this as the central aim of the new, radical industrial epoch which fully embraces iron and concrete, is led by inventors and engineers, and is liberated from historical styles. This modern conception of beauty is motivated by a desire for truth, simplicity, and unity. It implies the cooperation of art and industry. Art improves industry and industry disseminates more art. As Paulsson argues, "The arts industrialize in order to obtain beautiful forms; industry becomes artistic in order to achieve closer contact with contemporary technology and thereby obtain new goals and an expanded field of operation."[72]

"Skönhet och kvalitet" (Beauty and quality) is the title and theme of chapter three. Paulsson describes the economic significance and impact of the competitive marketplace on production. He contends that the copy is never as good as the original and that by demanding quality and excellence Swedish producers can compete with foreign manufacturers, as well as achieve distinction.[73] One way in which to obtain this result is through standardization. But Paulsson argues that quality is more than just good materials and production methods. It also implies that wares have good form. They must be affordable, simple, and tasteful.

Chapter four, "Utlandet" (The foreign), examines the relationship between modern taste and the international market. Paulsson focuses specifically on the impact of the Deutscher Werkbund and its links to German nationalism before the First World War. By emphasizing quality and the artist's role in industry, Germany achieved international recognition for its applied arts and became the envy of other countries, while German industry achieved economic strength.

Svenska Slöjdföreningen is discussed in chapter five. Paulsson outlines the way in which this organization sought to introduce the Werkbund ideology into Sweden. He notes the significance of the 1917 Home Exhibition at the Liljevalchs art gallery in Stockholm as a "definitive transition from isolated individual production to a collective generation's single-minded work for a design tradition founded on a broad social base.[74] He stresses Swedish culture's radical democratic tastes, and the optimistic desire to unite artists with industry. Simon Gate and Edward Hald's glass production is mentioned as a prime example of this tendency.

Chapter six, entitled "Konstnären" (The artist), examines the ambivalent attitudes of artists toward industry. The younger artists, according to Paulsson, are more willing to cooperate with industry, whereas the older generation view this as a limitation on their creative freedom. He argues that "they want to have their complete freedom in everything."[75] This older generation is more closely tied to the craft tradition.

Fig. 3-10. Exhibition Hall 19 (Swedish Glass) at the 1930 Stockholm Exhibition (From Erik Gunnar Asplund, "Stockholmsutställningen 1930-utställningshallarna," *Byggmästaren* 9 [1930], p. 142). Asplund noted that "the fenestration of the hall of glass is two-sided, which was considered necessary in order to illuminate the glass as much as possible   but [we determined that] one should simply exhibit glass in good ordinary light!" (ibid, p. 138).

They view their pieces as unique and not mechanically reproducible. Paulsson argues that when artists and industry join together in a mutual agreement, new and original styles become possible. This implies that the artist be willing to create forms that are not dependent upon him for their artistic effect, but that a machine can reproduce in large quantities in a logical and controlled manner.

Paulsson devotes chapter seven to "Framställaren" (The producer-manufacturer). He extends his ideas from the home to the factory and recognizes the need to please the factory worker. Paulsson argues that by improving working conditions, providing more educational opportunities, and establishing a greater artistic presence in the workplace, the workers themselves will have a greater sense of beauty. They will produce better products, take greater pride in their work, and become more discriminating consumers. He

describes the tension between the traditional craftsman working by hand in a small workshop and the modern laborer employing machines in the factory. In both cases if the workers strive for quality and establish high goals for themselves, they will produce beautiful wares. This results in important savings to society, a stronger sense of national identity, and a decline in foreign imports.

Chapter eight, entitled "Säljaren" (The seller), discusses the relationship between the consumer, factory owner, and merchant. Paulsson analyzes mass purchasing habits and is especially interested in how the profit motive affects the quality of goods sold. He also discusses modes of display, especially the role of the storefront window and its impact on an object's appearance. According to him, "when a beautiful ware stands alone or among other beautiful things they preserve its beauty, when it is placed among ugly wares it appears ugly due to its isolation."[76] He argues that in order to entice those of modest means to purchase finer goods (at sometimes greater costs), instead of the cheap imitations of inferior quality, they must be paid their wages on a different schedule. Instead of once a week, they must realize the possibility of a larger outlay and the need to save instead of living from hand to mouth. Paulsson recognizes that "they would rather purchase something five times for ten kroner than once for fifty."[77] In particular he praises the farmers who plan their purchases for the entire year based on the income from the fall harvest. He decries the gaudy wares (kitsch) that are popular in rural shops. According to him, they are a "cultural sickness," and along with the large department stores full of similar things, they must be entirely eliminated.[78]

The final chapter, entitled "Samhället" (The society), discusses the broad implications of his ideas. He recognizes that an improved relationship between art and industry has deep social consequences for the Swedish people. It results in a fundamental change in human beings, as well as the social and cultural structures of society. Like Ellen Key, Paulsson recognizes the vital role of education for improving social taste. He concludes with the optimistic proclamation that the next generation will be better prepared than the present one to meet the task of making all objects more beautiful.

Aesthetic Demands, Social Needs, and Modern Swedish Glass

In retrospect the aesthetic reforms of Ellen Key and Gregor Paulsson have a complex and somewhat paradoxical relationship to the development of modern Swedish design. Their radical reforms frequently encountered opposition and resistance from pessimists, skeptics, and conservatives alike. The greatest impediment to their success, however, was perhaps Swedish society itself (and the weakness of human nature). As Paulsson always noted, artistic form is inseparable from its social context. He also admitted somewhat reluctantly that "form is conservative" and can take a very long time to unfold. Yet what good is beautiful form in an imperfect world? Unfortunately, not all members of society want what is best for them or their fellow citizens. Questions of beauty lose their importance when people are merely interested in survival or feel their personal identity threatened by the larger social collective. Some members of society regard beauty, order, simplicity, and coziness as sterile, boring, and threatening. The small and relatively homogenous Swedish population no doubt played an important role in helping to establish the aesthetic reforms of Ellen Key and Gregor Paulsson, but they also encountered resistance.

It is easy to view Key as a precursor to functional-

Individen och massan . . .

Det personliga eller det allmängiltiga?
Kvalitet eller kvantitet?
— en olöslig frågeställning, ty vi kan icke komma ifrån kollektivitetens faktum lika litet som vi kan komma ifrån individens fordran på självständigt liv.
Problemet heter i våra dagar:
kvantitet *och* kvalitet, massa *och* individ.
Det är nödvändigt att söka lösa det även i byggnadskonsten och konstindustrin.

Fig. 3-11. Frontispiece in *acceptera* (Stockholm, 1931). The text reads, "the individual or the masses . . . the personal or the collective? Quality or quantity? A question posed without solution, for we cannot escape the fact of our collectivity anymore than we can escape the individual demand for autonomous life. In our day the problem is called: the individual *and* the masses, the personal *and* the collective. It is necessary to find a solution even in architecture and artistic handicrafts."

ism, especially given her emphasis on functional utility, as well as her demand that design logically reflect purpose. Ellen Key discussed glass only briefly in *Skönhet för alla* where she argued that "indeed the simpler the form of the glass, the more beauty it has as a rule, and the trophy cup remains perhaps the most beautiful of all."[79] In addition to these brief remarks, in a later essay Key praised Alf Wallander's glass designs, as well as his broad social commitment. Gregor Paulsson, on the other hand, wrote extensively about Swedish glass and recognized its potential impact on the Swedish home.

In 1925 Orrefors had earned its international reputation at the Paris Exposition des Arts Décoratifs et Industriels Modernes as a manufacturer of expensive, high-quality, exclusive designs in large part due to its

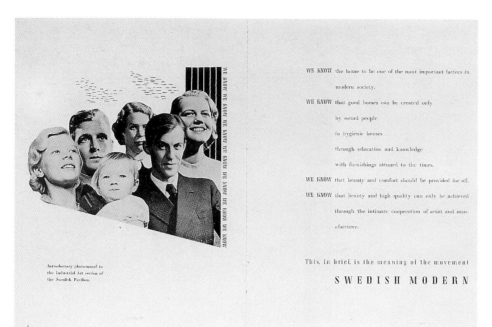

WE KNOW the home to be one of the most important factors in modern society.

WE KNOW that good homes can be created only by sound people in hygienic houses through education and knowledge with furnishings attuned to the times.

WE KNOW that beauty and comfort should be provided for all.

WE KNOW that beauty and high quality can only be achieved through the intimate cooperation of artist and manufacturer.

This, in brief, is the meaning of the movement

SWEDISH MODERN

Fig. 3-12. Photomural at the entrance to the Industrial Art section of the Swedish Pavilion, New York World's Fair, 1939. (From Åke Stavenow, et al., eds., *Swedish Arts and Crafts / Swedish Modern—A Movement Toward Sanity in Design,* exhib. cat. [New York: Royal Swedish Commission, 1939], pp. 4–5)

perfect combination of art and industry. The collaboration was considered "perfect" in the sense that the artists were eminently aware of their importance and success, the essential role they played. Five years later the display of glass at the 1930 Stockholm Exhibition acknowledged the fundamental tension between the exclusive and ordinary, the expensive and affordable, and the sharp contrast between luxurious, decorative fantasy and practical reality (fig. 3-10). Within Asplund's special Exhibition Hall, the elegant, sophisticated, and expensive works created by Edward Hald and Simon Gate stood in sharp contrast to the common, ordinary, but eminently affordable glass table services featured elsewhere in the exhibition. Ironically it was the former that became better known and thereby increased the prestige of the Swedish glass industry despite the fact that Hald and Gate worked in both art glass and everyday ware. In a review of the 1930 Stockholm Exhibition Jacob Bang praised the famous art glass of Hald and Gate but argued that the affordable, functional everyday glass displayed in the "collective" section was the only thing really new and truly "in pact with the essential aims of the exhibition."[80] Bang suggested that this *bruksglas* ("everyday glass") should have received greater recognition, and that factories should aim to cultivate it in the future. Paulsson also recognized this difficulty. He proudly accepted the international success of Swedish glass, while lamenting its departure from the daily life of the larger public and his own aesthetic philosophy. It is ironic that the affordable, functional, everyday objects intended for the common man did not make Swedish industrial arts famous. Instead it was the expensive, unique, individual luxury items such as Orrefors engraved glass.

As an apologia for functionalism, the 1931 manifesto *acceptera* sought to mediate the tension between mass-produced wares and unique, luxury items. Its central issue was a demand for socially responsible architecture and design, which reconciled quality and quantity, beauty and utility, the individual and collective (fig. 3-11). In 1932 Sweden's first Social Democratic government appeared, heralding the advent of the Scandinavian welfare state. Its egalitarian, reform-oriented programs were considered a sane "middle way" between capitalism and socialism.[81] The sociologists Gunnar Myrdal and his wife, Alva, were closely linked to the functionalists' circle, especially to Sven Markelius and Uno Åhrén. They shared a common impetus to develop affordable, attractive, and practical housing, and they especially recognized the impact of the housing issue on children, women, and the family.[82] Their radical proposal for collective housing, designed to ease the mother's burden and child's welfare, was completely consistent with Ellen Key's precepts and ideals.

At the New York World's Fair in 1939 glass was also prominently featured in the Swedish Pavilion designed by Sven Markelius (fig. 3-12). The aesthetic reforms of Key and Paulsson were transformed here into the concept of "Swedish Modern" with its emphasis on sanity, beauty, comfort, affordability, and quality. Within this short interval the tension between the exclusive and the ordinary was sharply diminished, and a new orientation had emerged. The simple and unpretentious gradually assumed dominance, and the initial grandeur and "grace" of the art glass lost some of its novelty. Both categories of glass came to be regarded as essential features of the ever-evolving ideal of

Swedish beauty. Glass became an object of distinct, national artistic value, a symbol of modern Sweden. It also achieved an important position in the ordinary Swedish home. In the words of one critic, it had "become a source of joy providing everyday comfort and beauty . . . ."[83] Beauty came to be regarded as a significant social factor in Sweden because it increased one's well-being, sense of joy, and standard of living. Ellen Key's notion of *samhällsskönheten* ("social beauty") as a dynamic cultural force, which affects all aspects of our daily life, public as well as private, was a prophetic and profound insight into the future course of Swedish design.

I am grateful to several individuals for assistance with this project: Barbara Miller Lane, my exemplary dissertation adviser, over the years has shared her vast knowledge of Ellen Key, Scandinavian architecture, and modern European history; Marion John Nelson has likewise provided encouragement, friendship, and many stimulating discussions of Scandinavian art; Kathryn Casey and Marit Bratli Sheffield read and commented upon the manuscript; Marianne Tiblin, Leslie Grove, Solveig Zempel, Leo G. Mazow, Anne Helmreich, Anne-Marie Schaaf, Charles A. Burke, and Widar Halén expeditiously met my obscure bibliographic requests and assisted with photographs; and finally Derek Ostergard provided the opportunity to pursue this topic and made valuable comments on an earlier draft.

All translations, unless otherwise noted, are by the author.

1. Ellen Key, *Skönhet för alla*, 4th ed. (Stockholm: Bonniers, 1908), p. 30 [Och framför allt bör man ej tro att skönhet endast är en lycka, som några få erhållit].

2. Ibid., pp. 5-6 [Och den enda möjligheten att alla verkligen för billigt pris skola kunna erhålla vackra saker, det är att fabrikanterna—särskilt av möbler, tapeter, tyger, glas, porslin och metallsaker—sätta sig i forbindelse med konstslöjdens idkare, så att dessa åt allt, från och med det enklaste och minsta t.ex. tändstickslådan och till det största, giva vackra former och lämpliga prydnader. Först då intet fult finnes att få köpa; då det vackra är lika billigt som det fula nu är, kan skönhet för alla bli en full verklighet].

3. Ibid., p. 5 [Och den smak, som hos dem på 70-90-talet gjort sig gällande, har varit den mest grant tarvliga tyska, ej blott i det yttre utan även i det inre.]

4. Ibid., p. 23 [Vill man ha ett lättfattligt namn på god smak bör man taga ärlighet].

5. International impulses from England, Germany, France, Belgium, and Japan, among others, had a significant impact on modern Scandinavian design. In addition to the key figures already discussed, Gustav Upmark, Carin Wästberg, Lars I. Wahlman, Fritz von Dardel, Paul Mebes, Émile Gallé, Alfred Lichtwark, Henry Havard, Hans Makart, Josef Hoffmann, Heinrich Tessenow, Hans Poelzig, Viollet-le-Duc, Christopher Dresser, and Walter Crane also deserve mention. See Elisabet Stavenow-Hidemark, "Hur Svenskt Var Det Svenska?" *Fataburen. Nordiska Museets och Skansens årsbok* (1991), pp. 44–64; and Bo Grandien, "Det skönas värld eller Venus i såskoppen," *Form* 82, nos. 2-3 (1985), pp. 12–28.

6. Norwegian translation by Nicolay Nicolaysen, *Kunsten i hus* (Kristiania, Norway: Cammermeyer, 1872); Swedish translation *Konsten i hemmet* (1876), parts of which appeared earlier in *Tidsskrift för hemmet* (1874-75). See Gunilla Frick, *Svenska Slöjdföreningen och konstindustrin före 1905*, Handlingar 91 (Stockholm: Nordiska museets, 1978).

7. Muthesius lectured on the Werkbund ideology during a visit to Stockholm in 1911. See Gunilla Frick, *Konstnär i industrin*, (Stockholm: Nordiska museet Handlingar:106, 1986), p. 12.

8. For the Swedish translation see Hermann Muthesius, *Stilarkitektur och byggnadskonst*, trans. Axel Lindegren (Stockholm, 1910); for Norwegian see idem, *Stilarkitektur og bygningskunst*, trans. Henrik Grosch (Kristiania, Norway: Cammermeyer, 1909); for English see idem, *Style-Architecture and Building-Art*, trans. Stanford Anderson (Santa Monica, CA: The Getty Center, 1994).

9. Hermann Muthesius, *Das englische Haus: Entwicklung Bedingungen, Anlage, Aufbau, Einrichtung und Innenraum*, 3 vols. (Berlin: Wasmuth, 1904–05).

10. Adolf Loos, "Ornament und Verbrechen" (1908); reprint in idem, *Trotzdem 1900–1930* (Innsbruck: Brenner Verlag, 1931). For an English translation see "Ornament and Crime" in Ludwig Münz and Gustav Künstler, *Adolf Loos* (New York: Praeger, 1966); and Adolf Loos, *Spoken into the Void: Collected Essays, 1897–1900*, trans. J. O. Newman and J. H. Smith (Cambridge, MA: MIT Press, 1982).

11. See Clive Ashwin, "The Nordic Connection—Aspects of Interchange Between Britain and Scandinavia," *Studio International* 195, no. 997 (Nov/Dec 1982), pp. 20–30.

12. *Idun* was founded as an illustrated weekly magazine for "women and the home" in 1887 by Frithiof Hellberg. The title refers to the goddess of eternal youth in Nordic mythology, the wife of Brage.

13. Gregor Paulsson also criticized Morris's commitment to the individual artist-artisan, his strong links to historical tradition, and, above all, his dislike for technology.

14. Key traced her ancestry to the Mackey clan of Scotland who had emigrated to Sweden. She traveled to England and Scotland in 1900.

15. Ellen Key, *Lyckan och Skönheten* [Livslinjer III] (Stockholm: Bonniers, 1925).

16. See Ulf Wittrock,"Key, Ellen Karolina Sofia," in *Svenskt Biografisk Lexikon*, vol. 21, ed. Erik Grill (Stockholm: Bonniers, 1975-77), pp.90-98.

17. For Key's intellectual roots see Ulf Wittrock, *Ellen Keys väg från kristendom till livstro* (Uppsala, Sweden: Appelbergs, 1953). The folk high-school movement was founded in Denmark by N. F. S. Grundtvig in the 1830s. Its aims were religious, patriotic, and romantic and directed towards the enlightenment of the peasantry through the study of Old Norse literature, national poetry and history, and a rejection of the classical educational system.

18. For a useful summary of Key's philosophical position see Romy Ambjörnsen, "En Skön, Ny Värld-Om Ellen Keys visioner och en senare tids verklighet," *Fataburen. Nordiska Museets och Skansens årsbok* (1991), pp. 260–96.

19. Founded by Anton Nyström in 1880, Stockholms Arbetarinstitut was one of the first such institutions dedicated to the intellectual improvement of the common laborer by means of free lectures on historical and scientific topics.

20. For Key's relationship to Richard Bergh and their polemical exchanges over beauty, Scandinavian nationalism, and other matters see Birgitta Rapp, *Richard Bergh-Konstnär och kulturpolitiker, 1890-1915* (Stockholm: Tryck Gotab, 1978).

For a discussion of Key and Carl Larsson's relationship to the group of Norwegian national romantic artists known as the Lysaker-Circle see Tone Skedsmo, "Hos kunstnere, polarforskere og mesener," *Kunst og Kultur* 65, no. 3 (1982), pp. 131–51.

21. For Key's impact on American audiences and her alleged relationship to Frank Lloyd Wright see Lena Johanneson, "Ellen Key, Mamah Bouton Borthwick and Frank Lloyd Wright: Notes on the historiography of non-existing history," *NORA: Nordic Journal of Women's Studies* 3, no. 2 (1995), pp. 126–36.

22. Axel Key assisted Artur Hazelius in the creation of the Skansen open-air folk museum, which officially opened in 1891, and was a leading force in the Norse Revivalist movement. His famous Villa Bråvalla near Gustavsberg was built in the Romantic Viking Revival or Old Norse style. See Bo Grandien, *Rönndruvans Glöd*, Handlingar no. 107 (Stockholm: Nordiska museet, 1987).

23. The first edition appeared in February 1899. It went through many subsequent editions and was included in the popular series *Verdandis småskrifter* (1888–1954) published by the Verdandi Student Society, a "folk movement" that had been founded in Uppsala in 1882 to promote freedom of speech, liberal debate, and radical thought. Hulda Garborg apparently translated *Skönhet för alla* into Norwegian. Garborg and her husband, famed Norwegian writer Arne Garborg, maintained close contact with Ellen Key over the years. See Widar Halén,"Gerhard Munthe and 'The Movement that from Japan is Moving Across Europe Now'," *Scandinavian Journal of Design History,* no. 4 (1994), pp. 36-37; and Tor Obrestad, *Hulda* (Oslo: Gyldendal, 1992). I am grateful to Widar Halén for assistance with this reference.

24. First published in *Iduns julnummer* (1897).

25. See Carl August Ehrensvärd, *De fria Konsters philosophi* (1786), reprint (Stockholm: Sallskapet Bokvannerna, 1974).

26. Key, *Skönhet för alla*, p. 4 [att var sak skall motsvara det ändamål, för vilket den är till!].

27. Ibid., p. 4 [. . .fylla sitt ändamål med enkelhet och lätthet, finhet och uttrycksfullhet, annars har den ej uppnåt skönheten, oaktat den motsvarar nyttans krav].

28. Ibid., p. 5 [Framför allt måste det bliva olika, allt efter de personers behov, som skola bebo hemmet].

29. Ibid., p. 7 [Ett rum får en själ först när en människa där röjer sin själ; nar det visar oss vad denna människa minnes och älskar, huru hon dagligen lever och arbetar].

30. Ibid., pp. 12-13 [Det är sammanhanget, överensstämmelsen, som först och främst gör dessa rum vackra].

31. Ibid., p. 18 [(Det) är gott råd att låta allt så mycket som möjligt behålla den av materialet själv betingade, naturliga formen och färgen].

32. Ibid., p. 31 [Den skönhet, som nås med den minsta möjliga tidsförlust och kostnad, är för de enkla hem, om vilka här talas, den mest värdefulla skönheten].

33. Ibid., p. 32 [Den verkliga smaken är den, som förstär att skapa ett tilltalande helhetsintryck ur de mest olika förhållanden och med de mest skilda medel. Den verkilga smaken är slutligen den ädla smaken, som vet att måtta och enhet äro villkoren för skönhet såvel i hemmet som i det övriga konstnärliga skapandet].

34. Ibid., p. 34 [Den personliga smaken utbildas bäst genom att man runt omkring sig ser det konstsköna och lär sig att uppskatta det].

35. For an excellent analysis of the folk museum within the context of modernity and changing modes of visual spectatorship see Mark B. Sandberg, "Effigy and Narrative: Looking into the Nineteenth-Century Folk Museum," *Cinema and the Invention of Modern Life*, ed. Leo Charney and Vanessa R. Schwartz (Berkeley: University of California Press, 1995), pp. 320–61.

36. Key, *Skönet för alla*, p. 12 [Den nya tiden har ju många nya behov och många nya medel att tillfredsställa dem].

37. The Scandinavian conception of the "folk" lacks many of the pejorative connotations of English. Key used it to refer to the Swedish nation at large, as well as the rural population. See Ellen Key, "Folket och konsten," *Varia* 1 (1900); and idem, *Folkbildningsarbetet, särskilt med hänsyn till skönhetsinnets odling* (Uppsala: Tidens Förlag, 1906).

38. Key, *Skönet för alla*, p. 36 [Varken land eller stad äro saledes lottlösa, när det gäller skönheten!].

39. Ibid., p. 36 [Ingen konst, ingen lyx Kunna giva äkta behag åt det rika hem, där den innerliga skönhetskänslan och skönhetsglädjen saknas].

40. Ibid., p. 14 [de som där ha pengar ha ingen smak och de som ha smak ha inga pengar].

41. First published in *Julbloss* (1891).

42. First published in *Iduns julnummer* (1896).

43. Ellen Key, *Barnets århundrade*, 2 vols. (Stockholm, 1900). For an English translation see idem, *The Century of the Child*, trans. Marie Franzos, preface by Havelock Ellis (New York G. P. Putnam, 1909).

44. Written originally in 1870, it was first published in *Iduns julnummer* (1895).

45. Key, *Skönhet för alla*, p. 20 [makten av lugna, varma glada färger, som ej endast stegra de friskas livsenergi utan även verka stillande på nervsjuka]. Her views of color warrant further consideration. They seem closely related to the widely held belief in her time in a distinct "Nordic color-instinct."

46. See Ingeborg Glambek, *Kunsten, Nytten og Moralen: Kunstindustri og husflid i Norge, 1800-1900* (Oslo: Solum, 1988). The Norwegian equivalent is *husflid* although even here certain nuances pertain due to its strong nationalist implications and unique status in Norwegian museums of applied art as opposed to ethnological collections. Paulsson argued that the primary aim of *konstslöjd* (artistic handicrafts) or *konstindustri* (applied arts) was "to connect beauty to the products with which we surround ourselves in our daily life" (Gregor Paulsson, *Den nya arkitekturen* [Stockholm: Norstedt, 1916], p. 151 [Vad är egentligen konstslöjd, konstindustri? Det är en princip, som går ut på att forbinda skönhet med de produkter, varmed vi omge oss i vårt dagliga liv].

47. See Elisabet Stavenow-Hidemark, "Hemmet som konstverk. Heminredning i teori och praktik på 1870-och 80-talen," *Fataburen. Nordiska museets och Skansens årsbok* (1984), pp. 129–48.

48. For Dietrichson's contributions see Ingeborg Glambek, "One of the age's noblest cultural movements," *Scandinavian Journal of Design History* 1 (1991), pp. 47–76; Stavenow-Hidemark, "Hemmet som konstverk"; Bo Grandien, *Rönndruvans Glöd*, Handlingar 107 (Stockholm: Nordiska museet, 1987); Ludvig Looström,"Lorentz Dietrichson och Svenska Slöjdföreningen," *Svenska Slöjdföreningens Tidskrift*, no. 12 (1917), pp. 22–24; Arne Eggum, "Lorentz Dietrichson som kunstpolitiker under naturalismens frembrudd," *Kunst og Kultur* 64, no. 3 (1981), pp. 133–59; and Fredrik Paasche, "Dietrichson, Lorentz Henrik Segelcke," in *Norsk Biografisk Leksikon*, vol. 3, ed. Edvard Bull (Oslo: Aschehoug, 1927), pp. 322–30.

49. Lorentz Dietrichson, *Det skönas verld*, 2 vols. (Stockholm, 1867–1879).

50. Dietrichson was strongly influenced by the work of Gottfried Semper and Jacob von Falke and helped to popularize their ideas in Scandinavia.

51. See Carl G. Laurin, "Konsten i skolan och konsten i hemmet," *Föreningen Heimdals folkskrifter* 63 (1899).

52. See Carl Hernmarch, "Folcker, Gustav Erik," in *Svenskt Biografiskt Lexicon*, vol. 16, ed. Erik Gill (Stockholm: 1964–66), pp. 254–55.

53. Alf Wallander, "Om Smaken i Våra Svenska Hem," *Varia* 11 (1900), pp. 727–31.

54. Elna Tenow, *Solidar*, 3 vols. (Stockholm, 1905-07). Also see Elisabet Stavenow-Hidemark, "Hygienism kring sekelskiftet," *Fataburen. Nordiska Museets och Skansens årsbok* (1970), pp. 47–54.

55. Ragnar Östberg, *Ett hem* (Stockholm: Bonniers, 1905).

56. Similar developments in Norway include Hulda Garborg, *Heimestell* (Kristiania, Norway: "Den 17de Mai," 1899); and N. K. Bay, *Egne hjem* (Kristiania: Cammermeyer, 1903).

57. For an excellent analysis of the Skønvirke movement see Claire Elaine Selkurt, "The Classical Influence in Early Twentieth Century Danish Furniture Design" (Ph.D. diss., University of Minnesota, 1979). The periodical of the *Skønvirke* was published in Copenhagen from 1914 to 1927.

58. Key, *Skönhet för alla*, pp. 16-17.

59. Carl Larsson, *Ett Hem* (Stockholm: Bonniers, 1899). Larsson's work was immensely popular in Germany; see Cecilia Lengefeld, *Der Maler des glücklichen Heims: Zur Rezeption Carl Larssons im wilhelminischen Deutschland* (Heidelberg: Universitätsverlag C. Winter, 1993).

60. See Carl Malmsten, "Om Svensk Karaktär inom Vår Konstkultur—Särskildt i Hemmets Utdaning," *Svenska Slöjdföreningens Tidskrift*, no. 10 (1915), pp. 163–74; and ibid., no. 11 (1916), pp. 83–95.

61. August Brunius, "Carl Larsson och en nationell möbelstil," *Svenska Slöjdföreningens Tidskrift*, no. 7 (1911), pp. 22–26.

62. See Hans Pettersson, "Paulsson, Nils Bernhard Gregor," in *Svenskt Biografisk Leksikon*, vol. 28, ed. Göran Nilzén (Stockholm, 1994), pp. 756–64.

63. Gregor Paulsson, *Vackrare Vardagsvara* (Stockholm: Svenska Slöjdföreningen, 1919), p. 8 [Det existerar ett nödvändigt samband mellan dem och den tids politiska och sociala karaktär, under vilken de kommo till].

64. See Margaret Iversen, *Alois Riegl: Art History and Theory* (Cambridge: MIT Press, 1993).

65. Pettersson, "Paulsson, Nils Bernhard Gregor," p. 757; Gregor Paulsson, *Upplevt* (Stockholm, 1974).

66. The first Nobel prize, awarded in 1901, helped to increase Sweden's international prestige as did the Stockholm Olympics of 1912. Sweden introduced universal suffrage in 1911, and was neutral during both world wars.

67. See Erik Wettergren, "Varia," *Svenska Slöjdföreningens Tidskrift*, no. 10 (1914), pp. 132–43.

68. See Carl Westman, "Totalomdöme," *Svenska Slöjdföreningens Tidskrift*, no. 12 (1917), pp. 69–72.

69. For a précis of many of these ideas see Gregor Paulsson,"Konst och industri," *Svenska Slöjdföreningens Tidskrift*, no. 14 (1918), pp. 11–21; and idem, "Anarki eller tidsstil," *Svenska Slöjdföreningens Tidskrift*, no. 11 (1915), pp. 1–12.

70. Paulsson, *Vackrare Vardagsvara*, p. 6 [Två personer inför samma föremål kunna ha rakt motsatta åsikter, en slipad kristallvas befinnes av den ene vara oerhört vacker, av den andre avskyvärd. Vem har rätt? Svar i viss mån båda].

71. Ibid., p. 9 [Men med enhetlig smak uppstår också enhetlighet över formen i hela samhället. Detta är den djupare betydelsen av satsen *Vackrare Vardagsvara*].

72. Ibid, p. 16 [Konsten industrin att få in vacker form, industrin konsten att komma i närmare kontakt med nutida teknik och därigenom få nya uppslag och större verksamhetsfält].

73. Paulsson seems committed to the belief that an excellent copy is never as good as an original—regardless of its condition.

74. Paulsson, *Vackrare Vardagsvara*, p. 27 [. . . en definitiv omsvängning från individers isolerade produktion till en samlad generations målmedvetna arbete för en på bred social grund lagd formkultur]. The New Home Exhibition at Ullevål Hageby in Oslo in 1920 was almost an exact reprise of the 1917 Liljevalchs Home Exhibition. See Carl W. Schnitler, "Den nye tid og den nye stil," in *Kunsten og den gode form* (Oslo: Gyldendal, 1927).

75. Ibid., p.38 [De vilja i allt ha sin fullkomliga frihet].

76. Ibid., p. 47 [Då en vacker vara står ensam eller bland andra vackra varor, bibehåller den sin skönhet, då den kommer bland fula, blir den genom sin isolering själv ful].

77. Ibid., p. 47 [De köpa hellre fem gånger för tio kronor än en gång för femtio].

78. Ibid., p. 49 [Naturligtvis är en utveckling till skapande av bättre vardagsvaror över lag endast möjlig genom att de små specialaffärerna och de stora kvalitetsvaruhusen på konkurrensesn vag helt undantränga varuhussen ar bon-marché-typen samt andra och tredje klassens småaffärer i förstäder och på landsbygden].

79. Key, *Skönhet för alla*, p. 28 [Ju enklare formen på ett glas är, desto vackrare är det i regeln, och pokalfornen förblir troligen den vackraste].

80. Jacob E. Bang, "Glasset paa Stockholmsudstillingen," *Nyt Tidskrift for Kunstindustri* 3, no. 9 (September 1930), p. 145 [Det er ikke for meget sagt, at denne lille Samling Glas var det eneste virkeligt nye i Stockholmerudstillingens Glasafdeling, det eneste der virkeligt var i Pagt med Udstillingens Aand].

81. See Marquis W. Childs, *Sweden: The Middle Way* (New Haven: Yale University Press, 1936).

82. For the ties between the Myrdals and Markelius see Eva Rudberg, *Sven Markelius, Architect* (Stockholm: Arkitektur Förlag, 1989). The Myrdals' relationships to the functionalists group warrant further study.

83. Åke H. Hult, "Glaset och publiken" in *Modernt Svenskt Glas*, ed. Gregor Paulsson (Stockholm: Jonson and Winter, 1943), p. 251 [Glaset som material har vunnit en god ställning i det svenska hemmet. Det har i vida kretsar kommit att utgöra en källa till glädje som en faktor för vardagslivets trevnad och skönheten i hemmet].

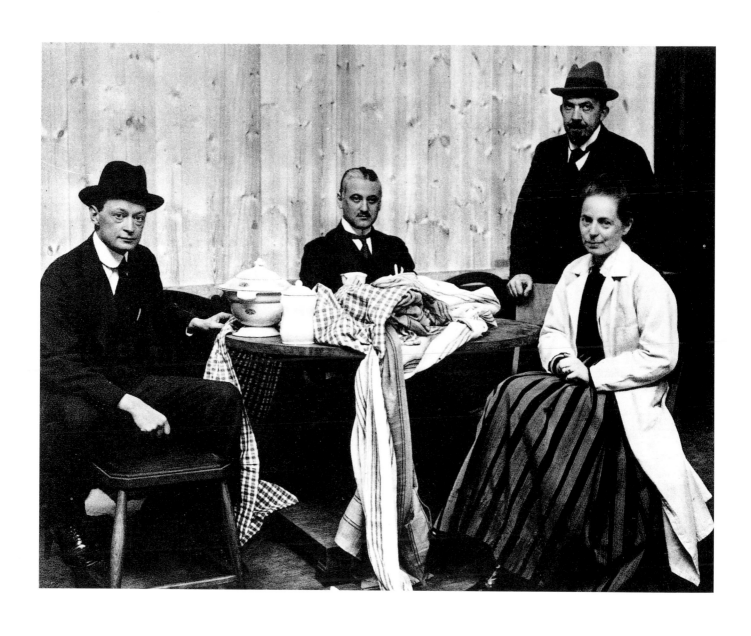

CHAPTER FOUR

The Emergence of Swedish Modern Design, 1917–1939

Anne-Marie Ericsson

Fig. 4-1. Organizers of the Home Exhibition which was held at the Liljevalchs Konsthall, Stockholm, 1917: *from left*, Erik Wettergren, August Nachmanson (treasurer), David Blomberg (commissioner), and Elsa Gullberg. On the table are textiles and Wilhelm Kåge ceramics. (Svensk Form, Bildarkivet, Stockholm)

The period between the two world wars was the golden age of modern Swedish design. The First World War left Swedish industry poised for development. Swedish neutrality had assured that the factories and plants remained virtually intact, although in need of modernization by the end of the war. The traditional craft industries—glass, ceramics, metal, textiles, and furniture—were in need of an aesthetic modernization as well. This would be achieved through the efforts of a small, dedicated group of intellectuals (fig. 4-1). The "tools" they would use to secure Sweden a leading role in international design were the nation's finest young modernist artists, and their progress would be evident at each of the national and international expositions that occurred during the period. Of equal importance was the development of a social agenda in the arts, a concern of the modern movement internationally. In Sweden this became manifest in design imperatives under the rubric of functionalism that included improved housing for all and well-made mass-produced objects. The design initiative was facilitated by a social climate that favored progress and from which the concept of Sweden as the "people's home" slowly emerged. By 1939 "Swedish Grace" and "Swedish Modern," terms coined to describe the Swedish design response to modernism, had achieved international renown.[1]

The Baltic Exhibition of 1914

The so-called Baltic Exhibition in Malmö[2] was meant to encourage trade among the countries bordering on the Baltic Sea. For Malmö, Sweden, a growing industrial city, it provided an opportunity to establish itself as a commercial center. For Sweden as a whole it was a way to help recoup its identity after the loss of Finland to Russia in 1905 and Norwegian independence. Although the exhibition was still somewhat regional, it represents a turning point in Swedish design. Traditionally it marks the height of criticism of Sweden's decorative arts, and it served as a catalyst for bringing art and industry closer together.[3]

At Malmö the applied arts industries adhered to outmoded Art Nouveau design. The design community had not yet formulated a social agenda. The exhibitors presented luxury products including heavy furniture, conventional silver services, and elaborate sets of porcelain with eighteenth-century decoration.[4] They appeared to be conservative compared with the playful designs of the Danish exhibitors and could not compete commercially with the major German exhibitors.[5] A group of young Swedish artists, craftsmen, and scholars were especially critical of the Swedish pavilion at Malmö, their position inspired by the example of the Deutsche Werkbund which had been founded in Munich in 1907. Its goal was to unite the efforts of architects, artists, and craftsmen with industry to improve the quality of mass-produced designs.[6]

As a group the critics at Malmö were members of the innermost circle of Svenska Slöjdföreningen (The Swedish Society of Craft and Industrial Design), Sweden's counterpart to the Werkbund.[7] Most of them had been born in the 1880s and were self-taught in the arts through independent study and travel. They shared a belief that design could have a positive impact on everyday life.[8] One of the leaders of this group was Erik Wettergren, Slöjdföreningen's new secretary and editor of its journal between 1913 and 1918. He was among the first to criticize the Swedish applied arts industry by accusing industry of stripping objects of their inherent material qualities.[9] According to Wettergren, mass production was deadening to objects, while craft production evoked a greater vitality. His arguments derived in part from the English Arts and Crafts movement, but they were also inspired by the debate in Swedish architectural circles over the integrity of materials in architectural design and construction.[10]

Another of Slöjdföreningen's critics was Gregor Paulsson whose essay "Anarki eller tidsstil" (Anarchy or period style) attacked the use of period styles as a design principle and called for new design solutions as required by mass production and the industrial society.[11] Paulsson's most important contribution was the publication of Vackrare Vardagsvara (More beautiful things for everyday use; 1919).[12] In it he argued that for the design of decorative arts products the applied arts industries should rely on modernist artists, who were thought to have an understanding of modern industrial needs, rather than craftspeople, who represented traditional attitudes toward the design and manufacturing processes.

To facilitate the placement of artists as designers for industry, a kind of specialized employment agency was founded at Svenska Slöjdföreningen. Directed by Elsa Gullberg, a textile artist at the Högre Konstindustriella Skolan (School for Advanced Studies in Industrial Design) in Stockholm,[13] it had been inspired by the Vermittlungsstelle für angewandte Kunst (Employment Agency for the Applied Arts) in Munich. Gullberg, another of Svenska Slöjdföreningen's inner circle, had established an informal network of influential members of Sweden's cultural and business communities. Through this small, but powerful and discriminating group, Svenska Slöjdföreningen was able to match the talents of artists to particular industries.[14] Thus, for example, when Swedish artist Arthur Percy returned from France to Stockholm, Gullberg, who had known his earlier work, suggested that he visit the owner of the Gefle Porslinsfabrik. Percy was hired and subsequently worked there for more than thirty years.[15] He typified the kind of artist Paulsson identified as being most suited to go into industry.[16]

In the debate following the Baltic Exhibition Swedish manufacturers defended their work by asserting that they had always attempted to be responsive to the times and had long supported artists.[17] In addition they claimed to have been faced with more difficult economic conditions at the time than many manufacturers were having to deal with on the Continent.[18] Although some critics, artists, and manufacturers showed their dissatisfaction by resigning from Svenska Slöjdföreningen, others remained and worked to adapt and update the Society's mission.

The manufacturers were correct in asserting that artists had been involved in Swedish industry for some time. In 1868 August Malmström, for example, had designed a porcelain service for Gustavsberg Porslinsfabrik based on pre-Christian, Nordic prototypes with dragon motifs.[19] Around the turn of the century Alf Wallander worked for Rörstrand, Gunnar Wennerberg for Gustavsberg, and both men worked for Kosta Glassworks as well. Their "Swedish" Art Nouveau floral decorations for glass and porcelain had a remarkable freshness that is recognized as a turning point in Swedish design even though it is derived from Continental Art Nouveau decoration. Sweden's major architects from the turn of the century also designed furniture, porcelain, pewter, and silver, but mostly as special orders for expositions.

These earlier efforts at collaboration were based on artists working outside the factory, often in other cities, in their own studios. They did not participate in the production process at the factory nor did they help to devise manufacturing techniques to aid the production of their work. The critics responded to this situation by advocating a new relationship between artists and industry in which the artist would choreograph the entire process of production, working closely with technicians such as master glassblowers, from design to finished object.

In 1915 cooperation between Svenska Slöjdföreningen and industry was further assured through new

Fig. 4-2. Gunnar Asplund's kitchen installation for the 1917 Home Exhibition. The color scheme was based on shades of blue and white. (Svensk Form, Bildarkivet, Stockholm)

Fig. 4-3. Table service called "Turbine," designed by Edward Hald, 1917. The name derived from Hald's rationalization of the decoration which was applied by rotating the ware on a potter's wheel. (Svensk Form, Bildarkivet, Stockholm)

statutes that gave higher priority to mass-produced goods than to handicrafts. The change can be charted in the society's journal, *Svenska Slöjdföreningen Tidskrift*. Beginning in the 1920s, under the editorial direction of Gregor Paulsson, the journal devoted more space to essays and commentary on mass production in the applied arts industry than to traditional handicrafts.[20] Furthermore, a change in direction was stimulated by economic incentives and the recognition by all parties that it would be profitable to pursue a closer collaboration between artists and manufacturers. The progressive critics argued that such a move would make Swedish products more competitive with the applied arts industry on the Continent. Swedish manufacturers would be best served by concentrating on artistic quality. In support of this new design philosophy an active program of exhibitions was inaugurated to demonstrate Swedish design excellence. This change in design philosophy also instigated a fierce debate within the Swedish design community in which those who supported progressive design and new production faced off against those who aligned with craft production.

The Home Exhibition of 1917

Svenska Slöjdföreningen's first goal after the debacle of the Baltic Exhibition was to organize a design exhibition that responded to Sweden's severe housing crisis. To try and find solutions to the housing situation architects and designers were invited to submit projects for small apartments and interiors. The best of these would be constructed as part of Hem-utställningen (The Home Exhibition) of 1917. The problem was in finding manufacturers who were willing to produce high-quality goods at low cost in order to service a broader market that until then was not considered sufficiently important to require good design.

The Home Exhibition must be understood within the context of the First World War and the international economic situation it spawned. Despite Swedish neutrality the nation had felt the effects of war through, for example, isolation from the international marketplace. While some businesses had actually profited from the war years, many others had been adversely affected, and poverty and housing shortages were widespread.

The exhibition opened in the fall of 1917 at the Liljevalchs Konsthall in Stockholm. The interior installations served not only as design solutions to housing shortages but as showcases for household glass, porcelain, and textiles. There was an impressive list of artists and designers who participated, many at the beginning of what would be long, fruitful careers in the applied arts industry: architects Gunnar Asplund (fig. 4-2) and Uno Åhrén, both of whom also designed fur-

Fig. 4-4. Urn, designed by Ivar Johnsson; produced by Näfveqvarn, 1923; cast iron. This was exhibited at the 1923 Gothenburg Jubilee Exhibition; its neoclassical motif, a depiction of Diana the Huntress, typifies "Swedish Grace."

niture; furniture designer Carl Malmsten; textile designer Elsa Gullberg; ceramicists Wilhelm Kåge and Edgar Böckman; and glass artists Edvin Ollers, Simon Gate, and Edward Hald, who also designed ceramics.

Through their work they introduced a new type of artistic vision into the applied arts. Asplund, Malmsten, and Åhrén, for example, designed their installations as small apartments in an informal vernacular style, which they thought the new industrial worker class would appreciate. Edward Hald designed a table service called "Turbine" (fig. 4-3) which came to represent a type of machine aesthetic that was compatible with the times. Wilhelm Kåge's table service, later called "Arbetarservisen" (Worker's service), although few workers could afford it, was made at Gustavsberg with a machine originally designed for multicolor printing. It was a blue-and-white pattern that was considered appropriate for low-income households. Edvin Ollers designed glassware that relied for its aesthetic impact on blisters or bubbles caused by impurities in the glass made during the First World War when there was a shortage in Sweden of high-quality silica. Kåge and sophisticated viewers appreciated the "flaws," but

Kosta's glassmakers disapproved of this kind of glass, which to them represented poor quality.

The textiles for the Home Exhibition were intended to be both attractive and durable. When Elsa Gullberg found it difficult to persuade textile manufacturers to work to her specifications, she founded a studio devoted to making small handweavings or crayon sketches of fabric swatches to determine designs that could be adapted by the textile industry. She was backed in this endeavor by Nordiska Kompaniet, Sweden's leading department store.[21]

Although many visitors and critics interpreted the new look displayed at the Home Exhibition as typically Swedish, in fact Swedish artists had long been inspired by outside sources, including major design journals such as *The Studio*, an English publication, as well as European design models, especially those from Germany and Austria.[22] Travel and study also gave Swedish artists a connection to progressive trends and movements on the Continent.[23]

Svenska Slöjdföreningen's social agenda for the exhibition was strengthened through its association with the Centralförbund för Socialt Arbete (Central Organization for Social Work). Despite the mission of the 1917 exhibition to address the housing crisis it could not offer a realistic solution to the problem. The organizers were all from the upper or middle classes and accepted without question Ellen Key's idealistic philosophy that education and "beauty" would ameliorate the abysmal living conditions of the working class. Few visitors from the working class could in fact afford the kind of interiors or objects on display. Nevertheless the Home Exhibition marks a seminal moment in Swedish design. Out of it a new applied arts industry emerged that would soon be producing objects and designs recognized internationally as "Swedish Grace."[24]

Prelude to the Paris Exposition of 1925
In 1920 artists who had exhibited at the Home Exhibition founded their own society, Föreningen Verkstaden (The Workshop Society,) and held another exhibition at the Liljevalchs Konsthall. Unlike the Home Exhibition, the 1920 show attempted to reach a middle-income clientele.[25] Three years later the city of Gothenburg, Sweden, celebrated its 300th anniversary by hosting a major industrial exposition.[26] The exhibition organizers returned to a conservative approach to design, emphasizing traditional luxury objects. Notably absent from the exhibition were everyday items evocative of the Svenska Slöjdföreningen agenda.[27] The applied arts pavilion, located in a secluded part of the fairgrounds, was designed by Hakon Ahlberg. It was divided into small rooms, each of which was used to display examples of one of the decorative arts. In this restrictive space new glass designs by Orrefors and

Fig. 4-5. The Swedish glass and porcelain display in the Grand Palais, Paris Exposition des Arts Décoratifs et Industriels Modernes, 1925. Alf Munthe's canopy, with embroidery executed at the Thyra Grafström textile factory, forms one entrance to the room. (Svensk Form, Bildarkivet, Stockholm)

Kosta glassworks were featured. They were richly decorated with engraved motifs that moved around the form cinemagraphically. The work exhibited by Kosta and Orrefors made Gothenburg a triumph for the Swedish glass industry.

The decade of the 1920s was a period of transition as Swedish design moved toward the functionalist aesthetic of the 1930s. The true significance of the Gothenburg Jubilee Exhibition of 1923 is that it reveals the prevalence of neoclassicism in Swedish architecture and design. This aesthetic can be seen in a variety of work: in Alf Munthe's embroidery work for the Skandia Cinema which was designed by Gunnar Asplund in 1922–23; in Asplund's furniture for Stockholm's new City Hall designed by Ragnar Östberg; in Svenskt Tenn's gray satin-finish pewter objects that were reminiscent of eighteenth-century farm implements; and in cast-iron garden urns (fig. 4-4) and fountains, manufactured by Näfveqvarn, which recalled late-eighteenth-century design.[28]

Swedish Design at the Paris Exposition of 1925

The 1923 Gothenburg Jubilee Exhibition served as a dress rehearsal for the Swedish contribution to the 1925 Exposition des Arts Décoratifs et Industriels Modernes in Paris. Although Sweden's participation was initially jeopardized by an unfavorable economy, Svenska Slöjdföreningen managed to acquire funding from the State for a national pavilion designed by Carl Bergsten and for Gregor Paulsson to serve as the "design commissioner." (Each applied arts exhibitor was encouraged to contribute and was responsible for its own costs.) Ultimately Swedish exhibitions were to be seen in the Swedish pavilion and Grand Palais (fig. 4-5), as well as in shops along the Boulevard des Invalides.

The Swedish pavilion featured decorative arts by the country's leading designers and manufacturers, pursuing a neoclassical aesthetic similar to that displayed at Gothenburg. Uno Åhrén's "Lady's Salon"

Fig. 4-6. Chair, designed by Gunnar Asplund, 1925; bentwood, leather with gold stamping.

installation, for example, was distinctly neoclassical or Empire, as if meant for a modern-day Madame Récamier. Carl Hörvik designed a long sofa in neo-Biedermeier style and a cabinet with a gilt interior. Simon Gate's monumental Baroque-inspired covered urn stood in the entrance hall. There were examples of engraved glass for Orrefors by Gate as well as Hald.[29] For the Swedish glass and porcelain exhibition in the Grand Palais, Alf Munthe designed an elaborate canopied entrance that included a textile made at the renowned Thyra Grafström workshop in Stockholm. It was strongly influenced by eighteenth-century chinoiserie, an idiom that was popular in Sweden in the mid-1920s.[30]

The Swedish design achievement was highly acclaimed by the international press, and the nation was awarded thirty-one grand prizes. Paulsson attributed this success to the quality of the inexpensive mass-produced items while other critics emphasized the role of luxury goods.[31] The most significant outcome for Sweden was the rise to international promi-nence of the Swedish design industries. French interest was extensive. Leading periodicals such as *Art et Décoration* and *L'Amour de l'art* published articles on Sweden's contributions to the exposition.[32] Fifteen thousand copies of the catalogue were printed, and Paulsson's 1919 book, *Vackrare Vardagsvara*, was trans-lated into French (but never published).[33] Erik Wettergren gained international renown with his book on the 1925 Paris Exposition, *L'Art décoratif moderne en Suède* (Modern decorative art in Sweden) in which he championed the role of eighteenth-century Swedish craft production in the creation of modern design.[34]

Wettergren's position was in sharp contrast to the perspective offered by Uno Åhrén who would become a leading exponent of progressive Swedish design. Following the exhibition Åhrén published an impas-sioned defense of modernism entitled "Brytningar" (Ruptures).[35] He emphasized the need for industrial production and argued that Le Corbusier's Pavillon de l'Esprit Nouveau at the Paris Exposition represented the importance of industry's role in everyday life. The functional aspects of design deserved the highest con-sideration: a chair should offer a place to sit, not mas-querade as art (fig. 4-6).[36] Åhrén's article provided a mild foretaste of the uproar that would follow the opening of the 1930 Stockholm Exhibition (Stockholmsutställningen 1930 av konstindustri, kon-sthantverk och hemslöjd).

The Stockholm Exhibition of 1930

In 1927, the year of the Deutsche Werkbund's Stuttgart exhibition, "Die Wohnung" (The Dwelling), Svenska Slöjdföreningen proposed an exhibition to be present-ed in Stockholm in 1930. Its purpose, formulated by the exhibition's general commissioner, Gregor Paulsson, was to demonstrate the Swedish contribution to modern industrial design and low-cost housing.[37] The exhibition represented the culmination of ideas introduced by the Society at the 1917 Home Exhibition. Gunnar Asplund served as the exhibition's chief architect, and breaking with tradition, he orga-nized the displays of mass-produced objects in a sep-arate area, away from traditional Swedish crafts, and gave them a more prominent place. This was an impor-tant innovation. Paulsson knew that unless mass-pro-duced objects had their own exhibition spaces they would be overshadowed by luxury products. In tex-tiles, for example, displays were arranged by tech-nique with hand-woven textiles shown in the craft sec-tion, separate from machine-made designs.[38] Also, rather than display glass and ceramics hierarchically in vertical pyramids of shelves, the customary arrange-ment dating to the nineteenth century, at Stockholm they were exhibited on more "democratic" horizontal shelves and tables (fig. 4-7).

It was difficult for some of the applied arts industries

Fig. 4-7. Porcelain exhibits arranged by maker at the 1930 Stockholm Exhibition. Another area focused on the methods and benefits of standardization. (Svensk Form, Bildarkivet, Stockholm)

to produce new designs that met the exhibition committee's criteria in time for the exhibition itself. Some, such as the porcelain factories, already had established product lines that would be difficult to retool and augment. At Gustavsberg, however, Wilhelm Kåge's design for a table service called "Praktika" (fig. 4-8) had standardized parts. Although it was not ready in time for the 1930 exhibition, the service captured the ideological foundation put forth by Paulsson.

Furniture designs demonstrated a return to concerns for minimum housing space. The late 1920s were marked by renewed economic problems. Building projects were difficult for young architects to secure and many turned to the applied arts, especially furniture design. For a brief time Gemla Fabrik and Bodafors Möbelfabrik, two of Sweden's foremost furniture manufacturers, featured designs by many of the country's leading architects, including Asplund, Åhrén, Hörvik, and Markelius. Most of their designs were made primarily for the 1930 Stockholm Exhibition. None of these prototypes was considered a major

Fig. 4-8. Table service called "Praktika," designed by Wilhelm Kåge; produced by Gustavsberg, 1933. The lids doubled as deep serving dishes, and the service was designed to stack compactly for the most efficient use of space in small, functionalist kitchens.

design by the critics, and few if any went into actual production. Tubular-steel chairs, for example, which had been inspired by Marcel Breuer's work, provoked one critic-cartoonist to draw them converted to toboggans,[39] and Sven Markelius's stacking chairs were deemed practical but not attractive. Their impact instead was in paving the way for Sweden's younger generation of designers—Bruno Mathsson, Axel Larsson, and Elias Svedberg.[40]

The industry/craft debate was fueled by the Stockholm Exhibition. Progressive designers who were associated with functionalist design advocated mass-produced, low-cost objects grounded in a strong social agenda. Traditionalists argued for the preservation of craft techniques in modern design. By 1930 international modernism had drawn very few supporters in Sweden.[41] It was not surprising, therefore, that Swedish artists, architects, and designers tried to avoid using the term modernism, which was a concept increasingly associated with "style." They preferred the term functionalism instead, which transformed the issue from one of aesthetics to a social imperative. It was around this time that "Swedish Grace" began to be used to describe the modernist response to design in Sweden. It was applied to designs that still allowed for surface decoration and continued to be inspired by the neo-classical forms prevalent during the 1920s in Sweden. In the late 1930s, "Swedish Modern" was introduced by English and American journalists to designate modernist designs that were more concerned with overall form than with surface decoration which was often limited to an expressive use of color.

Shortly after the opening of the Stockholm Exhibition, the lines of debate had been drawn, with Paulsson representing the functionalists and Carl Malmsten, one of Sweden's premier furniture designers, the traditionalists.[42] They were dubbed "Funkis" and "Tradis" in the press of the day. Malmsten condemned the "mechanization and cold intellectualism" of the Stockholm Exhibition.[43] Many architects and designers agreed, feeling betrayed by Svenska Slöjdföreningen which, through its criteria for exhibitors, had forced them to surrender their art to massproduction. They were not particularly interested in making everyday articles more attractive, but rather in continuing to produce luxury products for an elite clientele. Malmsten was joined by members of the old guard, including architects Carl Bergsten, Ivar Tengbom, and Ragnar Östberg; sculptor Carl Milles; textile designer Elsa Gullberg; and writers Elin Wägner and Torsten Fogelquist. Gullberg's alignment with the traditionalists was surprising considering the often radical nature of her own work and her commitment to a social agenda through commissions to design for schools and hospitals. She may have felt a responsibility toward the artists she had placed in the applied arts industry, or she may have considered Paulsson's position to be too rigid. In expressing the group's dismay Fogelquist wrote, "Could there be anything more absurd than a manufacturer who specializes in art design jeopardizing its production, or at least the individual, more personal expressions of its artists, just to serve the almighty, controlling, annihilating machine?"[44]

The functionalists continued to support standardization and rationalization in design, rallying around Paulsson's 1919 concept of "more beautiful things for everyday use."[45] In 1931 Paulsson, Walter Gahn, Eskil Sundahl, Gunnar Asplund, Uno Åhrén, and Sven Markelius published acceptera (Accept), a manifesto in support of the design agenda established by the Stockholm Exhibition. Among the illustrations they included a simple table service that fulfilled the design imperatives shared by the group, and in an echo of Vackrare Vardagsvara, the caption reads, "The everyday item should be of use to us, unpretentious, quiet, and appealing."[46]

The Triumph of "Swedish Modern"

The 1929 Wall Street crash and ensuing economic collapse were paralleled in Sweden by the so-called Kreuger crash of 1932.[47] Fear of unemployment in the design community prevailed, while economic setbacks seemed to stimulate innovative product design. Within the porcelain industry, for example, table services began to be standardized and consolidated, with fewer forms making up a service. Old designs were actually recolored in monochromatic hues to look more "modern." In the process the lines between economic necessity and fashionable adaptation became blurred.

In new designs artists paid greater attention to production issues, which in many cases meant reducing or eliminating surface decoration. In 1933 Arthur Percy introduced one of his most successful functionalist table services, called "Celadon" after the generic Chinese ceramics that inspired it.[48] Another Percy design, "Veronica" (fig. 4-9), straddles the line between functionalism and traditional work. Wilhelm Kåge created some thirty austere services decorated only with bands of color, such as a table service called "Atlanta" (1937), which had blue bands.[49] At the glassworks, some artists, especially those who thought that glass should be treated sculpturally as mass and not as ground for surface decoration,[50] largely abandoned engraving for their art glass, although engraved glass continued to be an important part of the production line.

Surrealism and realism, which marked Swedish painting in the 1930s, also influenced the applied arts. Artists borrowed motifs from the surrealists to incorporate into their work. Realism offered a more relaxed, humane approach to functionalism, and representation-

Fig. 4-9. Plate from a table service called "Veronica," designed by Arthur Percy, 1933–36. This represents the kind of service decoration prevalent in the early 1930s. (Private collection)

al motifs such as plant forms began to be used again as decoration. As further evidence of the changing attitudes within the design community, Slöjdföreningen's journal, which had been renamed *Form* in 1932, began to include commentary on the nineteenth-century Arts and Crafts work of William Morris.

In the mid-thirties a flourishing textile art emerged in Swedish design. This may be attributed in part to the opportunities afforded by the somewhat spartan interiors of international modernism. Traditionalists saw col-

orful textiles as a way to soften and humanize these interiors, and the design and development of textiles became another facet of the power struggle between Funkis and Tradis in Svenska Slöjdföreningen. Artists and textile designers soon formed close alliances. Gullberg, who founded a block-printing firm in 1934, engaged several artists to design patterns for her, including Carl Malmsten, Alf Munthe, Arthur Percy, and the somewhat younger Vicke Lindstrand. Percy proved to be an extraordinary pattern designer, with a facility for rich patterns.

An especially fruitful collaboration was between Estrid Ericson of Svenskt Tenn, Sweden's foremost design firm, and Josef Frank, an architect who had emigrated from Vienna in 1933 fearing the threat of Nazism. With his connections to European modernism Frank exercised more freedom in his use of decoration than most of his Swedish counterparts. Frank's approach to architecture and interior design, however, was widely divergent from the leading proponents of the modern movement.[51]

The first public showing of Frank's work for Svenskt Tenn occurred at the 1934 design exhibition at the Liljevalchs Konsthall in Stockholm. In response to functionalist design characterized by machine-inspired forms and a decisive lack of decoration, Frank created a highly elaborate display. The focal point of the installation was a monumental sofa (fig. 4-10) that evoked Frank's interest in comfort as a principal feature of interior decoration. The Liljevalchs exhibition embodied Frank's unique use of color and pattern and his reliance on historial design and Western and non-Western sources to create a distinctly modern design aesthetic. His humanistic approach, strong decorative sense, and fusion of historical and contemporary influ-

Fig. 4-10. Sofa, designed by Josef Frank; produced by Svenskt Tenn, 1934 (this example, 1995). Exhibited in the 1934 "Stil och Standard" exhibition at the Liljevalchs Konstahll in Stockholm, the sofa was upholstered in a different, slightly more traditional, but equally rich textile. Frank's use of textile patterns may have contributed to the expansion of textile design in the mid-1930s.

Fig. 4-11. Chair, designed by Bruno Mathsson; produced by Karl Mathsson AB, 1931; bent beechwood, cotton webbing. This was a prototype; the first finished model was exhibited at the 1934 "Stil och Standard" exhibition at the Liljevalchs Konsthall in Stockholm.

ences were among the main characteristics of Swedish Modern design.

Around 1935 several new talents, notably furniture designers Bruno Mathsson and Elias Svedberg and textile designer Astrid Sampe, also began to have an impact on the direction of Swedish design. They viewed modernism as less problematic than their predecessors had and showed that it was possible to work austerely without having the "artistic element" disappear. Like Frank they demonstrated a freer relationship to modernism, working decoratively without being reactionary.

Mathsson gained recognition in 1934 when he introduced an armchair made of bent, laminated wood and cotton webbing (fig. 4-11).[52] Among his primary concerns as a designer were durability and comfort, and in his later years he chose leather and steel which provided even greater durability. He was equally interested in the technical aspects of manufacturing his designs and thus represents the new kind of applied artist whom Paulsson had envisioned more than a

decade earlier, that is, one who has both art skills and a knowledge of the manufacturing process.

In 1937 Nordiska Kompaniet, Sweden's leading department store, hired Astrid Sampe to design textiles for its customers, and as a result she established Textilkammaren, Nordiska's experimental textile workshop. Her first designs under this label were made on handlooms but she soon transferred production to the textile industry, relying on various large textile manufacturers: Almedahl at Dalsjöfors produced towels; Kasthall at Kinna made carpets; and her printed textiles were realized at Erik Ljungbergs Textiltryck i Floda outside Gothenburg where many of the Svenskt Tenn designs by Josef Frank were also produced. Among the artists who worked for Sampe at Nordiska were Sven Markelius, Sven-Erik Skawonius, Tyra Lundgren, painter Karl Axel Pehrson, Finnish artist Viola Gråsten, and Danish architect Arne Jacobsen.

The collaboration between textile manufacturers and Sampe was a reflection of the change that had occurred in industry since the 1917 Home Exhibition when Elsa Gullberg had tried unsuccessfully to forge a connection between textile arts and industry. Sampe's textile workshop at Nordiska was a modern design studio in which this rationalist designer experimented with new materials and techniques and collaborated with modern artists specifically hired to work on textile patterns.

Sampe had first attracted international attention as a designer at the Paris Exposition of 1937, where she exhibited with a young furniture designer, Elias Svedberg (fig. 4-12). She represents the beginning of the peak period in modern Swedish design, a period that would reach fruition after the Second World War. By the late 1930s earlier visions of a new relationship between the artist and industry seemed almost tangible. Instead of the artist as autocrat, dictating design and production, however, it was a far more equitable relationship. Artists and manufacturers had come to know each other and their mutual needs, and there was increasing cooperation between producers.

The 1937 Swedish pavilion at the Paris Exposition Internationale des Arts et Techniques dans la Vie Moderne had been designed by Sven-Ivar Lind, who had studied with Asplund. Swedish critics derided the design as too severe,[53] but foreign visitors found it interesting, with a spaciousness and "Nordic gravity" as well as high-quality, inexpensive examples of Swedish decorative arts.[54] Two years later, Sweden participated in the 1939 New York World's Fair, calling its contribution "Swedish Modern: A Movement Toward Sanity in Design."[55] The Swedish pavilion, designed by Sven Markelius, offered new interpretations of modernism for many of the visitors (fig. 4-13). Among the room installations was a "cottage room" on which Elias Svedberg and Astrid Sampe again collaborated.[56] It

Fig. 4-12 Installation by Astrid Sampe and Elias Svedberg for the 1937 Paris Exposition. (Svensk Form, Bildarkivet, Stockholm)

had light pine furniture, blue or yellow patterned upholstery, and other textiles.[57] Another noteworthy installation was an interior designed by Josef Frank and Estrid Ericsson for Svenskt Tenn.[58] Its bold combination of geometric patterns and its kidney- shaped desk as well as low sofa and other furniture were harbingers of Swedish design in the 1950s and an early example of Swedish Modern design.

The Swedish pavilion was among the most popular at the fair, receiving wide attention in the press, and "Swedish Modern" had captured the imagination of the American public. It offered a more humanistic approach to modern design than the streamlined, machine-age objects shown in other World's Fair pavilions.

By the end of the 1930s Swedish design had established its place in the forefront of international design. Beginning with the 1917 Home Exhibition Swedish designers had been moving closer to answering Paulsson's call for "more beautiful objects for everyday use." There had been an ongoing debate over industry vs craft, machine-made vs handmade, throughout the period. Comparing Svedberg's "cottage room" installation of 1939 with Asplund's "apartment kitchen" of 1917 (see fig. 4-2) reveals the achievements of

Fig. 4-13. Plate, Table Service called "Blå Vinranka" (blue grapevine), designed by Arthur Percy, 1939; stoneware. In contrast to the streamlining and more abstract interpretations of modernism seen at the 1939 New York World's Fair, Percy's design, like others in the Swedish pavilion, represented a more humanistic approach. (Private collection)

Swedish designers and manufacturers on either side of this debate over two decades. Although they were nearer to reaching the goal of creating inexpensive, mass-produced quality objects for everyday life, there was still much ground to cover. Most of the items shown at the New York World's Fair during that last summer before the Second World War were either made by hand or by small-scale production methods.[59] It would not be until after 1945 that the next phase of Swedish design would begin, during which many artistic ideals, such as small-scale production, would be abandoned and the trend toward mass production would move forward.

1. The expression "Swedish Grace" was coined by the English journalist P. Morton Shand ("Stockholm 1930," *Architectural Review* 68, no. 405 [1930], pp. 67–72). The origin of "Swedish Modern" is less certain; it came into usage among the English-speaking press at the time of the 1937 Paris Exposition.

2. Participants were Russia (including Finland and the Baltic states), Denmark, and Germany. Examples of the fine and applied arts as well as industrial products were shown. The Russian art exhibition included works by Kandinsky, among others. Sweden's introduction to expositions of arts and industry had occurred a generation earlier, at the so-called Crystal Palace Exhibition in London in 1851. The first Scandinavian exposition was held in Stockholm in 1866, the year the Nationalmuseum opened. Swedish achievements in glass and the other applied arts were shown at other pivotal expositions in the nineteenth century, including the 1876 and 1900 Paris expositions.

3. For criticism of the Swedish displays at Malmö see *Svenska Slöjdföreningens Tidskrift,* yearbook (1914) and ibid. (1915).

4. Rörstrand's porcelain factory, which was established in 1726, preferred using its own old eighteenth-century patterns. Among the exhibitors were Svensk Hemslöjd and Svenska Hemslöjdföreningarnas Riksförbund, Gustavsbergs Porslinsfabrik, De Svenska Kristallglasbruken (which included the Kosta, Eda, Alsterfors, Alsterbro, and Reijmyre glassworks), and Nordiska Kompaniet (NK). See Anne-Marie Ericsson, "Konstindustri och konsthantverk," in *Baltiska utställningen, Malmö, 1914* (Lund, Sweden: Signum, 1989), pp. 139 *ff.*

5. Danish manufacturers included Bing & Gröndahl, Royal Danish, and Georg Jensen; Germany was represented by Meissen and Rosenthal among others.

6. See Gilian Naylor, "The Werkbund," in *Bauhaus Reassessed: Sources and Design Theory* (London: Herbert Press, 1985), pp. 37 *ff.*

7. Svenska Slöjdföreningen was founded in 1845 as an organization to support craft workers; its name was changed to Föreningen Svensk Form (The Swedish Design Federation) in 1974 (Svensk Form archive, Stockholm Stadsarkiv).

8. See chap. 3 in this volume.

9. Erik Wettergren, "Varia," *Svenska Slöjdföreningens Tidskrift,* yearbook (1914) pp. 132 *ff.* Wettergren served as director of the Nationalmuseum, Stockholm, from 1942 to 1950.

10. Ferdinand Boberg, the doyen of Swedish exhibition architecture and student of Louis Sullivan, was thought to exercise a pernicious influence and was virtually shunned by Sweden's architectural community. His last major work was at the Baltic Exhibition.

11. Gregor Paulsson, "Anarki eller tidsstil," *Svenska Slöjdföreningens Tidskrift* 11, no. 1 (1915), pp. 1-2. Paulsson was possibly one of the few committed modernists in Sweden before 1920. As Svenska Slöjdföreningen's director between 1920 and 1934, he was responsible for launching functionalism at the 1930 Stockholm Exhibition. See chap. 3 in this volume.

12. Gregor Paulsson, *Vackrare Vardagsvara* (Stockholm: Svenska Slöjdföreningen, 1919).

13. Today the school is known as Konstfack. Gullberg first worked for Svensk Hemslöjd, where she modernized the wealth of folk patterns and provided the company with quality and forms that were suited to the modern era. Gullberg stayed at the SSF until 1925, when she was commissioned to design textiles for Stockholm's new Concert Hall. In 1927 she started her own firm, Elsa Gullberg Textilier och Inredning. See *Elsa Gullberg, textil pionjär,* Nationalmusei katalog 523 (Stockholm: Nationalmuseum, 1989); and Barbro Hovstadius, "Elsa Gullberg," in *Svenska textilier, 1890–1990* (Lund, Sweden: Signum, 1994).

14. There were also negative aspects to Slöjdföreningens presence in art and industry: porcelain manufactured during the 1920s, for example, which was submitted to exhibition juries, often bears the stamp, "SSF." Not everyone liked this quality control system.

15. Anne-Marie Ericsson, *Arthur Percy: konstnär och formgivare* (Stockholm, 1980), pp. 37 *ff.*

16. Percy, who had studied with Matisse in Paris, was considered an "expressionist" with a decorative bent. Between 1910 and 1920 the term *expressionism* was used in Sweden in a very broad sense to describe the generation of painters and sculptors who had studied at the Kungliga Akademien för de fria konsterna (Royal Academy of Art) in Stockholm.

17. For selected manufacturers' letters responding to Wettergren's criticism, see "Schismen," *Svenska Slöjdföreningens Tidskrift,* yearbook (1915), pp. 36–50. The original letters are in the Svensk Form archive, Stadsarkivet, Stockholm.

18. For an overview of economic policies and industrial developments in Sweden, see chaps. 1 and 2 in this volume.

19. The service, which is known as "Dragon Porcelain" or "National style," was inspired by the runes and snakelike markings on ancient stones. See Inga Arnö-Berg, *Serviser från Gustavsberg,* 2nd ed. (Stockholm: ICA bokförlag: 1985).

20. After 1932, the *Svenska Slöjdföreningens Tidskrift* was renamed *Form.*

21. *Elsa Gullberg,* p. 18.

22. Elisabet and Ove Hidemark, "Kontinenten och Sverige: influenser på arkitektur och konsthandverk omkring 1917," *Fataburen* (1968), pp. 71 *ff.* Carl Larsson's house in Sundborn, for example, and the books he wrote about it were influenced by British design that appeared in *The Studio.* Also see chap. 3 in this volume.

23. Among the young Swedish artists living abroad were many who later made their careers in the decorative arts. The silversmiths Jacob Angman and Wiwen Nilsson, for example, studied in southern Europe with its remnants of a classical past, while most architects turned to Berlin and Vienna to expand their skills. A few, notably Ferdinand Boberg and Carl Hörvik, visited Great Britain and the United States. For these and the other young Swedish artists, traveling and studying abroad offered an opportunity to experience a kind of urban atmosphere virtually unknown in Sweden at the time. Until the end of the Second World War, Stockholm was a fairly small city with a few monumental buildings and "boulevards" but without a diverse assortment of theaters, restaurants, and art galleries. Cabaret and café society in the international sense did not exist.

24. See n. 1.

25. Architect Gunnar Asplund's "music room" installation, with a red grand piano and blue walls, was one of the most colorful exhibits.

26. Its celebration had been delayed two years by the First World War.

27. *Fataburen* (1968), p. 111.

28. *Svenska Slöjdföreningens Tidskrift,* yearbook (1924), pp. 1, *ff.* The last major project of 1920s neoclassicism was the design of the ocean liner M/S *Kungsholm* (completed in 1928), with interiors by Carl Bergsten. Its furnishings included an engraved glass tabletop by Edvard Hald, carpets and upholstery designs by Elsa Gullberg and Märta Måås-Fjetterström, and cast-iron objects, table services, intarsia, and frescoes by Sweden's leading artists and designers. The ship was used to transport troops during the Second World War after first being stripped of its interior fittings in New York. Their whereabouts are unknown.

29. Some of this glass may have been acquired by the Musée de la Ville de Paris. A tureen by Arthur Percy was purchased by the Metropolitan Museum of Art, New York, but some of the inexpensive glass and porcelain services were presumably purchased by private individuals, not museums. Arthur Hald, son of Edward Hald, who served as editor of the *Svenska Slöjdföreningens Tidskrift* and director of the society, initiated research into the disposition of everyday items at the Paris Exposition, but his work was cut short by his death in 1994.

30. Munthe later shifted to more abstract motifs in his textile designs which were described as "soft architecture."

31. Paulsson also wrote that he regarded the 1920s as the applied arts decade. See *Fataburen* (1968), pp. 112 *ff.*

32. Many of these articles were by Paul Desfeuilles, a professor of Scandinavian literature and linguistics at the university in Caen.

33. *Exposition internationale des arts décoratifs et industriels modernes à Paris 1925: Section de la Suède* (Stockholm: Svenska Slöjdföreningen, 1925). For the translation of *Vackrare Vardagsvara* see "Paris 1925, Publication du musée de Malmö," trans. Virgile Pinot (Svensk Form archive, Stadsarkivet, Stockholm).

34. Erik Wettergren, *L'Art décoratif moderne en Suède* (Malmö, Sweden, 1925); idem, *The Modern Decorative Arts of Sweden*, trans. Tage Palm and ed. Edward Russel (London: Country Life, 1927). A German translation was published in 1926.

35. Uno Åhrén, "Brytningar," *Svenska Slöjdföreningen Tidskrift,* yearbook (1925), p. 1 *ff.* Åhrén's article constituted a showdown with progressive art and echoed Adolf Loos's earlier arguments in "Ornament und Verbrechen" ([1908]; reprint in Adolf Loos, *Trotzdem 1900–1930* [Innsbruck: Brenner Verlag, 1931]). There are also interesting comparisons between "Brytningar" and "Varia," Wettergren's critical commentary on the Baltic Exposition a decade earlier. The major difference between the two arguments is that while Wettergren honored traditional craftsmanship, Åhrén was exploring the possibilities of modern design. See Wettergren, "Varia," pp. 132 *ff.*

36. Many of the major adherents to modernism exhibited in Paris, such as Le Corbusier and Josef Frank, who would immigrate to Sweden in 1933.

37. One of the key figures behind this effort was Paulsson, who, since the 1917 Home Exhibition, had remained committed to the belief that quality, mass-produced objects were appropriate for everyday life. During the 1920s he had become increasingly disenchanted with the proliferation of luxury products based on stylistic formulas. This, he cautioned in a 1928 lecture in Stockholm, was little short of a return to the past. Paulsson delivered his talk at Svenska Slöjdföreningen on October 25, 1928. For a transcript see "Stockholmsutställningen 1939," Svensk Form archive, Stadsarkivet, Stockholm.

38. Paulsson, *Upplevt* (Stockholm, 1974), pp. 119 *ff.*

39. Sketch by Bertil Almqvist, *Aftonbladet* (Summer 1930).

40. See Per G. Råberg, "Vardagsvaran," in *Funktionalistiskt genombrott: Radikal miljödebatt i Sverige, 1825–31*, utgiven i samarbete med Sveriges Arkitektur museum [English summary] (Stockholm: PA Norstedt & Söner, 1970). ·

41. In painting and sculpture the reception given modern art was lukewarm at best. When works by such artists as Mondrian, Arp, and Léger were displayed in the restaurant at the 1930 Stockholm Exhibition, almost nothing was sold. As a result, Otto G. Carlsund, who had financed the painting and sculpture exhibition, was forced into bankruptcy and experienced personal humiliation. He was a member of the Art Concret group that had been founded by Theo van Doesburg in 1929 in Paris. See "Konkretism," in *Konsten i focus*, vol. 2 (Stockholm: Almqvist & Wiksell, 1971), p. 218.

42. Josef Sachs, head of Nordiska Kompaniet, described Malmsten as probably suffering from a "nervous breakdown," according to Paulsson (*Upplevt*, p. 123). The controversy continued into the 1930s. In 1934 Malmsten challenged Paulsson as director of the society, and Paulsson ultimately resigned, having been offered a position the same year as professor of art history at the prestigious Uppsala University, Sweden's premier higher educational institution.

43. In an article in *Svenska Slöjdföreningen Tidskrift,* yearbook (1931), pp. 124 *ff.*

44. Torsten Fogelberg, *Dagens Nyheter* 21, no. 3 (1930) ["Kan man tänka sig någonting mer absurt än en ledning för ett företag som har konsthantverk på sitt program och vill förinta detta konsthantverk eller åtminstone det personliga eller individuella häri, för att tjäna den suveräna, monopoliserade, allt annat utträngande fabriksvaran"].

45. Paulsson, *Vackrare Vardagsvara.*

46. Gregor Paulsson et al., *acceptera* (Stockholm: Tidens Förlag, 1931).

47. The Svenska Tändstickaksitebolaget, a match manufacturer, went bankrupt in 1932, and its managing director, Ivar Kreuger, committed suicide (see chap. 1, n. 14, in this volume).

48. At the same time, however, Percy stubbornly continued to incorporate traditional surface decoration such as bouquets and wreathes into his work. "Blå Vinranka" (Blue Grapevine"), for example, a table service that was introduced at the 1939 New York World's Fair, incorporated plant motifs.

49. Kåge also developed a more streamlined contour in his work, as in "De mjuka formernas servis" (The soft-shapes service; 1940).

50. Swedish designers were urged to learn from French glassmakers such as Baccarat. Tage Zickerman, "Nutida Glaskonst," *Svenska Slöjdföreningens Tidskrift,* yearbook (1927), pp. 1–46.

51. Kristina Wängberg-Eriksson, *Josef Frank, Livsträd i krigets skugga* (Lund, Sweden: Signum, 1994), p. 74. Frank designed furniture and textiles for Svenskt Tenn until his death in 1966.

52. That Mathsson used wood and not steel tubing was not surprising given that his father owned a carpentry workshop in Småland. It was there that Mathsson acquired carpentry skills, but in other ways he was self-taught, studying twentieth-century art and design in books ordered from the library of the Röhsska, a museum of design in Gothenburg. See Ingrid Böhn-Jullander, *Bruno Mathsson* (Lund, Sweden: Signum, 1992), p. 28.

53. For the architect's statement, see Sven-Ivar Lind, "Vår Paviljong på Parisutställningen," *Form* (1937), p. 1.

54. P. Morton Shand, "Svenska paviljongen i Paris sedd genom engelska ögon," *Form* (1937), pp. 153 *ff.*

55. Åke Stavenow et al., eds., *Swedish Arts and Crafts / Swedish Modern—A Movement Toward Sanity in Design,* exhib. cat. (New York: Royal Swedish Commission, New York World's Fair, 1939).

56. The other installations were by Josef Frank, G. A. Berg, Axel Larsson, and Carl Malmsten.

57. A fireplace, map of the archipelago, and model sailboat suggest that this was meant to be a beach house. For a sketch (by Harrie Wood) of the installation, see *Country Life* (June 1939), reprinted in *Form* (1939), p. 134.

58. Nina Stritzler-Levine, ed., *Josef Frank, Architect and Designer: An Alternative Vision of the Modern Home,* exhib. cat. (New York and London: The Bard Graduate Center for Studies in the Decorative Arts / Yale University Press, 1996).

59. Dag Widman, *Konsthantverk, konstindustri, design 1895–1975* (Stockholm, 1975), p. 68.

CHAPTER FIVE

Glass in the Context of Contemporary Swedish Painting, 1918–1930

Nina Weibull

In the early years of the twentieth century the art trade in Sweden constituted a relatively modest phenomenon. It was concentrated primarily in Stockholm and, to a lesser degree, in Gothenburg, a prosperous mercantile city on Sweden's west coast. According to August Brunius, one of the period's leading critics, Hallins Konsthandel in Stockholm was the first art gallery in the area,[1] a pioneering enterprise where one could purchase "reproductions, graphics, a bit of sculpture, and a few modern paintings."[2] Younger exhibitors were also welcomed there. At the end of the First World War the art trade expanded and art dealers established themselves along Stockholm's fashionable Strandvägen. Four new art galleries were dedicated mainly to progressive art, and Brunius declared that Stockholm was becoming increasingly sophisticated, at least on the surface.[3]

Until around 1917 the selection of art in Stockholm was extensive, and the quality varied greatly. For most Swedes wishing to purchase art, the choice was limited either to the work of the leading Swedish artists—Anders Zorn, Carl Larsson, and Bruno Liljefors—who were schooled in the tradition of French *plein-air* painters or to the inferior imitations and sentimental landscapes reminiscent of tinted photographs. The offerings reflected the powerful influence of the so-called Konstnärsförbundet (The Artists Federation) at the beginning of the twentieth century. The federation promoted Swedish landscape art, preferably nocturnes. Against this conservative background, any progressive modernist efforts in the new galleries seemed to be nothing less than shocking novelty.

The earliest group of modern painters, known as "De Unga" (The Young Ones), first exhibited together at Hallins Konsthandel in March 1909. De Unga included both traditionalists and revolutionaries, some of whom had trained with Henri Matisse in Paris between 1908 and 1911. One of those who took part in the 1909 exhibition was Edward Hald who would soon join Orrefors Glassworks and eventually become one of the preeminent Swedish glass artists of the twentieth century. The painters Isaac Grünewald and Leander Engström were also among the young radicals showing with the De Unga group in 1909. Three years later, in 1912, they

Fig. 5-1. The Svensk-Franska Konstgalleriet, Stockholm, 1919, with an installation of Swedish and French modernist paintings, reproductions of late-nineteenth-century French paintings, and, in the vitrine against the far wall, glass objects from Orrefors Glassworks.

were among the founding members of a new group, "De Åtta" (The Eight), which included Nils Dardel and Sigrid Hjertén, wife of Isaac Grünewald and the only woman artist in the group. Despite the artists' efforts to distance themselves from traditional painting, the 1909 De Unga exhibition was still essentially conservative, reflecting the traditionalism of the Konstnärsförbundet rather than the liberating aesthetics of Cézanne and Matisse. In two succeeding exhibitions at the Hallins Konsthandel, held in 1910 and 1911, some of the De Unga artists showed more modernist works, only to be met with criticism and incomprehension.[4]

Although Edward Hald had not participated in the 1912 exhibition of the De Åtta group, his paintings were included at the 1915 exhibition, *Schwedische Expressionisten* (Swedish Expressionism), at Herwarth Walden's Der Sturm gallery in Berlin.[5] Walden had been a strong advocate of futurism, and by 1915 the influential Grünewald had also become interested in this movement.[6] Hald's paintings were shown at the suggestion of the futurist Gösta Adrian-Nilsson (known as GAN) who was acquainted with Walden and, together with Gregor Paulsson, had provided the impetus for the Berlin exhibition. Paulsson would become a major link between artists and the decorative arts.[7]

Prior to the opening of the exhibition, there was considerable competition and debate among the artists, and many of the founding members of De Åtta, such as GAN, Dardel, Engström, and Einar Jolin, were eventually forced by Grünewald to withdraw from the 1915 exhibition, in part so that Sigrid Hjertén could be included. The work of Grünewald and Hjertén had been greatly influenced by Matisse, who was a major inspiration to Swedish painters between 1910 and 1920.

In addition to De Unga and De Åtta, there were

coalitions of other painters who supported each other and exhibited together but were less radical in their approach to painting. One of these groups, established by Birger Simonsson, Tor Bjurström, Hilding Linnqvist, and Erik Hallström, relied on traditional subject matter such as naive, idyllic village scenes and genre painting. Another group, which included De Åtta artists Jolin and Dardel, was known for a sophisticated "naive" manner with classical stylistic traits and, in Dardel's case, surrealist elements as well.[8] Thus by the end of the First World War, many progressive Swedish artists had organized into groups, and from these groups would later emerge several individuals who would make important contributions to the decorative arts.

The Fine and Decorative Arts: Glass on Display in Stockholm

In "Den svenska konsthandeln" (The Swedish art trade), August Brunius singled out the Cirkeln Konsthall on Biblioteksgatan and the Svensk-Franska Konstgalleriet at 26 Sturegatan in Stockholm as being especially noteworthy.[9] The Svensk-Franska Konstgalleriet was established in 1918 by Gösta Olsson, who had been in Paris during the First World War where he had established a remarkable network of contacts as well as a taste for modern French art.[10] His gallery became a primary connection between avant-garde French and Swedish art. During the 1920s it was Sweden's most important venue for nineteenth- and twentieth-century progressive art, regularly featuring work by Daumier, Renoir, Gauguin, Pissarro, Cézanne, Matisse, Bonnard, and Modigliani.

The gallery also showed modern Swedish glass, particularly that made by Orrefors Glassworks (fig. 5-1). This began after a 1917 exhibition of Orrefors's work at the Nordiska Kompaniet (NK), Sweden's most prestigious department store. Simon Gate and Edward Hald, who were by then the two leading artists at the factory, invited Olsson to the glassworks, and apparently they made an agreement whereby Orrefors would pay for the design of a permanent display case at the gallery while Olsson would attempt to sell Swedish art glass in France through his many connections.[11] In March 1919 the first exhibition showing both contemporary painting and art glass went on view at the Svensk-Franska Konstgalleriet. The work represented the progressive interpretation of glass as a work of art. Graal glass and engraved crystal were shown alongside work by Picasso and Maurice de Vlaminck and Swedish painters Einar Jolin and Simon Gate.[12] Contemporary critics who commented on the exhibition, however, distinguished between the paintings and the glass, reflecting the ongoing bias characteristic of the period.

Another glass artist who received attention in the Swedish press at this time was Edvin Ollers who had begun his career as a painter. In 1917 Svenska Slöjdföreningen (The Swedish Society of Craft and Industrial Design) had recommended him to the Kosta Glassworks.[13] Thanks to Ollers, Kosta received critical acclaim for the colored glassware the factory introduced at Hemutställningen (The Home Exhibition), which was held at the Liljevalchs gallery the same year. Ollers modeled his designs after eighteenth-century glass in the collections of the Nationalmuseum and the Statens Historiska Museum in Stockholm. The prototypes shown at the Home Exhibition were made with a glass melt that included impurities causing it to bubble. When the glass went into production at Kosta, a purer melt was used and much of the aesthetic appeal of the original was lost.

In a review that appeared in a Gothenburg newspaper, Brunius referred to a 1919 exhibition of paintings and painted earthenware by Ollers shown at the Cirkeln gallery, noting the apparent "cooperation between the applied arts and industry" that this work represented.[14] Ollers was one of a number of artists who worked in both ceramics and glass. Brunius credited the interchange between Swedish artists and glassblowers for the rapid advances in the design of both luxury and utilitarian glass. Glassblowers were, in effect, skilled artists. Many glass manufacturers, however, were not supportive of the new artistic efforts. This had been evident in Kosta's opposition to Ollers's insistence on retaining the impurities in the glass for artistic effects. Brunius, however, encouraged Ollers to continue his experiments in revitalizing eighteenth-century forms, using earthenware as a medium rather than glass and collaborating with a receptive ceramics factory.[15] This did not happen. The freely decorated earthenware that Ollers produced for Upssala-Ekeby in 1918 and exhibited at the Cirkeln gallery was admired by the critics and the public but was not put into production. Elisabeth Thorman, another art critic, summed up the problematic relationship between artists and industry when she described the breakdown between Upsala-Ekeby and Ollers whereby "they let the artist buy his own work for a high price, then they washed their hands of him and wanted no more to do with him or his ceramics."[16] Ollers became one of the many trained painters whose work was marginalized. Appointed a drawing teacher at the Tekniska Skolan (School of Technology), he also wrote art criticism from 1922 to 1923.[17] His contribution to Swedish applied arts was limited after this period.

Art versus Industry

Despite the collaborative efforts of Svenska Slöjdföreningen, artists remained reluctant to ally themselves with industry. Relatively few individuals responded either to Svenska Slöjdföreningen's call for artists to work with industry or to the Society's attempts to secure a new favorable status for artists.[18] The reasons for this are difficult to define.

Demography provides at least part of the answer. Most Swedish artists were from modest backgrounds. The majority of them received their formal education either at the Tekniska Skolan, where they were trained as drawing instructors, technical artists, or craftsmen, or at the Konstakademien (Academy of Art), where they were encouraged to become independent artists. The success of individual painters depended on finding a good dealer to present their work and on receiving positive criticism. Very few artists succeeded in attracting the attention of collectors, who were themselves small in number. A few artists, such as Grünewald and the sculptor Carl Milles, became wealthy from their art. Hilding Linnqvist, Nils Dardel, and Otte Sköld were under contract to Gösta Olsson at the Svensk-Franska and were able to sustain good incomes. Success enabled artists to travel abroad where they gained wider aesthetic experience and came in direct contact with progressive developments in the arts on the Continent. During the 1920s many Swedish artists traveled to France and Italy. For the most part, however, contemporary commentary indicates that, during periods of economic depression in the 1920s and 1930s, most of Sweden's artists lived in poverty. In 1923 the government proposed distributing 250,000 kronor from state lottery funds to needy artists as something of a relief effort.[19]

Simon Gate was one of the few artists who agreed to collaborate with industry; ultimately he became one of Sweden's leading glass artists. Trained as a draftsman at the Tekniska Skolan, he intended to establish a career as a portrait painter and went on to study painting at the Konstakademien where he met two of Sweden's foremost narrative painters, Gustaf

Cederström and Georg von Rosen. They were both representatives of the conservative ideal. Gate remained committed to this academic training throughout his career, drawing from it for inspiration. He consistently incorporated classical figures, for example, into his engravings on glass, and he created small molded plaster figurines of mythical beings such as the Faun and Nymph (fig. 5-2). Such subjects were appropriate to the neoclassical forms he used for his crystal pieces in the 1920s.

The art theoretician and historian Gregor Paulsson was a strong advocate of artists working for industry. In his seminal manifesto, *Vackrare Vardagsvara* (More beautiful things for everyday use; 1919), he acted as a propagandist, arguing that industry could be further developed by artists. The decorative qualities of contemporary art and the new means of expression then being explored in the arts could fuel the applied arts. Years later, when Paulsson summarized the period between the 1917 Home Exhibition at Liljevalchs Konsthall and the 1923 Jubilee Exhibition in Gothenburg, Sweden, he noted that artists had not gone to work for industry in the numbers he had envisioned. The reason he posited for this was that artists initially did not see themselves as serving society but rather as serving beauty.[20] Even at this early stage, functionalism was considered counter to aesthetics.

Paulsson's position was supported by Edward Hald's brief but illuminating reply to the question of assessing the so-called independent arts, handicrafts, and the mission of the applied arts industry, respectively: "We [who went to work in industry] were regarded with a certain disdain. The work was viewed as a lesser form of artistic activity that was suitable for those with less ability. There was seldom any recognition of an intellectual or social agenda."[21]

In a 1925 essay on the relationship between good "independent" art and good "applied" handicraft, August Brunius came up with a variant of the beauty-versus-function dilemma that Paulsson had identified. He wrote, "A 1925 man [who is pleased with all types of simplifying shortcuts and good tools] becomes angry when he sees the engraved decoration on a piece of art glass disappear as he fills it with water and arranges a bunch of flowers—i.e., when the object is utilitarian, its artistic quality disappears!"[22] This summarizes the conflict between function and decoration. In his remarks Brunius quoted both Austrian architect Adolf Loos who said, "ornamentation is a custom as outmoded as tattooing," and British art critic Roger Fry who called decoration an "artistic eczema."[23] The promotion of form over ornament was central to debates by the art community in Sweden and culminated in the radical functionalism of the 1930s.

Another explanation for artists' resistance to working with industry might be found in the status quo. Progressive intellectuals such as Paulsson and Hald were excited by the prospect of establishing a new venue for the creation of art within industry. Most artists of the period, however, continued to support the nineteenth-century, romantic vision of artists pursuing individuality and independence, a view they probably shared with the majority of Swedish manufacturers at the time.

The Romantic Heritage of the Late Nineteenth Century: Under the Sign of the Rose Hip

In his major study, *L'Art décoratif moderne en Suède* (Modern decorative art in Sweden), Erik Wettergren discussed the applied arts displayed in the Swedish pavilion at the 1925 Paris exposition.[24] Wettergren, the curator of decorative arts at the Nationalmuseum in Stockholm, was primarily interested in the luxury crafts. He compared the Swedish craft tradition to a tree with three major roots. The first consisted of traditional vernacular handicrafts. The second was the indigenous expression that had evolved from a transformation of French rococo and neoclassical design in the late eighteenth century. The strength and harmonious rigor that characterized French art and culture of the period was readily incorporated into a vernacular Swedish expression. The third root was entirely modern, the result, Wettergren claimed, of the purifying influence of rationalism and sensible taste on nineteenth-century industrial eclecticism.

Fig. 5-2. Faun and nymph, by Simon Gate, 1915/20; plaster. (Private collection)

Fig. 5-3. *Gåslisa, Herdinnana vision* (Gåslisa, The Vision of the Shepherdess, by Ernst Josephson, ca. 1890; oil on panel. (Prince Eugen's Waldemarsudde)

According to Wettergren, if Meissonnier's rococo and Delafosse's neoclassicism could be compared to magnificent roses, the Swedish counterpart was the simple rose hip, the wild briar of Swedish romanticism. The cultivated French rose versus the wild Swedish rose was analogous to the opposing ideals of classicism and romanticism. The wild briar was also an apposite symbol for the Swedish national character; it was "the sign of poverty and the charm and purity of the wilds."[25] Between 1910 and 1930, the "rustic" aesthetic represented by the wild rose found extensive expression in interior designs and in designs for ceramics, glass, metalwork, and textiles.

In painting, this aesthetic manifested itself variously during the interwar years. The brief period from 1918 to 1920 was characterized by Swedish naivism, an intimately romantic idiom that paid homage to a dreamy mysticism and a longing for simple, beloved, traditional objects such as the cut-glass designs of the late nineteenth century. Naivism also found expression in the engraved decoration on some of the art glass produced during this period.[26] In painting, naive, largely self-taught techniques were explored in response to international modernism, which in Sweden was limited to expressionism and exercises in futurism and cubism.

The naive movement was inspired in large measure by the work of Ernst Josephson, an early romantic visionary of the 1880s and 1890s, whose work also influenced Swedish expressionists. Josephson painted the wild rose itself in a luminous and mystical canvas, *Gåslisa, Herdinnana vision* (Gåslisa, The Vision of the Shepherdess, ca. 1890; fig. 5-3). The rose is executed as if it were a piece of jewelry, a rare treasure, presented by nature to the young girl who kneels before her vision. This figure represents a merging of Swedish folk tradition and the popular, romantic interpretation of the Virgin Mary.

The leading exponent of naive painting, however, was Hilding Linnqvist, who was Josephson's most immediate successor. After a brief period as a student at the Tekniska Skolan and the Konstakademien, Linnqvist worked on his own, drawing from nature and studying engravings at the Nationalmuseum. He also did restoration work. In 1918 a selection of his small-scale paintings, such as *Stilleben med hyaciter* (Still Life with Hyacinths, 1917) was exhibited at at the Liljevalchs Konsthall in the Yngre svenska konstnärer (Young

Fig. 5-4. *Smycken och kristall* (Jewelry and Crystal), by Hilding Linnqvist, 1919; oil on canvas. (Private collection)

Swedish Artists) exhibition. Also shown were works by Leander Engström, Edward Hald, Vera Nilsson, Gösta Sandels, and Otte Sköld, among others. Linnqvist's dreamy, fairy-tale–like landscapes and still lifes featuring depictions of traditional, cut or engraved glassware and wildflowers were well received by the public (fig. 5-4). During the 1920s he became one of the Svensk-Franska Konstgalleriet's most popular artists. Linnqvist, like fellow naive painter Erik Hallström, whose painting *Ångsblommor* (Wildflowers, 1918) also includes a glass vase, was inspired by medieval Swedish frescoes and provincial eighteenth- and nineteenth-century paintings that were essentially vernacular.

After several of the naivists traveled to the Continent in the early 1920s, they began to incorporate elements of French and Italian classicism into their work. The romantic cottage garden, for example, a favorite subject for both Linnqvist and Hallström in the late 1910s, was replaced by views of formal gardens such as those outside the villas of southern Europe.[27]

Expressionism, Orientalism, Late Fauvism: Like a Singing Tree

If the naivists sought to express the dream world of emotion and memory, the many artists who came under the influence of Henri Matisse strove to emulate his attention to an intellectual order (balance in form, harmony, and color) and to painting as dialogue between outer and inner observations. The use of simplified line, rhythmic form, and bold, decorative colors was transformed into highly individual styles by the many Swedish artists who studied with Matisse in the early part of the twentieth century. These included Isaac Grünewald, Sigrid Hjertén, and Edward Hald, who would contribute substantially to the decorative arts with their designs for ceramics, glass, and textiles.[28]

In April 1918 Isaac Grünewald gave a lecture at the Estetiska Föreningen (Society for Aesthetic Study) in Uppsala. It was published the same year under the title, *Den nya renässansen inom konsten* (The new renaissance in art). In it he began with a flourish, exclaiming, "Simplification, grandeur, expressiveness, clarity: behold the watchwords of contemporary art." Under this rubric, he continued by bringing together phenomena as diverse as neolithic cave paintings, Indian and Egyptian sculpture, Persian miniature paintings, "primitive" African art, sixteenth-century Italian art, the paintings of Delacroix, Cézanne, and Matisse, and even Ernst Josephson, whom he called "the first, even if unconscious, expressionist in modern times."

By then Grünewald had assimilated the fluid linear drawing technique Josephson had discovered in an encounter with the spirit or fantasy world in 1888–89 (which led Josephson to a mental breakdown). This is evident in Grünewald's ink drawings whose subject is a pastiche of Josephson's "psychotic" sketches.[29] Decorative painting, however, offered greater latitude to the young, ambitious Grünewald. In 1913 he submitted an entry to the competition for the decoration of the registrar's office of Ragnar Östberg's Stockholm City Hall (completed in 1923). His plan was to create his own version of Matisse's *La Joie de Vivre* (1905–06, The Barnes Foundation). Two years later, in 1915, he completed *Det sjungande trädet* (The Singing Tree; fig. 5-5), by which time he had found his own dynamic approach. The subject is the Berselii Park in Stockholm. The black trunk of the tree curves upward through golden afternoon light that has colored the shadows a cool green; the crown of the tree pulses with warm red on cool pink. Like characters in a comedy, a woman with a parasol and a small boy wearing a striped jersey pull each other in opposite directions. The composition's arabesque lines, however, have more in common with the decorative manner of native, Dalecarlian, narrative painting of the eighteenth and nineteenth centuries than they do with Matisse's sophisticated orientalism.[30]

Painting on porcelain was another area that attracted contemporary painters. In 1916 Isaac Grünewald and

Sigrid Hjertén exhibited together at the Gummeson gallery on Strandvägen in Stockholm. Grünewald showed paintings of Stockholm city scenes and floral subjects, and Hjertén displayed painted porcelain she had created for Rörstrand. August Brunius was enthusiastic about Hjertén's work, commenting, "From these painted dishes and boxes the purity and strength of the gift of color shines through. . . . One also sees what charm there is in the boldness of execution—just as in old Persian ceramics—instead of the ornamental mechanical feel that has become customary in a large segment of the ceramics field."[31] Hjertén had a special talent for decoration but never put her designs for porcelain into mass production, nor did she ever attempt to create art glass. In essence she considered herself a painter who had been trained as a textile artist. At Grünewald's suggestion, Hjertén abandoned her plans to study tapestries in England and instead went with him to Paris to work under Henri Matisse who further encouraged her talent.[32]

In 1911, the year she married Isaac Grünewald, Hjertén wrote an article entitled "Modern och österländsk konst" (Modern and oriental art),[33] in which she developed the argument that the qualities of Chinese and Persian art are to be found in the masters of modernism, Cézanne, Matisse, Braque, and Picasso. She formulated "elementary laws" for contemporary art: "the consistent simplification of lines in order to obtain the greatest possible expressiveness, the subordination of proportion to the demands of the composition, concentration on the strongest moments of a movement in the part of the figure performing the movement, the supremacy of color over tone. . . . The curve is the tune of the work, and its consistency must in no way be disturbed by the figure."[34]

The subject matter in Hjertén's painting between 1910 and 1920 often combines, as rival principles, modernism's interest in depicting the life model as an impersonal arrangement of volume, line, and color, and traditional genre painting. In *Brunetten och Blondinen* (The Brunette and the Blonde, 1912) and *Iván i fåtöljen* (Iván Sitting in an Armchair, 1915), for example, the room itself becomes expressive.[35] In another portrait of her son, *Iván med leksakshäst* (Iván With a Wooden Horse, 1918; fig. 5-6), Hjertén is clearly on the verge of finding the harmony between her delicate palette and

Fig. 5-5. *Det sjungande trädet* (The Singing Tree), by Isaac Grünewald, 1915; oil on canvas. (Norrköping Museum)

the characteristic, dynamically diagonal composition with a simplified curved "Persian" form.

It has been said that Sigrid Hjertén "anticipated the ideal home of our time, with the window open to society."[36] The relationship, however, between her studio/parlor and the vast "room" of society glimpsed through her window was one of tense contrast rather than ideal harmony. From the beginning most Swedish art critics did not understand Hjertén's art and even treated it with disdain. In 1912 Brunius, who eventually became one of her few supporters, described her paintings as mildly derivative.[37] But a few years later, when comparing her art to Grünewald's at the 1918 Expressionistutställningen (Expressionist Exposition) at the Liljevalchs Konsthall, he had clearly changed his mind, finding her art to be "far from an imitation of Isaac Grünewald. Hertjén's paintings, the *Interiör* (Interior), *Den svarta kängan* (The Black Shoe), *Badstrand* (Beach), *Barnen vid dammen* (Children at the Pond), and especially *Den blå skottkärran* (The Blue Wheelbarrow) and *Den lille sjuklingen* (The Little Invalid), are exquisite works of a most coloristic imagi-

nation."[38] General recognition of her talent for composition and special skill with color came only in the mid-1930s, after she had stopped painting. Among Matisse's Swedish students, the only truly independent Fauvist was Sigrid Hjertén.

Edward Hald had known the Grünewalds since his student days in Paris in 1908–09. For Hald the encounter with Matisse's aesthetic was not as decisive as it had been for Isaac Grünewald. Hald's Paris experiences were more significant in providing a place for him in the "De Unga" group and for giving him the opportunity to visit museums and study paintings by Ingres, Delacroix, Puvis de Chavannes, Cézanne, and particularly Vuillard and Bonnard. Hald's first solo exhibition, in 1914, consisted of interiors and landscapes as well as studies of nude bathers, which he had painted during a few summers spent on the island of Utö, near Stockholm. These summer scenes were later shown in the 1915 Schwedische Expressionisten (Swedish Expressionism) exhibition at Der Sturm Gallery in Berlin. In 1917, the year in which Hald was hired by Orrefors, he attracted critical attention with an exhibi-

Fig. 5-6. *Iván med leksakshäst* (Iván With a Wooden Horse) by Sigrid Hjertén, 1918; oil on canvas. (Private collection)

Fig. 5-7. *Det koniska berget* (The Conical Mountain), by Edward Hald, 1921; oil on canvas. (Private collection)

tion of paintings at the Lund University Art Museum. His modernist "discrete" approach was praised as was his sense of line and decorative unity.[39] From 1917 until 1944, the year he left Orrefors, Hald devoted his energies to creating art glass. It was not until 1947 that he exhibited his paintings again, in a major showing of his work at Konstnärshuset (The Artists' House) in Stockholm.

Considering the intimately realistic painting that Hald produced between 1910 and 1920, his bravura display of late Fauvism, *Det koniska berget* (The Conical Mountain, 1921; fig. 5-7), comes as a surprise. Highly intense German expressionist color is combined with a simplification of form in the manner of Matisse. At a time when contemporary Swedish art in some circles was returning to the classical language of form, Hald opted to situate his nude figures, symbols of

freedom and sensuality, in an arcadian landscape. Here the aqueduct of antiquity coexists with a mountain peak reminiscent of neogothic forms; the surrounding landscape includes trees in the shape of arabesques (the large one to the left recalls Grünewald's "singing tree") and sunbathers who are painted in the jewellike colors of a stained-glass window. Interestingly, the darker female figure is drawn with the same highlit double outline as in Hald's earlier design for the engraved glass vase called "Girls Playing Ball" (1919/1920). Perhaps *Det koniska berget* should be viewed as a sweeping farewell from an artist to a medium to which he would only return decades later.

The Triumph of Cubism and Classicism: Nils Dardel and Arvid Fougstedt

At the autumn 1918 exhibition of work by De Unga and

Fig. 5-8. *Visit hos excentrisk dam* (A Visit to an Eccentric Lady), by Nils Dardel, 1920; watercolor. (Private collection)

at the Autumn Salon, both held at Liljevalchs Konsthall, the public encountered the most recent trends in Swedish painting, which were conventionally figurative. Evidence of modernist trends such as futurism, dadaism, and constructivism was scarce. The Autumn Salon included traditional landscapes and portraits whose styles recalled French painting, from impressionism to seminal works by Cézanne and Picasso. The impact of Matisse had lessened. The naivists' compositions amused the public with their wealth of details, narrative depictions, and determination to capture the unsophisticates who still inhabited the city and its environs. A superficial, classicizing cubism represented by Georg Pauli, a painter of the 1890s, and the young Otte Sköld, who had lived in Copenhagen during the First World War, attracted attention and protests. Two collages by Sköld (a dust jacket for a book and a design for bottle labels) were particularly ridiculed. "Why not hang a knitting needle here using a piece of iron wire tied to the frame?" a less-informed critic suggested, thus anticipating Duchamp's "ready-mades." Arvid Fougstedt, in his programmatic painting, *David i Ingres ateljé* (David in Ingres's Studio; 1918), introduced the new neoclassicism featuring deep perspective, posed figures that were distinctly delineated, sculptural form, and subdued colors. This type of painting came to dominate the 1920s under the name of *ny saklighet* (new objectivity).

Nils Dardel, a painter who explored many different forms of modernism, also exhibited in the 1918 Autumn Salon. Dardel had traveled to Paris in 1910, studied briefly with Matisse, and continued to work independently. He was at home in the artistic milieu of Paris, associating with Jean Cocteau, Pierre Bonnard, and Pablo Picasso, among others. In 1912 and 1913 Dardel had worked in a cubist idiom and later experimented with naive painting before settling on his colorful linear style. In 1917 he traveled to North America and Japan, and his work became influenced by

Fig. 5-9. *Mauritz Stiller*, by Arvid Fougstedt, 1920; oil on glass. (Sandrew's Film Company, Sweden)

Japanese drawing and painting. Around 1920 he focused on fantastic and whimsical subjects, often ironic or bizarre and frightening. These works reflect Dardel's own conflict-ridden emotional life and ambiguous sexuality, while simultaneously evoking contemporary artistic trends.

One of the most refined examples of Dardel's symbolically and aesthetically rich pictorial world is the watercolor version of the large painting, *Visit hos excentrisk dam* (A Visit to an Eccentric Lady, 1920; fig. 5-8). In it, a young woman with the countenance of a Renaissance madonna hovers between self-disclosure and concealment, mirroring the artist's own emotional struggles. A young man (possibly the artist himself) hangs from the studio skylight. Like the hanged man, a rabbit dangles from a fishing line, eye to eye with a large snake or worm whose contour is repeated in the lines of the tree—a surrealistic version of Grünewald's singing tree. In this drama there are symbols of masculinity and femininity, humanity and bestiality that act out emotional poses—submission and aggression,

temptation and endangerment, dreamlike fascination and naked cruelty.

In two canvases—the enigmatically comic, *Columbi ägg* (Egg of Columbus, 1924) and the eerie *Paranoikern* (The Paranoiac, 1925)—Dardel's painting comes close to the Freudian-inspired Surrealism that André Breton's circle was then developing in Paris. But unlike the Surrealists of that group—René Magritte, Salvador Dalí, Max Ernst, Man Ray, and Meret Oppenheim—Dardel created symbolic expressions of an emotional fantasy world at once full of innocence and hard-bitten perversion. It is perhaps closer in mood to the work of the American artist Florine Stettheimer.[40]

Arvid Fougstedt represents a return to the early French neoclassicism of David and Ingres. Fougstedt lived in Paris during the First World War, where he was on the fringes of the circle of young artists that included Picasso and Modigliani. He returned to Stockholm in 1917 and made his debut there in 1919 with an exhibition of paintings and drawings. The critics praised

Fig. 5-10. *Tidsbild—Gypsie Bar, Quartier Latin* (Period Picture—Gypsy Bar, Latin Quarter), by Otte Sköld, 1925; oil on canvas. (Private collection)

both his technical maturity and his ability to convey style and contemporary social attitudes with great immediacy.

Inspired by Picasso's classical 1915 drawing of the art dealer Vollard, Fougstedt painted a portrait of the Swedish film director Mauritz Stiller in 1919–20 (fig. 5-9).[41] The precision with which Picasso rendered his Ingres-inspired pencil drawing was decisive for Fougstedt's own direction, particularly in its distinctive treatment of volume. Fougstedt, however, adds a detailed treatment of the textiles and a lush palette. Picasso was neither a traditionalist nor a surrealist, yet André Breton began his essay on the relationship between painting and Surrealism by referring to Picasso the classicist: "Surrealism had to pass 'where Picasso had passed and will pass again.' "[42]

Stiller demanded that his portrait be painted on glass (*verre eglomisé*), which was an expensive technique whereby the artist had to work "backward," applying the highlights and details first.[43] It required both time and a high level of skill. In the painting Stiller's face is skillfully modeled with a thin brush in a manner similar to the line painting that had inspired Dardel in Japan in 1917.[44] The armchair's pistachio

green upholstery is balanced by the pale violet tasseled shawl and the dominant red Persian carpet, a combination of colors reminiscent of Matisse. In the background is a Chinese cabinet with intarsia decoration on the drawers. Overall the portrait is a unique aesthetic document of the era with considerable coloristic luminosity, due in part to the special effect achieved by the *eglomisé* technique. It makes reference not only to Picasso's drawing but also to the traditional bourgeois portrait that originated in the Netherlands in the seventeenth century.

There is a basic difference between the approaches to neoclassicism taken by Dardel and Fougstedt in 1918–20 and by Simon Gate at Orrefors at the same time. Gate focused on variations of well-known subjects, such as Botticelli's *Venus*, which were appropriate to the luxury objects he was producing. Dardel and Fougstedt were applying classicism to an entirely new image of the modern individual as a person who was disciplined, organized, and clear-minded (qualities of classicism), as well as eccentric, introverted, and sensual (in the Ingres tradition). Neither Dardel nor Fougstedt applied their talents or translated their visions into objects of the decorative arts.

The Persistence of the Classical Vocabulary

The historicist reactions of Swedish painters to expressionism during the early to mid-1920s were not only based in French neoclassicism and vernacular painting. Artists also looked to the masters of the fifteenth and sixteenth centuries for inspiration. Like Fougstedt, Otte Sköld, who was primarily interested in form and had worked in a cubist manner, became drawn to the artists of the Flemish Renaissance — Memling, Brueghel, Holbein, and Clouet. After living in Copenhagen during the First World War, Sköld went to Paris in 1920 where he lived for many years. He painted a number of still lifes in the Dutch seventeenth-century tradition, but the intense social life of Paris also provided him with subjects, as in the adroit composition, *Tidsbild — Gypsie Bar, Quartier Latin* (Period Picture — Gypsy Bar, Latin Quarter, 1925; fig. 5-10). The subject is a compact synthesis of three different barroom interiors. The painting can be seen as a response to Pieter Brueghel's *Peasant Dance*, which was both accessible and closed to the viewer. *Tidsbild —Gypsie Bar* also mediates between what is open and what is concealed from the viewer. The mechanical repetition of arms, faces, plastered-down hair, and hats is a deft stylistic manipulation, depicting a crowd of couples engaged in various activities — dancing, smoking, drinking, or kissing. They are "fixed like a heap of bacteria under the lens of a microscope."[45]

While Sköld focused on issues of painterly form, Vera Nilsson incorporated personal symbolism into her bold, expressionist paintings of the 1920s and 1930s. Characteristic of her work of the 1920s is a burnished coloring. In *Såpbubblor* (Soap Bubbles, 1927; fig. 5-11), Nilsson expresses her anquish over the social and political tensions in Europe between the two world wars. Nilsson had achieved a major success in 1922 when she took part in an exhibition at Liljevalchs Konsthall in which "Falangen" (The Phalanx) artists' group was first shown. Falangen was an initiative of Nils Dardel and Otte Sköld; it included the elite of Swedish painters, thirteen men and one woman. Nilsson's deeply moving expressionism was liberated by encounters with the work of Vincent van Gogh and the sensualist oeuvre of Renoir. Gösta Olsson at the Svensk-Franska judged Nilsson's painting to be the best in the country.

Among Swedish painters, the victory of the eclectic classicism of the 1920s over the expressionism of the previous decade was not based solely on cubism's breakthrough in the academies of art. Also at issue was the fact that after 1919 it became possible to travel south to the Continent. Young artists enthusiastically studied the great sixteenth- and seventeenth-century traditions and did so with the help of new teachers. Maj Bring, who had painted with Matisse in 1911, described her new impressions of 1922: "André Lhote had opened a school in Montparnasse that Scandinavians enjoyed attending. . . . Lhote's theories of composition were not new, they were still the same as those of which, for example, Raphael had made use.

Fig. 5-11. *Såpbubblor* (Soap Bubbles), by Vera Nilsson, 1927; oil on canvas. (Nationalmuseum, Stockholm)

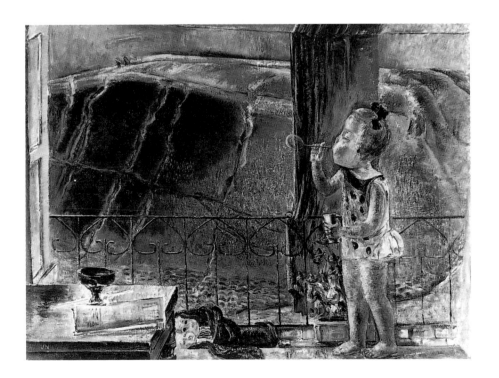

Fig. 5-12. *Självporträtt/I vit turban* (Self-portrait/In a White Turban), by Tyra Lundgren, 1921; oil on panel. (Moderna Museet)

. . . I would instead call [his cubism] a classicism in modern dress. I then copied a small painting by Raphael at the Louvre and it was interesting to see how Raphael in the tiniest detail observed the rules we had picked up at the school in Lhote's house."[46]

Tyra Lundgren, an artist who designed art glass at Kosta Glassworks beginning in 1935, painted the purely classical *Självporträtt/I vit turban* (Self-portrait/In a White Turban, 1921; fig. 5-12) during her first year as a student of Lhote's. She had a higher opinion of Lhote's teaching and theoretical skills than of his painting. The composition of her self-portrait might, at first glance, suggest Jan van Eyck's *Man With a Red Turban*, but the sculptural modeling places it in the Italian fifteenth-century portrait tradition. The determination to monumentalize rather than beautify is obvious and supports the artist's own comment: "A number of my paintings could just as well have been sculptures."[47] Lundgren was trained in ceramics and worked as a designer for the Rörstrand and Lidköping Porcelain Factories (until 1930), Arabia in Helsinki (until 1937), Sèvres outside of Paris (until 1939), and Gustavsberg (1939–49). Yet it was mainly in Italy, in Rome's premier artistic circles

and with Venini in the glassworks on Murano, that she found her artistic home. Lundgren herself wrote, "One evening in Venice I bumped into a dazzlingly white, gold-laced Italian officer who invited me for a romantic gondola ride on Venice's dark, glittering waters. He was Paolo Venini, with whom I had only corresponded up to that point. I came across the industrious Venini the next day on the glassworkers' island of Murano in his own factory. . . . So when Venini said, 'Regard my factory as your own, join me and if you come you'll borrow my best master,' I accepted the challenge and began to experiment with Bobolo, one of Venini's best glassblowers. That's the way it started. I came with fresh eyes and an imagination about materials."[48]

The interest in classical styles and the retreat from experimental modes in the later 1920s and early 1930s gave way to a conservative attitude toward the possibility of genuine collaboration between artists and industrial design. In 1935 Otte Sköld was appointed a professor at the Konstakademien. He later became the academy's director and also the director of the Nationalmuseum. In his first speech at the Konstakademien he asked, "Why should art be more social than music? Do we perhaps use music to create only psalms, religious hymns, national or international war songs, marches, dances, and jazz? Art, when it is itself, is a *free* creation. . . . Just as a game is a free invention, with no other task save the game's own, so art is and so art ought to be liberated from all new direct missions."[49] Sköld opposed the idea of merging the Konstakademien with the Tekniska Skolan; an Orrefors vase or a photograph, he believed, was not on the same "spiritual level" as a first-class painting.

In 1936 the successful Tyra Lundgren expressed the same reservations: "For twenty years now, we in Sweden have totally focused on the useful, on giving what was functional an attractive form and on putting a low price on well-made objects. But why should we combine this socially directed industry with art? Is art something useful? . . . Our mania for calling each and every tasteful creation art has in truth had double-edged consequences. If on one hand it has somewhat elevated the simpler taste of the general public, then on the other the taste of those with more education has been leveled. . . . An object that is supposed to delight the eye with its surface and its own beauty, regardless of other functions, must be accorded great care and be expensive."[50]

In the mid-1930s Sköld and Lundgren represented their time just as Edward Hald and Gregor Paulsson had in 1917. Interestingly, after two decades, the elitist point of view that was linked to traditional, classical ideals emphasizing distinctions between high and low art, between independent and commissioned artists, came to prevail over the bold new way of thinking, of equalizing and removing boundaries. For Sköld and

Fig. 5-13. *Tidsbild* (Picture of the Period), by Sven X:et Erixson, 1937; oil on canvas. (Moderna Museet)

Lundgren the Italian tradition of form was deeply inspiring and they both felt bound to guard its ideals of beauty and independence.

Swedish Artists in the International Arena

In the years just before the Second World War, Swedish artists continued to journey to the Continent. Edward Hald, Nils Dardel, Otte Sköld, and Tyra Lundgren were equally at home in Paris, Rome, Venice, or other European cities as in their native land. They represented the cosmopolitanism that had developed in the Swedish community. Vera Nilsson and other Swedish artists such as Sven Erixson shared a somewhat different philosophy, not solely aesthetic but radical and all-encompassing, springing from a passion for social justice and humanism.

In 1922 Erixson, who had trained at the Tekniska Skolan, won first prize in a design competition sponsored by the Kosta Glassworks. On one of his winning pieces of crystal, he had quoted a line from a poem by a Swedish Renaissance bishop: "Freedom is the best thing that can be sought around the world by the one who can take it."[51] From 1929 to 1931, Erixson was a guest artist at Kosta where he produced richly decorated glass.[52] Because of financial difficulties, however,

neither the artist nor the management of the glassworks established a permanent collaboration. Instead, most of Erixson's work consisted of easel and monumental painting for large-scale glass mosaic panels and theater decoration. For Erixson, like other artists of his generation, the conflict between art and craft seemed to have lost much of its sting. His reason for not continuing at the glassworks was simply that painting was his preferred medium.

As Ernst Josephson before him, Erixson expressed his love of life and nature powerfully and subjectively, and his art is viewed by the broad public as being very Swedish. In a darkly dramatic painting, *Tidsbild* (Picture of the Period, 1937; fig. 5-13), Erixson captures the mood at Slussen's, a dynamic structure in the middle of downtown Stockholm, where people are drawn like moths to the newspaper headlines "War," "Spain," "Murder." On the facade of a building in the background a lighted neon "SF" (Svensk Filmindustri) beckons, advertising an escape from reality. International catastrophe was just two years in the future and with it would come an abrupt halt to progress in the arts throughout Europe and indeed most of the world.

1. According to August Brunius, from 1910 to around 1920, Hallins Konsthandel was for a time the only dealer in art objects in this area. The gallery was located on Drottninggatan, a principal thoroughfare in Stockholm since the seventeenth century.

2. August Brunius, "Den svenska konsthandeln," *Göteborgs Handelstidning* (January 3, 1919). During the First World War Brunius wrote for *Svenska Dagbladet* and was editor of its arts pages. Between 1920 and 1923 he wrote for the *Göteborgs Handelstidning* and after 1923 returned to *Svenska Dagbladet*. His political liberalism characterized his work as a critic, and he became the leading spokesman for his generation of artists.

3. Ibid.

4. Gösta Lilja, *Det Moderna måleriet i svensk kritik, 1905–1914* (Malmö, 1955), pp. 120–28, 137–44.

5. In 1912 Walden had exhibited Italian futurism; starting in 1917 he espoused the cause of the Berlin Dadaists.

6. Bengt Lärkner, *Det internationella avantgardet och Sverige, 1914–1925* (Malmö: Stenvall, 1984), pp. 122–26.

7. Gregor Paulsson studied art in Berlin (1909–12) and was knowledgeable about modernist art on the Continent. As director of Svenska Slöjdföreningen (1920–34) he oversaw such major events as the 1930 Stockholm Exhibition. In 1934 he was appointed professor of art history at Uppsala University. Also see chap. 3 in this volume.

8. The well-composed landscapes and refined still lifes of Einar Jolin coincide with Matisse's statement, "Je cherche le calme." In contrast, Dardel charged his paintings with symbolism, gradually developing an idealized purity of form and line.

9. Brunius, "Den svenska konsthandeln."

10. Olsson had worked in Paris as a physical therapist during the war.

11. Gösta Olsson [and Kristina Jacobsson], *Från Ling till Picasso: En konsthandlares minnen* (Stockholm: Bonniers, 1965), p. 70. Orrefors eventually cancelled the agreement with the Svensk-Franska Konstgalleriet, choosing to sell glass at Nordiska Kompaniet (NK), Sweden's leading department store. The same year a selection of engraved crystal was also exhibited at the Artium, an art gallery in Stockholm.

12. This was not the first time that graal glass designed by Simon Gate had been exhibited with contemporary painting. In the autumn of 1917 there had been an exhibition of painting and small sculpture with progressive furniture and art glass at the gallery of Konstföreningen (The Art Federation). The artists who exhibited—Torsten Palm, Alf Munthe, and Victor Axelsson—were dubbed "De Intima" (The Intimates) by Brunius. They were of the same generation as De Unga but, unlike them, had not gone to Paris; instead they had remained in Stockholm, primarily in the Smedsudden area on Lake Mälaren at the city's northwest edge. The intimate landscape artistry of Corot was their ideal. According to Brunius, "Carl Malmsten's furniture and Simon Gate's art glass go particularly well with this art. There is the same feel for quality in the detail and for the intimate total work that emerges from the best paintings."

13. Erik Wettergren, "Kostaglaset 1917–1942: Samarbetet med konstnärer," in *Kosta Glasbruk, 1742–1942*, Jubileumsskrift utgiven av Kosta glasbruk med anledning av dess 200-åriga verksamhet (Stockholm: [Kosta], 1942), p. 178; Dag Widman, "Edvin Ollers—en av 1917 års män," *Form* 3/4 (1960).

14. August Brunius, "Det konstindustriella samarbetet," *Göteborgs Handelstidning* (April 1, 1919).

15. Ibid.

16. A. Elisabeth Thorman was an art critic who wrote for one of the daily newspapers. See *Stockholms Dagblad* (May 19, 1919).

17. Ollers began at the Tekniska Skolan as an assisant teacher (1912–35); after 1935 he was the school's leading drawing instructor until it was reorganized as the Konstfackskolan in 1946, after which he remained as professor of drawing.

18. "[The] artists engaged in the applied arts industry benefited from what were extremely favorable conditions and could figuratively sit down at a sumptuously laid table. This was also the most important reason why a number of independent artists such as Hald left the economically uncertain field of painting for the somewhat more secure applied arts industry" (Ulf Hård af Segerstad, "Han stannade till festens slut," *Svenska Dagbladet* [September 24, 1983]). This is somewhat inaccurate, however, as fewer than a dozen artists actually became involved with industrial design.

19. Both Brunius and Ollers viewed such efforts as insufficient and unwelcome charity and suggested that government support be directed toward the purchase of public artworks. Starting with a government bill in 1937, Sweden would introduce formalized art support by establishing the Statens Konstråd (State Art Council), whose mission was and still is to purchase works created by the country's artists and thereby disperse commissions at a cost of 1 percent of the total cost of each new public building. The Konstråd has been successful in reaching this twofold goal.

20. Gregor Paulsson, "Stilepok utan morgondag," *Fataburen* (1968).

21. Edward Hald, "Att balansera situationen," *Form* 41 (1945).

22. August Brunius, "Tiden och tidens konsthantverk: ett ord till försvar ochtill angrepp," *Svenska Dagbladet* (July 27, 1925).

23. Loos and Fry as cited in ibid. Brunius probably quoted from Adolf Loos, "Ornament und Verbrechen" (1908); reprint in idem, *Trotzdem 1900–1930* (Innsbruck: Brenner Verlag, 1931).

24. Erik Wettergren, *L'Art décoratif moderne en Suède* (Malmö, Sweden: Malmö Museum, 1925).

25. Carl Jonas Love Almqvist (1793–1866) was a leading Swedish romantic writer. His works were collected under the title, see *Törnrosens bok* (1832–42; 1839–50). The briar symbolizes a naive innocence and devotion to God.

26. See, for example, Edward Hald's *Fiskdammen* ("The Fish Pond, 1923) and *Kärleksstigen* ("The Love Path," 1923), as well as a 1923 plate by Sven Persson and G. Thorell with an engraving of a park with fountain and willow trees (Wettergren, "Kostaglaset," fig. 78).

27. Hallström's most famous painting, *Rörstrands porslinsfabrik, 1918*, however, was inspired by the neighborhood on the outskirts of Stockholm where he and Linnqvist had grown up. Hald and other artists created ceramic tableware at Rörstrand's. The factory closed in 1926 when the company moved to Gothenburg; in 1932 it moved again, to Lidköping.

28. As Edward Hald recalled, Matisse the teacher seemed "like a hospital doctor in his white medical smock who went around and made diagnoses of the patients—the students. He talked about important subjects, about balance in form, and about contrasts and relationships in color. There was something hygienically fresh about his painters' school and the big studio in the Cloître Sacré-Coeur in the Boulevard des Invalides." "Il faut distinguer" [one must choose]," Matisse once said to Hald, who adopted this as a motto throughout his career (Arthur Hald and Erik Wettergren, eds., *Simon Gate, Edward Hald: En Skildring av människorna och konstnärerna* [Stockholm: Svenska Slöjdföreningen, Norstedts, 1948]), p. 22.

29. See, for example, the drawing of a couple in an embrace (Nationalmuseum, Stockholm, inv. no. NM H 191/1918).

30. The basic shape in *Det sjungande trädet* is repeated as a modernist sign of celebration and vitality by Edward Hald in his bowl called "Fireworks" (1921).

31. August Brunius, "Konst," *Svenska Dagbladet* (October 3, 1916).

32. When one of Hjertén's schoolmates looked up the elderly Matisse, the painter remembered the Grünewalds well. Of Sigrid, he said: "'Elle était très douée.' [She was very gifted] That was an opinion that I never heard him say about any other of his students" (Maj Bring, *Motsols: Memoarer* [Gothenburg, Bokförlaget Treangel, 1986], p. 125). Wassily Kandinsky was more reserved; in a 1916 letter to Gabriele Münter, who was then exhibiting in Stockholm and knew the Grünewalds, he wrote, "Tu ne dois pas envier Mme Grünewald à cause de son talent pour la composition. . . . le tableaux de la dame sont beaux, mais pas assez pesant' [You needn't envy Mme Grünewald for her talent. . . . her paintings are fine but not very substantial] (Vivian Endicott Barnett, *Kandinsky och Sverige* [Malmö and Stockholm: Malmö Museum / Moderna Museet, 1989], pp. 76–77).

33. Sigrid Hjertén, "Modern och österländsk konst," *Svenska Dagbladet* (February 24, 1911).

34. Ibid.

35. *Brunetten och Blondinen* is in the Sundsvall Museum; *Iván i fåtöljen* is in a private collection.

36. Carlo Derkert, *Nordisk målarkonst: Det moderna måleriets genombrott* (Stockholm: Ehlin, 1951). Derkert distinguishes between Hjertén's "ideal home" and the 1900 version defined by painter Carl Larsson. For further discussion of Larsson and ideals of the home, see chap. 3 in this volume.

37. August Brunius, "De åtta," *Svenska Dagbladet* (June 2, 1912).

38. Idem, "Expressionisterna i Konsthallen," *Svenska Dagbladet* (May 15, 1918).

39. Beate Sydhoff, "Målaren Edward Hald," in *Edward Hald: Målare, Konstindustripionjär*, exhib. cat. (Stockholm: Nationalmuseum, 1983).

40. See, for example, Florine Stettheimer, *Spring Sale at Bendel's*, 1921 (Philadelphia Museum of Art).

41. Stiller was then at the height of his career, with several internationally acclaimed films to his credit. In 1923 he directed a young Greta Garbo in *Gösta Berlings saga* and in 1925 would introduce her to the Hollywood film industry. The Picasso drawing of Vollard is in The Metropolitan Museum of Art (Elisha Whittelsey Fund). Fougstedt visited Picasso's studio (which he also sketched), calling it "as big as a church," with close to 500 canvases on the walls. When Picasso pointed out a mammoth canvas, Fougstedt responded:

"'No, look at an Ingres!' I said, picking up a drawing that was on the nearby table. 'I painted it, I just finished it yesterday. Ça m'embête,' he added, 'I'll do a series like this and exhibit it after the war.' I first looked in astonishment at the canvas, which exhibited the wildest cubism, then at the drawing. The latter was a portrait of the art dealer Vollard; using a pencil that was sharp as a needle, he had modeled the most delicate shadows in the face and carefully delineated each and every eyelash" (Arvid Fougstedt, *Svenska Dagbladet* [December 1915], cited in Bengt O. Österblom, *Arvid Fougstedt* [Stockholm: Wahlström & Widstrand, 1946], pp. 77–80).

42. It first appeared in *La Révolution surréaliste* (1925–27); cited in Briony Fer, David Batchelor, and Paul Wood, *Realism, Rationalism, Surrealism: Art Between the Wars*, The Open University: Modern Art, Practices and Debates (New Haven and London: Yale University Press, 1993), p. 173.

43. Stiller agreed to an extraordinary fee of 2,500 kronor and an open deadline for the portrait to be painted; it now hangs in the offices of the Sandrew's film company.

44. Dardel would also paint Stiller's portrait; see, for example, *Eleganter i Japan* ("Elegant People in Japan," 1918; private collection) and *Den döende dandyn* ("The Dying Dandy," 1918; Moderna Museet, Stockholm).

45. Erik Blomberg, *Naivister och realister* (Stockholm: Aldus/Bonnier, 1962), p. 20.

46. Bring, *Motsols*, p. 125.

47. Maj Modin, "Tyra Lundgrens självporträtt åren 1920–35," Ph.D. diss. (Uppsala University, 1977), p. 23.

48. Tyra Lundgren, "Mitt liv i konst," *Julpost* 45 (1968), p. 21.

49. Rolf Söderberg, *Otte Sköld* (Stockholm: Sveriges Allmänna Konstföreningen, 1968), pp. 145–46.

50. Trya Lundgren, "Vi är inte så bra som vi tror," *Stockholmstidningen* (April 4, 1936).

51. Blomberg, *Naivister och realister*, p. 53.

52. His work is in the collection of the Kosta Museum. Some were included in "Xet Sven Erixson i Tumba och Stockholm," a retrospective exhibition at the Stockholms Stadsmuseum held in 1995.

CHAPTER SIX

A Brief History of Swedish Glass

Gunnel Holmér

Fig. 6-1. Interior of the Kungsholm Glassworks, copy of a painting by Pehr Hilleström, 18th/early 19th century; oil on canvas. (Smålands Museum, Växjö)

Handmade glass has been produced in Sweden for about five centuries. During this time, despite its somewhat remote location, Sweden has been well connected with the mainstream of developments in art and craft in Europe and elsewhere. Until the eighteenth century, glass was a luxury product, accessible only to a small, wealthy segment of society. In the nineteenth century technological innovations in manufacturing processes made glass cheaper to produce, and glass objects soon became part of everyday life. Glassworks, especially in southeast Sweden, proliferated, spawning factory towns and industrial societies whose members were dependent on glassmaking for their livelihood either directly or indirectly. Since 1900, despite socioeconomic and political upheavals, Sweden's glass industry has survived and even flourished. Sixteen glassworks are still devoted to craft production of some kind for both mass-produced items and art glass. Thanks to the close cooperation between artists and artisans, Swedish glass in the twentieth century has established its own identity and gained an international reputation for excellence.

Origins of Swedish Glass

Sometime in the fourteenth or fifteenth century, monks belonging to the order of Saint Birgitta at Vadstena Abbey, Sweden, began producing glass for church windows.[1] Glass for secular use at this time was imported and thus very expensive. The first reliable evidence dates the manufacture of blown glass for domestic use in Sweden to the sixteenth century when the Swedish king, Gustav Vasa, brought two Venetian glassblowers to Stockholm in an effort to reduce the need for costly imports.[2] By 1700 approximately twenty glassworks had been established in Sweden. Their founders were members of the court and aristocracy, but the skilled glassworkers were recruited mainly from Germany and Italy,[3] lending a German or Venetian character to Sweden's early glass production. While most were situated in central areas of the country, especially Stockholm and its environs, a number of glassworks had been constructed in southern Sweden during the seventeenth

Fig. 6-4. Römer glass engraved with the royal arms, Kungsholm Glassworks, 1717; free-blown glass. (Smålands Museum, Växjö)

laurel branches on the front, often with a sun or star on the reverse.[18]

The Henrikstorp Glassworks in southern Sweden initially produced only bottles, jars, and other types of simple household glass made of brown and green glass. Starting in 1715 colorless glass was also blown there, and typical products were drinking bowls, jugs, goblets, and two-handled dishes.[19] As at Kungsholm, the engravers at Henrikstorp were German. They worked in a highly stylized ornamental idiom based on plant motifs, producing monograms surrounded by laurel branches, among other designs. Henrikstorp glass, which was generally simpler than Kungsholm designs, was popular among city dwellers and peasants.

Sales to the general public were made primarily through itinerant salesmen (fig. 6-5), but also directly from outlets with sales staff working on commission in major cities such as Stockholm and Gothenberg.[20] Glassworks owners also sometimes sold the glass personally to people of rank and to public institutions. In 1744, for example, Kosta delivered window glass to the royal palace in Stockholm, and in the next year they produced a dozen wineglasses for the Swedish king.[21] Swedish glassware even reached St. Petersburg and Riga as the circle of customers expanded in the Baltic region.[22]

The Nineteenth Century

During the first half of the nineteenth century new glassworks were constructed while others closed. Reijmyre (established in 1810) and Eda (1833), among others, survived into the twentieth century. Presumably some of these glassworks replaced Finnish glassworks that Sweden had lost during the 1808–09 war with Russia.[23] The steady decline of Kungsholm's production could also have stimulated the founding of new glassworks. In any event, glassworkers from Kungsholm, including cutters and engravers, were hired at Reijmyre and other glassworks.[24] Just as in the previous century, these new businesses were founded by noblemen or senior civil servants and were located throughout the country, although a concentration in western Sweden could already be detected. The factories were situated near streams and rivers that provided the waterpower needed to run the glass-cutting machines and the punch press used to crush raw materials.

Some new glass factories in this area were actually started by workers from nearby glassworks or from neighboring Norway.[25] Most nineteenth-century glassworks, however, were established in the second half of the century when it became customary for factory personnel with limited capital and access to local labor to start their own companies. Rural shopkeepers and peasants also started glassworks.[26] Most of these were established in southern and central Sweden, with a significant concentration in the Småland region. Between 1850 and 1900 seventy-seven glassworks started up, and of these more than half (forty-five) were located in this region, which became known as "The Kingdom of Glass." Today fifteen of Sweden's sixteen glassworks are in southeast Småland.

It was especially common for Kosta's glassblowers to leave the factory and form their own companies. In the spring of 1876 the manager at Kosta wrote somewhat anxiously that "the glassworks' glassblowers are now busy setting up factories so that finally there will be a glassworks in every homestead."[27] This was not an idle concern. Before 1900 Kosta was the source, directly or indirectly, of eighteen new glassworks to which it lost many skilled workers. The shortage of skilled manpower was so widespread that in the 1870s Kosta could not capitalize on a favorable economy and

Fig. 6-5. Itinerant glass seller, artist unknown, 18th century; oil on canvas. (Smålands Museum, Växjö)

even attempted again to recruit foreign glassworkers.[28] By the end of the nineteenth century, this trend had abated, and far fewer glassworkers left Kosta to start their own glassworks. Increased construction costs once again made new factories affordable only to very wealthy individuals.

The large forests in Småland made it the ideal region for the glass industry whose furnaces required extraordinary quantities of fuel. As in earlier times many nineteenth-century glassworks owned their own forests. During economic downturns, they sometimes raised capital by selling wood to finance the purchase of raw materials or other necessities.[29] Local peasants, who often earned extra income by making deliveries of wood, encouraged the establishment of new glassworks by donating wood or investing capital.[30] Previously many had supplied charcoal to the ironworks in Småland. Since the Middle Ages iron ore had been extracted from the lakes and bogs in Småland, but beginning in the 1860s iron production had moved to other areas where ore was extracted from rocks. In the wake of the "great ironworks death," some ironworks converted to other industries such as glass. Orrefors,

for example, had begun as an ironworks in 1726 and converted to glass production in 1898. The transition was facilitated by similarities between the patriarchal conditions and social hierarchies in both industries.

Another prerequisite for running a glassworks was adequate manpower. The nineteenth century in Sweden can be characterized as the "century of the population explosion," during which the population more than doubled, jumping from 2.347 million in 1800 to over 5.186 million in 1900,[31] with the greatest increase among the poorest sector. Most Swedes earned their living in agriculture, but few actually owned land, making them dependent on local landowners for employment. The scarcity of agricultural work prompted close to one million Swedes, many from Småland, to emigrate, mostly to North America between 1865 and 1914.[32] Others sought jobs in the cities and in industry, and each year many made seasonal labor migrations throughout the country. In Småland the glass business became an important alternative to agriculture.

Many glassworks in Småland and elsewhere were forced to close after only a few years, and even today ware, packing, and inspecting. Generally they chose to work at the glassworks where they could earn a higher cash wage than domestic work until they were married.

The director of the glassworks managed the operation and its finances, as in any business. At small glassworks owners usually acted as directors, and if they were knowledgeable about making glass, they sometimes helped in the smelting house as well. Much of their business was otherwise conducted away from the factory.

The Factory Town as Community

Newly established glassworks were small, self-contained societies until well into the twentieth century (fig. 6-7). Food crops were grown in company fields; grain was ground at the company mill; the company store sold goods on credit (often leading to unusual debts that made it impossible for workers to seek employment elsewhere). All tools were made in the company smithy: the wood for new buildings and repairs was sawed at the company sawmill. Some glassworks shared access to existing mills, sawmills, and smithies.

As more workers found employment in Swedish glassworks, genuine industrial societies developed, and improved transportation became important for both the factories and the small company towns around them. In the mid-1870s an expanding national railway network facilitated travel and transportation of raw materials and finished products to and from the glassworks. The factories grew apace with the railroads. Train travel made it easy for various craftsmen and dealers to move or change employment. There was greater independence in the workforce leading to fundamental changes in industry.

Immediately after 1900 workers established their own cooperative societies and opened their own stores whose profits were distributed among the members every year. Credit was discouraged so that workers would learn to run their homes on a budget in accordance with wages. To keep prices low, goods were delivered directly to the store by the larger merchants or wholesalers.

Initially the glassworks had not planned to build worker housing; many owners had limited capital and could afford to construct only the essential industrial buildings. At the end of the nineteenth century, however, in response to housing shortages and to give workers an incentive to stay in their factory jobs, multifamily dwellings were built, sometimes in rows on both sides of a straight road that led directly to the blowing room. They were usually poorly constructed, however, with apartment units that were small, drafty, and difficult to keep clean. Each unit consisted of one room and a kitchen, but master-blowers lived in slightly larger

quarters consisting of two rooms and a kitchen. In some cases families shared cooking facilities. Each housing complex had a woodshed, privy, and other outbuildings plus various farm buildings. At Kosta as early as 1889 workers could buy plots of land and build their own homes,[38] but this was unusual until the twentieth century, and even then master-blowers were usually the only workers who could afford to construct their own houses.[39]

Overcrowding and poor domestic living conditions meant that most socializing occurred outside the confines of the complex, and often in connection with civic groups, the unions, or other organizations. The Temperance Movement, for example, developed a strong presence in most Swedish factories. Alcohol abuse created difficult social problems in Sweden. In 1879 the first Swedish chapter of the International Order of Good Templars (IOGT) was founded, and soon temperance lodges were established at most glassworks. They encouraged the creation of glee clubs, theater groups, and the like, and also started study circles and libraries. In many places, there were newly built "people's houses" and "people's parks." Beginning in the 1880s Sweden's industrial workers began to organize unions and to enter politics.[40] These activities also provided a social forum for factory workers.

Nineteenth-Century Glass Forms and Techniques

During the nineteenth century Sweden's production of glass expanded considerably. A number of new forms were introduced and by around 1800 noticeable English influences were seen in both form and decoration. Conical-shaped carafes and oviform wineglasses, for example, became popular, as did the use of blue glass. In addition opaque white, footed glass vessels, often with painted designs, were produced at several glassworks.

The production line at the Cedersberg Glassworks, which closed in 1838, typifies the types of glass then being made. A rectangular brandy flask engraved with tulips, birds, genre scenes, dates, or monograms was the most common (fig. 6-8). This type of bottle, which often came with a custom-made travel case, was also produced in Germany and England and became quite common in Sweden when brandy consumption increased during the eighteenth and nineteenth centuries and glass products became more accessible.[41] In addition Cedersberg stock included vinegar bottles, beakers, tankards, drinking glasses, and other wineglasses, as well as blue glass and green glass in the form of saucers, plates, and bottles.[42]

The first cut crystal in Sweden was imported from England. Facet-cut glass became more common on pots, bowls, carafes, drinking glasses, and the like.[43]

Fig. 6-8. Brandy flasks, possibly produced at Cedersberg Glassworks, first half of the 19th century; free-blown engraved glass (far right), mold-blown engraved glass (others). (Smålands Museum, Växjö)

Beginning in the 1830s engraving, which had begun in the eighteenth century, was usually restricted to bottles and other simple objects.[44] Because few clients could afford expensive crystal, most products were simple household glass. Perfume bottles and pitchers for serving punch, however, were also among the new items. Dressing table accessories became common in Sweden by the middle of the century, their use having spread from France and England. The introduction of pitchers for punch also presumably reflected new habits. Hot punch had been specially prepared in bowls until the 1840s when a wine company began to manufacture and sell ready-made punch in bottles. It gradually became preferable to chill this beverage, and people began to serve it from special pitchers instead of directly from the bottle.[45]

By mid-century cut-glass objects were produced in greater quantity, with models that were Bohemian, Belgian, and French in origin. During the 1870s "olive" cutting—so called because each cut was olive-shaped—became popular for high-footed bowls and pumpkinlike carafes with long, thin necks.[46] This carafe form was based on early Venetian models which had been adapted in England in the 1840s. In the 1870s thin-walled wineglasses with engraved designs went into production and were offered in catalogues from both Kosta and Reijmyre.[47] In addition there were painted, opaque glass vessels, primarily vases, of unknown origins.

The nineteenth century was marked by a number of technical advances at the Swedish glassworks. Blowing into fixed molds was introduced in the 1820s which meant that imitation cut glass could be inexpensively produced. The technique facilitated the production of ribbed decorations on wineglasses or other forms (fig. 6-9). A decade later pressed glass began to be manufactured. In 1836 a professor at the Teknologiska Institutet (Technological Institute) in Stockholm

Fig. 6-9. Carafes, second half of the 19th century; optic-blown and mold-blown glass. These models were produced at several Swedish glassworks. (Smålands Museum, Växjö)

returned from the Continent with drawings for glass presses and samples of pressed glass. He sold the country's first glass press to Reijmyre Glassworks, and in 1839 a smith at Kosta made a pressing machine.[48] Molds based on foreign models, primarily French or Bohemian, were soon being produced in Sweden, and many were also imported. Before long most Swedish glassworks offered pressed glass.

In the 1870s the Swedish glass business experienced a boom period in the wake of widespread industrialization. The demand for glass products steadily increased until supplies were nearly exhausted. Technical advances made it possible to increase production while keeping costs down, and customers were soon accommodated. Machines took over some steps, but classic handicraft production remained. German inventor Friedrich Siemans's new type of glass furnace, fueled by gas instead of wood, helped to increase production significantly. The Siemens furnace system achieved complete gasification of solid fuel. In the old furnaces smoke from combustion had been released through roof hoods or chimneys; in the new system heat was redirected into the furnace instead as the draft air was also heated.[49] The new furnaces reduced smelting time, allowed for larger furnaces, and reduced fuel consumption. Eda installed the new furnace in 1859, Reijmyre in 1872, and Kosta in 1888.[50]

The 1870s also saw the introduction of cracking-off machines that greatly increased capacity, especially in the production of service glass.[51] Until then most glass had been flared, meaning that the opening had been cut off and smoothed by hand while the molten glass was still hot. With cracked-off glass the opening was made after the glass had cooled. The top part was then removed by first tracing with a diamond stylus and then placing the glass on a turntable that rotated beside a gas jet. Reacting to the heat, the glass split along the scored line. The sharp edge was leveled by cutting and warming. Special departments, often staffed by women, were responsible for this part of production.

In the 1880s and 1890s miter-cut crystal based on English and American models and including ornamental pieces and large service sets came into fashion.[52] However, most people had to make do with more traditional types of glass and with less expensive pressed glass made to resemble cut glass. Estate inventories from the end of the nineteenth century provide examples ture of the most common objects in Swedish households at this time. The estate of one peasant, for example, included brandy flasks and glasses, carafes, creamers, sugar bowls, cake plates, various drinking glasses, saltcellars, candelabra, jam jars, and plates. Of these only the sugar bowl and creamer were in daily use; others were reserved for visitors and special occasions, and much of the inventory consisted of pressed glass.[53]

Methods for decorating glass developed further. At Kosta the old pedal-run cutting chairs were abandoned in the 1840s when the firm shifted to waterpower. In the late 1850s the cutting operation ran on steam.[54] Several years later Reijmyre Glassworks also acquired a steam machine for its cutting work. Kosta installed an additional cutting machine a few years later, and by 1895 there were about 200 cutting chairs at the glassworks.[55] Starting in the 1880s it became common for drinking glasses to have acid-etched patterns, produced with stencils and pantographs. Etching became an inexpensive alternative to engraving, which had now returned to favor on delicate glass.[56]

Clearly these technical advances benefited table glass. In the early nineteenth century, services of glassware in the modern sense were only beginning to be formulated. It was more usual for a single wineglass and one beer glass to be considered adequate, even on formal occasions. Starting at mid-century, however, the forms in a service began to increase, as reflected in the glassworks' product catalogues, and each guest might have five to ten glasses. The 1877 Reijmyre price list mentions sixty-eight service models by name, such as "Serrano" or "Gambetta," most of which were adopted from the Continental models.[57] Some products, such as items for the dressing table, had nothing to do with setting a table but were offered as part of the service anyway. The proliferation of restaurants in the late nineteenth century also had an impact on increased demand for glassware.

Social customs had changed, and among more affluent segments of society large dinner parties, where many different dishes and beverages were served, became the norm. Recalling these occasions, the son of Carl Wilhelm Scheutz (who ran the Alsterbro Glassworks from 1896 to 1907) wrote:

> When there were big parties there was ample food and drink. In those days the supply of wild game, fish, and shellfish for households that were self-sufficient was considerably greater than it is now. Housewives were very knowledgeable about practical things especially when it came to producing the delicacies of the smörgåsbord table. There were servants to see to everyone's needs. The preparations for parties were thorough and the result more than impressive. As far as I can remember, light wines were not served when there were banquets. At the smörgåsbord table you had your choice of schnapps and beer and then, with dessert, a glass of Madeira. An alcoholic punch or cognac were served with the coffee and cigar boxes were passed among the gentlemen.[58]

The Swedish glassworks that had come into existence during the second half of the nineteenth century offered fairly similar product lines. By 1900, however, specialization had begun, and window and bottle glass, which were in some demand, came to be produced primarily in large firms outside of Småland. Increased efficiency through mechanization was essential to combat tough foreign competition, and only those firms that were large enough to invest in modernizing their plants survived.[59] In the Småland region specialization was less pronounced, and mixed craft production lingered into the twentieth century. Gradually, however, the region's glassmakers produced less and less window and bottle glass, focusing instead on hand-made art glass and more simple household glass.

Sales and Marketing Strategies

During the nineteenth century the demand for domestic glassware increased significantly. Door-to-door salesmen still circulated, but some glassworks also sold through outlets in various towns. Businesses were helped by expanded freedom of trade; as of 1864 anyone was "authorized to engage in trading or manufacturing in town or country."[60] Previously such activity had been strictly regulated. Among glassworks competition became intense. A nineteenth-century innovation was the printing of sales catalogues. Retail merchants ordered goods for their customers from these catalogues and price lists as well as from itinerant salesmen. Thanks to improved roads and railways, deliveries could be made to stores in remote locations. Several of the larger glassworks opened their own stores. Newspaper advertisements also attracted buyers, and glass products were exhibited widely at international design and trade expositions in Sweden and abroad.

At the end of the nineteenth century the leading glassworks producing glass for domestic use were Kosta, Eda, and Reijmyre. Competition among the glassworks in the 1870s was commented on by the manager at Kosta, who wrote, "In Stockholm I visited the larger glass stores and the Industrial Exposition and found that the Reijmyre Glassworks had made significant advances in recent years. The Eda Glassworks also appeared determined to follow in time but Limmared's production was of fairly mediocre quality and Hofmantorp's appeared to be unknown. Although Kosta's production does credit to itself, I found that one has to be on one's guard because the question is whether Reijmyre isn't better than Kosta."[61]

The larger glassworks had better products and greater resources for sales and marketing than the smaller ones. Despite the fact that many of the small glassworks had a steady client base in the Swedish capital, they were little known there. The Alsterbro Glassworks, for example, only established its sales office in Stockholm in the late 1930s,[62] whereas Kosta had opened one shop there in 1866 and had a representative who showed the product line to various retailers throughout the country.[63] The new firms competed with Kosta for a share of the market for domestic glass, while the small glassworks survived by concentrating on a limited production line that proved to be profitable. Because the Kosta factory was well equipped and able to produce technically superior glass, it attracted a wide clientele. It provided simple domestic glass for customers of modest means and more expensive, high-quality glass for its wealthy clients. By 1900 Kosta was the largest glassworks in the region, with approximately five hundred employees, whereas the average for other glassworks in Småland was forty-five.[64]

Until the early 1880s Swedish glassworks could not satisfy the national demand for domestic glassware, and approximately 25 percent of the glass purchased in Sweden was imported. Most of the imports were special objects and luxury glass from Bohemia. The flow of imports and exports, however, was governed not just by consumers' needs but also by customs duties. When this tax was reduced in the 1870s, imports benefited, whereas an increase in the 1890s resulted in fewer imports and more exports.[65] The British market for Swedish-made tumblers, sherry and

port glasses, and goblets, among other items, became increasingly important to Sweden's glassworks. There were also sales to Germany and the other Nordic countries,[66] and, thanks to improved railways, Kosta even made sales to Russia and India.[67] These foreign contracts also provided inspiration for new models and decoration.

As sales increased Swedish glass developed an impeccable reputation at home and abroad. In 1897 the Swedish glassworks exhibited their products to 1.2 million visitors at the art and industrial exposition that was held in Stockholm (fig. 6-10),[68] prompting one critic to write: "When it comes to the clarity and solidity of their products, what the Swedish glassworks produce can without doubt measure up to those produced abroad. What one misses in them is new design, i.e. imagination. In this respect it would be desirable for our glassworks to do as the porcelain factories did—to get artistic minds interested in their field."[69] A year later Kosta hired the Swedish artist Gunnar G:son Wennerberg to design glassware, and by the international exposition in Paris in 1900 the glassworks had introduced a collection with a new style.[70]

The Twentieth Century

The early twentieth century was a difficult time for the Swedish glass industry. Prices for raw materials rose, foreign sales dropped, and competition increased. In 1903 Reijmyre, Kosta, Eda, Alsterfors, Flöxhult, and Alsterbro merged to form the AB De Svenska Kristallglasbruken (Association of Swedish Crystal Manufacturers). By joining together the firms would be able to set up a joint sales organization and adapt production to meet demand.[71] In 1912 the Svenska Hushållsglasfabrikanters Förening (Federation of Swedish Household Glass Manufacturers) was established. Its statutes read in part: "By both regulating prices for household glass on the domestic market and preventing illegal competition, the purpose of the federation is to promote the export of glass for domestic and medical use, to intervene in members' purchase of raw materials, and to help in promoting members' economic interests." About twenty Swedish glassworks joined and in the first year issued a joint price list covering plain, cut, and pressed glass.[72] Comparable federations were founded in the window and the container glass industries.

Economic problems persisted in Swedish glassworks and other industries until the late 1940s. Despite a policy of neutrality, Sweden suffered during the two world wars. The country was cut off from the outside world, and exports of glass products and imports of raw materials dwindled. During the first half of the 1920s as well, the price of imported glass fell, which adversely affected sales of domestic glass. High wages, the cost of rail freight, and the expense of importing raw materials and other necessities from Germany, England, Belgium, and France exerted a negative effect on prices. The most successful items were art glass of high quality and craftsmanship.[73] In the 1930s the situation improved somewhat but the worldwide depression affected glassworks everywhere. The situation was described in a 1934 issue of the trade journal, *Glas och Porslin*:

The mass-produced item, that pure consumer good, is produced in excess by every glassworks. The result has been the usual, unrestrained competition among glassworks, promptly, of course, seized upon by buyers, and which

Fig. 6-11. Edward Hald (left) and master glassblower Gustaf Bergkvist, ca. 1940.

furthermore has depressed prices, and the profit margin has declined or is not there at all. The federation's [Svenska Hushållsglasfabrikanters Förening] chances of determining prices are effectively undercut by what is to be sure a small number of major glassworks which are still not part of the organization. Furthermore, highly qualified goods, for which the competition evidently becomes less severe and which therefore make more profitable prices possible, consist almost exclusively of the pure luxury product. And as such they, like exports, are clearly sensitive to changes in economic conditions. Thus it should not be surprising that the current crisis has hit glassworks harder than any other Swedish industry.[74]

Despite economic problems, more and more glassworks came to employ artists. Thanks to Svenska Slöjdföreningen (The Swedish Society of Craft and

Fig. 6-12. Painting a glass globe for an electric light fixture at the Pukeberg Glassworks, 1937.

Industrial Design) and its employment agency, artists such as Simon Gate and Edward Hald (fig. 6-11) were placed at Orrefors in 1916 and 1917, respectively, and Edvin Ollers at Kosta in 1917, specifically to design new items for the 1917 Hemutställningen (Home Exhibition) in Stockholm. The many national and international expositions gave the glassworks the incentive to create high-quality art glass for exhibition and prompted many of the smaller glassworks to work with artists to renew their stock designs. Without the expertise of skilled craftsmen, however, artists and the glass works that employed them were not always able to realize their designs. Despite all other influences, production was long dominated by traditional models. At the Baltic Exposition in Malmö in 1914 an abundance of miter-cut glass was exhibited alongside household glass, lighting glass, chemical and technical glass, and other traditional works.[75] Product catalogues from the 1930s and 1940s show household glass as well as smooth, cut, and engraved glassware services and decorative glass. As late as 1950 production at the Boda Glassworks, for example, generally continued traditions established in preceding decades. Thus restaurant glass dominated among soda glass and cut glassware services along with more traditional types of cut pieces in crystal.[76]

With the widespread use of the kerosene lamp, lamp chimneys had become part of the regular production of many glassworks. In the twentieth century, as electric lights began to reach more and more homes, the demand for lighting glass increased. Pukeberg and Rosdala, which had led in the manufacture of earlier lighting glass, adapted their products to the needs of the new era (fig. 6-12). Beginning in the 1920s glass fittings for electrical appliances were produced under Edward Hald's direction at Orrefors, and in the 1930s production was started at Fåglavik,

Fig. 6-13. Glassblowers who specialized in the production of handmade window glass at the Gyllenfors Glassworks in the 1880s.

Flygsfors, and Engshyttan.[77] In the first decades of the twentieth century economic problems led to a number of closures in Småland, and many skilled glassworkers lost their jobs. During temporary closures staff continued to live on the premises, where they occasionally engaged in agriculture, forestry, or roadbuilding. When glass production resumed, manpower was thus close at hand.[78]

Production of handmade sheet glass for windows (fig. 6-13) disappeared from Småland when the last cylinder glass was blown at Ramnåsa in 1934, but the Emmaboda Glassworks, which converted to producing machine-made window glass, was able to survive. Despite almost constant overproduction, except during the first and second world wars and the stiff competition that came with them, new companies continued to be started by former glassworkers. The Älghult Glassworks, for example, opened in 1933, when general unemployment was high and there was no problem finding skilled staff. During the 1930s the firm produced mostly household and medical glass, with large exports to Great Britain, Ireland, America, and New

Zealand, among other countries.[79] (In 1938 exports accounted for 60 percent of production.) One of Älghult's founders remembered the difficulty in breaking into the market in the beginning; for an entire year he could not pay himself any wages. During the Second World War, exports ceased and there were difficulties importing essential raw materials. Among other things, soda was replaced by salt.[80] As at many other glassworks during this period, production at Älghult was partly shifted to the manufacture of glass jars used in food processing. Although many workers were drafted into a branch of the armed services, the Älghult Glassworks survived, and in 1945 was able to advertise "its line of plain and cut household glass, ornamental glass, glass for preserves, medical glass, and hospital glass."

Some defunct glassworks were revived by converting from window glass to glass for domestic use. The Gullaskruf Glassworks, for example, reappeared in 1927 and established a reputation for making solid pressed glass, including everything from parts for the automobile industry and laboratory equipment to kitchen utensils and various types of blown glass. Just before the Stockholm Exhibition of 1930, Gullaskruf hired the artist Hugo Gehlin to design pressed and blown glass for everyday use and enameled and hand-made art glass which established the glassworks' singular identity. At about the same time, Gullaskruf expanded into the foreign market (fig. 6-14), and until 1940 around 45 percent of its sales were exports to North America, England, Norway, Denmark, Switzerland, Canada, South America, Australia, and South Africa.[81] On several occasions American customers sent over their own samples and instructions for making glass.

The immediate postwar era was a highly successful period for the Swedish glass industry as exports resumed virtually unopposed until the countries ravaged by war rebuilt their own glassworks and competition increased. Gradually household glass dwindled as other materials, such as plastic, replaced glass for certain forms. In the 1950s Swedish glassmakers began to focus on production of handmade service glass and other objects, as well as on art glass.

Increased imports of cheap glass coupled with a shortage of development capital at the small glassworks forced some factories to close in the late 1960s and 1970s. Others merged to form large companies. With their combined strength they commanded the resources to develop glassmaking technology and to enlarge production, making increased exports possible. The most recent merger occurred in 1990 when Kosta Boda AB and Orrefors AB became Orrefors Kosta Boda AB. The new firm encompasses several older glassworks: Orrefors, Sandvik, Kosta, Boda, Åfors, and the subsidiary SEA. As the century comes to a close, Sweden still boasts several independent glassmakers —Älghult, Bergdala, Gullaskruf, Johansfors, Lindshammar, Målerås, Nybro, Reijmyre, Rosdala, and Skruf—and their artistic achievements have kept the Swedish glassworks in the forefront of the glass industry worldwide.

Fig. 6-14. Page from the Gullaskruf Glassworks' catalogue, ca. 1930s. These objects were available for export; the decanter and tumbler at the top were designed by William Stenberg, Gullaskruf's owner, and the decanter called ''Brandyfish'' by Hugo Gehlin.

1. For a facsimile of the monastery's records, see *Diarium Vadstenense* (Copenhagen: Ernst Nygren, 1963). Also see Olof Nordström, ''Vadstena kloster —Sveriges första glashytta?'' *Glasteknisk tidskrift*, no. 1 (1988), p. 2; idem, ''Glas och glastillverkning i Sverige från medeltid till 1800-talets början,'' *Glasteknisk tidskrift*, no. 2 (1990), p. 53.

2. Jan Erik Anderbjörk and Åke Nisbeth, *Gammalt glas* (Uppsala, Sweden: ICA-förlaget, 1968), p. 9.

3. Olof Nordström, *Glasbruk och hyttor i Sverige, 1555–1985*, Smålands museums skriftserie, no. 2. (Växjö, Sweden: Smålands museum, 1986), pp. 2–3.

4. Heribert Seitz, *Glaset förr och nu* (Stockholm: Albert Bonniers Forlag, 1933), pp. 111–12.

5. Ibid., pp. 107–8.

6. *Limmared, 1740–1940* (Ulricehamn, Sweden: AB Fredr. Brusewitz, 1940), p. 103; Bengt Westberg, ''Casimirsborgs glasbruk, 1757–1811: En industri i Tjust

för 175 år sedan,'' *Tjustbygden Kulturhistoriska Förenings Årsbok* (1961), pp. 5–6.

7. Folke Rosengren, ''Ledning och ekonomisk utreckling,'' in *Kosta Glasbruk, 1742–1942*, Jubileumsskrift utgiven av Kosta glasbruk med anledning av dess 200-åriga verksamhet (Stockholm: [Kosta], 1942), p. 18.

8. Torbjörn Fogelberg, *Sandö glasbruk, 1750–1928*, (Sundsvall, Sweden: [T. Fogelberg], 1968), p. 9.

9. Sven E. Noréen and Henrik Graebe, *Henrikstorp: Det skånska glasbruket, 1691–1760* (Gothenburg, Sweden: Skånska Ättiksfabriken AB, 1964), p. 39; Olof Nordström, ''1700-talet—glasets användning vidgas,'' *Glasteknisk tidskrift*, no. 3 (1991), p. 115.

10. *Limmared, 1740–1940*, p. 13.

11. Torbjörn Fogelberg, *Ettarps glasbruk, 1736–1756*, Årsbok för kulturhistoria och hembygdsvård i Hallands län, no. 66. (Halmstad and Varberg: Hallands läns-muséer, 1983), p. 54; idem, *Björknäs glasbruk: Nackas första främlingsholoni*,

(Stockholm: Nackaboken, 1989), p. 109; Noréen and Graebe, *Henrikstorp*, 1964, p. 41; Westberg, *Casimirsborgs glasbruk*, pp. 15 ff.

12. Limmared's earliest documents date to the 1780s and 1790s. *Limmared, 1740–1940*, p. 52; Jan Erik Anderbjörk, "Glasblåsare och annan hyttpersonal," in *Kosta Glasbruk*, p. 152; Noréen and Graebe, *Henrikstorp*, p. 41.

13. In the Kosta Glassworks archives contracts dating from 1757 and 1797 with various glassblowers spell out specific privileges, such as transportation to church for Roman Catholics (Anderbjörk, "Glasblåsare och annan hyttperson-al," pp. 144, 147–51; Fogelberg, *Sandö glasbruk*, p. 47). Furthermore, in various documents from the Björknäs Glassworks dating from the period 1736–1742, mention is made of German glassblowers enjoying economic benefits. See Olof Nordström, *Svensk glasindustri, 1550–1960: Lokaliserings—och arbet-skraftsproblem*, Meddelanden från Lunds universitets geografiska institution, diss. no. 41 (Lund University, 1962), pp. 33–34.

14. Anderbjörk and Nisbeth, *Gammalt glas*, pp. 44–46.

15. Arvid Baeckström, "Göteborgs Glasbruk, 1761-1808 och glashandel i Göteborg före 1820," *Meddelanden från Industrimuséet i Göteborg*, no. 5 (1962), pp. 22–24; Torbjörn Fogelberg and Åke Nisbeth, *Liljedahls glasbruk*, Småskrifter utgivna av Värmlands museum, no. 14 (1979), pp. 128 ff.

16. Edward Strömberg, "Kostaglasets teknik; Kostaglaet 1742–1942," in *Kosta Glasbruk*, p. 129.

17. Anderbjörk and Nisbeth, *Gammalt glas*, p. 46.

18. Ibid., pp. 23, 28–29; Nordström, "1700-talet—glasets användning vidgas," p. 117; Seitz, *Glaset förr och nu*, pp. 109–10.

19. Anderbjörk and Nisbeth, *Gammalt glas*, pp. 34–38; Noréen and Graebe, *Henrikstorp*, pp. 85 ff. and 121 ff.

20. Torbjörn Fogelberg, *Om glasförare tiden från omkring 1740 till 1820-talets början*, Smålands museums skriftserie, no. 1 (1985), pp. 1–23; Nordström, "1700-talet—glasets användning vidgas," p. 117; Noréen and Graebe, *Henrikstorp*, p. 42; Westberg, *Casimirsborgs glasbruk*, pp. 7, 13–14; Heribert Seitz, "Cedersbergs glasbruk och dess tillberkningar, 1781–1938," offprint, *Meddelanden från Östergötlands Fornminnes—och Museiförening* (1933–34), p. 75.

21. Rosengren, *Ledning och ekonomisk utreckling*, pp. 19, 24; Strömberg, "Kostaglasets teknik," 1942, p. 119.

22. Rosengren, *Ledning och ekonomisk utreckling*, pp. 24–25.

23. The first Finnish glassworks, which was established in Uusikaupunki (Nystad) in 1681, was short-lived. Conditions were more propitious for Åviks Glassworks, which was established in 1748. For slightly more than three decades it was Finland's only glassworks and most of its products were sold in Sweden. In the 1780s Mariedal, Torsnäs, and Olhava were established and in the 1790s, Notsjö. The larger firms had agents in both Finland and Sweden (mostly in Stockholm but also in Gothenburg). Following the end of the war in 1809, Finnish customs goods could be sold duty-free in Sweden for another few years. In 1817, however, Sweden imposed a 5 percent customs duty which was doubled eleven years later to protect domestic Swedish production. Increasingly the need for glass products in Sweden was met by domestic pro-duction—not least from newly established firms. See Kertuu Niilonen, *Finskt glas* (Helsinki, Finland: Tammi, 1966), pp. 5, 7; and Jacob Seela, "Kring Finlands äldre glasindustri-Flaskor och buteljer under 200 år," annual report (Turku, Finland: Åbo stadshistoriska museum, 1970–71).

24. Production at Kungsholm had declined in response to increased competi-tion from glassworks that had been established during the previous century throughout the country, eight of which were still in operation when Kungsholm closed in 1815. The market was no longer concentrated in Stockholm and the surrounding area. Another factor contributing to Kungsholm's decline was the growing popularity of cut glass inspired by English models. To meet this demand, the company employed a large number of cutters and cutter's apprentices at great expense which only added to the company's economic problems. See Heribert Seitz, *Äldre svenska glas med graverad dekor—En undersökning av det bevarade 1700-talsbeståndet*, Nordiska Muséets handbok no. 5 [English summary] (Stockholm: Nordiska muséet, 1936), pp. 53–54; and Anderbjörk and Nisbeth, *Gammalt glas*, pp. 54–55, 65.

25. Nordström, *Svensk glasindustri, 1550–1960*, p. 58.

26. Nordström, *Glasbruk och hyttor*, pp. 7–8, ll.

27. Torbjörn Fogelberg, "Småglasindustriens lokalisering och struktur, 1870–1920," pt. 1, *Glasteknisk tidskrift*, no. 6 (1962), p. 162.

28. Torbjörn Fogelberg, "Om Kosta glasbruk och den småländska glasbruks-bygdens uppkomst," *Glasteknisk tidskrift*, no. 5 (1961), p. 151.

29. Ibid., no. 4, p. 125.

30. Ninety percent of the shares in Skruf's glassworks, for example, were pur-chased by peasants who owned forests in the surrounding area (Nordström, *Svensk glasindustri, 1550–1960*, p. 75).

31. Franklin D. Scott, *Sweden: The Nation's History*, epilogue by Steven Koblik, rev. ed. (Carbondale and Edwardsville, Ill.: Southern Illinois University Press, 1988), p. 339; Jörgen Weibull, *Swedish History in Outline* (Stockholm: The Swedish Institute, 1993), p. 82.

32. Cottage life in Småland in the 1880s was not easy: "A little bit of herring or meat to have with potatoes accounted for the better portion of the day's food, which in hard times was reduced to coarse bread and potato dipped in salt. When the cows' milk ran dry, people had to make do with drinking beer or the molasses they used on porridge" (Sten Carlsson, "Rationalisering inom jord-bruket, 1870–1920," in *Emigrationen och det industriella genombrottet*, Den svenska historien, vol. 13 [Stockholm: Albert Bonnniers förlag, 1979], p. 136; Weibull, *Swedish History in Outline*, p. 85).

33. Torbjörn Fogelberg, "Småglasindustriens lokalisering och struktur, 1870–1920," pt. 2, *Glasteknisk tidskrift*, no. 1 (1963), p. 17.

34. Nordström, *Svensk glasindustri, 1550–1960*, pp. 108–10.

35. Torbjörn Fogelberg, *Ett sekel i belysningens tjänst: Rosdala glasbruk, 1895–1995* (Växjö: Rosdala glasbruk, 1994), pp. 43–44.

36. "I skenet av en glasugn: Åfors glasbuk och samhälle 1876-1978 (Kalmar 1980)" in "I Glasriket: människan - miljön - framtiden" [a study project of the ABF and Svenska Fabriksarbetareförbundet in Kalmar and Kronobergs, lan 1982], p. 2.

37. In 1900 the provisions of this law were tightened. See Torbjörn Fogelberg, *Den minderåriga arbetskraften inom glasindustrin under 1800-talet och tiden omkring sekelskiftet* (Växjö: Kronobergs läns hembygdsförbund, 1973), pp. 138, 187.

38. Nordström, *Svensk glasindustri, 1550–1960*, p. 116.

39. Ibid., p. 126.

40. The first trade union at a Småland glassworks was established in 1893 at Kosta. For further discussion of the trade union movement see chapter 2 in this volume and *Glasindustrins Arbetsgivareförbund, 1908–1958* (Växjö: Glas-industrins Arbetsgivareförbund, 1958), pp. 18–20, 36; Torbjörn Fogelberg, *Fackföreningsrörelsens genombrottsskede vid glasbruken under perioden från och med omkring 1890 till och med år 1907* (Växjö: Kronobergs läns hem-bygdsförbund, 1973), p. 106.

41. In 1755 King Gustaf III decided that the production of brandy should be governed by the state, which thereby encouraged increased brandy consump-tion. Twelve years later, a change occurred that permitted brewing for home use under certain circumstances, and in 1809 it was decided that anyone could produce and sell brandy (Seitz, "Cedersbergs glasbruk," pp. 104–106).

42. Ann-Sofi Topelius, *Glas från Cedersbergs glasbruk*, exhib. cat. (Linköping, Sweden: Länsmuséet, 1981), pp. 8 ff.

43. Elisa Steenberg, "Svenskt adertonhundratalsglas: en konsthistorisk studie," Ph.D. diss. (Stockholm, 1953), p. 245.

44. From product catalogues we can see that engraved glass occupied a rela-tively obscure position at this time. In Kosta catalogues from the 1850s no engraved glass is pictured though this could be made to order. In the 1853 Reijmyre catalogue only a few carafes, wine glasses, and mugs with engraved decoration are shown. See ibid., p. 60.

45. Ibid., pp. 26–27.

46. Ibid., p. 51.

47. Anderbjörk and Nisbeth, *Gammalt glas*, p. 88.

48. Ibid., pp. 75–76.

49. Torbjörn Fogelberg, "Smältugnar och deras konstruktion vid de svenska glasbruken under tiden fram till första världskrigets slut," pt. 2, *Glasteknisk Tidskrift*, no. 1 (1993). Air for combustion comes in through a chamber (A) with hot bricks; it is heated to 800–900 degrees Celsius, and smoke is extracted through a similar chamber (B) with cold stones, which are thereby heated up. After about a half-hour, a stream of air is sent through the furnace, sucked into the now warm chamber (B) and the smoke drawn out through the cooled-off chamber (A). 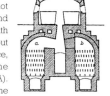 This shift occurred each half-hour and the heat in the smoke was thereby "regenerated" (Mogens Schlüter, et al., *Dansk glas, 1825–1925* [Copenhagen: Nyt Nordisk Forlag, 1979], p. 385).

50. Anderbjörk and Nisbeth, *Gammalt glas*, p. 88.

51. Steenberg, *Svenskt adertonhundratalsglas*, p. 170.

52. Anderbjörk and Nisbeth, *Gammalt glas*, p. 95.

53. Steenberg, *Svenskt adertonhundratalsglas*, p. 107.

54. Strömberg, "Kostaglasets teknik," 1942, pp. 110–11; Olof Nordström, *Kosta: främling i järnbruksbygd / Kosta, 1742–1942: 250 Years of Craftsmanship* (Malmö: Kosta Boda, 1992), p. 27.

55. Nordström, *Kosta: främling i järnbruksbygd,* p. 31.

56. Steenberg, *Svenskt adertonhundratalsglas,* pp. 260–61, 275.

57. Ibid., p. 57.

58. Torbjörn Fogelberg and Carl Ivar Scheutz, *Alsterbro glasbruk 1871–1961,* Kalmusserien no. 6 (Kalmar: Kalmar läns museum, 1981), pp. 66–67.

59. Nordström, *Svensk glasindustri, 1550–1960,* p. 94.

60. "Från skråtidens slutskede," in *De första Bernadotterna: Vårt moderna statsskick växer fram,* Den svenska historien, vol. 12 (Stockholm: Albert Bonniers förlag, 1979), p. 102.

61. Fogelberg, "Om Kosta glasbruk," no. 5, p. 152.

62. Fogelberg and Scheutz, *Alsterbro glasbruk,* 1981, p. 140.

63. Nordström, *Kosta: främling i järnbruksbygd,* p. 26; Rosengren, *Ledning och ekonomisk utreckling,* p. 48.

64. Nordström, *Svensk glasindustri, 1550–1960,* p. 81.

65. Ibid., pp. 80–81.

66. Fogelberg and Scheutz, *Alsterbro glasbruk,* pp. 131–36.

67. Nordström, *Kosta: främling i järnbruksbygd,* p. 27.

68. Fredrik Strandberg, "Stockholmsutställningen 1897," in *Emigrationen och det industriella genombrottet,* Den svenska historien, vol. 13 (Stockholm: Albert Bonniers Förlag, Stockholm, 1968–1979). For the poor in various parts of Sweden trips to Stockholm on so-called people's trains were organized.

69. *Svensk slöjdföreningen Meddelanden* (1898).

70. After some years Wennerberg left Kosta; although his artistic glass had made up but a small portion of Kosta's production, his efforts represent the first collaboration between art and industry at a Swedish glassworks.

71. Rosengren, *Ledning och ekonomisk utreckling,* p. 53.

72. Jan Erik Anderbjörk, "Svenska Hushållsglasfabrikanters Förening," in *Svenska Glasbruksföreningen SHF-SG, 1912–1962* (Växjö, Sweden: Svenska Glasbruksföreningen, 1962), pp. 5, 27–29, 192.

73. Jan Erik Anderbjörk, "Bildandet av SHF och dess första verksamnetsår," in ibid., pp. 46–47, 51.

74. Ibid., p. 51; *Glas och Porslin,* no. 7 (1934).

75. Anderbjörk and Nisbeth, *Gammalt glas,* p. 104.

76. See "Handcut Crystal," sale catalogue, Boda Glassworks, 1954; and [untitled], sale catalogue, Boda Glassworks, 1955.

77. Ernst Harrisen, "Belysningsglasbruken," in Anderbjörk, *Glasblåsare,* pp. 143 ff.

78. Nordström, *Svensk glasindustri, 1550–1960,* p. 132.

79. *Baromtern* (November 27, 1945).

80. "Ett glasrike i Glasriket: Älghults socken," in "I Glasriket - människan - miljön - framtiden" [a study project of the ABF och Svenska Fabriksarbetaren-förbundet in Kalmar and Kronobergs län, 1982], p. 54.

81. Jan Erik Anderbjörk, ed., *Gullaskrufs glasbruk, 1927–1952* (Gothenburg, Sweden: [Gullaskrufs glasbruk], 1952), pp. 20–23, 26, 28.

Hall-Armatur
i mattat blått kristall glas
beslagen matt-försilvrade
Skala 1:2

Orrefors maj 1926
Simon Gate

102

CHAPTER SEVEN

Lighting Design at Orrefors Glassworks, 1920–1940

Gunnel Holmér

In the nineteenth century a typical Swedish glass factory produced a wide variety of work, including decorative objects, domestic glassware, jars and bottles, and lighting fixtures. Gradually, however, as the factories expanded, some—Rosdala, Pukeberg, Flerohopp, Idesjö, Färe, Sibbhult, Fåglavik, and Limmared—began to specialize in lighting devices, and by the turn of the century, there was considerable competition.[1] They primarily manufactured the oil receptacles and chimneys for kerosene lamps, but in the twentieth century, as electricity became more common, the factories expanded their range of forms and models in response to the new technology. The Rosdala and Pukeberg glassworks eventually assumed the lead as manufacturers of commercial lighting fixtures that were sold in quantity both in Sweden and abroad.

The production of lighting fixtures reached an important turning point in the 1920s when artists at Orrefors began to take an interest in their design (fig. 7-1). In 1921 a special edition of *Svenska Slöjdföreningens Tidskrift*, the publication of Svenska Slöjdföreningen (The Swedish Society of Craft and Industrial Design) included drawings of two lamps with engraved glass by Edward Hald (fig. 7-2).[2] In subsequent years Hald and Simon Gate would create one-of-a-kind lighting designs at Orrefors that came closer to art glass than any of the products of the glassworks specializing in lighting fixtures.

In 1926 Orrefors made a special marketing appeal primarily to architects.[3] The mailing included photographs of ornately decorated chandeliers and blown-glass details (fig. 7-3) as well as other electric lighting fixtures, ranging from simple hanging lamps with cut decoration to elaborate chandeliers such as Model GD9 designed by Simon Gate (see fig. 7-1). The working parts—electric lightbulbs and fittings—were deliberately masked or hidden. Customers were informed that Orrefors kept some models in stock but others required special orders or could be customized to suit a client's needs. The glass melt used was often tinted brown, yellow, or blue, although white lamps were also quite popular.

One problem with the early electric lighting devices for domestic use was that

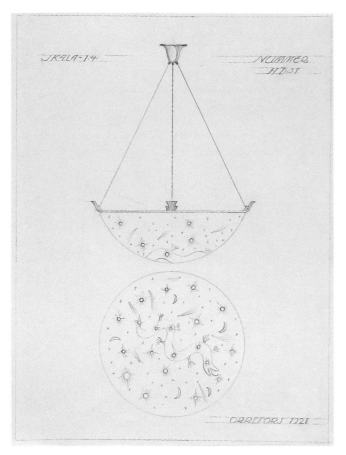

Fig. 7-2. Design for a lamp (Model HD 38); Orrefors, 1928. Although the drawing is dated 1928, the first lamp of this type was actually produced around 1920. (Orrefors Museum)

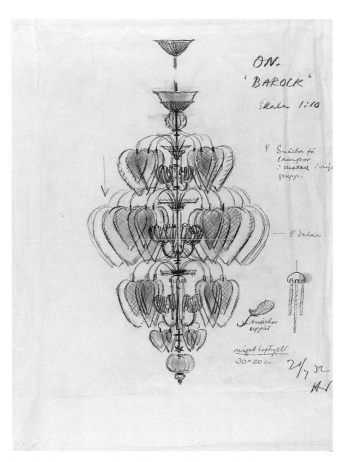

Fig. 7-4. Design for a chandelier called "Baroque"; Orrefors. (Orrefors Museum)

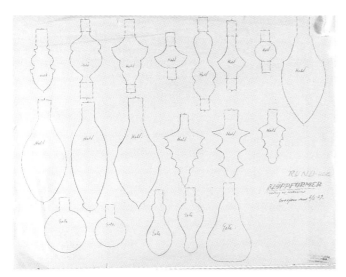

Fig. 7-3. Designs for blown-glass details; Orrefors, ca. 1929. (Orrefors Museum)

they diffused light very poorly. The forms that had been practical for candles or oil lamps continued to be used for new electrical fixtures (fig. 7-4), even when they might be inappropriate. Design innovations were clearly warranted, and designers began by focusing on the technical aspects of lighting rather than aesthetic considerations. In 1928 a critic writing in *Svenska Slöjdföreningens Tidskrift* drew attention to the problem and the inadequacy of some of the solutions:

> Somewhat better adapted to the nature of electrical light than ordinary chandeliers are the now-common glass bowls in which light bulbs are mounted. The most expensive ones are manufactured by Orrefors to designs by Simon Gate and Edward Hald. Unfortunately, these artists approach this field in the same way they approach the design of grand urns and other decorative pieces. Their lighting bowls, too, are at their best during the daylight hours, when they have no function. When they are lit, the artistic ornamenta-

tion is utterly compromised by the light of the bulbs, which illuminate the bowl unevenly and are irritating and often blinding. The glass must be matte on both sides to avoid glare.[4]

Edward Hald, who was especially responsive to demands for better lighting designs, had in fact recognized the aesthetic and technical potential of matte lampshades several years earlier. At the 1925 Paris Exposition des Arts Décoratifs et Industriels Modernes, he had shown lamps on which the pattern had been acid-etched directly on a roughly polished glass surface. The matte finish produced in this manner, which permitted light to pass through while reducing the glare, was far better suited to lighting fixtures than transparent glass. The matte surface also provided a good base for "satin" cut-glass decoration.[5]

One approach to room lighting consisted of ceiling panels made with a grid of ornamented glass panes mounted in a wood or cast-iron frame.[6] A light bulb mounted above each pane provided the light source. These ceiling panels were installed in reception rooms, restaurants, and other public spaces. In one example (fig. 7-5), designed in 1927 for Orrefors, Edward Hald specified a matte, yellow glass embellished with motifs including smokestacks, steamships, lions with sabers, the sun, and the initials "DFOK." Although the actual client is unknown, the motifs suggest a connection to industry.

In the late 1920s Hald created several innovative lighting designs. He introduced austere, functional models, free of unnecessary decoration. Among the early examples of these was a hanging lamp, designed in 1926, with a shade and globe of bone-white glass. Another design, the "P.H. Model" (1929), was called "a technically adequate model with regards to the quality of light."[7] In 1929 Hald also designed the yellow-tinted, matte "Saturn" lamp, a globe encircled by a ring of sheet glass.[8]

In the 1930s Hald continued to concentrate on improving the functional aspects of lighting. This is evident in the notations on his drawings. Some make recommendations for eliminating glare or for ensuring the proper diffusion of light.[9] On the drawing of a frosted opal glass shade from 1932 (fig. 7-6), Hald's notations (under the heading, "The point of it all") call for the glassblower to blow the globe in a single piece, with the "overblow used as underside! Glare controlled by turned-over edges, as much as needed." Through its simple form, this lamp, which was basically a variation of the "P.H. Model," could be mass produced, making it less expensive for the consumer than the more elaborate chandeliers. The absence of decoration reflected Hald's focus on the lamp form purely as an effective source of light and not as a decoration in itself.

Hald collaborated on many designs with Orrefors's

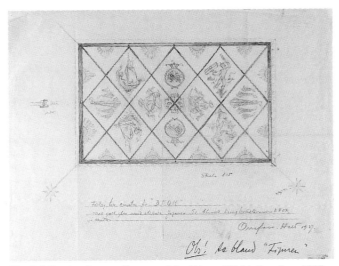

Fig. 7-5. Design for a ceiling panel, by Edward Hald; Orrefors, 1927. (Orrefors Museum)

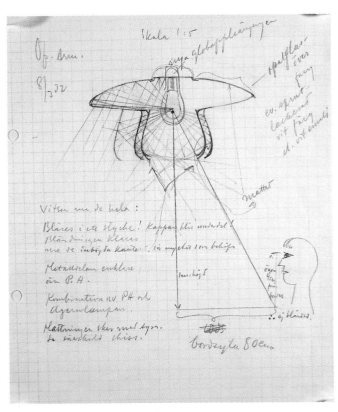

Fig. 7-6. Design for a functional lighting fixture, by Edward Hald; Orrefors, 1932. (Smålands Museum, Växjö)

Fig. 7-7. The "Haldislamp" as shown in the Orrefors sale catalogue, 1937. (Småland museums arkiv)

Fig. 7-8. Design for a chandelier, by Edward Hald; Orrefors, 1931. (Orrefors Museum)

production supervisor, Robert Ihs, who had joined Orrefors in 1930. Ihs had a reputation for technical wizardry, and under his direction, a special department was established for the manufacture of lighting devices. Among the designs Hald and Ihs worked on together was the "Haldislamp" (fig. 7-7), designed in 1931 and probably named after both men ("Hald" and "I[h]s").[10] In another 1931 design Hald experimented with glass plates in an elaborate engraved chandelier made to resemble a birdcage (fig. 7-8).

Some of the glassblowers at Orrefors were assigned to work on lighting fixtures. Around 1930 one of the four shops that produced bottles was converted to a production facility solely for globes and shades for simpler lighting fixtures. Erik Sejnäs, a gaffer in the shop, describing the colored glass used in lighting, recalled that "we could have a bone-white underlay, or we could have dark or light yellow. Gate often picked 'Havana,' which was a dark color. He wanted to create a soft light, but in fact the color seemed to absorb a lot of light."[11]

An Orrefors sale catalogue from the mid-1930s reveals that many models designed during the previous decade continued to be made, although new ideas in lighting had also been introduced in the interim. The 1937 sale catalogue includes lighting fixtures that were distinctly modernist in appearance.[12] At the time Hald, Gate, and occasionally Vicke Lindstrand, who started at Orrefors in 1928, were the principal designers of lighting devices. Their creations were destined for both commercial and residential buildings, with specific forms for designated interiors. The simplest hanging devices of opal glass were for use in dining rooms, offices, and stairwells. More elaborate chandeliers were hung in living rooms and bedrooms (figs. 7-9 and 7-10). Models consisting of one or more glass disks or panes, hung horizontally, seem to have been especially popular (fig. 7-11). These were often painted or decorated with sandblasted patterns and called by such names as "The Four Winds," "The Five Continents," "Gemini," "Zodiac," and "Grapes." Both English and Swedish descriptions were used in the catalogue, evidence of the growing international market for Swedish glass. One lampshade with a checked pattern was even called "The Scotch Lamp."

Although the items in the 1937 catalogue were intended primarily for domestic interiors, some were also appropriate for use in public spaces. Orrefors was frequently commissioned by architects and interior designers to create lighting devices for restaurants, cinemas, theaters, hotels, and other public spaces.[13] Their major commissions included lighting fixtures for the Stockholm Concert Hall (1925), Stockholm City Library (1928), the ocean liner M/S *Kungsholm* (1928), and the Gothenburg Concert Hall (1935). One critic lavished praise on the "Saturn" lamps that were

Fig. 7-9. Two examples of chandeliers in which globes or bowls are combined with sheet glass as shown in the Orrefors sale catalogue, 1937. (Småland museums arkiv)

Fig. 7-11. Examples of sheet-glass ceiling lamps as shown in the Orrefors sale catalogue, 1937. (Småland museums arkiv)

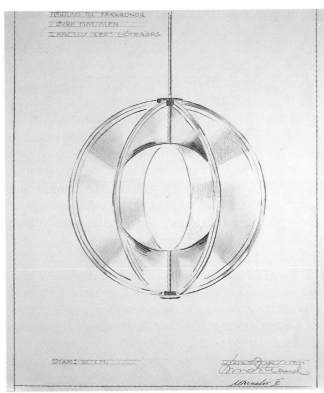

Fig. 7-10. Design for a chandelier, by Vicke Lindstrand; Orrefors, 1935. According to the inscription this was meant for the "Carolus Rex" dining hall in Gothenburg. (Smålands Museum, Växjö)

installed in the Biorama Cinema located in Kalmar, describing them as ". . . the first thing one sees. The central section of the ceiling is dark, reminiscent of a night sky, and in the firmament, to extend the metaphor, are suns and stars that radiate light with enchanting brilliance."[14]

Orrefors also produced a variety of wall sconces and lamp bases of which "the blanks were yellow, clear, or opalescent white and came from the Ramnåsa window glassworks where there was a huge stock. Different models were then cut from the sheets to be sandblasted. This was one of Nils Landberg's specialties."[15] The Ramnåsa Glassworks, located about 35 miles from Orrefors, was the last glassworks in Sweden that produced window glass by hand. When it closed in 1934, Orrefors bought the entire stock of glass plate for the Orrefors lighting department. Landberg, who had studied engraving at the Orrefors school, started at the factory as an apprentice in the engraving shop.[16] Beginning in 1936 he was given greater independence as an artist. He worked with Vicke Lindstrand on the monumental sandblasted window called "Technology and the Future" which was installed over the entrance to the Swedish pavilion at the 1937 Paris Exposition des Arts et Techniques dans la Vie Moderne. He also

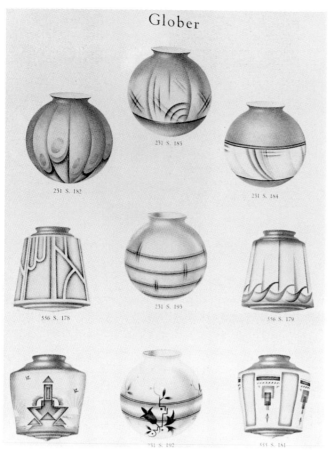

Glober

231 S. 182   231 S. 183   231 S. 184

556 S. 178   231 S. 193   556 S. 179

231 S. 192   555 S. 181

Fig. 7-12. Painted globes as shown in the Rosdala Glassworks sale catalogue, 1938. (Småland museums arkiv)

contributed to the Orrefors work shown at the New York World's Fair in 1939.

In addition to its public commissions and sales through its product catalogues Orrefors marketed its work through the lighting department of Nordiska Kompaniet (NK), the leading Stockholm department store. NK lighting fixtures were assembled from shades and other glass components designed by the artists of Orrefors.[17] The headquarters of the Swedish Match Company (erected 1926–28), for example, which was designed by architect Ivar Tengbom, was fitted with ceiling lamps of engraved glass and bronze ordered through NK. Tengbom selected bronze figures by sculptor Ansgar Almquist and glass globes with decoration by Simon Gate.[18] Many other leaders of Swedish design also contributed to this project, including Carl Malmsten, who designed the furniture, and Elsa Gullberg, who supplied textiles for the interiors.

Affluent private clients also placed custom orders through NK. Their requirements could be quite specific. In one private commission in the 1930s Erik Tidstrand, an architect who worked for NK, wrote:

Our customer would like an extremely beautiful bowl. His room is a fine gentleman's salon, furnished in a neoclassical Louis XVI style, modernized, designed by Malmsten. The customer is a sportsman, a hunter and an angler, and the walls will probably be hung with Liljefors paintings. Recently, we received another bowl from you in a light orange hue and violet—the pale, light color would be suitable here, but for such a demanding design as will be required for this bowl, it is probable that an opaque colored glass will be required. The customer requested that Mr. Hald sketch a bowl. The ornamentation of the bowl we leave entirely at your discretion; we have merely proposed some metal fittings to hold the bowl in the correct position, as the drawing shows.[19]

Like the most prestigious art glass produced at Orrefors, the luxury lighting glass required the collaboration of the firm's master-blowers including Gustaf Bergqvist and his highly skilled staff. It was precisely the high quality of these one-of-a-kind pieces made at Orrefors during the 1920s and 1930s that set the factory apart from the other Swedish glassworks specializing in lighting fixtures. The simpler Orrefors lighting products, however, found stiff competition from the Rosdala and Pukeberg glassworks which had long production runs. Rosdala was well known for high-quality opal glass, and beginning in the early 1930s, its specialty was lighting glass with painted decoration. The Rosdala catalogue for 1938 includes traditional globes, bowls, and shades (fig. 7-12).[20]

A Pukeberg price list from the late 1920s also includes the customary shades for table and hanging lamps (fig. 7-13).[21] As the 1930 Stockholm Exhibition neared, however, Pukeberg's owners at AB Arvid Böhlmark lamp factory in Stockholm, decided to use the exhibition to improve their position among the lighting producers in Scandinavia.[22] Their efforts were apparently successful, and in 1936 the factory issued a catalogue that included many functional or modernist lighting designs. They were very similar to the Orrefors product line and undoubtedly made Pukeberg more competitive in the marketplace. In addition to bowls and globes that echoed the Orrefors designs, Pukeberg's lighting fixtures included patterned glass panels, as well as ceiling lamps constructed from horizontally hung glass panes. During the 1930s lighting glass was also manufactured at Flygsfors, Engshyttan, and Fåglavik.[23]

Despite the increased competition, especially for buyers of inexpensive, mass-produced lamps, Orrefors continued to be successful in marketing its lighting fixtures. Orrefors glass was still considered the most prestigious to own. The glassworks employed a large enough staff of both artists and craftsmen to meet

Fig. 7-13. Chandeliers as
shown in the Pukeberg
sale catalogue, 1936.
(Småland museums arkiv)

  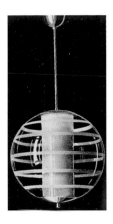

the demand for a wide variety of lighting, both mass-produced and custom-made, for domestic use, businesses, and public spaces. No other Swedish glassworks at this time had such resources. In 1936 sculptor Edvin Öhrström was hired, and among his first assignments was the design of a lamp for the Malmö Museum.[24] Eventually he was made one of the artistic directors for the factory's lighting department. Swedish lighting designer Carl Fagerlund joined the Orrefors art staff in 1946, at a time when the firm was embark-

ing on a program of expansion. Over the next three decades the glassworks continued to manufacture lighting fixtures, transferring production in 1975 to Flygsfors, which had been acquired by Orrefors. When Flygsfors closed in 1979, Orrefors discontinued its production of lighting glass, bringing to an end a rich and varied chapter in its history.[25] The lighting devices it produced represent one aspect of the spirit of cooperation that developed between Swedish art and industry between the two world wars.

1. Torbjörn Fogelberg, *Ett sekel i belysningens tjänst: Rosdala glasbruk, 1895–1995* (Växjö: Rosdala glasbruk, 1994), p. 189.

2. Erik Wettergren, "Orreforsglas," in Gregor Paulsson, ed., *Svenska Slöjdföreningens Specialnummer* 1 (Stockholm: AB Gunnar Tisells Förlag, 1921), pp. 14–15.

3. These drawings can be found in the archives of the Småland Museum and Orrefors Glassworks.

4. Nils G. Wollin, "Elektrisk belysningsarmatur," *Svenska Slöjdföreningens Tidskrift* (1928).

5. Arthur Hald and Erik Wettergren, eds., *Simon Gate, Edward Hald: En Skildring av människorna och konstnärerna* (Stockholm: Svenska Slöjdföreningen, Norstedts, 1948), p. 137.

6. The Orrefors archives contains several examples of drawings for these ceiling panels.

7. Uno Åhrén, "Standardization and personality," *Svenska Slöjdföreningens Tidskrift* (1929), p. 48.

8. Hald and Wettergren, *Simon Gate, Edward Hald*, p. 137.

9. These drawings are in the archives of the Smålands Museum.

10. Hald and Wettergren, *Simon Gate, Edward Hald*, p. 137; Ann Marie Herlitz-Gezelius, *Orrefors—ett svenskt glasbruk* (Stockholm: Bokförlaget Atlantis, 1984), p. 127.

11. Erik Sejnäs (b. 1910), former gaffer in the lighting shop at Orrefors: personal communication.

12. *Orrefors Belysningsarmatur* [sale catalogue], Orrefors, 1937.

13. Hald and Wettergren, *Simon Gate, Edward Hald*.

14. Commentary that appeared in the newspaper, *Kalmar Läns Tidning* (February 18, 1933).

15. Åke Nilsson (b. 1910), former employee of the lighting shop at Orrefors: personal communication.

16. Hald made alterations on many of Landberg's sketches, and both men's signatures can often be found in the lower right-hand corner. These drawings are in the archives of the Småland Museum. Also see Helena Dahlbäck Lutteman, "Storhetstid med världsrykte: 1917—andra världsriget," in Jan Brunius et al., *Svenskt Glas* (Stockholm: Wahlström & Widstrand, 1991), p. 117.

17. Drawings in the Orrefors archives.

18. Wollin, "Elektrisk belysningsarmatur," p. 29.

19. Drawings and orders in the Orrefors archives.

20. *Katalog å glasvaror för elektrisk belsning.* (Norrhult, Sweden: [Rosdala Glassworks], 1938).

21. *Glasvaror för elektrisk belysningsarmatur från Pukebergs glasbruk*, sale catalogue no. 119 (Stockholm: Arvid Böhlmarks Lampfabrik, 1927).

22. Erik Andrén, *Aktiebolaget Arvid Böhlmarks Lampfabrik, 1872–1937* (Stockholm: Arvid Böhlmarks Lampfabrik, 1937), pp. 104–105.

23. See *Flygsfors, 1930–1955* (published by the glassworks, 1955); *Engshyttan, 1934–1954: Efter 20 år—en tillbakablick på AB Engshyttans tillkomst och utveckling* (published by the glassworks, 1954); *Priskurant från AB Fåglaviks Glasbruk* (published by the glassworks, 1938).

24. For a discussion of Öhrström's contributions to the Orrefors production see chap. 9 in this volume.

25. By 1996, Rosdala Glassworks had become the only Swedish factory engaged in the production of lighting glass.

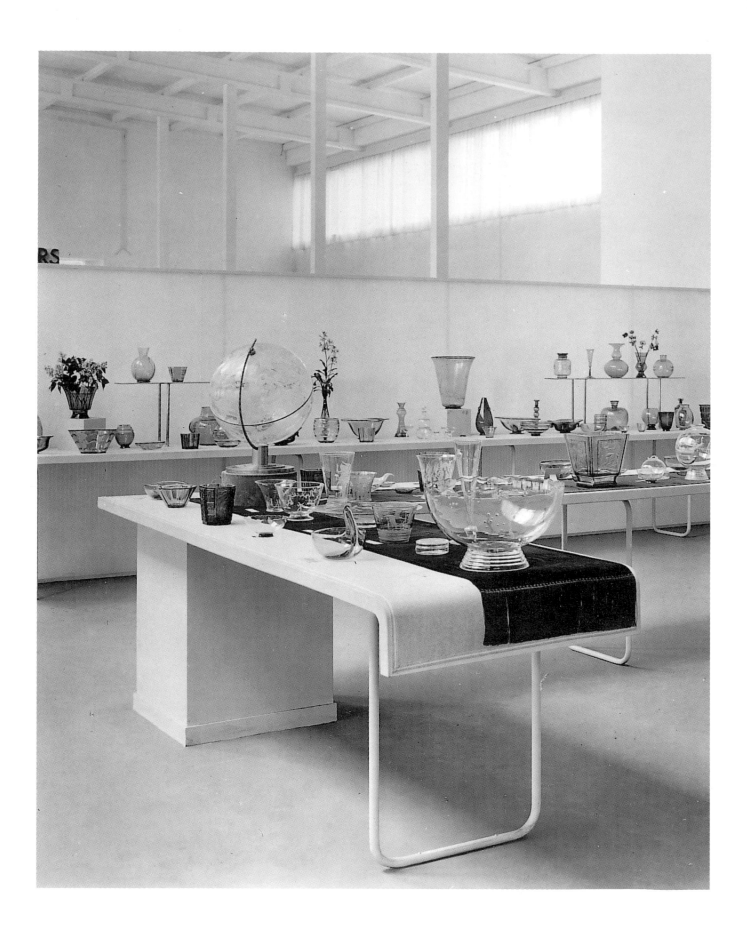

CHAPTER EIGHT

Swedish Glass Between the World Wars

Elsebeth Welander-Berggren

Detail of fig. 8-9. Orrefors Glassworks installation at the 1930 Stockholm Exhibition.

During the first half of the twentieth century, the Swedish glassworks initiated revolutionary aesthetic changes. The reasons for a burgeoning glass production, particularly during the First World War, are difficult to pinpoint. By 1914 the industry boasted an unparalleled corps of expert craftspeople, including glassblowers, cutters, and engravers. Their sophisticated skills and the relatively new practice by the glassworks of hiring artists to design glassware yielded consummate artistry and positive results. Swedish neutrality during the First World War allowed artists to work under better conditions than their counterparts on the Continent, but the war also deprived Sweden's glass industry of its most important source of silica (essential to production) and created labor difficulties in the factories. New developments occurred nonetheless as the war intensified the initiative for quality, low-cost designs. Another contributing factor in the development of Sweden's glass art was the industry's participation in the many international expositions of applied arts. One of these, the Stockholm Exhibition of 1897, had a powerful impact on the arts in Sweden in the early part of the twentieth century. Although the exhibition was far from global in scope, it included both Scandinavian and international sections, and it set the stage for epic changes in Sweden's glass industry.

The Swedish Glassworks and Glass Production

At the beginning of the twentieth century there were sixty-three glassworks operating in Sweden, the great majority of them in Småland, a province dubbed the *Glasriket*, or "Kingdom of Glass."[1] Most of them produced domestic glassware, window glass, bottles, and glass for the chemical and engineering industries.[2] Art glass represented only a small percentage of their production. By 1939, the number of glassworks had increased significantly; no fewer than ninety-nine factories were in operation, with the greatest concentration still in Småland. The expansion of the country's railways facilitated shipments of components and raw materials for glass production to the factories, and it became equally convenient to transport finished products to consumers.[3]

Hyttan

Kosta

1924.

Fig. 8-1. Postcard view of the Kosta Glassworks, ca. 1924. (Archives, Kosta Glassworks)

The Swedish glassworks have always struggled financially; this has been the case historically, and so it remains today. In 1903, in an attempt to improve profitability and competitiveness, several of the companies jointly established the AB De Svenska Kristallglasbruken (Association of Swedish Crystal Manufacturers).[4] Each factory continued to operate independently, but until the association ended in 1931 they shared the same goal: to permit effective common marketing as evident in their joint production catalogues.

Production figures and employment records for the years prior to 1940 are scarce. In 1914, however, the Kristallglasbruken recorded annual sales of 2.5 million kronor, half of which was accounted for by exports.[5] Their collected labor force numbered 1,300, and together the various glassworks owned 60 crucibles and 400 cutting machines. Färe Glassworks, with 140 employees, operated on a significantly more modest scale. Pukeberg had 300 employees, and Limmared, with annual sales of 450,000 kronor, had 175 workers, while Reijmyre employed 400.

At Orrefors and Kosta (fig. 8-1), the two largest glassworks, production figures and employee records for the years between the two world wars would perhaps be most revealing, but the available literature offers little documentation. Extant records indicate that Kosta's production during the 1920s was approximately twice that of Orrefors.[6] In 1931 Orrefors had 300 employees,[7] and its first annual report, from 1938, shows share capital of 1 million kronor and a net profit of 40,372 kronor. Kosta's share capital was 800,000 kronor in 1937, with a net profit that year of 12,184 kronor. Orrefors had overtaken Kosta thanks in part to its close collaboration with artists and designers in the production of art glass and to its development of the "graal" and "ariel" techniques.

Eda Glassworks flourished from 1910 to 1923, with sales resulting in annual profits of 100,000 to 300,000 kronor. By 1924, however, their profits were down to 2,000 kronor, and after 1927 when Edvard and Gerda Strömberg bought the company, it began recording annual losses whose causes cannot be isolated. During the Strömberg's first year of ownership, losses were 69,000 kronor; in 1931, their worst year, partly attributable to the worldwide economic depression, losses reached 222,000 kronor. Before the Strömbergs' tenure Eda had sold pressed glass and carnival glass; after 1927 the goal became production of elegant, modern pieces. Gerda Strömberg, who created many of Eda's designs, endorsed a distinctly modern aesthetic characterized by austere geometric forms. This work may have been too progressive for the market because Eda's glass was difficult to sell at that time.[8]

During its early years of operation, Pukeberg had virtually no exports, but in 1913 the factory began shipping large quantities of glass to England. The English increasingly turned to Swedish glassworks for mass-produced goods, as Britain's previous suppliers on the Continent were derailed by the First World War. In 1914 Pukeberg recorded sales of some 433,000 kronor, and by 1917 their sales were up to 1.1 million kronor, which increased to 2,165,000 by 1920. Glass for kerosene lamps and lighting products accounted for the majority of sales, while tableware represented a smaller percentage.[9]

Sandvik Glassworks had 48 employees in 1898. Ten years later their labor force had increased only slightly to 54 employees, but by 1919, after Edward Hald and Simon Gate had begun designing for Sandvik, the production staff numbered 110 employees, falling to 95 by 1939.[10] In 1939 Sandvik exported 55 percent of its production to some thirty countries.[11]

Boda Glassworks, like all the others, experienced a great deal of financial difficulty during the First World War.[12] Company records from 1914 show that it had stopped exporting smaller glass pieces altogether, and during the war years it concentrated on production of preserve jars, which kept production levels high enough to maintain full employment.[13] Production at all the Swedish glassworks was an anxious affair during the war years because sand and soda were imported solely from Germany. To maintain production levels, the glassworks began using sulfate glass, and the designs by Hald and Gate that were made at Sandvik are most interesting.

Swedish Glass Artists Between the Wars

Contemporary reviews of major Swedish glass exhibitions during the interwar period are colored by nationalistic fervor. Despite an impression often conveyed by these reviews that Swedish art glass developed in isolation, away from the vibrant experimentalism of glass art in the rest of the world, this was not the case. Swedish glass was anchored in the outer world, and foreign influences played a vital role in shaping the Swedish tradition.

ORREFORS GLASSWORKS. The first artist associated with Orrefors was Simon Gate (fig. 8-2), who was made the company's art director in 1916. Educated in Stockholm at the Tekniska Högskolan (College of Technology; 1902–05) and the Kungliga Konstakademien (Royal Academy of Art; 1905–09),[14] Gate was a charismatic and energetic innovator. Together with master-blower Knut Bergqvist (fig. 8-3), who came to Orrefors from Kosta in 1914, Gate stretched the technological and aesthetic boundaries of casing glass, developing his own graal glass technique in 1916. He also worked extensively in engraved glass, then a neglected art form.[15] His work evokes both baroque dynamism and classical restraint.

A prolific designer, Gate produced a remarkable body of work at Orrefors, including presentation pieces for international exhibitions and royal gifts and commissions. Among his creations were monumental vessels, such as an urn called "Triton" (1917), a bowl called "Bacchanalia" (1925), and the "Paris Cup" (1925), as well as elegant sulfate glass from the 1930s that was etched and engraved. He produced vast amounts of tableware for Sweden's royal family and others and in 1935 designed the glass presented to the Crown Prince of Denmark as a wedding gift. His legacy reveals his great talent as a designer; a devotee of the medium, he can be called a thinker who thought in glass.[16]

Edward Hald was educated at a school of business

Fig. 8-2. Gustaf Abels engraving the bowl called "Bacchanalia," which was designed by Simon Gate and first shown at the 1925 Paris Exposition des Arts Décoratifs et Industriels Modernes. When Gate inspected the newly finished piece, he accidentally broke it and a new one had to be completed by Abels in time for the exhibition. Abels called this the most exasperating work he had ever done. (Archives, Orrefors Glassworks)

Fig. 8-3. Master-glassblower Knut Bergqvist at Orrefors, 1920s. (Archives, Orrefors Glassworks)

Craft and Industrial Design) in Gothenburg, Lindstrand came to Orrefors in 1928, remaining there until 1940. He was a dynamic and innovative designer, developing many new techniques, such as the so-called ariel technique, on which he collaborated with Edvin Öhrström and master-blower Knut Petersson. Producing the first ariel vases in 1937,[18] Lindstrand's approach was playful, bold, and immediate. In the 1930s he designed vases decorated with enamel-painted faces, such as a vase called "The Four Continents," and among his most dramatic creations were thick, deeply engraved vessels of optic glass decorated with pearl divers and shark fishermen. In 1936 a series of vases introduced "mycenae," a decoration created with vaporized carborundum powder, another Lindstrand innovation.

Edvin Öhrström started at Orrefors in 1936. He had studied at the Tekniska Högskolan, Stockholm, from 1925 to 1928 and attended the Konstakademien from 1928 to 1932.[19] Öhrström preferred heavy, monumental glass. He created a new technique of "throwing" in order to produce the desired blocklike forms[20] and was a master of ariel.[21]

In 1925 Nils Landberg came to Orrefors, after attending the Konstslöjdskolan (School of Design) in Gothenburg. He began as an engraver but was made a glassworks designer in 1934. Sven Palmqvist came to Orrefors in 1927 as a student at the factory's engraving school, completing his studies in 1930. He attended the Tekniska Högskolan from 1932 to 1934 and studied sculpture at the Kungliga Konstakademien. The greatest successes of Landberg and Palmqvist would come later, during and after the Second World War.[22]

KOSTA GLASSWORKS. In 1917, as the Hemutställningen (Home Exhibition) at Liljevalchs Konsthall neared, Kosta hired Edvin Ollers in an effort to compete with Orrefors in creating art glass. Ollers had trained as a drawing instructor at the Högskolan för Industriell Konst (College of Industrial Design) in Stockholm from 1906 to 1910, later studying painting at Vahlands Målerskola (Vahlands School of Painting) in Gothenburg. Over the course of his career, he worked for many of the glassworks: at Kosta (until 1918); Reijmyre (1918–19); Elme (1926–30); Limmared (1929–40); Kosta again (1931–32); Alsterfors (1930–34); and Åfors (1934–40). At Kosta he created elegant freeblown vases, bowls, and tableware, working in bubblestippled green and blue soda glass with elegant yet robust applied decoration.[23] This was an unusual application of soda glass, the cheapest glass, which was used most frequently for windows and other mundane products.

Kosta also employed the sculptor, engraver, and graphic artist Karl Hultström from 1919 to 1924, and the painter Lennart Nyblom. Kosta sponsored a design competition prior to the 1923 Gothenburg Jubilee Exhibition. The winner was painter Sven Erixson (usu-

in Leipzig, Germany (1903–05), and studied architecture in Dresden and painting in Stockholm, Copenhagen, and Paris (under Henri Matisse). Hald made his artistic debut in Stockholm in 1909. In 1917 he began designing porcelain for Rörstrand and glass for Orrefors (fig. 8-4), where he eventually became an art consultant and managing director (1933–44). He remained a designer at Orrefors from 1947 until the 1970s.

Hald's glass designs were innovative and masterly. He brought a fresh, whimsical quality to Orrefors glass, notably in such touchstone pieces as a bowl called "Girls Playing Ball" (1920), a vase called "Fireworks" (1921), and a celestial globe designed for the 1930 Stockholm Exhibition.[17] Hald further developed the graal technique, producing the first pieces in his new version of the technique in about 1936. Like Simon Gate, Hald designed many tableware series; his functional glass for Sandvik was especially popular.

If Gate and Hald were the leading designers at Orrefors in the 1920s and 1930s, Vicke Lindstrand and Edvin Öhrström represent the next generation of Orrefors artists. After training at the Svenska Slöjdföreningens Skola (School of the Swedish Society of ally known as "X-et"), who worked at the glassworks throughout 1923 and again from 1929 to 1931.[24]

Although Kosta hired the finest glassblowers and engravers, the factory lacked an art director until 1929. After the Paris exposition in 1925, at which Orrefors was widely recognized as the foremost Swedish glassworks, Kosta sought to elevate its art glass production. In preparation for a 1927 exhibition at the Metropolitan Museum of Art in New York, Kosta hired the painter and graphic artist Ewald Dahlskog in the autumn of 1926. Like many other designers of the period, Dahlskog had trained at the Tekniska Högskolan (1908 –12) and the Kungliga Konstakademien (1913–18) in Stockholm. A month after arriving at Kosta, he unveiled a collection that sent a shock wave through the entire glass community. He remained at the factory for four extraordinary years during which he radically transformed the production of art glass. Rather than look to Orrefors for ideas, he created a bold, expressive idiom of his own, using cut decoration of a sort never before seen. He offered resounding proof that cut crystal need not be boring, effete, and lifeless but could be used to express a modern aesthetic.[25] Among Dahlskog's best-known works is the bowl called "Carrousel" which he designed in 1926. His glass had none of the delicate classicism that dominated the 1920s; instead, it anticipated the more vigorous expressions of the 1930s.[26]

Elis Bergh was the leading artistic force at Kosta from 1929 to 1950. After attending the Tekniska Högskolan in Stockholm (1897–99), he continued his studies at the Högskolan för Industriell Konst and served as an assistant to the royal architect, Agi Lindgren, in 1903 and 1904. Following studies in Germany, he worked as a designer at Böhlmarks lamp factory for ten years and in 1921 at AB Hallberg, a goldsmith. At Kosta "Bergh crystal" became legendary; it is characterized by harmonious, thick-walled faceted pieces, often in blue-green hues.[27] Although his glass may not have been particularly revolutionary, Bergh provided Kosta with stable, ongoing leadership. He left a legacy of over 2,600 designs, the most important being his many elegant tableware series.[28]

In 1934 Sven-Erik Skawonius began a brief tenure, lasting just a year, at Kosta. He also had trained at the Tekniska Högskolan and the Kungliga Konstakademien (1927–30).[29] A brilliant and versatile artist, he expanded on the faceting innovations begun by Dahlskog, designing surrealistic new patterns. Skawonius reintroduced sandblasting, which achieved deeper decorative relief effects in the walls of the vessels.[30]

Tyra Lundgren was one of the first women to design art glass. She began her training at the Tekniska Högskolan (1914–18) and Kungliga Konstakademien (1918–22) and studied sculpture in Vienna in 1920 and painting at André Lhote's atelier in Paris in 1920 and 1921. Lundgren also worked as a ceramics designer

Fig. 8-4. Poster by Edward Hald, 1917. It announces an Orrefors exhibition that was held in Norway. (Svensk Form Bildarkivet, Stockholm)

from 1934 to 1939 for the Sèvres factory in Paris and spent a formative year at the end of the 1930s at the Venini Glassworks in Venice. At Kosta she designed a variety of vases and bowls with deep sandblasted patterns in a high cameo technique and motifs including distinctive, stylized fish, birds, and classical female figures.[31]

REIJMYRE GLASSWORKS. Edvin Ollers came to Reijmyre in 1918, staying just one year. His creations, especially his vases, were strongly rooted in the neoclassicism of the eighteenth century. Unlike his designs for Kosta the previous year where he had used soda glass, at Reijmyre he exploited more homogeneous melts, and his color scale shifted somewhat, toward mild honey-yellow and Prussian blue.[32] The architect Sten Branzell and painter Axel Törneman also worked at Reijmyre — Branzell beginning in 1922 and Törneman a year later. Together they designed the "City Hall Cup," which was donated to the city of Stockholm and displayed at the newly built City Hall in 1923. The cup, free-blown from a blue-green melt, was nearly human size, its cover crowned by a spouting dolphin.[33]

Reijmyre went bankrupt in 1932 but was revived five years later by glass artist Monica Bratt-Wijkander,

Fig. 8-5. The Reijmyre Glassworks display at the Stockholm Exhibition of 1897. (Östergötlands Länsmuseum)

and production restarted in 1938. Bratt-Wijkander's designs were graceful and harmonious, with a rich palette of red, blue, or green. Unlike many of her contemporaries at Kosta and Orrefors, she was not interested in creating presentation or exhibition pieces. Instead she devoted herself and the Reijmyre factory to functional glassware.[34]

EDA AND STRÖMBERGSHYTTAN GLASSWORKS. Eda's design in the twentieth century has been dominated by Gerda Strömberg, who produced art glass at Eda from 1927 to 1933. She continued her efforts at Strömbergshyttan Glassworks from 1935 until her death in 1960. Her art glass was almost always devoid of external decoration. The vessel walls were thick and light-distorting, often faceted with large, wide cuts. She used glass melts of various colors, sometimes clear, sometimes topaz or beryl.[35] She preferred to produce her designs from start to finish in the blowing room.[36]

GULLASKRUF GLASSWORKS. Just before the Stockholm Exhibition of 1930, the managing director of Gullaskruf, Wilhelm Stenberg, hired the painter and graphic artist Hugo Gehlin to help the company produce signature glass for this important exposition. Gehlin sought to revive the tradition of painting glass with enamel and produced free-blown bowls and bottles that are tributes to the glassblower's art, building on two centuries of tradition.[37]

Glass at the Major Exhibitions Between the World Wars

International exhibitions of the applied arts served as stepping stones in the development of Swedish art glass. The Stockholm Exhibition of 1897 was especially significant in this progression, signaling the start of an energetic effort by the Swedish glassworks to catch up and compete with the makers of contemporary art glass on the Continent.

While some reviewers of the exhibition, such as Ludvig Looström, secretary of Svenska Slöjdföreningen, were confident in their high praise of the glass that was displayed (fig. 8-5),[38] many others, such as Pietro Krohn, director of the Kunstindustrimuséet (Museum of Decorative Arts) in Copenhagen, were harshly critical of the highly decorated Swedish glass. Three of the major Swedish glassworks—Kosta, Reijmyre, and Eda—exhibited heavy crystal bowls, cups, vases, and carafes, the surfaces covered with faceted cuts.[39] (Kosta included a bowl with a red overlay that represents one of the first examples of French casing technique employed in Sweden.[40]) Although the melt used in the ware that was exhibited was of high quality and the faceted pieces showed great technical skill, they lacked the freshness and vitality of work by Emile Gallé, E. B. Lévillé, and L. C. Tiffany, among others.

In 1898 E. G. Folcker, who became curator of applied arts at the Nationalmuseum in Stockholm in 1900, further defined the problem: ". . . one finds that they [the glassworks] are in need of a new design sensibility—they lack imagination. In this respect, it would be desirable for our glassworks to go the same route the ceramics factories have gone with such great success—that of seeking to interest artists in their plight. Examples are to be found abroad of the benefits such a policy can bring."[41]

The challenge to engage artists had been made and the response from the glass industry was immediate. Kosta, who had already employed artist Axel

Enoch Boman in 1895, hired Gunnar G:son Wennerberg in 1898,[42] Karl Lindeberg in 1907, and Alf Wallander in 1908 (who was also approached by Reijmyre Glassworks), and other glassworks followed suit.[43] The positive results of their efforts were soon seen in the international exhibitions of the early twentieth century: in Paris (1900),[44] Turin (1902), St. Petersburg (1908), Stockholm (1909), and Malmö (1914), among others.[45]

The 1914 Baltic Exhibition at Malmö sparked renewed debate over the direction being pursued by Sweden's applied arts industries. Critics complained, on one hand, about the sporadic nature of the collaboration between artists and manufacturers and, on the other, about the inability of artists to design objects for mass production. The Baltic Exhibition included a great deal of faceted glass that met with an indifferent response from the general public but was more harshly criticized by reviewers. Svenska Slöjdföreningen's new secretary Erik Wettergren argued that the repetitive faceted cuts essentially annihilated the surfaces of the objects, that Swedish overlay glass was raw and inharmonious in its coloring, and that the naturalistic decoration was uninspired. His final judgment was unambiguous and severe: "What is called for here is an out-and-out revolution, or, if that is impossible, the complete cessation of operations."[46]

Svenska Slöjdföreningen, which had organized the Baltic Exhibition, was restructured shortly afterward as a result of the controversy. In 1915 Gregor Paulsson, who had also been critical of the Swedish applied arts at Malmö, contributed a polemical essay to the Society's journal.[47] Many considered it nothing less than a call to arms in which Paulsson exhorted his readers to redefine the role of the applied arts in society:

> It can be said with no fear of contradiction that Swedish arts and crafts are currently at a critical juncture. . . . Is our era without taste? . . . As industry matured and became a major power, people were so intoxicated by it that, in their haste, they forgot there was such a thing as beauty, too. . . . The anarchy we see now is nothing more than a lack of cooperation. But [cooperation] must be achieved; the artisans must place themselves at the service of the designers, and the designers, in turn, must not regard the artisan's work as an inessential secondary consideration.[48]

Following the Baltic Exhibition there was a concerted effort to establish a social agenda for the applied arts. This idea was not new. In 1907 the Deutscher Werkbund (German Work Association) had been founded in Berlin to foster cooperation between German artists, theoreticians, designers, and manufac-

turers as a way of developing aesthetically appealing mass-produced objects of high quality. In Sweden the leading supporters of this manner of reform were Wettergren, Paulsson, and Elsa Gullberg, a designer and textile artist. Gullberg was instrumental in establishing and directing a kind of employment agency connected to Svenska Slöjdföreningen. Modeled directly on a similar branch of the Deutscher Werkbund, this arm of the Society placed artists and designers at various factories in an attempt to elevate product design. In this way Gullberg, who was tireless in her efforts, found positions for Simon Gate at Orrefors in 1916 and Edward Hald there in 1917. She also secured a place for Edvin Ollers at Kosta around the same time.

In the wake of the Baltic Exhibition, Slöjdföreningen decided to organize another exhibition to address the issues raised by critics of the 1914 displays. The result was the Home Exhibition, which came to be associated with Paulsson's concept of vackrare vardagsvara (more beautiful things for everyday use).[49] It opened at the Liljevalchs Konsthall in Stockholm in the autumn of 1917 and showcased the applied arts, including quality mass-produced tableware that was both inexpensive and functional. Many of the designs were created by Gate, Hald, and Ollers in their new positions at the Orrefors and Kosta glassworks.

The new glass garnered considerable praise. The functional bowls, wine glasses, and carafes by Ollers for Kosta were heralded in particular as an important step forward.[50] His robust bubble-stippled, greenish glassware, inspired by simple Swedish vernacular design, took center stage.[51] At last, declared the critics, here was glass designed not for the elite few but for the masses. Neither the reviewers nor the artists, however, had counted on the complete disinterest with which the general public greeted this new work. Gate's pale blue vases and wineglasses were also overlooked by his intended audience. Instead, the public preferred the more conventional faceted wineglasses in imitation of the luxury glassware made for the upper echelons of society. They chose to purchase richly embellished pieces with mass-produced designs from the catalogue issued by Åhlen & Holm, a mail-order company.[52] This dismissal of the new, rough, colored glass was not altogether surprising. Plain, colored glass, usually brown, was for beer and wine bottles, not glassware to grace an elegant table. At the Home Exhibition only the upper classes and intellectuals were enthusiastic enough about the distinctly modern work of Gate and Ollers to purchase it.[53]

Following the First World War, exhibitions were organized at a dizzying rate as the glassworks and other applied arts industries vied to introduce new products and showcase the young artists engaged in their factories. New collections were shown at

Nordiska Kompaniet (NK), the main department store in Stockholm, which had become a venue for modern design. Swedish glass may not have been transformed overnight, but its development moved forward with unprecedented speed. Orrefors assumed an undisputed leading role. Graal glass, a technical tour de force of glassblowing in which the decoration is sometimes encased in a layer of glass, was introduced in 1916 when the technique was used to produce a single glass object at Orrefors. Although a year later production was up to 421 pieces and Orrefors was offering designs in brilliant red, altogether the factory produced only 1,396 glasses using the graal technique between 1916 and 1931.[54]

The playful, engraved designs of Hald and Gate brought Orrefors a series of critical successes. After the Home Exhibition the two artists continued to develop engraved glass at Orrefors. Engraving had virtually disappeared from the Swedish glass industry until Hald and Gate revived it, rediscovering the craft and exploring its artistic potential anew. Engraved glass would be the factory's most successful product line for many years to come, establishing Orrefors' international reputation.[55]

The Gothenburg Jubilee Exhibition of 1923 featured work from Orrefors (fig. 8-6) and the AB De Svenska Kristallglasbruken. Orrefors dominated both the exhibition and the press coverage, and the factory's installation came to symbolize the new alliance of art and industry.[56] Among the showpieces of the Orrefors display were free-blown footed cups in shades of smoky gray, deep red, and blue semicrystal with a delicate optic-blown bowl, "balustrade" stem, and wide foot.[57] Simon Gate and master-blower Knut Bergqvist, who collaborated on these pieces especially for the exhibition, christened their work "Palace glass," of which Orrefors produced some 275 pieces.[58]

In 1924 the Society won critical acclaim for its installation of Swedish applied arts at the Utställning av Svenskt konsthantverk och Konstindustri (Exhibition of Swedish Handicraft and Applied Arts) in Helsinki. Swedish glass was recognized for its masterly design and execution. As one reviewer wrote, ". . . as for the glass itself—its triumph was swift and absolute. Who

Fig. 8-6. The Orrefors Glassworks display at the Gothenburg Exhibition of 1923. (Svensk Form Bildarkivet, Stockholm)

Fig. 8-7. The glass display at the Swedish pavilion, Exposition des Arts Décoratifs et Industriels Modernes, Paris, 1925. (Svensk Form Bildarkivet, Stockholm)

could resist the charm of these airy pieces, seemingly conjured up with playful ease? What has happened in Sweden must be almost unparalleled, bringing into being a production of this scope and quality in just a few short years."[59]

The ultimate test of the Swedish glass industry occurred at the Paris Exposition des Arts Décoratifs et Industriels Modernes, in 1925. For the first time Orrefors displayed its most progressive art glass as part of a major international forum (fig. 8-7). The results were decidedly positive, and the factory was awarded many gold medals and stellar reviews. "Orrefors glass in Paris," read one headline, "came, was seen, and conquered."[60] After the exposition Gregor Paulsson was unstinting in his praise for their efforts: "Now that Orrefors, with this exposition, has won for itself an unchallenged international reputation —a reputation, one hopes, that its technical and financial management will do everything in their power to expand—it must be said that their achievement is

essentially unparalleled: in some eight years' time, creating from nothing the world's finest art glassworks."[61]

After the success of Swedish glass in Paris, Slöjdföreningen organized for a smaller version of the Paris exhibition to be shown in New York City and elsewhere in the United States in 1927. Held at the Metropolitan Museum of Art, the Exhibition of Swedish Contemporary Decorative Arts was well received, and as in Paris, the art glass was singled out for praise. Of Gate's glass the *New York Times* wrote: "He has achieved the height of perfection in this glass service created for the crown prince of Sweden."[62]

In 1928 several leading artists—including Mårta Måås-Fjetterström, Prince Eugen, Carl Milles, Simon Gate, and Edward Hald—were invited to participate in an exhibition in Amsterdam. The same year, the M/S *Kungsholm* made its maiden voyage. Outfitted with prime examples of the latest in Swedish applied arts, the liner served as a floating showcase for Swedish arts and industry. Hald and Gate had been commis-

Fig. 8-8. Glass hall at the Stockholm Exhibition of 1930. (Svensk Form Bildarkivet, Stockholm)

sioned to design lighting fixtures, mirrors, and tables.[63]

One of the landmark expositions of modern design in Sweden between the world wars was the Stockholm Exhibition of 1930 (fig. 8-8). It drew the entire Swedish applied arts world with a program that was based on functionalism and had its roots in the 1917 Home Exhibition. The goal was to emphasize functional objects inspired by industrial design rather than craft production.[64] Kosta featured some forty glasses by Sven Erixson, while Elis Bergh, Sten Branzell, and Ewald Dahlskog contributed crystal tableware and decorative glass. At the Orrefors display there were "graal glass, stately gift items, decorative glass, and tableware, including both luxury pieces and handsome objects for everyday living."[65] Gate's vase called "Four Winds" and Hald's celestial globe (fig. 8-9) were exhibited for the first time, and Vicke Lindstrand's painted and engraved vases were also shown.

At the time of the Stockholm Exhibition, Edvin Ollers was the art director at both the AB Fred. Brusewitz

Glassworks in Limmared and Elme Glassworks in Älmhult. Eda Glassworks displayed a large selection of glass by Gerda Strömberg, and Gullaskruf contributed glass by Hugo Gehlin. Hofmanstorps New Glassworks showed domestic and decorative glass designed by Carl Alexanderson while Pukeberg Glassworks AB Arvid Böhlmarks showed lighting and domestic glass designed by Harald Notini. Johansfors, Målerås, Skruf, and Åfors glassworks also participated.[66]

Department stores were highly instrumental in the dissemination of modern design. Nordiska Kompaniet (NK) in Stockholm regularly mounted exhibitions of Swedish and international decorative arts. They often featured glass by the Swedish glassworks, prompting immediate analysis and appraisal. *Form*, as the journal of the Svenska Slöjdföreningen had been renamed in 1932, regularly published reviews of these exhibitions. They bear the stamp of the functionalist ideas and reflect the beliefs promulgated in the social manifestos of the time, but they also provide an invaluable record of their era and include important analyses of Swedish glass production. In 1934, after Kosta showed the glass of Sven-Erik Skawonius at NK, *Form* responded enthusiastically: "It can be said without exaggeration that this is an enormously important addition to Swedish glass art."[67] In 1936, when Orrefors was the focus of an NK exhibition, *Form* also lauded the results: "It is a simple fact that Orrefors' latest performance (with 'Mycenae,' graal and engraved glass) is a new artistic triumph, following the many preceding it. This is all the more pleasing given that we have an important meeting to look forward to in Paris next year. To hold the territory they have won, the Swedish applied arts will have to marshal all their forces to the utmost."[68]

At the 1937 Paris exposition Orrefors presented new work by Hald and Knut Bergqvist, who had further refined their graal technique to create thick-walled vases with maritime and piscine motifs that was known as "fish graal." English critic P. Morton Shand, however, also singled out the work of Gerda Strömberg, writing that her "cut-glass vases are among the very few glass vases I would ever wish to own."[69] Ariel glass, another technical innovation, was also first shown in 1937, and by the Second World War, 220 pieces had been made.[70]

The last major international expositions before the outbreak of the Second World War were those in New York and San Francisco in 1939.[71] The catalogue accompanying the Swedish exhibition at the New York World's Fair illustrated objects from the glass and applied art installations. Those at the glass display (fig. 8-10) included thick-walled engraved vases de-

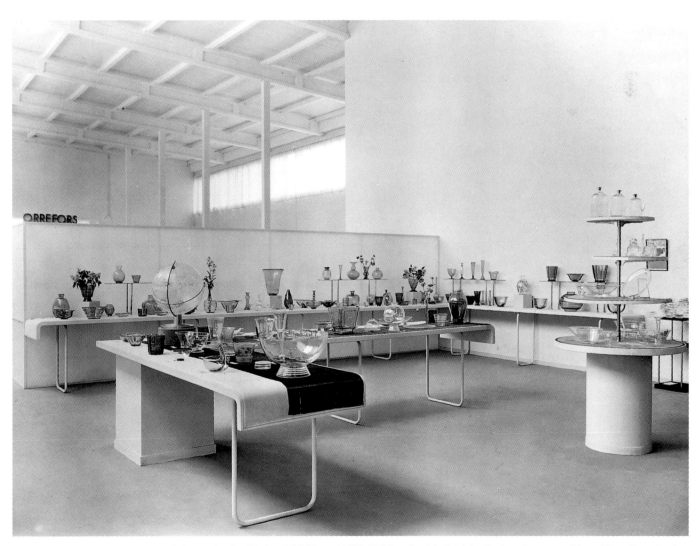

Fig. 8-9. Orrefors Glassworks installation at the Stockholm Exhibition of 1930. Hald's celestial globe is displayed on one of the tables. (Svensk Form Bildarkivet, Stockholm)

Fig. 8-10. The glass display in the Swedish pavilion at the New York World's Fair, 1939. Åfors, Kosta, Orrefors, and Strömbergshyttan contributed work; the textile was designed by Astrid Sampe. (From *Form* [1939])

signed by Simon Gate, Vicke Lindstrand, and Sven Palmqvist; ariel and graal glass by Edvin Öhrström; free-blown vases and wineglasses by Nils Landberg; and many tableware and domestic glass services by Gate and Lindstrand.[72] Kosta showed tableware services by Elis Bergh, while Strömbergshyttan displayed vases and glass services by Gerda Strömberg, and Edvin Ollers at Åfors contributed thick-walled, broadly faceted vases and free-blown bowls. The New York and San Francisco exhibitions marked the last occasions until after the Second World War at which Swedish glass artists were featured as a group before an international audience.

The progress made by Swedish art glass between the two world wars was monumental, led by artists and powered by industry. They made forays in many directions, including revisits to the past to modernize techniques such as engraving. There had been pioneering efforts to introduce new ways of working. The graal, ariel, and mycenae techniques, for example, offered stunning new possibilities to artists and manufacturers. At the same time there had also been a revolution in thinking about glass and the other objects of everyday life. On one hand, a social agenda had been developed around the concept of "more beautiful things for everyday use," while on the other hand, glass had been elevated from everyday object to art. These two directions—quality mass-produced glassware and unique art glass—represent a true union of art and industry and together have assured the survival of the Swedish glassworks to the present day.

1. In addition to Orrefors (1898–) and Kosta (1742–), the glassworks most relevant to this exhibition are: Reijmyre (1812–1926, 1932–); Eda (1835–1933, 1935–39, 1943–53); Boda (1864–); Pukeberg (1871–); Åfors (1876–); Strömbergshyttan (1876–1979); Flygsfors (1889–1920, 1930–79); Sandvik (1889–); Målerås (1890–1903, 1917–22, 1924–); Johansfors (1891–); Gullaskruf (1893–1921, 1927–83); Skruf (1897–1980, 1981–); and Elme (1917–70) (Olof Nordström, *Glasbruk och hyttor i Sverige, 1555–1855*, Smålands museum skriftserie, no. 2. [Växjö: Smålands museum, 1986], pp. 54–63). For further information, see the appendix in this volume.

2. Nordström, *Glasbruk och hyttor*, pp. 54–63.

3. Ibid., p. 11.

4. The founding members were Kosta, Reijmyre, Eda, Alsterfors, Flöxhult and Alsterbro, Johanstorp, Gyllenfors, and Geijersfors.

5. This information is drawn from the catalogue for the Baltic Exhibition in Malmö in 1914 (*Officiell Berättelse över Baltiska utställningen* [Malmö: Fölagsaktrebolages Malmö Boktryckerier, 1914]), pp. 540–45.

6. M. Artéus, ed., *Kosta 250 år*, Jubileumsskrift (Malmö: Tryckeriteknik i Malmö AB, 1992), p. 53.

7. Arthur Hald and Erik Wettergren, eds., *Simon Gate, Edward Hald: En Skildring av människorna och konstnärerna* (Stockholm: Svenska Slöjdföreningen, Norstedts, 1948), p. 113.

8. Torbjörn Fogelberg and Gunnar Lersjö, *Eda glasbruk, 1830–1953* (Arvika: Varmlands museum, 1977), pp. 77–78.

9. Sune Ambrosiani, *Pukebergs glasbruk* (Stockholm: Nordisk, 1946), pp. 108, 114.

10. *Glas-Kultur-Samhälle: 120 år i Hovmantorp* (Nybro, Sweden: ABF Lessebo, 1980), p. 20. Comparative records for Sandvik in 1919 are not available.

11. Ibid., p. 46.

12. During the period between 1914 and 1939, the arts community throughout Europe suffered from the effects of two world wars, as well as the Great Depression of the 1930s. See chaps. 1 and 2 in this volume.

13. *Generationers arbete på Boda glasbruk* (Nybro, Sweden: ABF Lessebo, 1982), p. 28. Comparative records for 1939 are not available.

14. Helmut Ricke and Ulrich Gronert, *Glas in Schweden, 1915–1960* (Munich: Prestel Verlag, 1986), p. 269.

15. Alastair Duncan, *Orrefors Glass* (Woodbridge, Eng.: Antique Collectors' Club, 1995), p. 81.

16. Heribert Seitz, *Glaset förr och nu* (Stockholm: Albert Borriers Förlag, 1933), p. 134.

17. Ricke and Gronert, *Glas in Schweden*, p. 270. One critic wrote, "Standing before this great celestial globe, with its bluish, faintly chilly hues of almost majestic grandeur, one might well ask—is it possible to demand more of human knowledge?" (Seitz, *Glaset förr och nu*, p. 135).

18. Lars Thor, *Legend i glas: En bok om Vicke Lindstrand* (Stockholm: Liber Förlag, 1982), p. 101; Ricke and Gronert, *Glas in Schweden*, 1986, p. 137

19. Ibid., p. 270

20. Märta Stina Danielsson, ed., *Svenskt glas* (Stockholm: Wahlström and Widstrand, 1991), p. 115.

21. In fact one of Öhrström's ariel vases sold at auction in 1988 for almost a million kronor, the most ever paid for Swedish art glass (Auction catalogue, AB Bukowski, Stockholm [May 1988], lot 741).

22. Ricke and Gronert, *Glas in Schweden*, p. 270

23. Ibid.

24. Danielsson, *Svenskt glas*, p. 100.

25. Gregor Paulsson, ed., *Modernt svenskt glas* (Stockholm: Jonson and Winter, 1943), p. 151.

26. Artéus, *Kosta 250 år*, p. 55.

27. Seitz, *Glaset förr och nu*, p. 136.

28. Artéus, *Kosta 250 år*, p. 58. Most of these designs are for drinking glasses; they are now in Kosta's archives.

29. Ricke and Gronert, *Glas in Schweden*, p. 271.

30. Paulsson, *Modernt svenskt glas*, p. 153.

31. Ricke and Gronert, *Glas in Schweden*, p. 270; Paulsson, *Modernt svenskt glas*, p. 155.

32. Danielsson, *Svenskt glas*, p. 99.

33. Paulsson, *Modernt svenskt glas*, p. 150.

34. Ricke and Gronert, *Glas in Schweden*, p. 270.

35. Paulsson, *Modernt svenskt glas*, p. 176.

36. Ibid., p. 179.

37. Ibid., p. 180.

38. Looström wrote, "The section of the arts and handicrafts exhibition which afforded us the most delightful surprise was glass manufacture. Starting from humble origins, the glass industry has progressed slowly and methodically, now and again bringing new works to the marketplace, simple tableware series and decorative pieces, and at last winning the unreserved sympathies and faith of the public. When the collected forces of the Swedish glassworks appeared at the exhibition, their triumph was absolute" (Ludvig Looström, *Stockholms Allmänna Konst- and Industriutställning 1897* [Stockholm: 1899–1900], p. 589). Svenska Slöjdföreningen concurred, suggesting that only a table laid with shining damask, brilliant silver, and glittering crystal was artistically correct (E. G. Folcker, "Kosta och Orrefors," *Svenska Slöjdföreningen tidskrift*, [1917], p. 88).

39. Looström, *Stockholms Allmänna*, pp. 588, 590–91.

40. It is now in the collection of the Nationalmuseum, Stockholm; Paulsson, *Modernt svenskt glas*, p. 51.

41. *Svenska Slöjdföreningen tidskrift*, no. 1 (1898), p. 53.

42. It was not surprising that Wennerberg was among the first to be hired by Kosta. While in Paris in 1897 he had written to Prince Eugen, son of King Oscar II: "The glass industry here is just as superior as one might possibly imagine. I think the gentlemen at Kosta ought to try their techniques, and with the help of an artist, such as me, for example, they could really do some lovely things" (quoted in Danielsson, *Svenskt glas*, p. 60).

43. Reijmyre was another leader in hiring artists, engaging Anna Boberg and Betzy Åhlström in 1901 and Ferdinand Boberg in 1907, among others (ibid., p. 66). Wallander was approached by Reijmyre and Kosta around 1908, and since the two glassworks had both been members of the Svenska Kristallglasbruken since 1903, there were no objections to his designing for both of them.

44. At the 1900 Paris exhibition Kosta displayed Art Nouveau glass by Wennerberg; although it did not create a sensation compared to the work of Emile Gallé and Daum, it was well received in Sweden (ibid., p. 63). Gallé's marqueterie de verre was a major inspiration; in this technique the gather was rolled in bits of colored glass, variegated glass rods were sometimes applied to it, and it was then heated and marvered. The cast-on decor was often cut afterward. The result was thick-walled glass with a smooth surface that resembled the later graal glass, which also had decoration inserted into the melt (ibid., p. 66).

45. The glass exhibitors included AB Förenade Kristallglasbruken, Färe, Pukeberg, Karlstads, Limmared, and Sandvik (*Officiell Berättelse över Baltiska utställningen*, p. 540).

46. Erik Wettergren, [untitled], *Svenska Slöjdföreningen tidskrift* (1914), p. 137–38.

47. Gregor Paulsson, "Anarki eller tidsstil," *Svenska Slöjdföreningen tidskrift* 11, no. 1 (1915), pp. 1–2.

48. Ibid., passim.

49. Gregor Paulsson, *Vackrare Vardagsvara* (Stockholm: Svenska Slöjdföreningen, 1919).

50. *Svenska Slödföreningens Hemutställning*, exhib. cat. (Stockholm: Liljevalchs förlag, 1917) and archive of the Nationalmuseum, Stockholm.

51. Hald and Wettergren, *Simon Gate, Edward Hald*, p. 41.

52. Åhlen & Holm was a mail-order company.

53. *Svenska Slöjdföreningen tidskrift* (1917), pp. 87–93.

54. Production of graal glass was resumed in 1936, but of a different type of graal glass, continuing until 1981, with a total of 23,681 pieces produced during the period (Ricke and Gronert, *Glas in Schweden*, 1986, p. 273).

55. Seitz, *Glaset förr och nu*, p. 133.

56. *Svenska Slöjdföreningen Konstindustriutställning*, exhib. cat. (Gothenburg: Svenska Slöjdföreningen, 1923), p. 22.

57. Hald and Wettergren, *Simon Gate, Edward Hald*, p. 70.

58. Ricke and Gronert, *Glas in Schweden*, p. 277.

59. *Svenska Slöjdföreningen tidskrift* 2, no. 20 (1924), p. 65.

60. Hald and Wettergren, *Simon Gate, Edward Hald*, p. 81.

61. Ibid., p. 84.

62. Ibid., p. 91.

63. Ibid., p. 96.

64. Ibid., p. 103.

65. *Stockholmsutställningen 1930 av konstindustri, konsthandverk och hemslöjd*, exhib. cat. (Uppsala, Sweden: Almquist & Wiksells boktryckeri, 1930).

66. Ibid.

67. Sven-Erik Skawonius and Gregor Paulsson, "Glas från Kosta," *Form* (1934), p. 234.

68. *Form* (1936), p. 149.

69. P. Morton Shand, "The Swedish Pavilion in Paris through English Eyes," *Form* (1937), p. 153.

70. Ricke and Gronert, *Glas in Schweden*, p. 282.

71. For further information on the New York World's Fair and the Golden Gate International Exposition, San Francisco, see chapter 11 in this volume.

72. Åke Stavenow, et al., eds., *Swedish Arts and Crafts/Swedish Modern: A Movement Toward Sanity in Design*, exhib. cat. (New York: Royal Swedish Commission, New York World's Fair, 1939).

CHAPTER NINE

Orrefors Glass in Public Spaces

Märta Holkers

Fig. 9-1. The entrance to the Swedish pavilion at the 1937 Paris Exposition Internationale des Arts et Techniques with a monumental window designed by Vicke Lindstrand for Orrefors.

During the years between the world wars the Orrefors Glassworks received numerous commissions to produce glass for public spaces. This work greatly enhanced the factory's status as a world leader in the creation of modern art glass, and it further solidified the growing relationship between Orrefors and Sweden's foremost designers. Through collaboration with Simon Gate and Edward Hald, Orrefors achieved major technical and aesthetic breathroughs in this domain. Its commissions ranged from monumental windows to small panels for doors, from drinking fountains to lighting fixtures[1]; and its clients included city governments, private industry, and religious groups. Despite the factory's achievements and its prodigious reputation, however, little attention has been paid by historians to this aspect of the Orrefors production.

Orrefors architectural work gained momentum, as did much of its other art glass, through exposure at the international exhibitions (fig. 9-1). These venues provided a unique environment for large-scale projects and an opportunity for the glassworks to realize special orders. For the 1923 Gothenburg Jubilee Exhibition, Edward Hald created a graceful glass fountain for the main exhibition pavilion that served as a focal point in the stair hall.[2] Two years later at the Paris Exposition des Arts Décoratifs et Industriels Modernes Orrefors produced richly embellished chandeliers designed by Gate and Hald for the Swedish exhibition room in the Grand Palais. Made of translucent blue glass, each chandelier was engraved with stylized leaf forms.[3] Hald, who often incorporated architectonic motifs and interior views as decorative elements in his engraved designs, included a variation of this chandelier form on his covered vessel, "Masquerade Ball," made the same year (fig. 9-2). Hald's interest in lighting fixtures had been evident as early as 1919 when he designed several lamp fixtures with engraved decoration. These proved too costly to make, however, and did not go into regular production.[4]

The Paris chandeliers earned widespread acclaim for Orrefors and led to a major public commission to create a modified version as well as other lighting fix-

Fig. 9-2. "Masquerade Ball," by Edward Hald, Orrefors, 1925; engraved glass.

Fig. 9-3. Chandelier for the Stockholm Concert Hall, by Edward Hald, Orrefors, 1926.

tures a year later for the new Stockholms konserthus (Stockholm Concert Hall; fig. 9-3), which was designed by Ivar Tengbom, 1923–26.[5] A striking feature of the Concert Hall is the contrast between the austere facade of the building and the lavish interiors which epitomized the graceful neoclassical design then prevalent in Sweden.[6] For the chandeliers Gate and Hald substituted a delicate lilac hue for the blue glass that had been used in Paris. The scale, luminosity, and exquisite color of the glass made these fixtures among the Concert Hall's most prominent design features, and they were warmly reviewed. Critic Axel L. Romdahl wrote, "Hald and Gate, the Orrefors design team, both

deserve praise for this remarkably effective composition." Commenting on the technical innovations being pursued at Orrefors, he singled out fixtures installed along one of the theater's promenades as having been "pretreated by a new method developed at Orrefors which has enabled the soft glow emitted by the lamp to combine with the blue of the glass itself and produce a light which is very close to daylight."[7] The Concert Hall showcased other examples of the Orrefors expertise. Three mirrors reminiscent of eighteenth-century Venetian forms with foliated frames were designed by Carl Malmsten and engraved by Edward Hald.[8]

After the success of the Concert Hall commission

Orrefors issued a small catalogue primarily for "architects and other interested parties" in which the factory offered twenty-two designs for electrical lighting fixtures available in beige, light blue, or ivory-colored glass.[9] Among these were some of the Concert Hall models as well as various other designs specified for large spaces including ballrooms and restaurants.

Simon Gate continued to design primarily luxury chandeliers in the neoclassical manner of the Concert Hall pieces.[10] He even replicated the Concert Hall chandelier for his own home.[11] Edward Hald, however, became a more ardent supporter of functionalism as it was outlined by Gregor Paulsson, director of Svenska Slöjdföreningen (The Swedish Society of Craft and Industrial Design), in a speech given on October 25, 1928 to discuss the social agenda of the planned 1930 Stockholm Exhibition.[12] The ideal, said Paulsson, had been pioneered at "Die Wohnung" (The Dwelling), the exhibition held in Stuttgart in 1927, where "rationalization" had been demonstrated throughout the applied arts and a new, efficient style of architecture had been introduced that was "commonly known as functionalism." New times, proclaimed Paulsson, were just around the corner.[13] The Stockholm Exhibition planned for 1930 would focus on the aesthetics of mass production, returning to the themes of the earlier Home Exhibition of 1917 and the ideals Paulsson had presented in his seminal book *Vackrare Vardagsvara* (More beautiful things for everyday use).[14]

Hald's lamp designs for Orrefors became exemplars of functionalism.[15] In 1928 he exhibited distinctly modern light fixtures at the Liljevalchs Konsthall, and he continued to design in this manner throughout the 1930s. By 1937 the Orrefors catalogue of available lighting fixtures included several of his ceiling lamps, such as "The Four Winds," "Diana," "Turbine," and "Saturn," which as the name implies was a ringed globe.[16]

Like most of the Swedish glassworks Orrefors had produced window glass, but never in quantity, and not as an important part of the factory's production. Only when window glass was transformed into custom-made art glass and associated with the factory's architectural commissions did it become noteworthy. The achievements of Orrefors in this area during the 1930s greatly added to the prestige of the company.

The ecclesiastical commissions that Orrefors accepted became a special interest of Simon Gate. In 1934 he created a window for the Kviberg Chapel in Gothenburg (figs. 9-4 and 9-5). The memorial chapel was designed by architect R. O. Swensson,[17] and like many other buildings in Gothenburg is of yellow brick. Its otherwise understated interior, which includes two large gilded angels by the sculptor Carl Berger, features a tall, narrow window designed by Gate, depicting an elaborate Resurrection scene. In most cases

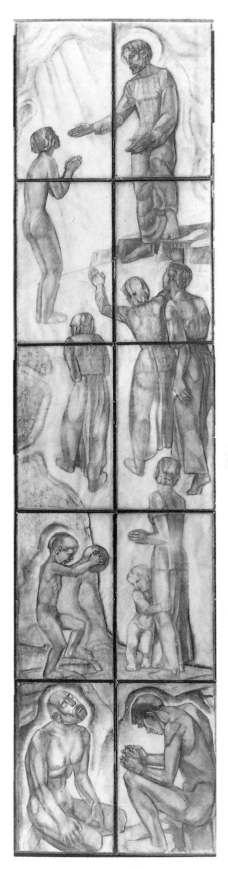

Fig. 9-4. Drawing for a window in Kviberg Chapel, Gothenburg, by Simon Gate, Orrefors, 1934.

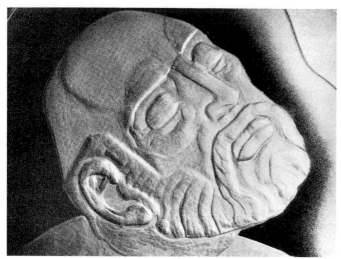

Fig. 9-5. Window in Kviberg Chapel, Gothenburg (detail) by Simon Gate, Orrefors, 1934.

Fig. 9-6. Drinking fountain (replica) for the Gothenburg Concert Hall; original by Simon Gate, Orrefors, 1935.

designers at Orrefors left the actual engraving process to the highly skilled professionals at the factory who followed the artist's sketches and templates. For this window, however, Gate himself completed much of the technical work. After the figures had been sandblasted, he used an engraving wheel to thin the glass and obtain a precise range of muted color. The intensity of color is directly dependent on the thickness of the glass.[18]

Gate's window for the Kviberg Chapel was a momentous achievement and a turning point for Orrefors. The critics were unanimous in their praise, especially for the subtle palette that Gate used. One reviewer, writing in *Form*, described the window as having "no colors at all, except for a nuance of grayish pink. The effect is something altogether new. We are so used to the explosion of color in church windows that we have a hard time imagining that the monumental glass window offers other possibilities, too. Gate's and Orrefors' window is something brand new, something better suited to the modern room than was the old multicolored grandeur."[19]

The triumph of this architectural collaboration contributed to making monumental windows an Orrefors specialty. A year later the factory received one of its most important assignments of the 1930s. Orrefors was commissioned to produce several decorative windows for the new Göteborgs konserthus (Gothenburg Concert Hall), as well as lighting fixtures and an impressive drinking fountain (fig. 9-6).[20]

The Gothenburg Concert Hall, in the center of the city, forms one corner of a cultural triangle, with the museum of art and city theater, at Götaplatsen, the city's main plaza. The building, designed by Nils Einar Eriksson, is characterized by an understated, modernist monumentality with an auditorium renowned for fine acoustics.[21] Axel B. Larsson, who had gained a reputation for his functional, graceful furniture designs at the 1930 Stockholm Exhibition,[22] completed the interiors in collaboration with leading Swedish artists and craftspeople. Larsson's modern interior scheme exemplifies the "Swedish Modern" aesthetic that would soon become known internationally.[23] Its sophistication and artistry corresponded with the importance attached to music in Gothenburg.[24]

At Orrefors, Simon Gate, Edward Hald, Sven Palmqvist, and Vicke Lindstrand all participated in this important commission. Gate contributed five window designs with musical motifs that were engraved by Sven Palmqvist (figs. 9-7 and 9-8). Hald explored the myth of Orpheus, depicting him playing his lyre for a gathering of wild animals (fig. 9-9). Vicke Lindstrand's design also pursued a musical theme.[25]

Orrefors also produced the Concert Hall's glass lighting fixtures, such as the magnificent chandeliers by Gate (fig. 9-10), which are hanging in the lobby, as

Figs. 9-7, 9-8. Windows for the Gothenburg
Concert Hall, by Simon Gate, Orrefors,
1935; engraving by Sven Palmqvist.

Fig. 9-9. Window for the Gothenburg
Concert Hall, by Edward Hald, Orrefors,
1935.

Fig. 9-10. Chandelier for the main lobby of the Gothenburg Concert Hall, by Simon Gate, Orrefors, 1935.

Fig. 9-11. Light fixture for the Gothenburg Concert Hall, Orrefors, 1935.

well as functionalist ceiling lamps (fig. 9-11) in other areas, all of which complimented the spare interiors. These more modern designs were markedly different from the neoclassical chandeliers and other lighting introduced a decade earlier at the 1925 Paris Exposition and repeated in the Stockholm Concert Hall in 1926.

Once again Orrefors art glass for a public space was a critical success. After the opening ceremonies art critic Axel Romdahl praised the quality of the glass, writing, "Aside from the cabinetry and architectural details made of wood, it is glass artisanry that has the starring role in this building's interior decoration."[26] He recognized the technical challenges of the commission, observing that "Orrefors' artistic forces, in the persons of Hald, Gate, and Lindstrand, have been mobilized and have done their best to solve the problems set before them. Gate has designed the chandeliers in the lobby and has succeeded in expressing the festiveness that is so pleasing in the great works of past eras, yet in a design idiom that is unmistakably modern." According to Romdahl, "One finds a strange new species of decoration in the narrow windows of the north gallery, rendered in cut and engraved glass. . . . During the day, the effect is lovely. The decoration ensures that 'something is always happening' in the long wall of frosted glass. But in the evening, when the concert hall is most often used, they are rather less expressive, if not entirely mute. It might not be a bad idea to set up some sort of exterior light source, so that concert-goers can enjoy their full effect."[27]

In preparation for the 1937 Paris Exposition Internationale des Arts et Techniques dans la Vie Moderne, Edward Hald, who was then serving as Orrefors's managing director, engaged the young sculptor Edvin Öhrström to find new directions for the factory's art glass. With little knowledge of the technical aspects of glassmaking Öhrström joined the other

Fig. 9-12. The "Technology and the Future" window designed by Vicke Lindstrand, Orrefors for the Swedish pavilion at the 1937 Paris Exposition.

Fig. 9-13. "The Three Wise Men" window for the Båstad Church, by Simon Gate, 1936; engraved by Gösta Elgström.

young artists at Orrefors—Nils Landberg, Sven Palmqvist, and Vicke Lindstrand. His earliest project was a large hanging lamp for the Malmö museum; it was in the shape of a cut-crystal ball decorated with figures.[28]

Öhrström's arrival at Orrefors coincided with the company's intense preparations for the 1937 Paris exposition. He was the first sculptor employed by a Swedish glassworks especially to work with glass as a medium for sculpture.[29] As a sculptor, Öhrström had been trained to work with massive forms, but in the glassworks this kind of art glass had never before been seen. The other Orrefors artists followed Öhrström's lead, and their thicker, more colorful art glass became associated with the glassworks.[30]

To achieve his goals Öhrström began by developing new techniques for making thick-walled objects— turning the molten glass in wet wood forms. Examples of this turned glass, called *drejat glas*, were shown at the 1937 Paris exposition.[31] Orrefors also introduced art glass made with its new "ariel" technique. Some examples of this complicated, costly art glass were by Vicke Lindstrand, others by Öhrström who excelled in this technique. His heavy objects were frequently in colors that paralleled his interest in precious gems— the blues, greens, purples, and other hues of sapphire, emerald, amethyst, and agate.[32]

Orrefors was commissioned to produce a monumental window for the entrance to the 1937 Swedish pavilion in Paris, which had been designed by architect Sven Ivar Lind. To fulfill this commission Vicke Lindstrand created an allegorical interpretation called "Technology and the Future," much of which he personally sandblasted onto a pane that was almost 20 feet high (fig. 9-12).[33] Its installation just before the opening of the exposition was detailed in *Form*:

Fig. 9-14. Wall panel for the Halmstad courthouse, by Edvin Öhrström, 1938.

Today, the traffic jam was worse than usual. The cause was the arrival of the largest window in the pavilion. A tricky one-ton load, and all a single pane. Vicke Lindstrand, the designer, arrived in the company of his Orrefors colleague Nils Landberg to decorate the window, and he followed every step of the transport with nervous expectancy. The enormous truck turned in toward the pavilion. . . . But there was a long wait before the glass was in place. The process took a day and a half, and one can say without exaggeration that the tension was unbearable the entire time. Twenty extra men from the glass company, five supervisors, and several people from the pavilion worked to cut down branches, discuss the problem, and test various solutions until at last the enormous pane of glass was installed.[34]

The window was praised as a masterpiece of modern glass, becoming one of the most talked-about decorative elements of the pavilion.[35] Also noteworthy at the pavilion was an ecclesiastical commission that Gate had completed in 1936. His sandblasted, delicately sculptural window, which was executed by master craftsman Gösta Elgström, depicted the story of the Magi (fig. 9-13. Following its exhibition in Paris, the window was installed in the church in Båstad, Sweden.

In 1938, Öhrström was commissioned to create a decorative glass panel at Orrefors, measuring almost ten feet square, for the courthouse in his hometown of Halmstad, Sweden. The robust relief depicted a harbor scene with stevedores straining with a load of timber (fig. 9-14). The subject matter reflects Öhrström's inter-

est in the lives and experiences of the working class. The design was sandblasted in high relief, with some sections left transparent to create reflective highlights.[36] Like Simon Gate in earlier projects, Öhrström completed much of the technical work himself.

During 1939 Orrefors was involved in several installations of art glass. The glassworks was commissioned by the Swedish American Line to create salon doors for the M/S *Stockholm*. Simon Gate designed a suite of panes (figs. 9-15 and 9-16) depicting scenes of the city of Stockholm and the principal businesses of Sweden, including glassmaking.[37] Sandblasted and engraved by Orrefors master craftsmen, the panes were installed in the ocean liner which was built in Italy and launched in June 1939.[38]

This had not been the first commission granted Orrefors by the Swedish American Line, whose liners served as floating ambassadors for Swedish craft and applied art. An earlier vessel, the M/S *Kungsholm*, which was launched in 1928, epitomized these commissions. Its interiors and furnishings had been supervised by architect Carl Bergsten who engaged many of Sweden's leading artists for the project.[39] Orrefors was commissioned to create light fixtures, mirrors, and other accessories, many of which were designed by Gate and Hald.[40]

A major event in 1939 for the international applied arts industries was the New York World's Fair. The 1937 Paris Exposition had not even opened when the Swedish government received an invitation to the 1939 exposition.[41] The New York World's Fair opened on

Fig. 9-15. Simon Gate working on his door panel design for the M/S *Stockholm*.

Fig. 9-16. Door panel (detail) by Simon Gate, 1939.

Fig. 9-17. Monumental fountain designed by Vicke Lindstrand for the Swedish pavilion at the New York World's Fair, 1939.

April 30, 1939. Its motto was "Building the World of Tomorrow Today." The Swedish pavilion, designed by architect Sven Markelius, was immensely popular in part because its displays presented a more humanistic interpretation of modernism. Its centerpiece was the Orrefors fountain designed by Vicke Lindstrand and consisting of a grouping of massive glass columns that were made of stacks of glass sheets (fig. 9-17). The work was hailed for its innovative design and artistry.[42] According to one correspondent, "This original artwork signals an interesting new solution to the problem of fountain sculpture, weighing approximately six tons and standing three meters tall, with a base diameter of some two meters."[43] At night the fountain was lit by 3,000 bulbs creating a shimmering crystalline mass.[44] "With such a lighting scheme," wrote art critic Gustaf

Näsström, "the Orrefors fountain at the Swedish Pavilion is truly a sight to behold."[45]

The New York World's Fair was to be the last major international exhibition for many years to come. The Second World War broke out four months later, bringing to a close a dynamic era in the decorative arts. The architectural work that Orrefors and the other Swedish glassworks had produced during the interwar years had forged a strong alliance between art and industry, one that has continued to the present day.[46] Although some of the monumental works created in the period were later destroyed or removed, either during the war or as part of architectural reworkings, many have survived intact. These one-of-a-kind windows and wall panels typified the ornamentation of public spaces until the end of the Second World War. Sandblasted and engraved by the highly skilled professionals at Orrefors, they represent a high point in art glass, but they were also costly and time consuming. A quicker, cheaper way of decorating glass panels by etching soon replaced the laborious engraving process. Although etching never produced the same vivid qual-

ity as engraved glass, etched-glass windows and panels became ubiquitous in Swedish towns and cities. They were so common in fact that by the end of the 1940s the appeal of frosted glass in public spaces had been exhausted.

1. See, e.g., "Dekorativa fönster och lampor," Orrefors sale catalogue (1944), Archives of Orrefors Glassworks.

2. Axel L. Romdahl, "Konstindustrihallen i Göteborg," Svenska Slöjdföreningens Tidskrift (1923), p. 113.

3. Gregor Paulsson, "Sverige i Paris," Svenska Slöjdföreningens Tidskrift (1925), p. 107.

4. Ann Marie Herlitz-Gezelius, Orrefors: Ett svenskt glasbruk (Stockholm: Atlantis, 1984), pp. 124 – 25. Later, a more economical technique of decorating the fixtures by etching and acid-polishing was developed.

5. In addition to the chandeliers in the stair lobby, Orrefors produced blue lamps for the dress circle corridor, small blue hanging lamps for the upper circle, and ceiling lamps for the cloakrooms.

6. This aesthetic came to be called "Swedish Grace," a term coined by the British journalist Morton Shand in Architectural Review (August 1930). Robert Hult, who worked for the architect Ivar Tengbom, supervised the interior in which he incorporated his own designs for gilt brass lighting fixtures. See Hélène Reuterswärd, "Inredningen i Stockholms Konserthus," Ph.D. diss. (Stockholm University, 1983), pp. 4, 7.

7. Axel L. Romdahl, "Konsthantverket i Stockholms Konserthus," Svenska Slöjdföreningens Tidskrift (1926), pp. 9, 13 – 16.

8. One of the mirrors still hangs in the royal foyer but two others have since been removed. See Reuterswärd, "Inredningen i Stockholms Konserthus," pp. 4 – 30.

9. Among these designs was Model HD6, which was identical to the blue bowls Hald had produced for the Concert Hall's dress circle promenade. See the Orrefors portfolio of loose drawings (1926) in the Royal Library (Kungliga bibliotekets avdelning för okatalogiserade tryck).

10. Sale catalogue, Stockholms Auktionsverk (November 1 – 3), p. 201, nos. 6061, 6062.

11. Reuterswärd, "Inredningen i Stockholms Konserthus," p. 10. For a photograph of this lamp see Arthur Hald and Erik Wettergren, eds., Simon Gate, Edward Hald (Stockholm: Svenska Slöjdföreningen, 1948), p. 89.

12. For a transcript of the speech see "Stockholmsutställningens Program," Svenska Slöjdföreningens Tidskrift (1928), pp. 109 – 116.

13. Ibid.

14. Gregor Paulsson, Vackrare Vardagsvara (Stockholm: Svenska Slöjdföreningen, 1919). For a fuller discussion of this book, see chap. 3 in this volume.

15. Herlitz-Gezelius, Orrefors, p. 124.

16. See "Orrefors, Belysningsarmatur," sale catalogue (1937), cat. no. 4, in the Royal Library (Kungliga bibliotekets avdelning för okatalogiserade tryck). Also see chap. 8, in this volume. Saturn was designed in 1929; the other designs listed in this essay are undated in the catalogue.

17. Architect Ragnar Ossian Swensson (b. 1882) worked in Gothenburg with his partner A. Bjerke from 1911 to 1922. In 1911 he took first prize for his design of landshövdingehus, a kind of residence specific to Gothenburg in which the ground floor is of brick and the two upper floors of timber.

18. Gustaf Munthe, "Kvibergskapellet," Form (1936), pp. 22 – 23.

19. Ibid.

20. Renovation of the building's interior in 1992 included restoration of the furniture and rugs. The drinking fountain, which had disappeared long ago, was replaced by a copy based on Simon Gate's original drawings and made at Orrefors.

21. Claes Caldenby, ed., Göteborgs konserthus: ett album, (Gothenburg: White arkitekter, 1992).

22. Axel B. Larsson (1898–1975) began his career as a designer at Svenska Möbelfabrikerna Bodafors in 1925. He worked there until 1956 and became

well known for designing furniture en suite. See Nationalencyclopedien, vol. 12 (Höganäs, Sweden: Bokförlaget Bra Böcker, 1993), p. 139.

23. The expression "Swedish Modern" was coined by American reporters who had visited the Swedish pavilion in Paris in 1937. The term was first used in Sweden in 1938. See G. A. Berg, "Swedish Modern," Form (1938), p. 163.

24. Caldenby, Göteborgs konserthus.

25. For additional examples of Vicke Lindstrand's glass panels see Alastair Duncan, Orrefors Glass (Suffolk, England: Antique Collectors' Club, 1995), p. 128.

26. Alex L. Romdahl, "Hantverket i Göteborgs Konserthus," Form (1935), p. 204.

27. Ibid.

28. Archives of Orrefors Glassworks, drawing no. 1312. The chandelier was entered in the drafting-room log on July 31, 1936, and again August 3, with the notation that the final draft had been produced.

29. Märta Holkers, Edvin Öhrström: Skulptör i glas (Stockholm: Carlsson Bokförlag, 1991), pp. 85 – 87.

30. Although sculptor Karl Hultström (1884–1973) worked as a designer at Kosta Glassworks from 1917 to 1919 and again from 1927 to 1928, he did not create sculptural work in glass as did Öhrström. See Ann Marie Herlitz-Gezelius, Kosta (Lund, Sweden: Bokförlaget Signum, 1987), pp. 42, 43, 45, 148.

31. Holkers, Edvin Öhrström, pp. 88–90.

32. Ibid., p. 19. Öhrström was the first to use such brilliant colors in glass; Sven Palmqvist later used a dynamic palette when he introduced his "Ravenna" technique in 1948.

33. Surprisingly, the large sheet of glass had been purchased from a glassworks in Belgium. See Lars Thor, Legend i Glas: En bok om Vicke Lindstrand (Stockholm: Liber Förlag, 1982), p. 38.

34. Svea Lindstrand, "Glimtar från en världsutställnings tillblivelse," Form (1937), pp. 139 – 40.

35. Åke Stavenow, "Sverige i Paris," Form (1937), p. 126. After the exposition the window was shipped to its owner, the Swedish Cooperative Union and Wholesale Society, but it was broken in transport. See Lars Thor, Legend i Glas: En bok om Vicke Lindstrand (Stockholm: Liber Förlag, 1982), p. 38.

36. The glass panel in Halmstad is still in place; it is also illustrated in "Orrefors' special catalogue of decorative windows and lamps" (1944), pp. 6 – 7. Shortly after the Halmstad commission Öhrström designed a glass panel for the offices of AB Turitz & Co. in Gothenburg. Measuring 67 by 31 1/2 in. (170 by 80 cm), it depicted three links in the chain of consumption, representing manufacturer, seller, and consumer. Unfortunately it disappeared when the firm changed owners in the 1990s. For an illustration of this work, dated 1940, see ibid., p. 8.

37. Hald and Wettergren, Simon Gate, Edward Hald, pp. 134, 135, 147.

38. The Stockholm was never delivered because of the outbreak of war. It served as a military storage vessel in Trieste until it was bombed and sunk in 1945. See Bonniers Lexikon, vol. 13, p. 603. A later Swedish passenger ship with the same name was also ill-fated: it collided with the Andrea Doria on July 25, 1956.

39. The ship's decorative details were dispersed during the Second World

War when it was commandeered by the U.S. Marines for troop transport. See Anne-Marie Ericsson, Svenskt 1920-tal: Konstindustri och konsthantverk (Lund, Sweden: Bokförlaget, 1984), p. 61.

40. Herlitz-Gezelius, Orrefors, p. 126.

41. Åke Stavenow, "Världsutställningarna och New York World's Fair, 1939," Form (1939), p. 72.

42. Lindstrand continued to pursue the theme established with this fountain, later creating monumental sculptures consisting of thousands of sheets of plate glass that were stacked, glued, and form-cut into shimmering greenish sculptures. Thor, Legend i Glas, pp. 106–18.

43. Report in the Swedish newspaper, Svenska Dagbladet (March 1939); and see Thor, Legend i Glas, p. 39.

44. Stavenow, "Världsutställningarna och New York World's Fair," p. 126.

45. Thor, Legend i Glas, p. 39.

46. During the war the glassworks continued to produce light fixtures and glass panels for hotels, restaurants, factories, and corporate boardrooms. In the mid-1940s Orrefors was manufacturing elaborate, luxury chandeliers, some of which were designated "alla Venezia," designed by resident Orrefors artists (Herlitz-Gezelius, Orrefors, pp. 127 – 29). These pieces from the 1940s have been described as "the glassworks' grandiloquent chandeliers, which evoke the festiveness of the baroque chandelier in a modern form" ("Decorative windows and lamps," Orrefors sale catalogue with a foreword by Åke Stavenow [1944]). And that is probably as far as it is possible to stray from "Swedish Grace" and "Swedish Modern."

CHAPTER TEN

Modern Swedish Glass in America, 1924–1939

Derek E. Ostergard

Fig. 10-1. Vase designed by Simon Gate; Orrefors, ca. 1926. This was among the engraved glass shown at the Metropolitan Museum of Art in New York in 1927. (Metropolitan Museum of Art, Purchase, Edward C. Moore, Jr., Gift, 1927; acc. no. 27.96.1)

Before the First World War, Swedish glass was unrecognized in the American marketplace, but by the start of the Second World War, it had come to be acknowledged as the leading representation of Swedish modernism in the United States. At the same time, apart from other Swedish modernist work, this glass earned its own autonomous profile in the international arena of progressive design. It was shown in several carefully orchestrated, nonprofit exhibitions in the United States during the 1920s and 1930s (fig. 10-1).[1] These shows are historically significant in that they introduced modern Swedish decorative arts to a large number of educated and affluent consumers. The shows were reviewed favorably by the press and were perceived by critics as presenting work that was relevant to the needs of many Americans. Importantly, soon after the appearance of this Swedish material in America, it also received the endorsement of numerous major institutions. Several American museums selected examples of modern Swedish decorative arts for their permanent collections from these exhibitions. This work was chosen for its intrinsic aesthetic and technical qualities, and because it was hoped that it might inspire American designers and manufacturers to move from their own conservative positions to modern product lines.[2] Despite the extensive appearance of this Swedish material in the United States during the interwar years (1918–39), only Swedish glass would have a measurable impact on American designers and their output.[3] The reasons for this situation are complex but readily understood in light of a multitude of cultural, aesthetic, and social considerations.

The Hierarchy of Ancestry and Taste: The Swedish Dilemma in America

In most respects, Sweden and the Swedish community in this country were enigmas to many Americans in the early twentieth century. In the United States the Swedish immigrants were primarily concentrated in the Midwest, which tended to isolate them somewhat from the rest of the country.[4] The Swedes, as part of the wave of immigrants who moved to the United States after the middle of the nineteenth century, had been unable to partake in many of the opportunities available to immigrant groups that had arrived earlier. Those Americans whose Dutch, English, and French ancestors had securely established themselves in the seventeenth and eighteenth centuries in politics, trade, and society left little room at the top of the national hierarchy by the time the Swedes began to arrive in appreciable numbers.

The culture of early twentieth-century Sweden itself was essentially unknown in the United States and lacked the status enjoyed by other nations such as France and England. With the reapportioning of Europe following the Treaty of Versailles in 1919, other newer nations, as well as the new Soviet Union, France, and Great Britain, dominated world news and the attention of Americans. Finally, the international perception of Sweden as a nation and a society became even more complicated during the 1920s, when it entered a period of considerable political, economic, social, and artistic transition.

The pronounced national prejudices of Americans for specific European cultures was also played out in the discriminatory habits of designers, manufacturers, and consumers in this country. Around the turn of the century and until the time of the First World War, the British Arts and Crafts movement helped to shape the thinking of the progressive architectural and design community in America. Many conservative middle- and upper-middle-class Americans sought to express their ancestry or social aspirations by relying on the more academic elements of the design community. These individuals purchased copies of seventeenth- and eighteenth-century English furnishings which were often executed in hybrid Jacobean, Georgian, and Tudor idioms.

At the same time many other members of the American artistic and design communities viewed Paris as the epicenter of taste. A considerable number of late-nineteenth and early-twentieth-century American painters and sculptors went to Paris to study, and the design community had equally strong ties to France.[5] Ogden Codman, Edith Wharton, Elsie de Wolfe, and other tastemakers promoted French objects and concepts in their publications, and several generations of American architects thought that the École des Beaux Arts in Paris was the crucible of architectural learning.[6] The most affluent American consumer usually venerated French taste above all throughout the first half of the twentieth century.[7]

Although the predilection for French concepts and merchandise persisted in the United States after the late 1920s, its overall significance to the American community was augmented by progressive design concepts and objects that had emerged in Germany and Central Europe after 1918.[8] This material gained considerable credibility in the United States, especially

in museum and academic circles by the end of the 1920s. Among the group of emerging avant-garde designers working in America in the 1920s and 1930s, many were of Central European birth or ancestry and likely to be receptive to these new concepts.[9]

This wave of Central European/German influence increased during the Depression, especially through the increased premium placed on functionalist work. In light of the global economic situation, the egalitarian goal of mass-produced, inexpensive objects that were devoid of expensive ornament received considerable support in museum and academic circles.[10] At the beginning of the 1930s, the Bauhaus school of design, considered by many educated Americans to be the epicenter of this design objective, received its first substantial showing in the United States in Cambridge, Massachusetts, at the Harvard Society for Contemporary Art.[11] After the middle of the 1930s, there was a substantial influx of former Bauhaus professors into the United States, the result of political and personal repression in Germany.[12] Many professionals in museum, academic, and design circles came under the influence of these individuals who arrived in the United States with reputations of near mythical proportions. Before the Second World War, the increasing premium placed upon these individuals was documented in a 1938 exhibition—Bauhaus, 1919–1928—which was assembled and shown by the Museum of Modern Art in New York City.[13]

To further complicate these circumstances, Swedish modernist work was not only competing with English, French, and German work for attention in the American marketplace, but often it was inextricably grouped with that larger and aesthetically diverse body of modernist decorative arts that was generally considered Scandinavian or Nordic. As a result, work of Finnish origin, such as that of Eliel Saarinen working in the United States and Alvar Aalto in Finland, often was considered Scandinavian in the 1930s, along with the Swedish work. The fact that the silversmith firm of Georg Jensen originated in Copenhagen, Denmark, had little relevance to most Americans.[14] It was all grouped together as "Scandinavian."

Promoters of Swedish design in America sought critical and commercial attention in a crowded and often temperamental marketplace. During the Depression, when much of this Swedish material was introduced for the first time, many sophisticated American consumers with an interest in modernism experienced a dramatic reduction in their buying power. Simultaneously, markets became increasingly conservative, and the challenge of bringing a new product from concept through production and to the consumer was a financial risk few American companies were prepared to take. A worthwhile aesthetic or technical concept from abroad may have been appreciated but was often avoided because of the limited and highly volatile market.

The Aesthetic Ambiguity of Swedish Modern Decorative Arts

Another significant reason for the lack of a discernible Swedish influence in this country lies in the Swedish decorative arts themselves. During the interwar period, Swedish modernism underwent three significant aesthetic transformations, leading to the perception of a lack of focus in this national body of work. Between the end of the First World War and the end of the 1920s, Swedish modern decorative arts were characterized by their reliance on neoclassical motifs, forms, and proportions that were often tempered by mannerist qualities. This early work was usually executed with a superb attention to detail resulting in substantial costs. Shown almost exclusively in upper-echelon stores and in the prestigious design and world's fairs of the era, this work was consistently recognized for its elitist associations.

Although this neoclassicism remained central to much Swedish progressive work until the Second World War, by the late 1920s it was augmented by functionalism and the austerity dictated by that particular approach to design. Influenced by earlier revolutionary developments on the Continent, several Swedish designers and architects moved quickly to produce buildings and objects that were in accord with this powerful tendency. This new wave in thinking emerged with considerable solidarity at the Stockholm Exhibition of 1930. The radical simplicity of the work shown there was the antithesis of the neoclassicism that had come to be considered modern and Swedish by the international consumer.

The pursuit of this utilitarian approach to design often encouraged the elimination of personal expression, and by the middle of the 1930s many Swedish artists and designers working in the decorative arts rejected it. Simultaneously, many individuals in the design community exploited the vocabulary of the Surrealists who had emerged in Western Europe in the 1920s. A biomorphic form language, the antithesis of the classical idiom, explored a non–compass-and-ruler approach to line and utilized forms and motifs often associated with the human unconscious. Many Swedish artists, especially those working in the glassworks, exploited this idiom. Thus, the considerable diversity of aesthetic expressions coming out of Sweden in a mere two decades made it difficult for most American designers and manufacturers to be influenced by any sustained and focused development in that nation's design.

In the larger world of twentieth-century decorative arts, it is difficult to assign an influence to a particular work or design concept due to the interconnectedness of that world. The ease of travel, the emergence of photography and its use by the growing fields of journalism and publishing, and the significance of trade and world fairs made the design field more international: the transferal of ideas became nearly instantaneous. The often hybrid nature of aesthetic innovations, especially after the turn of the century, also makes the search for the origin of an idea difficult. In the United States, in the midst of a barrage of new, nonindigenous concepts, elements of design vocabulary that may have been perceived by some as Swedish were actually borrowed from somewhere else or, conversely, credit for a Swedish idea was given elsewhere.[15]

During the 1920s and 1930s, the inroads made by Swedish products into the American retail establishment are difficult to measure. Apart from special exhibitions, Swedish work, when shown in retail settings, does not appear to have been marketed as Swedish in most cases, nor was it usually grouped with other Swedish pieces.[16] Swedish glass was sold with American glass as well as that of other nations. When Swedish furniture was retailed in the United States, it was rarely sold with Swedish textiles or other Swedish products. The sale of household furnishings was a compartmentalized and carefully controlled industry dominated by decorators, designers, and store owners.

Isolated in retail establishments from other Swedish goods, Swedish decorative arts rarely had a substantial aesthetic or conceptual impact based on their national origin. On a few occasions, American retailers sold foreign merchandise in national monolithic offerings devoted to modernism; however, these occurrences were rare and confined mostly to the second half of the 1920s.[17] Assessment of the impact of Swedish goods sold in the American marketplace is limited because of fragmented and poorly recorded documentation. In the end, the clearest area in which the appearance of Swedish material can be appraised is in ceremonial, not-for-profit exhibitions that were sent to the United States in the 1920s and 1930s.

The Early Years of Swedish Modernism

What makes the sudden appearance of modern Swedish decorative arts in America in the 1920s so remarkable is that the objects themselves had been a revelation to the Swedes just a few years before. The translation of this artistic flowering from a national to a global market was stunning. Initially much of this early progressive work was based on Swedish neoclassical designs of the late eighteenth century. The appearance of this new, but vaguely familiar work was reassuring to many Swedes who could readily discern its origins. Some of the more humble examples of emerging Swedish modernist work had their first cohesive exposure at the 1917 Hemutställningen (Home Exhibition) at the Liljevalchs Konsthall in Stockholm.

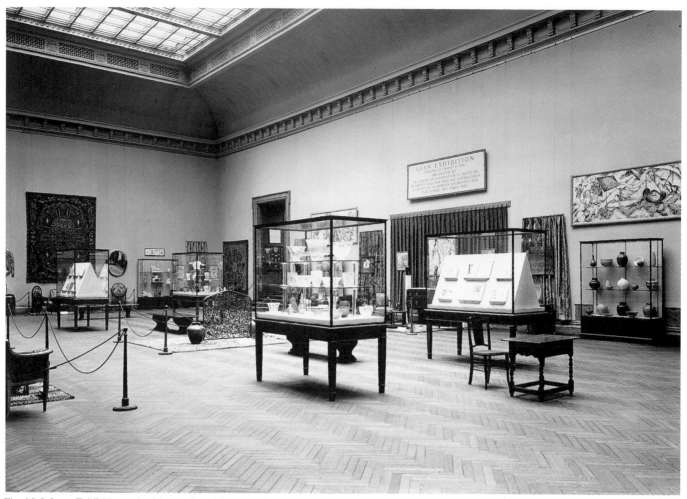

Fig. 10-2. Loan Exhibition at the Metropolitan Museum of Art, 1926. (The Metropolitan Museum of Art, New York)

Although individual pieces of modernist glass and furniture were seen in some shops and department stores in Sweden from that period on, it was not until the 300th anniversary of the founding of the city of Gothenburg in 1923 that a comprehensive showing was assembled.[18] In that enormous Jubilee Exposition, architecture, decorative arts, painting, and sculpture were presented in a unified manner so that there was an overwhelming aesthetic consistency to the exhibition. In the same year, the monumental Stockholm City Hall, designed by the architect Ragnar Östberg, opened with much of its lavish interior decorated in the new idiom. The exposure of this work occurred abroad almost simultaneously, although initially by means of design publications alone.[19] By 1925 at the Paris Exposition des Arts Décoratifs et Industriels Modernes, the Swedish Pavilion and the separate Swedish installations in the Grand Palais and in the Galerie des Invalides revealed this cohesive and mature vocabulary to an appreciative international audience. It would take a decade, however, from the time of the Liljevalchs Home Exhibition in 1917, and less than five years from the Gothenburg exhibition in 1923, for the Swedes to bring an official, monolithic assembly of their modernist venture to the United States.

Exhibition of Modern Swedish Decorative Arts in America in the 1920s

Before the organized showings of Swedish material in the late 1920s, there was a limited interest in America in the new developments in Swedish design, and especially glass, prior to the 1925 exposition in France. That support came primarily from a few principal museums that had either purchased, or received as gifts, examples of the new Swedish decorative arts. It does not appear as though these items were purchased from retail establishments in the United States, however, but rather from stores in Sweden.

One of the earliest of these purchases occurred in

1925 at the Art Institute of Chicago where a permanent collection of modern decorative art had been started in 1924.[20] The first piece of modern Swedish glass to enter the Art Institute's collection was an engraved decanter by Simon Gate that was put on display in Gunsaulus Hall at the museum in January 1925.[21]

The Metropolitan Museum of Art in New York City, however, became the epicenter for the promotion of Swedish modernism in the interwar era. Through special exhibitions, publications, and key acquisitions, the museum revealed its ongoing support. In 1924 the museum purchased an engraved bowl and undertray designed by Simon Gate and a standing cup and cover designed by Edward Hald for its permanent collection.[22] These appear to be the earliest examples of Swedish modern material to enter an American museum.

Following the Paris exposition in 1925, the Metropolitan Museum affirmed its emerging commitment to modernism and the decorative arts on several fronts in 1926.[23] Not only did the museum purchase several important pieces from the Paris exposition, but it also commissioned work from exhibitors at the fair and continued to host annual exhibitions of industrial art, a program it had initiated in 1917.[24] In 1926 the museum established a permanent gallery for the display of modern decorative arts and hosted a large exhibition of progressive decorative arts that had been shown in Paris in the previous year (fig. 10-2).[25] The show was dominated by French work; Swedish work was represented only by Orrefors glass, including a vase and undertray by Edward Hald called "Fireworks" and two vases by Simon Gate called "Heaven and Hell" and "Bacchanalia."[26]

Several months after the closing of the 1926 exhibition, the Metropolitan Museum presented a lavish offering devoted solely to Swedish modern art entitled "Exhibition of Swedish Contemporary Decorative Arts" (fig. 10-3). On view from January 18 to February 27, 1927, the exhibition traveled later that year to

Fig. 10-3. Exhibition of Swedish Contemporary Decorative Arts, The Metropolitan Museum of Art, New York, 1927. The installation designed by Carl Bergstrom includes Orrefors's lighting fixtures and a small display of art glass. (The Metropolitan Museum of Art, New York)

Fig. 10-4. Exhibition of Swedish Contemporary Decorative Arts, The Art Institute of Chicago, 1927. (Svensk Form, Bildarkivet, Stockholm.)

Detroit and Chicago (fig. 10-4).[27] Relying on the late nineteenth-century concept of *Gesamtkunstwerk*, or total work of art, the Swedes were responsible not only for the design and production of the objects, but also for the design and construction of the installation.[28] There was a perception that the material shown at the Metropolitan Museum was somehow not luxurious and was therefore more suitable for the tastes of the democratic American society.

Up until the Second World War, proponents of Swedish modern design would stress the similarities between Sweden and the United States. There was a sustained attempt to convince Americans that the simplicity of Swedish goods was somehow appropriate for the more informal American way of life. Even the introduction in the Metropolitan Museum of Art catalogue indirectly addressed this issue while simultaneously extracting Orrefors from the equation: "Sweden is not a rich country. There is, accordingly, little demand for articles of luxury. With a few exceptions, such, for instance, as some of the glass of Orrefors, contemporary Swedish decorative art is far from expensive or luxurious in character."[29]

The furniture by Carl Hörvik, made by Nordiska Kompaniet, and the wide assortment of hand-worked presentation silver in this exhibition at the Metropolitan Museum revealed the fallacy of this statement. From the elaborate ceramics of Wilhelm Kåge to the gold, silver, and enamel objects exhibited by Guldsmeds A.B. I Stockholm, it is apparent that the vast majority of the pieces in the exhibition were meant to dazzle the visitor with their luxuriousness. The Spartan qualities incorrectly ascribed to them were not evident.

During 1927 the Metropolitan Museum made several significant purchases of engraved glass from the exhibition, and these thirteen pieces became part of its permanent collection. One of these, a vase by Edward Hald (see fig. 10-1), was featured on the cover *The Metropolitan Museum of Art Bulletin* (January 1927). Engraved pieces constitute the bulk of these purchases, including some of the more elaborate designs executed by Orrefors during the 1920s. The museum also acquired three pieces of Orrefors's glass made with the "graal" technique, which was becoming increasingly out of fashion in the Swedish marketplace by the time of the Metropolitan Museum exhibition. It may be that the usually pale palette achieved through the graal process, as well as the rather limpid delineation of the ornamental motifs, contrasted with the bolder colors and hard-edged ornament usually associated with emerging avant-garde taste in America in the mid-1920s.

Orrefors glass was also directly marketed in the United States at this time by principals of the firm. In 1928 Edward Hald and J. H. Danius, the director of Orrefors, traveled throughout the United States to pro-

mote modern Swedish glass. Hald, who spoke English, lectured at museums and department stores on modern glass in Europe.[30] He was an influential spokesperson for Orrefors and was probably responsible for the ongoing placement and expansion of Orrefors glass in the American marketplace during that year. As a result, the presence of Orrefors glass, if not work by the other Swedish manufacturers, was increasingly evident in the china and glass departments of major department stores, as well as smaller firms specializing in the sale of gift items.[31]

A particularly significant installation utilizing Orrefors glass occurred during Hald's 1928 trip to the United States. While Eliel Saarinen was in the midst of his architectural plans for the enormous complex of buildings at the Cranbrook Academy of Art, he and George Booth, the benefactor of the school, received an impromptu visit from Hald and Danius.[32] Together, the four men modified an existing Orrefors model as a prototype for twenty light fixtures that Orrefors fabri-

Fig. 10-5. Dining hall of the Cranbrook Academy of Art, Michigan, ca. 1928–29, with lighting fixtures by Orrefors. (Cranbrook Academy of Art/Museum)

Fig. 10-6. First Class vestibule on the M/S *Kungsholm*.

cated for the main dining hall of the school (fig. 10-5). These multitiered fixtures, each nearly seven feet tall, were composed of a series of fluted, open, glass vases, linked by metal rods. The Cranbrook interiors, however, were seen only by a small, select group of Americans, and the impact of the Orrefors fixtures was diminished somewhat by the scale of the installation.

The introduction of Americans to another extensive installation of Swedish modern design occurred on December 3, 1928, when the M/S *Kungsholm* entered New York Harbor.[33] This transatlantic passenger ship, launched by the Swedish-American Line, followed the lead established by the French government, which had promoted French avant-garde design through its great ocean liners. In 1926 the *Isle de France* made its maiden voyage to the United States as a fully realized venture advertising progressive French furniture, glass, porcelain, art, and rugs. The Germans and English also utilized these transatlantic ships for the marketing of their national prestige through the use of modern design.

Although considerably more intimate and less emphatically modern than the interiors of French Line ships, those of the *Kungsholm* (fig. 10-6) were considered noteworthy for their bold color schemes and

reliance upon a severe but highly theatrical neoclassicism, the antithesis of the more lyrical neoclassicism developed by other Swedish designers such as Gunnar Asplund in the 1910s and 1920s. Under the artistic direction of the Swedish architect Carl Bergsten, the M/S *Kungsholm* presented the work of many of the major Swedish artists, workshops, and companies engaged in the production of modern decorative arts.[34] Furniture, textiles, ceramics, and floor coverings were all made in Sweden in accordance with the modernist theme. Although accorded considerable coverage in the American press, the ship was seen by only an affluent group of individuals who had to sail to Sweden. Within the decorating scheme of the ship itself, Orrefors contributed several substantial elements, including mirrors with engraved designs by Simon Gate, a glass-topped table with engraved signs of the zodiac by Edward Hald, lighting fixtures (produced through Nordiska Kompaniet), and engraved and cut vases, as well the glassware for the dining rooms.[35] A small booklet describing the ship was published several years later, presumably as a souvenir for passengers. Gustaf L. Munthe, the author of the pamphlet, was apologetically aware of the limitations of the ship. By the time the booklet was printed, the lavish and theatrical appearance of its interiors were in accordance neither with the global depression nor the state of aesthetic and social thinking in the world of avant- garde Swedish design. According to Munthe:

> The Kungsholm was completed in 1928, a year before the great world financial crisis began. Swedish arts and crafts were of an entirely different character then compared with the present day. The tradition of bygone days, a strong feeling for the gaily decorative as well as a decidedly personal manner of decoration were some of their principal characteristics. . . . One can readily understand why the Kungsholm has been called a floating museum. Ships are not supposed to be museums, but on the other hand, it is justifiable to make the interior of a large liner more luxurious and varied than would be considered appropriate for a similar interior on shore.[36]

The strident classicism of the interiors of the ship, stark and emphatically reminiscent of early-nineteenth-century neoclassicism, may be said to have been something of a revelation for American designers. With its bold ornament and striking color schemes, the ship's interiors may have had an influence on American interior designers such as Dorothy Draper, whose icy interiors of the 1930s, based on a monumental, reductivist classicism, bear some resemblance to those of the M/S *Kungsholm*.

In 1928 and 1929 the American Federation of the

Arts (AFA) circulated an exhibition of modern ceramics, made by both artisan and factory, which traveled to eight museums in the United States.[37] The Swedes, however, did not figure prominently in this assemblage. The Swedish section, consisting of thirteen entries, was dominated by ceramicists Arthur Carlson Percy and Wilhelm Kåge. In comparison the Germans exhibited eighty-one entries, the French seventy-nine, the United States seventy-one, the British fifty-nine, the Danish forty-nine and the Austrians forty-three. Dwarfed by the Danes as the only other Scandinavians who contributed to this show, the Swedes must not have been considered significant contributors by the organizers of this show of modernist work.

In 1929, nearly three years after hosting the exhibition of Swedish contemporary decorative arts, the Metropolitan Museum of Art in New York was again the first venue for a traveling exhibition of modern decorative arts entitled "International Exhibition: Contemporary Glass and Rugs." It traveled to museums in Boston, Philadelphia, Chicago, St. Louis, Pittsburgh, Dayton, Cincinnati, and Baltimore. Although the Swedish section was embedded in a exhibition that contained work from Austria, Denmark, England, France, Germany, Holland, Italy, and the United States, it nevertheless made a strong showing despite the fact that a recent workers's strike in Sweden prevented many impressive pieces of engraved glass from being included.[38]

In addition to the engraved glass that had critically triumphed at Gothenburg in 1923, Paris in 1925, and exhibitions and New York, Detroit, and Chicago in 1927, Orrefors also showed lighting fixtures and table glassware from their factory at Sandvik, which was known for its less expensive table services. The Metropolitan Museum of Art purchased a large fluted bowl by Simon Gate from the AFA exhibition.

The French section comprised the largest number of entries (196). The sheer variety of individual artists and factories that were shown by the French far exceeded that shown by other exhibitors.[39] The Germans were second with fifty-seven entries, and the Swedes were third with forty-four.[40] That the French had nearly four times as many entries as the Swedes was in part the result of the Francophile tastes of the Americans, and the inarguably diverse range of superlative art glass produced by the French. The size of the Swedish section may have been based on the general recognition of the technical and aesthetic limitations of the Swedish glass industry in the late 1920s with its most prestigious pieces mostly ornamented with engraving. Even Erik Wettergren, the preeminent promoter of Swedish modernism, had recognized the state of development of Swedish glass at the end of 1927, when he wrote:

The Swedish vitric-art is not so complicated as the French, which seems to issue from some mysterious and magic furnace, but despite its limited technical methods, it also covers an extensive field, for it is as well suited for the castle as the cottage, for the rooms of the museum as for the table of middle-class people or workmen. In its most costly engraved pieces it has a real, though somewhat distant kinship with what is undoubtably Europe's noblest vitric-art, namely Lobmeyr's, so full of tradition and modern spirit.[41]

This open recognition by a Swede of the place of Swedish glass in the international arena on the eve of the 1930s illustrates not only Wettergren's objectivity but also the need for Swedish glassmakers to broaden their range of technical and aesthetic expression if they were to continue to figure prominently in the design world. The AFA exhibition of glass documented the end of this important period at the Orrefors factory when engraved decoration still held center stage. Unfortunately this exhibition came several years too early in light of the dramatic artistic and technical growth that would occur within Swedish glass production in the 1930s.

Historically, the late 1920s were a transitional period for Orrefors because monumental shifts in the aesthetics, techniques, and, importantly, new personnel were about to occur at the factory. In particular, a young artist, Vicke Lindstrand, had joined the firm in 1928 and had yet to produce some of his most significant early work, which altered much of the firm's output. The piece called "Pearl Diver" reveals the new manner of simplified narrative engraving that would become a signature of the engraved work produced by the firm in the 1930s. The major transition in the engraved work of Simon Gate from his earlier, meticulously detailed designs to his bolder work of the very early 1930s had yet to occur under the influence of Lindstrand. Gate's fluid, biomorphic designs, which were introduced at the 1930 Stockholm Exhibition, had not yet been developed. The revision of the graal technique as well as the development of the revolutionary "ariel" and "mykene" techniques were still several years away from invention and production. Orrefors, poised on the cusp of a creative outburst in 1929/1930, gave no indication in the exhibitions of the late 1920s of the wealth of technical and aesthetic diversity that would soon occur. Nevertheless, the glass that was shown serves as a summation of a decade of phenomenal growth.

Swedish Modern Glass in America in the 1930s

The exhibition of Swedish modern decorative arts changed considerably in the 1930s, as did the promotion of much that was modernist and European in the United States. The immediate explanation for this lies in

Fig. 10-7. Interior of the Swedish pavilion at the Century of Progress exposition in Chicago, 1933–34.

the global economic situation: the overall return on the investment generated from the assembly and circulation of ambitious traveling shows of only decorative arts was no longer justifiable. Prestige, however great, was difficult to rationalize, much less measure, in terms of the economic outlay required by these exhibitions. In addition, by the 1930s, Swedish modernist goods, as well as other Continental pieces, were more available in American retail stores than they had been in the previous decade. Despite the guise of modernism they utilized, they were no longer as newsworthy as they had been in the 1920s, before the market had become saturated.

Perhaps more importantly, within the broad framework of the American design world there had been a rapid coming of age. By the late 1920s, American designers, as well as emigré designers working in America, had been called upon by critics, select consumers, and manufacturers to produce design idioms that were less dependent on European prototypes and that utilized native themes and concepts, while addressing the specific needs of American lifestyles.

Whether this was achieved without a certain unspoken reliance upon European prototypes is doubtful, but it remains certain that the days of the great traveling exhibitions of European modernist decorative arts were essentially over. From that time on, American organizations and institutions were more intent on showing American production to the public than they were in showing the work of non-nationals.

European work continued to be exhibited, but through the large international shows that occurred in the United States in the 1930s, specifically three principal expositions: A Century of Progress Fair, held in Chicago in 1933; Building the World of Tomorrow, in New York in 1939 and 1940; and The Golden Gate Exposition held in San Francisco in 1939 and 1940. Within those fairs, industrial design and handicrafts were embedded in the large interdisciplinary pavilions that promoted the cultural, political, ethnic, economic, and geographic resources of their respective nations. Although the promotion and sale of those goods allied with a national identity remained one of the significant motivations for manufacturers to exhibit at the fair, the overall theme of the expositions was beginning to change. Concepts such as progress, the future, and optimistic "blue sky" themes became the inspirational focus of these monumental and, as some felt, unnecessary exhibitions in the midst of hard times. The Chicago fair, assembled to commemorate the centennial of the city's founding, came at one of the lowest points of the Great Depression.[42]

The decorative arts section of the Swedish pavilion of the Chicago fair (fig. 10-7) documented the changes that had occurred in the Swedish design community since the Stockholm Exhibition in 1930.[43] The elegant neoclassicism that had triumphed at the 1923 Gothenburg Jubilee Exhibition and had established the reputation of Swedish modernism was suddenly no longer part of the equation for the future of modern Swedish decorative arts outside of Sweden. In many respects, there was a recognition among some designers and makers that modernist work that was aesthetically more austere and less dependent on historicist antecedents was the future route to financial and critical success. Through the use of designs suited to the standardization of the manufacturing process, well-made, competitively priced household goods could be distributed to a wider segment of the population. This was the essence of the Swedish installation of decorative arts in Chicago.[44] The glory of Swedish modern design of the 1920s had been rooted in the luxury trades. That market, although still significant to many makers in Sweden, was now augmented by the new aesthetic that addressed an entirely different, but ever-expanding niche in the marketplace: the educated, but economically restricted, consumer. In the great fairs of the early 1930s, basic aesthetic and technical quality mattered, but luxury did not. The catalogue for the Swedish decorative arts at the fair underscored this important shift. The new attitude was clearly expressed in the introduction to the catalogue:

> But time changes. If arts and crafts are to be entitled to exist, they must not concentrate on breaking their own record from a technical or artistic point of view. Working only on that line, it soon loses the track leading to the actual goal, that of providing the masses of people with glass, ceramics, furnitures [sic], silver and textile [sic] of high quality at reasonable prices. Industrial arts and home-crafts have to follow the old rule "Supply and demand."[45]

The glass that was illustrated in the catalogue of Swedish arts and crafts shown in Chicago may not have been fully representative of the shift in Swedish glass, but, nevertheless, with the exception of pieces of art glass engraved with figurative ornament, the selection consisted of relatively austere stemware.

In 1936 the Metropolitan Museum of Art revealed the extent of its commitment to modern Swedish decorative arts in an exhibition devoted to its vast holdings of glass borrowed from the different departments within the museum.[46] Spanning millennia and global in its presentation, the exhibition also included material of recent production. The modern Swedish glass, the oldest of which had entered the museum's collection only a little more than a decade before, was almost exclusively the output of Orrefors.[47] The Metropolitan Museum had not turned its back on the Swedish production even during the Depression; three of the pieces of glass on exhibit had been purchased since 1929. The exhibition devoted a vitrine to Swedish glass (fig. 10-8). With the exception of two small graal pieces and some cut glass, the Swedish glass on exhibit was engraved and none of it was solely utilitarian.[48] Again, as with the exhibition of contemporary glass and rugs circulated by the AFA in 1929 and 1930, this exhibition did not reveal the explosion of aesthetic and technical

Fig. 10-8. Vitrine with Swedish glass, including the bowl called "Vindrosen" designed by Edward Hald (bottom row, center), in the 1936 glass exhibition at the Metropolitan Museum of Art. (The Metropolitan Museum of Art, New York)

Fig. 10-9. Glass display in the Swedish pavilion at the New York World's Fair, 1939. (From Paulsson, *Modernt Svenskt Glas*)

innovations that was to take place at Orrefors in the 1930s, even though some of that explosion occurred in 1936. The new, heavy graal technique and the mykene technique, with their individual aesthetic expressions, were in the earliest stages of production when this exhibition opened in New York, and the "ariel" process had not yet been invented.

Three years later, in 1939, at the New York World's Fair, Americans had the opportunity to see the last great national offering of Swedish decorative arts before the Second World War. The Swedish Pavilion was centrally located off the exposition's principal walkway[49] near the heroic and dominating Trylon and Perisphere, the most memorable images of the exposition. The architecture of the Swedish pavilion was considerably more demure and was recognized by critics as being both progressive and allied with tradition. The organizers of the Swedish Pavilion had absorbed many of the lessons learned through the difficult years of the 1930s, especially at the Paris exposition of 1937, which had been particularly competitive in terms of the design and packaging of each pavilion. Perhaps more successfully than most of the installations presented by different nations, the Swedish Pavilion responded to the

fair's principal theme of "Building the World of Tomorrow."[50] Rather than utilizing futuristic themes as did many of the exhibitors, the Swedish pavilion was more rooted in the present with their pavilion. The organizers of the Swedish Pavilion sought to reveal the great social strides that the nation had made in the previous decade to secure a higher standard of living for its citizens. The production of well-designed goods had contributed enormously to that goal and the pavilion paid homage to that reality.

According to the official statement provided by the Swedish government, one of the points of Swedish Pavilion was the significance of the country's indigenous decorative arts.[51] These were considered essential to the pavilion, and they were used in several different ways: as overall furnishings of the interior including the restaurant; in the individual decorative arts installations for glass (fig. 10-9), ceramics, textiles, metalwork, and furniture that were located in the principal hall; and in the five individual room settings that were situated along a central corridor. This last portion of the pavilion included a drawing room by Carl Malmsten, a combined kitchen and living room for a farmhouse by G. A. Berg, and living room for a weekend lodge at the sea by Elias Svedberg. The reviews of the Swedish model rooms, in particular, cite qualities of simplicity and grace, superior workmanship, originality, lightness of effect, high quality, inherent honesty, as well as stating that they were functional, unpretentious and beautiful—assessments that any nationalistic critic, manufacturer or designer would most likely appropriate for describing the output of his or her own country or when seeking to be gracious about the work of a nonnational. In fact, many of these ambiguous words and expressions were used by the press when describing the contents of other pavilions, even when comparing the contents to indigenous taste and production. "The most interesting furniture items on the Fair grounds are to be found in the foreign concessions. The five model interiors at the Swedish Pavilion come first, because their design is applicable to the present American trend."[52]

The author of this article suggested that there were parallels between Swedish modernist furnishings and extant American modernist work, but not a dependency of the American material on the Swedish designs on display. It was generally held that American modernist work had entered its own mature phase and was capable of withstanding comparison with the work of the more established Swedes.

A comparison of the work shown at the Metropolitan Museum of Art in 1927 and the Swedish installation in New York twelve years later reveals that there had been no major shift in designers or manufacturers who where chosen to represent Sweden. Wilhelm Kåge, Elsa Gullberg, Carl Malmsten, Simon Gate, and

Edward Hald as well as Nordiska Kompaniet, Guldsmedsaktiebolaget, Orrefors, Kosta, and Rörstrand, who were among the exhibitors at the Metropolitan Museum in 1927, also appeared in the New York World's Fair in 1939. An examination of their work, however, does reveal a seismic change in the aesthetics of most of the work exhibited. At the 1939 international showing in New York, most exhibitions were based on functionalist principles. The graceful neoclassicism of the 1920s, although still popular in the Nordic countries and elsewhere, was out of place in the world of tomorrow in New York.

Textiles that relied on texture and color rather than woven and printed neoclassical motifs were now popular. The mannerist furnishings of the previous decade by Malmsten—for example, the saber legs and ambitious marquetry—were gone, replaced by pale wood forms, seating pieces low to the floor, and case pieces devoid of ornament. Even goldsmiths and silversmiths, traditionally attuned to the world of affluence, had eliminated many of the decorative elements so apparent years before. Only glass continued to show a clear allegiance to the earlier elitist work in terms of its use of extensive engraving, superlative crystal and elaborate new techniques.

The fidelity of Swedish progressive glass to its own recently fabricated traditions of elitism is understood in light of the fact that much of what was shown in the glass section was art glass. Art glass had not embraced the new functionalism, and functionalist glass would not hold the attention of the general public. The greater world of Swedish design may have changed significantly in the 1930s, but the principal glassworks such as Kosta and Orrefors would continue to rely upon their most virtuosic creations to garner attention. The glass shown at the fair was dominated by Orrefors, and its engraved glass still held the attention and respect of the reviewers.[53] In the official publication of the Royal Swedish Commission on the Swedish Pavilion, glass was lavishly illustrated and given pride of place. Luxury wares dominated the illustrations, including engraved work by Lindstrand, Gate, and Palmqvist, as well as two significant pieces of the new graal glass.[54] The monumental glass fountain by Vicke Lindstrand for Orrefors, however, was the principal piece of glass in the pavilion (fig. 10-10). Weighing nearly six tons, it captured the attention of the public. Internally illuminated, it was perhaps the largest functioning art glass ever made by Orrefors. Modeled on branches of coral, with large glass blossoms blown like open polyps, this piece was positioned prominently in the reflecting pool in the open courtyard of the pavilion.

The Golden Gate International Exhibition, held in San Francisco in 1939, honored the completion of the Golden Gate Bridge and the San Francisco–Oakland Bay Bridge. It lacked the dominating futuristic edge of the New York World's Fair. In its commemoration of the linking of the bay area of San Francisco, however, the fair was connected with the concept of advancement promoted by the Century of Progress exhibition held in Chicago six years before. Swedish modernist work was presented at the San Francisco fair under the guise of a national offering, but the installation itself had been assembled in the United States. The catalogue reveals that the lenders were private individuals and American retailers and wholesalers, primarily from the West Coast.[55] Neither the Swedish government nor the Svenska Slöjdföreningen appear to have been sponsors of the decorative arts section.

The decorative arts section of the exhibition, curated by the textile designer, Dorothy Wright Liebes,[56] presented a rich cross-section of Swedish modern design. Most of the objects and installations on view were sufficiently well known to sophisticated American audiences through magazines, department stores, and

Fig. 10-10. Fountain by Vicke Lindstrand in the central courtyard of the Swedish Pavilion at the New York World's Fair, 1939. (From Wurts, The New York World's Fair)

Fig. 10-11. Swedish pavilion at the Golden Gate Exposition, San Francisco, California, 1939. (From Huldt, Konsthantverk och hemslojkd i Sverige)

boutiques, as well as the other exhibitions of the 1930s. Nevertheless, the breadth of Swedish material was considerable and was installed in a complex series of model rooms and special installations. According to the object list, glass was the most significant entry in the Swedish section (fig. 10-11).[57] Many decorative-art historians have claimed that engraving ceased to be an important component of the output of the Swedish glass factories in the 1930s, but this was not the case. Technically superlative engraving, often tempered by a humorous subject matter and exquisite drafting, was still a hallmark of the work of several glassworks, especially Orrefors, in the San Francisco exhibition.[58]

The Impact of Swedish Glass on the Production of Glass in America

Swedish furniture, metalwork, textiles, and ceramics had little immediate or specific impact on American production during the 1920s and 1930s. The elaborate marquetry used on the furniture of Carl Hörvik and Carl Malmsten had no influence on North American work of the period. French textiles, as much as French fashion design, remained unrivaled in the minds of fashion-conscious Americans, leaving little room for Swedish material. Even the trademark ceramics of Arthur Percy and Wilhelm Kåge knew no progeny in the United States. The preeminent American silversmithing firms of Tiffany and Gorham, whose clientele was known for its conservatism in the twentieth century, rarely made significant forays into the aesthetics of Swedish modernism. When working in a progressive idiom, however, the firms tended to emulate the critically acclaimed work of Georg Jensen of Denmark.

By the end of the interwar era, although glass was as well received as other Swedish decorative arts in New York and San Francisco, it was imitated in a limited manner in the United States. The source of its appeal, however, did not lie in the new techniques and aesthetics that were shown in 1939. Its influence was revealed in the earlier work that had built the reputation of Swedish glass, specifically the firm of Orrefors, between 1917 and the end of the 1920s. Graal and engraved glass, both of which had been exhibited in the United States in the previous decade, would have the greatest impact in America in the interwar period.

In terms of the influence of Swedish modern glass on U.S. production, the most powerful, but essentially unspoken, connections were made over a period of two decades between Orrefors and the firm of Steuben Glass Works, founded in 1903 in Corning, New York, by the British-born glassmaker, Frederick Carder. A tireless experimenter in glass, Carder's own prodigious output often paralleled that of his contemporaries and competitors.[59]

At the Steuben Art Division of Corning Glass Works in the late 1920s, a stunning similarity between the Swedish modernist work and American production became evident. The "intarsia" glass developed by Carder and introduced in the late 1920s bears a striking resemblance to Orrefors graal pieces—in terms of their forms, colors, and delicate ornament. Graal glass from Orrefors had been shown for the first time officially in the United States at the Metropolitan Museum of Art in 1927, but it had been actively exhibited internationally since 1917 and illustrated on numerous occasions from the early 1920s.

Carder, when he was in his nineties, claimed that he had worked on a technique similar to his intarsia of the 1920s as early as 1916 or 1917.[60] In those early examples, he had laid out his decorative design in fragments of colored glass on the marver (a polished stone or metal slab) and then a gather (molten glass on a blowpipe) was rolled over this design in order to embed the pattern in the molten glass. This was reheated so that the fragments of colored glass eventually fused but retained their original decorative arrangement. At that point, the final form of the object was worked out by the blower. The Swedish technique was dramatically different in that it involved the use of an overlay on a blank, with the decorative design rendered by engraving, cutting, or an immersion in an acid bath before the piece was reheated and blown into a vessel form. For a variety of reasons, most likely those involving techniques of production, graal glass was considerably more expensive in the United States than intarsia glass.[61]

It was the means of attaining ornament, as much as the ornament itself, that attracted and then held the enthusiasm of the Americans when it came to Swedish glass. Specifically it was the Swedish use of the technique of engraving that had the greatest impact on American work. Engraving was not the personal domain of the Swedish glassworks, nor were Americans the only ones who appreciated this technique, but its impact on designers in the United States was profound

by the middle of the 1930s.[62]

Just as the Swedish glassworks had suffered from shortages of glassmaking materials during the First World War, Steuben was caught in a similar situation, and because of the company's inability to service the retail marketplace, it nearly collapsed. Sold in January 1918 to the Corning Glass Works, it was thereafter known as the Steuben Division of Corning Glass Works.

In 1933, the architect John Monteith Gates became Steuben's managing director. Before joining the firm, Gates had been an employee of the distinguished New York City architectural firm of Charles Platt and Sons, where he had won a 15,000 kronor first prize in a competition to redesign the center of Stockholm.[63] His awareness of Swedish circumstances must have been acute. In the same year that Gates joined the firm, Sidney Waugh, a sculptor, became head of the design department.

The following year marked the start of a period of extended development at Steuben whereby the old colored and richly ornamented glass was dropped from the line and replaced by heavy, clear lead crystal

Fig. 10-12. Vitrine with American glass, including the bowl called "Gazelle" (top, center) and the bowl called "Zodiac" (middle, center), in the 1936 glass exhibition at the Metropolitan Museum of Art. (The Metropolitan Museum of Art, New York).

engraved with designs. This expensive glass was produced in a limited edition. Waugh's popular "Gazelle Bowl" of 1935 is the most representative of this new line. The massive, powerfully articulated vessel was also reminiscent of the fundamental forms of some of the French glassmakers such as Aristide Colette as much as it was the work shown by such Swedish glassworks as Strömberg's and Orrefors. It was enhanced by a graceful, undulating frieze of engraved gazelles, an unmistakable reference to the Swedish work over the past decade and a half. With no substantial prototype for that manner of engraving—or aesthetic representation—in the American glass industry, the work that began to come out of Steuben by the middle of the 1930s was undeniably indebted to the work that had been produced at Orrefors.

Waugh's manner of rendering the gazelles was referential to the manner of engraving specified at Orrefors by Vicke Lindstrand, who was perhaps the most influential and innovative addition to the Orrefors design staff in the 1930s.[64] The "Europa Bowl," also by Waugh, has many of the heroic, boldly simplified elements that one sees in Lindstrand's reductivist, neoclassical work of the 1930s. The emphatically Swedish manner of engraving prescribed by Waugh is evident in the simple outlines of the subject matter that were given dimension by a series of deep, but relatively undetailed cuts into the lead crystal. As part of what could be called a carefully planned corporate strategy, examples of the "Gazelle Bowl" were presented as gifts by the firm to the Metropolitan Museum of Art and the Victoria and Albert Museum in London.

This dramatic shift in aesthetic policy at Steuben was apparent at the 1936 exhibition of glass at the Metropolitan Museum of Art (fig. 10-12). The presentation of recent American work consisted of a group of engraved pieces. Like all the glass in this exhibition, these pieces were part of the permanent collection of the museum, and it is easy to trace the dates of their entry into the collection. All the American pieces bore acquisition numbers identifying 1935 and 1936[65] as the years of their acquisition by the museum. A comparison of the vitrine of American work with the Swedish modern glass shown in the exhibition reveals a strong similarity between the two. It is only when the accession dates of the Swedish pieces are examined that the picture becomes complete. The Swedish pieces were acquired by the museum primarily in the middle 1920s, with additional pieces purchased in 1930 and 1934. The similarity between Hald's 1925 "Vindrosen" charger in the center of the vitrine and the 1935 "Zodiac" bowl by Waugh from Steuben is unmistakable. Steuben continued this development throughout the 1930s and after, in the postwar era. The lead established by the Swedes for upper-market glass of the 1930s is unmistakable.

Beyond the wealth of engraved pieces that had made Orrefors's reputation in the 1920s, many Swedish glassworks added to the repertoire of innovative luxury wares in the mid-1930s. This new work was deeply grounded in technical invention that it was years ahead of any American glassmaker's ability to integrate this material into their work. It may have been that this highly distinctive glass in ariel, late graal, and mykene techniques was too new for the American markets to be able to emulate so soon after its introduction in the United States.

Swedish art glass was extremely expensive to produce throughout the interwar years, and as a result most of it had a very limited production. In addition, the technical skill required to produce the heavy late graal, the mykene, and the ariel work and the high failure rate frequently encountered with the production of this work meant that few pieces were ever made. Those that were executed were sold at the high end of the retail markets.[66] In addition, the highly unusual appearance of these pieces also limited the market for them; they were not for every taste. In the first years after their introduction to the public, they were without parallel in the output of any other factory or studio in the international marketplace.

It has been frequently suggested that the technical means of production of these pieces was a mystery to other makers, but that seems highly unlikely. With the possible exception of the use of pulverized carborundum in the production of the mykene pieces, French, German, and American makers had all used the overlay technique and sandblasting, which were the principal components of the late graal and the ariel glass. A person skilled in the complexities of glass technology and production, such as Frederick Carder, would have been able to readily discern the means of production used to attain the effect of these remarkable pieces.

Despite the lack of evidence of a crossover of late innovative Swedish work into American markets, Swedish art glass was influential in the United States. This can be explained in part because glass was a material relatively amenable to change. The often immediate manner of its fabrication, especially in the area of art glass, enabled glassmakers and designers to respond to market changes more quickly than other craftsmen. It was also a material that had to be receptive to market changes. Other than utilitarian glass tableware, which became a component of most households by the early twentieth century, much of the glass production embraced by the modernists was in the realm of giftwares—ornamental vases, ashtrays, cocktail shakers, and the like. Often purchased by affluent consumers as individual pieces, this glass did not generally represent a major financial investment that a piece of furniture might, nor would an individual piece of glass dominate a room as a modernist rug might.

Glass could be readily executed in a wealth of forms and techniques and in a wide array of aesthetic expressions. The time required to make individual pieces of glass was considerably less than that needed to produce furniture, textiles, and ceramics. The luxury markets were often capricious and those involved in the production of glass were intimately aware of the quixotic character of their field and were prepared to alter their lines quickly.[67] The increasing importance of magazines and their illustrations and editorial comments could move markets dramatically. It was a critical component of the upper end of the the giftware market that its product could be transformed quickly if necessary to suit a market shift. The number of consumers at this level was limited and competition rigorous.

Recognition of audience was equally important at the large exhibitions. Glass that was sent out on exhibition almost invariably had to be within the realm of the luxury trades. Even simple stemware promoted as "inexpensive" was not for those of limited means. Few lower-income families had the means or the need to purchase a variety of wineglasses, champagne flutes, aperitif glasses, and other forms of stemware; they were created for those whose lifestyle required them.

Swedish glass captured the attention of Americans on the basis of its arresting designs, superlative quality, and just as importantly, its status as a luxury item. International exhibitions were forms of national propaganda, and luxury was a quality that was readily understood despite the language barrier. As early as 1927, Orrefors in America stood apart from the other Swedish glass, and in some respects, from the work of other Swedish modernists working in the decorative arts. Furniture, ceramics, metalwork, and textiles produced in Sweden in a modernist idiom changed over the twenty-year period of the interwar years and adjusted to the tribulations of the global economy, but Swedish glass appeared to adhere to the principles of quality and elitism that brought it such fame after the First World War. It integrated functionalist work into its

lines, but the form and its reputation thrived on the critical acclaim its art glass received.

Swedish glass may not have adjusted to the sweeping changes in the design world in the 1930s with the aesthetic and conceptual flexibility that other Swedish modernist decorative arts did. Orrefors and Kosta Boda, the two preeminent glassworks in Sweden, had geared their product lines to the luxury trades. For these firms to retool their lines in the midst of diminishing markets would have been fiscally unsound. With other glass companies well ensconced in the areas that produced middle and lower-end glass, such a move would have been unthinkable. Ultimately, in its complexities and consistencies, Swedish modern glass reflected the defining words of the official publication of the Swedish Pavilion at the 1939 New York World's Fair:

> Abroad, the Swedish efforts to create applied art attuned to modern man and his needs have been termed a style, Swedish Modern. However, by style is most often implied a distinct mode of presentation, something stationary and final. The present Swedish development in the field of industrial arts, on the other hand, is chiefly distinguished by its dynamic character. It is not a style, but rather a movement.[68]

Sweden's progressive glass was deeply indebted to that movement, and it made the single most important contribution to the international reputation of Swedish modern decorative arts in the interwar era. The reception of this glass in the American marketplace, perhaps the largest after Sweden, was sustained, enthusiastic, and widespread, and in some instances Swedish glass influenced the production of American glass. Although not always in tandem with concepts promoted within the Swedish design community during the 1920s and 1930s, this glass has come to exemplify the remarkable flowering in design that occurred during that critical era in the history of modernism.

1. The term *nonprofit* has been used to differentiate exhibitions from department store showings even though objects were invariably sold from exhibitions in order to recoup costs.

2. This was not a new phenomena but in fact followed the nineteenth-century procedure set by the South Kensington Museum in London (now the Victoria and Albert Museum).

3. Recent literature regarding American decorative arts of the interwar years reveals that the general curatorial consensus supports this notion. For a single citation on Sweden, see Richard Guy Wilson, Dianne H. Pilgrim, and Dickran Tashjian, *The Machine Age in America, 1918–1941* (New York: Harry N. Abrams, 1986), p. 278. For a citation on Edward Hald and the 1927 Swedish Contemporary Decorative Arts exhibition see Karen Davies, *At Home in Manhattan: Modern Decorative Arts, 1925 to the Depression* (New Haven: Yale University Press, 1983), p. 86. Also see Janet Kardon, ed., *Craft in the Machine Age, 1920–1945: The History of Twentieth-Century American Craft* (New York: American Craft Museum/Harry N. Abrams, 1995); David A. Hanks, *High Styles: Twentieth-*

Century American Design (New York: Whitney Museum of American Art/Summit Books, 1985); Martin Eidelber, ed., *Design 1935–1965: What Modern Was, Selections from the Liliane and David M. Stewart Collection* (Montreal and New York: Musée des arts décoratifs de Montreal/Harry N. Abrams, 1991).

4. Although nearly 1 million Swedes immigrated to the United States between the middle of the nineteenth century and 1929, they were primarily concentrated in Minnesota and often marginalized. They had a very small impact if any on American culture in general. They often stood apart, not only from the work produced in their own country, but from modernist developments in America as well. See Harald Runbloom and Hans Norman, eds., *From Sweden to America: A History of the Migration* (Uppsala: Acta Universitatis Upsaliensis, 1976); and chaps. 1 and 2 in this volume.

5. See Annette Blaugrund, *Paris 1889: American Artists at the Universal Exposition* (Philadelphia: Pennsylvania Academy of Fine Arts/Harry N. Abrams, 1989); Barbara Novak, *American Painting of the Nineteenth Century; Realism,*

Idealism, and the American Experience (New York: Praeger, 1989); Barbara Weinberg, *American Impressionism and Realism: The Painting of Modern Life, 1885–1915*, (New York: Metropolitan Museum of Art/Harry N. Abrams, 1994).

6. See Edith Wharton and Ogden Codman, *The Decoration of Houses*, reprint (New York; Norton, 1978); Elsie De Wolfe, *The House in Good Taste* (New York: The Century Company, 1913). On the École des Beuax-arts see *École Nationale Superieure des Beaux-arts*, (Cambridge, Massachusetts, 1995); and Arthur Drexler, ed., *The Architecture of the Ecole des Beaux-arts*, (New York: Museum of Modern Art, 1977).

7. In American retailing, French objects, French marketing concepts, and even French terminology were linked with commercial success. To a large degree, "Believing that the magical link to everything Parisian was a near guarantee of fashion-minded customers, the big retailers imported any and all promising French devices or ideas. Harry Selfridge of Field's (Marshall) visited Printemps and the Bon Marché in Paris for help in converting Field's into a major retail store. John and Rodman Wanamaker looked continually to Paris for fashion suggestions" (William Leach in *Land of Desire: Merchants, Power and the Rise of a New American Culture* [New York: Pantheon Books, 1993], p. 99).

8. In 1922 John Cotton Dana, a strong proponent of modernism in this country, was responsible for promoting interest in this area. He arranged an exhibition of German Werkbund products at the Newark Museum. A similar exhibition of Werkbund creations had been held in Newark in 1912.

9. Joseph Urban, Rudolf Schindler, Richard Neutra, Kem Weber, Paul Frankl, William Ackermann, Wally Vieseltier, Jock Peters, Peter Mueller-Munk, Tommi Parzinger, Walter Gropius, Anni and Josef Albers, Marcel Breuer, Herbert Bayer, Mies van der Rohe, Eugene Schoen, Walter Kantack, Walter von Nessen, Rena Rosenthal, Ely Jacques Kahn, Gilbert Rohde, Ilonka Karasz, Wolfgang and Paula Hoffmann, all worked in the United States during the interwar years.

10. This was not necessarily reflected in the additions made to the permanent collections of American museums.

11. This exhibition, which was on view from December 1930 through January 1931, included a small selection of decorative arts. See Nikolas Fox Weber, *Patron Saints: Five Rebels Who Opened America to a New Art, 1928–1943* (New York: Alfred A. Knopf, 1992), p. 118–21.

12. This group included Walter Gropius, Mies van der Rohe, Marcel Breuer, Anni and Josef Albers, and Lázsló Moholy-Nagy.

13. Henry Russell Hitchcock, *The International Style: Architecture Since 1922* (New York: W. W. Norton and Company, 1932); Franz Schulze, *Philip Johnson: Life and Work*, (New York: A. A. Knopf, 1994).

14. For an illustration of Swedish glass by Orrefors and flatware and hollowware by Georg Jensen see *House Beautiful* (April 1, 1940), p. 50. The accompanying text makes no mention of Denmark or Sweden.

15. This is the case with the Austrian architect and designer Josef Frank, who emigrated to Sweden in 1933. Frank brought with him a freedom of expression that was to have wide repercussions in Swedish interior design circles throughout the 1930s, and internationally thereafter. See Nina Stritzler-Levine, ed., *Josef Frank, Architect and Designer: An Alternative Vision of the Modern Home* (New Haven and London: Bard Graduate Center for Studies in the Decorative Arts/Yale University Press, 1996).

16. The inclusion of Swedish work in exhibitions in American department stores was limited perhaps because American department stores did not have branch offices in Sweden as they did elsewhere in Europe. Swedish work was not included in the 1927 Art-in-Trade Exposition at Macy's Department Store. This show, considered one of the most significant shows of modern European decorative arts in the 1920s, was assembled with the assistance of Robert W. deForest, president of the Board of Trustees at the Metropolitan Museum of Art. It was followed in 1928 at Macy's with "An International Exhibition of Art in Industry" in which Swedish items were shown. See Karen Davies, *At Home in Manhattan: Modern Decorative Arts, 1925 to the Depression* (New Haven: Yale University Press, 1983), p. 86.

17. For further information see Derek Ostergard, "The Sincerest Form of Flattery: The American Response to European Design," *Merchandising Interior Design: Methods of Furniture Fabrication in America Between the World Wars* (New Haven: Yale University School of Architecture, 1991).

18. Gothenburg's 300th anniversary was in 1921, but the exhibition was delayed two years.

19. See Guido Balsamo Stella, "Cristalli di Svezia," *Dedalo* (May 1921), pp. 822–30. This long, generously illustrated article includes a considerable amount of early, engraved modernist work from Orrefors. Some of the designs were only a few months old. This was the first issue of the magazine demonstrating the close links within the progressive design community (even between the marketing office of a factory and the editorial offices of a magazine) at the time. Also see "Applied Art in Sweden," *The Studio Yearbook* (1921), pp. 118–19; "Orrefors Bruk," *Dekorative Kunst* 34 (1925/26), pp. 69–76; and "Wirkung und Asthetik in der Raumkunst," ibid.

20. The Atlan Club Fund donated a piece of Orrefors glass; for a history of this organization see Sharon Darling, *Chicago Ceramics and Glass: An Illustrated History from 1871–1933* (Chicago: Chicago Historical Society, 1979), pp. 12–20, 26–27, 41, 72–75. The original collection included a amethyst-colored covered vase (1919) by Simon Gate on which were engravings of dancing nudes.

21. Accession number 1925.46; the seller was Nordiska Kompaniet, a Stockholm department store. See *Art Institute of Chicago Bulletin* (February 1925).

22. This information is courtesy of Jared Goss and Jane Adlin. The bowl and undertray by Simon Gate (acc. no. 24.176.1–2) was purchased for approximately $65 and the standing cup with cover by Edward Hald (acc. no. 24.176.3 a,b) cost $31. The difference in price may reflect the complexity of the engraving. Gate's depicts meticulously rendered human forms around the entire bowl, while Hald's relies upon a single female figure seated on a suspended swag amid stars.

23. For more information on this development at the Metropolitan Museum of Art, see R. Craig Miller, *Modern Design in the Metropolitan Museum of Art, 1890–1990*, (New York: The Metropolitan Museum of Art/Harry N. Abrams, 1990).

24. The most important objects purchased then by the Metropolitan Museum include a desk (acc. no. 25.209.1) by Louis Süe and André Mare and a cabinet (acc. no. 25.231.1) by Jacques Émile Ruhlmann (Tiffany Lee, The Metropolitan Museum of Art, New York: personal communication). See Miller, *Modern Design*, pp. 173, 175. Beginning with the 10th annual exhibition in 1926, the Metropolitan Museum stipulated that only original work, no reproductions or copies of decorative arts, could be exhibited in these exhibitions, further preparing the way for modern material to be shown in greater numbers at these exhibitions. See ibid., p. 23; and Karen Davies, *At Home in Manhattan: Modern Decorative Arts, 1925 to the Depression* (New Haven: Yale University Press, 1983)

25. This selection of modern decorative arts, sponsored by American Association of Museums, traveled to nine additional cities. *A Selected Collection of Objects from the International Exposition of Modern Decorative and Industrial Art at Paris 1925* (New York: The American Association of Museums, 1926)

26. The vase called "Heaven and Hell" in the Detroit Art Institute (acc. no. 26.404) may be the piece that was in the 1926 Metropolitan Museum of Art exhibition. In a photograph of the Metropolitan Museum installation, the vase was shown without an undertray.

27. *Exhibition of Swedish Contemporary Decorative Arts*, exhib. cat. (New York: The Metropolitan Museum of Art, 1927); Joseph Breck, "Swedish Contemporary Decorative Arts," *Bulletin of The Metropolitan Museum of Art* 22, no. 1 (January 1927). For the first mention of this exhibition see the *New York Times* (January 16, 1927), p. 11. Also see "Specimens of Modern Glassware in the Exhibition of Swedish Contemporary Decorative Arts on View Temporarily at the Metropolitan Museum of Art, New York," *The Glass Industry* (March 1927), p 65, illustrated; *Country Life* (February 1927), p. 68. For an account of the opening of the Swedish exhibition, see the *New York Times* (January 18, 1927), p. 22.

28. Robert W. de Forest, president of the Metropolitan Museum, said that ". . . its installation, arranged in Sweden and carried out entirely by the Swedes, is a lesson even to our own museum, which justly prides itself upon the artistic arrangements of its exhibitions" (*New York Times* [January 18, 1927], p. 22).

29. Breck, "Swedish Contemporary Decorative Arts," p. ix.

30. On his American tour, Hald lectured at the Metropolitan Museum of Art "in English on Modern European glass" (*The American Magazine of Art* [July 1928], n.p.).

31. It is not clear how Swedish glass was wholesaled in America in the 1920s or how contact was made between sales outlets and the factory. A variety of stores in New York City carried Orrefors and Sandvik glass throughout the 1920s and 1930s, including Georg Jensen and Bruce Butterfield, a gift shop in Greenwich Village that advertised glass from Sandvik (*House and Garden* [April 1928], n.p.).

32. See Robert Judson Clark, *Design in America: The Cranbrook Vision, 1925–1950*, (New York: Detroit Institute of Arts/The Metropolitan Museum of Art/Harry N. Abrams, 1983), p. 92; and Karen Serota, "The Story of Cranbrook," manuscript (Cranbrook Academy of Art, 1950).

33. An earlier liner, the M/S *Gripsholm*, arrived in New York on November 30, 1925, but its interiors were not intended as statements of modernity.

34. Bergsten had been the architect of the Swedish pavilion at the 1925 Paris exposition and had organized the installation of the 1927 exhibition at the Metropolitan Museum of Art. See Gustaf Lorentz Munthe, *Swedish Arts and Crafts on the M/S* Kungsholm, (Sweden: [Swedish American Line], [1935]).

35. Munthe, *Swedish Arts and Crafts on the M/S* Kungsholm.

36. Ibid., p. 5.

37. American Federation of Arts, *International Exhibition of Ceramic Art*, exhib. cat. (Portland, Maine: The Southworth Press, 1928).

38. For a brief discussion of Swedish glass and mention of the workers' strike, see "Introduction," in American Federation of Arts, *International Exhibition: Contemporary Glass and Rugs*, (Washington, D. C.: American Federation of Arts, 1929). The twelve organizers listed as members of the Swedish section were: Herman Lagercrantz (Swedish Ambassador to the United States), Olof H. Lamm (Consul General, New York City), Gregor Paulsson (Svenska Slöjdföreningen, Stockholm), Nils G. Wollin (Svenska Sljödföreningen, Stockholm), Froken E. von Walterstorff (Nordiska Museet, Stockholm), G. L. Munthe (Rohsska Konstslöjdmuseet, Gotenburg), J. E. Sachs (A/B Nordiska Kompaniet, Stockholm), Mr. Ernst Gustafson (Nordiska Kompaniet, Stockholm), Douglas Bisiker (Svenska Tandstick Aktiebolaget, Stockholm), Mr. and Mrs. J. Danius (Orrefors), and Mrs. Folke Ramström (Orrefors).

39. This analysis of the glass exhibited is based on the entries listed in the 1929 catalouge (ibid.).

40. The Austrians had thirty-nine entries; English, thirty-three; Americans, twenty-seven; Italians, nineteen; and Dutch, twelve. Many of these were groupings of glass objects.

41. Erik Wettergren, *The Modern Decorative Arts of Sweden* (Malmo, Sweden: Malmo Museum, 1927), p. 27. The thickness of the wall of Lobmeyr's engraved vessels, the bite of their engravers wheel, and the meticulous rendering of their engraving in general was different from the work produced at Orrefors.

42. It was located on 427 acres in Burnham Park and was open from May 27 to November 1, 1933 and from June 1 to November 1, 1934.

43. The 1930 Stockholm Exhibition, a display of modern Swedish art, architecture, and design, was recognized by some designers, critics, and consumers as a major turning point of modernism in Sweden. See chaps. 4 and 9 in this volume.

44. "The economical conditions are changed all over the world. The wealthier classes have had to limit their expenses, but they still have the inherent requirements of standard. Thanks to social inversion a greater mass of people now understands and appreciates an object of quality and good craftsmanship, and prefers to buy these to inferior quality products, if available at the same price" (Bengt Lundberg, *Arts and Crafts at the Swedish Chicago Exposition, 1933* [Stockholm: Centraltryckeriet, 1933], pp. 6–7).

45. Ibid., p. 6.

46. This exhibition was open from October 13 to November 27, 1936. I am indebted to Barbara File and Betsy Baldwin, archives of the Metropolitan Museum of Art, for this information. Also see Metropolitan Museum of Art, *A Special Exhibition of Glass from the Museum Collections* exhib. cat. (New York: The Metropolitan Museum, 1936).

47. The Orrefors objects in the exhibition bear the accession numbers: 24.176.1-2; 24.176.3 a,b; 27.96.1; 27.96.2 a,b; 27.96.3 a,b; 27.96.4; 27.96.5; 27.96.6; 27.96.7; 27.96.8; 27.96.9; 27.96.10; 30.134.4; 34.145.1; 34.145.2.

48. Despite claims by later twentieth-century glass historians that the engraved work diminished in importance in the 1930s, it was still heralded as the preeminent expression of the factory's output. See Metropolitan Museum of Art, *Special Exhibition of Glass*, fig. 40 and p. 44.

49. Erected on Market Street, the Swedish building was flanked by food processing firms—Standard Brands, National Dairy Products, and Continental Baking.

50. Richard Wurts, *The New York World's Fair 1939/1940*, (New York: Dover Publications, 1977), p. 3.

51. "The aim of the exhibition was to demonstrate briefly, first, the most important natural resources of Sweden, from the exploitation of which the Swedish people earn their living; second, the social welfare system, including public ownership of the chief public utilities, cooperatives of various types, and other modifications of private capitalism, known as the "Middle Way"; third, the modern Swedish decorative art and industrial arts, whose purpose is to make both homes and public buildings more attractive; and finally, the traditional Swedish way of preparing and serving food in an up-to-date restaurant" (Naboth Hedin, *Sweden at the New York World's Fair* [New York: The Royal Swedish Commission, 1939], n.p.).

52. *Furniture World* (June 15, 1939), cited in Hedin, *Sweden at the New York World's Fair*, n.p.

53. "An impressive part of the exhibition is the hall for arts and crafts. One whole side of the room consists of windows against which are shelves with all types of Swedish glass from engraved Orrefors pieces to heavy smoke-colored crystal from Strombergshyttan" (Elisabeth Aschehoug, *The* [New York] *Sun*, (June 24, 1939).

"On shelves across an immense high window, facing north, are set examples of the modern Swedish crystal glass, so delicately decorated, either by engravings or by figures blown in the material itself that they have become veritable works of art" (Hedin, *Sweden at the New York World's Fair*, n.p.).

54. A piece designed by Edvin Öhrström is incorrectly labeled as graal glass; it is an example of the new ariel technique (Ake Stavenow et al., eds., *Swedish Arts and Crafts: Swedish Modern-A Movement Towards Sanity in Design*, [New York: The Royal Swedish Commission, New York World's Fair, 1939], p. 15).

55. See Golden Gate International Exhibition, *Decorative Arts: Official Catalog, Department of Fine Arts, Division of Decorative Arts, Golden Gate International Exposition San Francisco*, (San Francisco San Francisco Bay Exposition Co.), 1939.

56. Ibid.

57. Of the few pieces identified by name, the vase called "Girls Playing Ball" (1920) was still considered sufficiently exciting to represent Orrefors's best output. The Swedish glass included work by all of the principal factories and designers of the 1920s and 1930s: (407) Elis Bergh; (412) Ewald Dahlskog; (417) Simon Gate; (420) Edward Hald; (425) Kosta-Reijmyre; (427) Nils Landberg; (429) Vicke Lindstrand; (433) Tyra Lundgren; (439) Edwin Öhrström; (440) Orrefors Bruks Aktiebolag; (441) Palmqvist; (450) Edward Strömberg (ibid., pp. 56–60).

58. "Engraving seems the specific trend in the factories of Sweden and Finland" (Elisabeth Moses, in Golden Gate International Exhibition, *Decorative Arts*, p. 55).

59. For Wettergren on Lobmeyr see Wettergren, *The Modern Decorative Arts of Sweden*, p. 27.

60. In a recent survey of Orrefors glass, Alastair Duncan speculates that the graal technique developed at Orrefors was actually inspired by Frederick Carder's early experiments with his own intarsia glass in his Corning, New York workshop. According to Duncan, Knut and Gustav Bergqvist made two trips to the United States in 1916 and visited Carder. It is not known if either of the Berqqvist spoke English nor is there any documentation in the way of passports, letters, or visas to support this contention which rests solely in the oral tradition (Alastair Duncan, *Orrefors Glass* [Woodbridge, England: Antique Collectors Club, 1995], pp. 30–31).

There is also no documentation in Carder's career for any successfully produced pieces of intarsia until the late 1920s. Carder experimented with similar techniques, but the first known pieces in intarsia did not appear until the 1929 AFA exhibition (American Federation of the Arts, *International Exhibition: Contemporary Glass and Rugs*, nos. 313, 319). For Carder's development of the intarsia process see Paul V. Gardner, *The Glass of Frederick Carder*, (New York: Crown Publishers, 1971), p. 73–75.

60. Ibid, pp. 73–75.

61. In the 1932 Steuben catalogue, three designs of intarsia ware are priced between $16 and $20; they may have been underpriced, however, to raise cash quickly or to relieve overcrowded storage space (Paul V. Gardner, *The Glass of Frederick Carder* [New York: Crown Publishers, 1971]). In 1927 the Metropolitan Museum of Art had purchased three pieces of Hald's graal glass from Orrefors for more money: acc. no. 27.96.8 for $51; acc. no. 27.96.9, for $46; and acc. no. 27.96.10 for $50 (Archives of the Metropolitan Museum of Art, New York).

62. Lobmeyr's designs, usually by Marianne Rath and Ena Rottenberg, were most highly praised by the critics—even Erik Wettergren in Sweden. Between the late nineteenth century and 1914, the United States had been one of the principal markets for cut glass which made it a logical place to sell the new glass.

63. See Mary Jean Madigan, *Steuben Glass: An American Tradition in Crystal* (New York: Harry N. Abrams, 1982), p. 74.

64. In the 1930s Steuben's shops were led by Swedish gaffers. Lindstrand had joined Orrefors in 1928, and his first substantial public showing was at the 1930 Stockholm Exhibition.

65. The pieces of American manufacture bear the accession numbers: 35.83; 35.94.1; 35.94.2; 35.94.3; 36.126.0; 36.126.1; 36.126.2-7; 36.126.8 a,b; 36.126.9.

66. The records at Orrefors for the making of these pieces indicate how few of these pieces were made. See Helmut Ricke, ed., *Schwedische Glasmanufakturen: Produktionskataloge, 1915–1960* (Munich: Prestel-Verlag, 1987).

67. Frederick Carder at Steuben Glassworks in Corning, New York, for example, offered an incredible diversity of forms to appeal to shifting trends in the market. Specialization was not part of corporate strategy. See Gardner, *Glass of Frederick Carder*.

68. See Stavenow et al., *Swedish Arts and Crafts*, p. 13.

Catalogue of the Exhibition

Derek E. Ostergard (DEO)
Nina Stritzler-Levine (NS-L)

Editor's note: The catalogue entries follow a chronological arrangement, illustrating the development of the Swedish glassworks over a forty-year period. The chronology has been established by the design date, but whenever possible, the production date of the example shown is also provided. In some cases objects have been taken out of chronological order to show conceptual or aesthetic relationships. The dimensions of the objects are given with height preceding diameter or width. At the end of each entry, initials identify the author. The references are cited in shortened form; full citations will be found in the bibliography.

1. Vase

ca. 1901–1902
Betzy Ählström
Blown, acid-etched, engraved,
marqueterie de verre; 6½ x 5⅝ in.
(16.5 x 14.3 cm)

Reijmyre Glassworks
Marks: "Reijmyre B. Ähm #56. K R[?]"

Collection Görander

The production of art glass in Europe at the turn of the century was dominated by the large glass factories and artist's ateliers in France. Emile Gallé, the leading aesthetic and technical innovator of art glass in the Art Nouveau idiom, was especially influential. The first examples of progressive Swedish engraved overlay work inspired by French designs were shown at the 1897 Stockholm Exhibition. Although considered a triumph at the time, they represented an aesthetic that did not last for very long in Swedish design. Their primary importance was in helping to establish a starting point for the development of progressive art glass in Sweden.

This vase by Betzy Ählström represents a significant change in direction from the 1897 overlay work. Its vibrant, organic form, richly embellished with colored glass, may lack the exactitude of many contemporary French pieces of art glass, but it reveals the confidence of a young designer unbound by market convention. Ählström worked at Reijmyre only for a brief period, from 1901 to 1902, but her work reveals a consistency in design and execution that equals many of the finest pieces being made in France. Her use of *marqueterie de verre*, a technique employed by Gallé, involved the "laying in" of individually selected pieces of glass into the molten gob on the pipe. The epiphyl-lum, a tropical plant, was new and exotic to most northern Europeans at the turn of the century, and its depiction was well suited to Ählström's revolutionary aesthetic.

Women had traditionally occupied the lowest positions in the hierarchy of the glass factories. They were usually employed in the packing of finished glass, not its actual design or production. Anna Boberg worked at Reijmyre in the same years as Betzy Ählström. They were the first of the few women to join the ranks of designers in the glass industry before the interwar years. DEO

References: Holmér and Riehnér, *Lyricism of Modern Design*, pp. 34, 224–25; László, *Konstglas*, pp. 30–31; Bukowskis Auction Catalogue (May 18–20, 1988), Lot 785.

2. Vase

Designed 1907–15
Karl Lindeberg
Blown, overlay, acid-etched, wheel cut,
engraved; 6¼ x 6¼ in. (16 x 16 cm)

Kosta Glassworks
Marks: "Vega"

Kosta Museum

The aesthetics of this vase and the technical means used to produce it are deeply indebted to avant-garde work produced at the French glassworks at the turn of the century. By the start of the First World War, however, there had been a rise in national consciousness in the Swedish design community, and Swedish critics were quick to condemn what they saw as a lack of creativity on the part of designers working for the Orrefors, Reijmyre, and Kosta glassworks.

During the early years of the twentieth century, Kosta was inclined to use designers who lived elsewhere and provided designs for the firm. Alf Wallander and Gunnar Wennerberg, for example, remained essentially detached from the day-to-day operation of the firm, while Karl Lindeberg, who designed this piece, was head of the engraving shop at Kosta and worked as a designer for the firm during his twenty-four years of employment there. Despite his employment at Kosta into the early 1930s, only his Art Nouveau designs are known. Lindeberg's work from before the First World War displays a consistency to which few other artists adhered. The size of his pieces tends to be small; he worked mostly with decorative pieces such as vases and bowls; and he usually worked in two colors—a colored overlay on a frosted white base.

Lindeberg was also known for his use of native Swedish flora and fauna as motifs on his glass. In that respect, his work was influenced by Emile Gallé who urged all designers of the decorative arts to seek inspiration from their environment. DEO

References: Artéus, ed., *Kosta: 250 Years of Craftsmanship*, pp. 50–51; Holmér and Riehnér, *Lyricism of Modern Design*, pp. 34, 224–25.

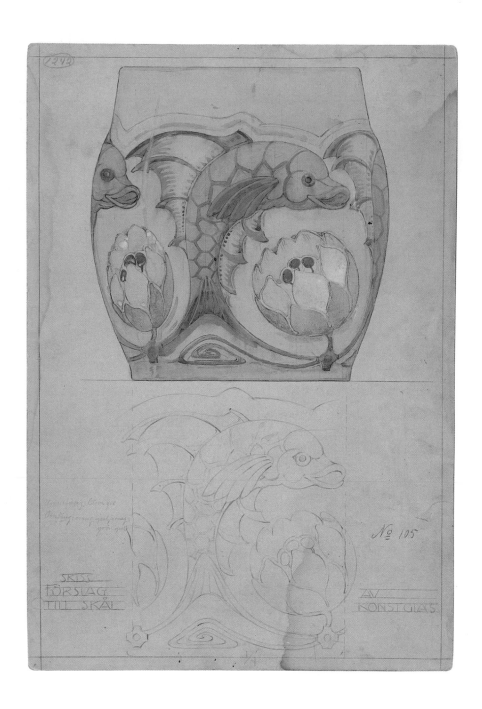

3. Drawing for Vase

ca. 1908
Fritz Blomqvist
Watercolor and pencil on paper; 19 x
12⁷⁄₈ in. (48.4 x 32.8 cm)

Inscription: "SKISS FÖRSLAG TILL SKÅL
AV KONSTGLAS No. 105/ Undefång:
Citrongul / "Överfång: orang opal,
orang & grön opal" [Drawing for
suggestion for bowl / of art glass
Number 105 / Underlay: lemon-yellow /
Overlay: orange opal, orange & green
opal]

Orrefors Museum
Inv. no. 1242

Blomqvist was only at Orrefors from
1914 to 1917 and apparently only during the summer months of 1916 and
1917. He came from the Technical
School in Stockholm to produce
designs after Johan Ekman assumed
the directorship of the glassworks;
Albert Ahlin was manager. Blomqvist
would have been present at the arrival
of the two young designers who rapidly came to dominate the production of
the firm—Simon Gate and Edward
Hald. The reason for Blomqvist's
departure is not known. It may have
been that, in the new climate of artists
designing for the decorative arts
industries, a draftsman occupied a
lower position than an artist in the
heirarchy of the firm, and thus he
decided to leave.

This superb rendering reflects
Blomqvist's considerable skill as a
draftsman. It may also be that this is
one of the drawings Blomqvist sent to
Kosta from Stockholm and that such
precise details were necessary to
direct the glassblowers in his absence.
The brief pencil notations, the only
written instructions, that have been
spontaneously scrawled across the
lower portion of the drawing indicate
the colored flashings required to produce this piece.

The drawing displays an originality
that was unusual for Swedish glass
between 1900 and 1914. The repeat of
a golden carp and waterlilies is tightly
unified through the shading of the
rose-tipped tails of the fish that are
linked with the bases of the flowers.
DEO

References: Duncan, *Orrefors Glass*, pp. 14
–16; Holmér and Riehnér, *Lyricism of
Modern Design*, pp. 36–37, 223–224;
Knutsson, *Swedish Art in Glass*.

4. Vase

ca. 1915
Knut Bergqvist, Heinrich Wollman
Blown, overlay, cut, engraved, acid-
etched; 9¹⁄₈ x 3⁷⁄₈ in. (23.3 x 9.7 cm)

Orrefors Glassworks
Marks: "ORREFORS"

Mrs. Agnes Hellner Collection,
Kungstenen Foundation, Stockholm
University

Inv. no. H4

In a critique of the Swedish glass shown at the 1914 Baltic Exhibition in Malmö, Sweden, the secretary of Svenska Slöjdföreningen (The Swedish Society of Craft and Industrial Design) criticized Swedish overlay work as crude and lacking in refined color sensibilities. This piece, with its single color overlay, symmetrical botanical ornament, and delicate detailing, repudiates those remarks. Aesthetically, it relates to designs produced at a number of Continental factories around the turn of the century. Catagorized as Art Nouveau, this work had become quickly debased by factories such as Daum Frères in Nancy, France, who mass-produced more commercial lines of art glass. By the First World War, when the Orrefors

vase was made, Art Nouveau decoration was increasingly out of favor in the marketplace. Shortly after the vase was produced, however, Orrefors itself would be in the midst of a major aesthetic revision of its output with a new emphasis on neoclassicism, and this manner of work would disappear entirely from the firm's line.

The clear glass core of this piece was flashed with an outer layer of green glass, and the form was blown into a mold and allowed to cool. After the design was traced onto the form, the outer layer of green glass was laboriously wheel-cut down to the clear glass core except where the botanical design was retained. The details of the floral and leaf elements were then engraved onto the piece,

and the clear background was acid-etched to achieve the subtle matte design that offsets the green elements. The acid-etched "Orrefors" insignia on the exterior wall of this vessel is unusual and reflects the French manner of openly marking their glass. Presumably this was an element demanded by French consumers, who perhaps saw this as reinforcing the status of the object.

Wollman, a craftsman who had emigrated from Bohemia to Sweden, most likely was responsible for the design of this piece which was executed, in part, by Knut Bergqvist, a master-blower from the rival Kosta glassworks. Both men joined Orrefors in 1914. DEO

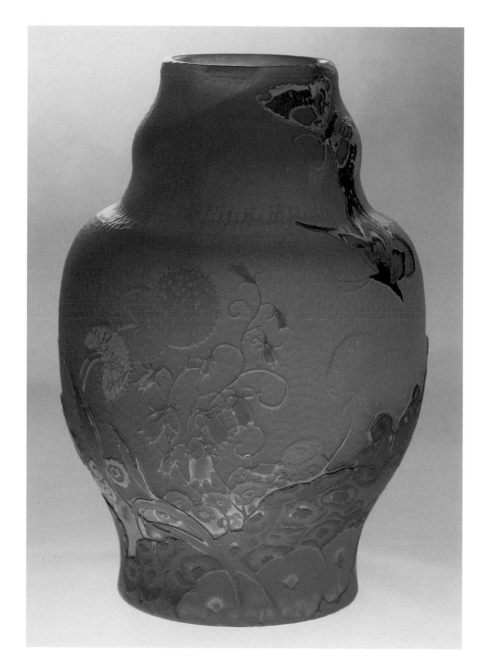

been executed personally by Simon Gate who rarely worked on the glass himself. By the time the vase was made, the overlay and cutting technique and this romantic aesthetic with its emphasis on naturalistic elements were becoming outdated. The techniques used, however, can be understood as laying the foundation for two of the principal means of glass decoration used at Orrefors for the next decade. The overlay technique was at the core of Orrefors graal glass that was critical to the firm's reputation in the late teens and early twenties. Copper wheels would be used, in part, for the engraved glass associated with the artistic prominence of the factory during the 1920s.

Gate was trained in Stockholm between 1902 and 1907 at the Konstfackskolan and Tekniska Skolan. After working briefly as a painter, he joined Orrefors in 1916, working as a designer until his death in 1945. Although frequently associated with a rich, academic manner of engraving, Gate experimented freely with the technical and aesthetic qualities of glass. In collaboration with Albert Ahlin and Knut Bergqvist, he developed the graal technique in 1916, one of the earliest innovations contributing to Orrefors's rise to fame in the late teens and early twenties. DEO

References: Duncan, *Orrefors Glass*, p. 20; Edenheim and Reihner, *Simon Gate, Edward Hald*, pp. 25, 29.

5. Vase

1916
Simon Gate, Knut Bergqvist, Heinrich Wollman
Blown, overlay, wheel cut, engraved;
11¾ x 7⅝ in. (28.8 x 19.5 cm)

Orrefors Glassworks
Marks: "Orrefors" / "KB71" [in pencil on thistles]

Mrs. Agnes Hellner Collection, Kungstenen Foundation, Stockholm University
Inv. no. H11

This massive vase is a tour de force of complex and multiple overlay work. The core of the vase was a large gob of purple glass. The glassblowers then flashed thin layers of white, blue, light green, and dark green glass over the core. The white, diaphanous spiral was achieved through an underlay technique wherein a white flashing was blown into the hollow form of the ves-

sel when it was nearly finished. This particular element makes it appear as though light is filtering from above into the scene depicted on the vase. Once the overlay had been completed and the final shape of the vase attained, the vase was allowed to cool very slowly to prevent it from shattering. Afterward, the laborious technique of cutting away the outer layers of glass with copper wheels to produce the decorative elements of the piece began. This manner of working the glass was exceptionally difficult, and the design had to be carefully worked out in a close collaboration between artist and master-blower. The layering of colored glass was carefully planned and overlaid with appropriate thicknesses so that the design could be executed as drawn.

Agnes Hellner, the daughter of Johan Ekman, director of Orrefors from 1913 to 1918, was the original owner of this vase. She claimed that it had

Fig. 5a. Vase by Daum Frères, Nancy, France. (Courtesy, Christie's New York)

6. Pair of glasses

Designed ca. 1916
Simon Gate
Blown, cut; $8^{7}/_{8}$ x $3^{1}/_{2}$ in. (22.5 x 8.9 cm)

Orrefors Glassworks
Marks: "G KB" [light red]; "Orrefors" [light brown]

Orrefors Museum

The basic generic design for this stemware originated in the work of Central European architects and designers just before the turn of the century. The subtle, undulating forms of these glasses appears in the work of Peter Behrens, who designed glasses in 1898 for the Benedikt von Poschinger Glassworks of Oberzwieselau, Germany. Josef Maria Olbrich's designs in this idiom were executed by E. Bakalowits & Söhn in Vienna in 1901, and several years later Koloman Moser's designs for glassware were made by Lobmeyr Glassworks in Vienna (fig. 6a).

By the First World War, the Swedish glass industry had become increasingly aware of the importance of the Continental factories and their aesthetic domination in the marketplace. Instead of developing a distinctive aesthetic of their own at this date, Orrefors wisely sought to follow fashion, even though it was somewhat outdated. At the same time, design critics and members of the powerful Svenska Slöjdföreningen (The Swedish Society of Craft and Industrial Design) also recognized the danger in slavish imitation in 1914. Their criticisms prompted an active search for an indigenous aesthetic that would result in the union of progressive Swedish artists with the design departments of Swedish applied arts manufacturers. This alliance would bring about a widespread flowering in the realm of Swedish design. DEO

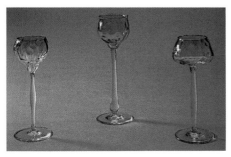

Fig. 6a. Wineglasses by Koloman Moser, 1903. (From Nervi, *Autriche, Suède et Finlande*)

7. Drawing for Pitcher and Glass

1916
Simon Gate
Pencil, pastel; 15$\frac{1}{8}$ x 14$\frac{1}{8}$ in. (38.4 x 36 cm)

Inscription: "Förslag till Te-servis I glas / S. Gate 1916" [Suggestion for Tea-set In glass /S. Gate 1916] [Stamp: Orrefors . . . Simon Gate n:r . . .]

Orrefors Museum

The extant drawings in the Orrefors archives from the early twentieth century reveal a finished quality usually lacking from drawings of the 1920s and 1930s. It may be that many of these designers had been trained to work in a more academic fashion, or that more fully executed drawings were required when designers worked in studios that were some distance from the factory. Their meticulously detailed renderings would be interpreted by the factory craftsmen. This changed significantly when designers began to live at the factories and participate in the day-to-day production of glass.

Glass-making techniques simplified considerably in the 1920s, with a new emphasis on clear, blown glass that was often decorated with engraving or painting. As a result drawings may have become less detailed, more elementary. The dramatic increase in the volume of new designs being introduced at Orrefors may have dictated that less time be spent on meticulously rendered drawings. Finally, the close collaboration between designers and glassworkers abrogated the need for detailed instruction.

What is consistent about most of the drawings in the Orrefors Archives dating from over a quarter of a century is their poor condition, the result of their repeated use in the blowing room and engraving studios. As working drawings, their only value was in their ability to instruct the craftsmen working in the glassworks. DEO

8. Pitcher and Glasses
1916
Simon Gate
Blown, cast-on elements; pitcher,
H. 14⅞ in. (37.8 cm)

Orrefors Glassworks
Marks: "S:G-KB"

Orrefors Museum
Not in the exhibition

A considerable effort was required to unite the different parts of this set, indicating the emphasis on the hand-working of glass at Orrefors at the time of the First World War. Despite the labor, time, and skill required to produce this glassware, it was not a costly presentation set. DEO

References: Hald and Wettergren, *Simon Gate, Edward Hald*, p. 35; Brunius et al., *Svenskt Glas*, p. 78.

9. Footed Bowl

1917

Simon Gate; blown by Knut Bergqvist;
engraved by Gustaf Abels
Blown, engraved; $3^7/_8$ x 5 in. (9.9 x
12.6 cm)

Orrefors Glassworks
Marks: "SG KB"

Mrs. Agnes Hellner Collection,
Kungstenen Foundation, Stockholm
University
Inv. no. H 461

According to Agnes Hellner (fig. 9a),
Johan Ekman's daughter who was
married to Johannes Hellner, another
director of Orrefors, this is one of the
earliest pieces of engraved glass produced by Orrefors. The classical
depiction of the woman in the lunette
is an indication of the new direction
about to be taken at the factory as it
produced fewer examples of late Art
Nouveau work. This small bowl must
be considered a transitional piece; the

engraving may be neoclassical, but
the translucent mottled blue glass is
reminiscent of the earlier Art Nouveau
work. Mottled glass tended to compete with the engraved image, and
beginning in 1917, the engravings
would be done primarily on clear, colorless glass.

The restrained engraving gives no
indication of the lavish and technically
accomplished engraving that would
begin to be produced at the factory in
the next few years. The first piece of
engraved glass by Gate is a 1917 bottle called "The Temple of Love" (in the
Orrefors Museum). Intaglio engraving
would become the dominant means of
decoration at the factory for the next
decade and a half until designers
working in the 1930s brought new
technical and aesthetic innovations.
When Ekman died in 1918, Orrefors
was taken over by his daughter who
owned the company until 1946.
Hellner was an astute collector and
owned many early pieces by Gate and

Hald, among other Orrefors designers.
Her large collection of Orrefors glass
was eventually presented to
Stockholm University. DEO

Reference:Edenheim and Reihnér, *Simon
Gate, Edward Hald*, p. 35

Fig. 9a. Simon Gate, Agnes Hellner, Edward
Hald, 1927. (From Wettergren and Hald,
Simon Gate, Edward Hald)

10. Footed Vase

1917
Edward Hald
Blown, engraved; $7^5/_8$ x $4^3/_8$ in. (19.5 x 11 cm)

Orrefors Glassworks
Marks: "Hd-KB"

Orrefors Museum

Simon Gate and Edward Hald would dominate Orrefors's production for nearly a quarter of a century following the start of the First World War. Gate arrived at Orrefors in 1916 and Hald the following year. This vase and cat. nos. 11 and 12 are among the earliest examples of their work. They reveal how rapidly the two artists developed individual aesthetic expressions that quickly pushed Orrefors to the forefront of international, innovative design. Until the late 1920s, when their technical and aesthetic work expanded dramatically into entirely new means of expression, both men were essentially recognized for their designs for intaglio engraving. In that process the design was cut into the surface of the vessel as opposed to cameo engraving in which the surface of the vessel was cut away to leave the design in relief. Gate's designs were often very deeply cut; they were catagorized as baroque in feeling—richly detailed, undulent, and frequently sensual. Hald's engraved designs were confined more to the surface of the glass and were a remarkable blending of the austere, the linear, and the humorous.

Despite the differences in the kind of engraving specified for their designs, the same production methods were used at the factory. After the design was delineated on the glass by means of an adhesive ink laid on a varnish, the engraver used a wide array of copper disks with different cutting edges which rotated at adjustable, high speeds. A mixture of oil and emery powder enabled the disk to achieve a significant "bite" into the glass.

The economical treatment of the ornament on the surface of Hald's piece (cat. no. 12), is indicative of almost all of his later work. In contrast to the richer, more sculptural depiction of a nude by Gate, Hald's work relied on a series of simple lines. He added whimsy to an otherwise dry image by placing a miniature version of the woman's face and breasts in reflection in the mirror. Realizing that such a simple engraving might be lost on the clear glass vase, Hald chose to add an engraved oval to capture the viewer's eye.

What is also apparent in the covered jar by Hald is his earlier training in the studio of Henri Matisse just before the First World War. The flat, linear nudes executed by Matisse had a powerful influence on the young Swede. Hald also trained as a designer at the Technische Akademie in Dresden. Like Gate, he worked for a period as a painter but became better known as a designer of glass and ceramics. DEO

11. Footed Vase
1917
Simon Gate
Graal; 9⅞ x 6⅛ in. (25 x 15.5 cm)

Orrefors Glassworks
Marks: "Graal Orrefors 1917 K.B. No. 438"

The Oslo Museum of Applied Art
Inv. no. OK 9273

Because the First World War severely curtailed the number of European markets open to Orrefors, the glassworks was forced to sell its new glass almost exclusively in the Scandinavian region. In 1917, even though Gate had been at the firm for little more than a year and Hald for less than one, Orrefors promoted their new designs vigorously in a series of exhibitions. Historically, the most important of these was the Home Exhibition at the Liljevalchs Konsthall in Stockholm. In terms of gaining a new, affluent clientele, however, the 1917 exhibition at the prestigious Stockholm department store, Nordiska Kompaniet (NK), garnered the most attention. There the director of the Museum of Applied

Arts in Oslo saw the new graal and engraved glass and requested that Orrefors send a selection of this glass to his museum.

The exhibition opened in Oslo on November 7, 1917; it later traveled to the museum in Bergen, Norway. Of the work shown, 202 pieces were by Gate and 39 pieces by Hald. Of the 241 pieces shown, 118 were made in the graal technique, which indicates the considerable commitment made to this new technique developed only the year before by Simon Gate and the master-blower, Knut Bergqvist. The Swedes based this new technique on the overlay technique made popular by Gallé and used by his factory in Nancy, France. A blank is created with

a central core of one color of glass, usually overlaid or flashed with one or more layers of contrasting, colored glass. Once allowed to cool, the blank is cut, etched, and/or engraved. Decorative designs are thus created by exposing the various layers of colored glass. The blank is reheated, blown, and worked, and allowed to cool to its final shape.

Apart from its very early date, Gate's graal vase (cat. no. 11) is remarkable for its high degree of technical execution. The principal section of the vase was composed of an orange glass core, overlaid with thin layers of pink, light green, and dark green glass. The precision of the depiction of the three figures and the

12. Footed Covered Jar

1917
Edward Hald
Blown, engraved, cast-on elements;
9⅝ x 5½ in. (24.5 x 14 cm)

Orrefors Glassworks
Marks: "Hd-KB"

The Oslo Museum of Applied Art
Inv. no. OK 9274

ionic columns is rare in the graal technique which usually imparts a more limpid quality to the design. In the reheating and blowing of the engraved blank into its final form, it was unusual for the design on the smaller blank to retain its integrity as the blank was expanded and worked into the finished product. Unlike later work, the outer layers of this vase were removed by cutting and engraving and not by the more economical technique of eliminating them with acid-etching. The somewhat crude nature of the borders of the colors that define the design indicate that a wheel was most likely used to cut away the layers to reveal the design before the final reheating and blowing of the piece.

The Hald covered jar (cat. no. 12) is equally remarkable. According to a December 22, 1917, entry in the acquisition book at the Oslo Museum of Applied Art, "This is the first work by Hald from the factory." The spontaneous quality of the engraving indicates the hand of someone not intimately aware of the complexities of working with a high-speed copper engraving disk. Other than the "KB" for Knut Bergqvist, the master-blower who created the form, there is no further indication that an engraver might have helped to decorate this piece. Hald would not use this exuberant means of engraving for long. Instead, he soon developed a more economical, precise manner of engraving. The

form of Hald's piece is indebted to somewhat earlier Central European art glass.

It is remarkable that these pieces were purchased by the museum for the same sum, 500 kronor each, a considerable amount for wartime Europe. The graal vase would have been much more labor intensive, given the time needed to accomplish its multiple overlay, and its considerable cutting, engraving, and final reshaping. DEO

References: Brunius et al., *Svenskt Glas*, p. 87; Edenheim and Reihnér, *Simon Gate, Edward Hald*, p. 49; [Oslo newspaper] *17 de Mai* (November 7, 1917), cited in acquisition book, Kunstindustrimuseet, Oslo, Norway.

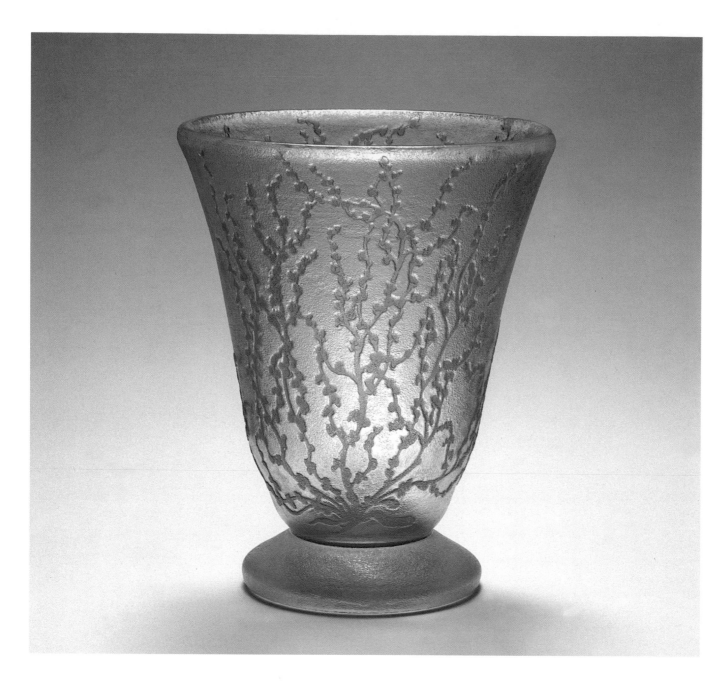

13. Footed Vase

1917
Edvin Ollers
Blown, overlay, etched; 7³/₄ x 6¹/₈
(19.8 x 15.7 cm)

Kosta Glassworks
Marks: "E.O. KOSTA 1917 Unik K2 [to
be done by hand]"

Nationalmuseum, Stockholm
Inv. no. NMK 236/1967

As a result of the efforts of Elsa Gullberg, a noted Swedish textile designer, Svenska Slöjdföreningen (The Swedish Society of Craft and Industrial Design) placed gifted artists with applied arts manufacturers, with the expressed intent of elevating the design of Swedish-made products.

Edvin Ollers, a painter and a drawing instructor at the School of Industrial Design in Stockholm, was one of the first to be employed through this system. In 1917 he was hired by Kosta Glassworks which was preparing to exhibit its work at the Home Exhibition at the Liljevalchs Konsthall in Stockholm. The organizers of the exhibition sought to provide Swedish consumers with well-made and well-designed domestic products which were affordable to a large segment of the public.

After the clear glass core of this vase was flashed with a thick overlay of yellow glass, the master-blower shaped the piece into a form designed by Ollers. His ornamental design was then traced on the yellow surface with the plant forms protected by an acid-resistent adhesive. The piece was then subjected to a series of baths in hydrofluoric acid which ate away the unprotected surfaces. Hydrofluoric acid, a powerful corrosive, had been discovered in Sweden in the 1760s by a German chemist, Karl Wilhelm Scheele. The frosted effect on this piece may have been achieved by mixing hydrofluoric acid with ammonia for several of the final baths.

The engraving on the underside of this vase indicates that this was a unique piece of art glass. DEO

References: Dahlback-Lutteman, ed., *Svenskt glas 1915–1960*, p. 47; Ricke and Gronert, *Glas in Schweden*, p. 189; Artéus, ed., *Kosta 250 Years*, p. 53.

14. Decanter, Vinegar Bottle, and Liquor Glass
1917
Simon Gate
Optic blown; decanter, 10³⁄₈ x 3³⁄₄ in. (26.5 x 9.4 cm); vinegar bottle, 7¹⁄₂ x 2³⁄₈ in. (19 x 5.9 cm); glass, 2¹⁄₂ x 2¹⁄₈ in. (6.8 x 5.4 cm)

Orrefors Glassworks

Orrefors Museum

The ribbing of some of these pieces is the result of the optic blowing technique. After the gob was taken from the gather and marvered, it was blown into a mold that had been cast with internal ridges. The air pressure, which forced the gob to expand into the mold, helped to impress the delicate ribs onto the glass. The manufacture of sulphate glass is a direct reflection of the wartime restrictions that prevented soda, one of the principal ingredients of glass, from entering Sweden, which had no indigenous stocks of this mineral. Germany, the principal supplier of soda to many European glassworks, was blocked from exporting this stock by wartime trade embargos. The use of sulphates, as a replacement for soda, imparted an irregular quality to the glass which contrasted with the prewar standard of precise, technically flawless glass. The sulphates also imparted a pale green tint to the glass which could be adjusted through the use of metallic oxides. It appears that sulphate glass was most commonly used for less expensive glass; and its use ceased by the 1920s. DEO

Reference: Edenheim and Reihnér, *Simon Gate, Edward Hald*, p. 34.

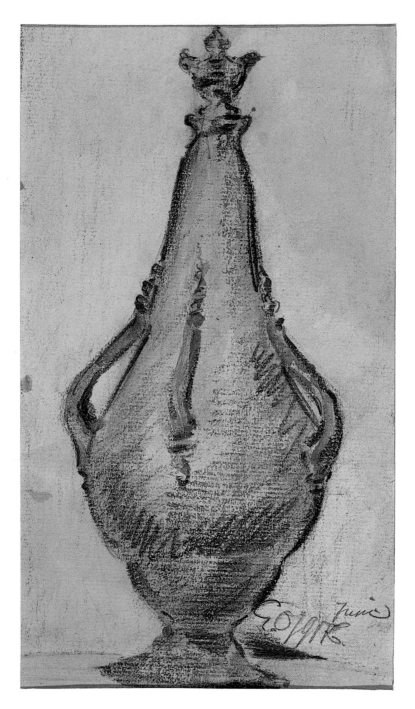

15. Drawing for Carafe

1917
Edvin Ollers
Pastel, watercolor, pencil; 10³/₈ x
5⁷/₈ in. (26.4 x 14.8 cm)

Inscription: "E.O. 1917 Juni" [E.O.
1917 June]

Kosta Museum

Few drawings by Edvin Ollers exist, but his ability to impart the vigorous, somewhat imprecise nature of the form he hoped to attain from glass is evident here. The twenty-nine-year-old Ollers was introduced to the management of the Kosta Glassworks by the influential Elsa Gullberg, a textile designer. Ollers, like Hald and Gate, had been a painter, and Gullberg and others thought that he would be able to bring the aesthetic sensibilities of an artist to the glass designed at Kosta. It appears as though the management of Kosta felt that there was a bohemian sensibility in his designs, rather than the artistic refinement that they had hoped to achieve. Apparently, Ollers's attempts to instill a more vigorous aesthetic into Kosta's line were not met with much favor from either management or workers. His pursuit of powerful new forms and use of a richer but less pure glass was perhaps undertaken too quickly. Despite the acclaim that his work received at the 1917 Home Exhibition, Ollers left Kosta later that year. He returned to the factory in 1931 for a year. DEO

Reference: Artéus, ed., *Kosta 250 Years*, p. 52.

16. Carafe and Assorted Glasses

1917

Edvin Ollers

Free-blown, cast-on elements; beer glass, 4⅝ x 2⅞ in. (11.7 x 7.3 cm); wineglass, 5⅜ x 3⅛ in. (13.5 x 7.8 cm); wineglass, 4⅝ x 2¼ in. (11.8 x 5.7 cm); cordial glass, 3⅞ x 2¼ in. (9.9 x 5.8 cm); carafe, 11⅛ x 6¼ in. (28.3 x 16 cm)

Kosta Glassworks

Smålands Museum, Swedish Glass Museum, Växjö
Inv. nos. M 8855 (beer glass); M 8854 (wineglass); M 12491 (cordial glass); M 12490 (wineglass); M 18970 (carafe)

The functional tableware designed by Ollers during his brief tenure at Kosta was first shown to a large audience in the 1917 Home Exhibition at the Liljevalchs Konsthall in Stockholm. Nearly two decades earlier, Ellen Key, a Swedish reformer, had published a highly influential group of essays entitled *Skönhet för alla* (Beauty for all; 1899) which provided the foundation for modern Swedish design. Key's principal tenets of good design for a beautiful home were simplicity, functionality, and individuality, and she stressed that these qualities should be available to all Swedes. These pieces by Kosta can be seen, in part, as having emerged from the design parameters set by her writings.

Ollers's tableware was inexpensive. Based on late-eighteenth and early-nineteenth century Swedish glassware, which was affordable only to the gentry and nobility, these later designs possessed aristocratic connotations that must have aided Kosta in its marketing efforts with status-conscious consumers. This association, possibly seen by some as effete, was offset by the colors and spontaneous effects achieved by the irregular quality of the glass. Most tableware at the time was made from clear glass, usually ornamented with deep facets or with hand-cut or machine-made historicist ornament. The irregular quality of Ollers's glass was achieved by throwing sand into the melt. It is reported that the workers at Kosta, whose products were respected for the purity and the quality of the glass, were embarrassed by having this "flawed" glass put on display. DEO

References: Holmérand Reihnér, *Lyricism of Modern Design*, p. 26; Ericsson, *Svenskt 1920–tal*, pp. 100–101; Artéus, ed., *Kosta 250 Years*, p. 120; Herlitz-Gezelius, *Kosta*, pp. 38–39; Ricke and Gronert, *Glas en Schweden*, p. 189.

17. Vase called "Triton"

ca. 1917
Simon Gate, Knut Bergqvist
Blown, wheel cut; 9 x 9⁷⁄₈ in. (23 x 25.4 cm)

Orrefors Glassworks

Mrs. Agnes Hellner Collection,
Kungstenen Foundation, Stockholm
University
Inv. no. H 547

Fig. 17a. Carl Milles, The Triton Fountain.
(Courtesy, Millesgården, Lidingö, Sweden)

The growing intimacy between Sweden's art community and its applied arts industries by around 1917 is fully evident in these vases, part of a group of cut-glass pieces that were called the "Triton" series. The sculptor Carl Milles was the most internationally recognized Swedish artist during much of the twentieth century. At the time these pieces were designed, Gate, then a young artist engaged by Orrefors to redesign its line, was well aware of artistic developments in Stockholm. In 1916 Milles had produced his Triton fountain with its vase-shaped, fluted base (fig. 17a). This fountain was purchased by Prince Eugen for his own residence in Stockholm. Prince Eugen was a gifted painter and the principal patron of Swedish artists in the early years of this century. Milles's statue was

18. Vase called "Triton"

Designed 1917, this example ca.
1919–20
Simon Gate
Blown, wheel cut; 11³⁄₈ x 8⁵⁄₈ in.
(28.8 x 22 cm)

Orrefors Glassworks
Marks: "SG KB"

Mrs. Agnes Hellner Collection,
Kungstenen Foundation, Stockholm
University
Inv. no. H 290

deemed "reminiscent of Bernini," and its rich, baroque form has obvious parallels in Gate's own work of the 1910s and 1920s. Within months of a January 1917 review of the fountain (including an illustration), Gate and Orrefors had introduced these cut-glass vases.

The black example relates most closely to the fountain base designed by Milles, and like the other examples from this series, it required meticulous handwork for the execution of the mechanistic flutes cut into the thick sides of the vessels. The precise execution of the first rib set the course for all succeeding wheel cuts from the lip to the base. Even the slightest deviation from this pattern destroyed the precision required by the design and meant that the piece had to be destroyed.

The transparent green example reveals an additional decorative effect achieved through an optical illusion not possible in the translucent black example and presumably not planned originally by Gate. Each of the deep cuts, known as "olive cuts," picks up and compresses the image of a multiple group of cuts from the opposite side of the vessel. This imparts the impression of delicate ribbing on each of the principal flutes on the vase. The cutting of the flutes on the green "Triton" vase is finer in quality than those on the black example—an indication that it may be a slightly later version, made after the glass cutters had improved their skills.

The production of these powerful, geometric forms was unusual at Orrefors, but it follows work designed in the early teens by individuals such as Josef Hoffmann for the Moser Glassworks in Karlsbad as well as other Bohemian glass firms. DEO

References: Brunius, "Milles Triton till Valdemarsudde," n.p.; Paulsson, ed., *Modernt Svenskt Glas*, p. 90, fig. 29; Duncan, *Orrefors Glass*, p. 35; Noever, ed., *Josef Hoffmann*, p. 268; Ricke and Gronert, *Glas in Schweden*, p. 70; Edenheim and Reihnér, *Simon Gate, Edward Hald*, p. 37; Dahlback-Lutteman, ed., *Svenskt Glas*, p. 82; "Aspects Nouveaux des arts en Suède," p. 183.

19. Dressing Set

ca. 1917/1918
Simon Gate
Blown, cast-on elements; tray, 1 x 11 x
9⅝ in. (2.5 x 28 x 24.6 cm); two
flacons, 6⅞ x 3⅛ in. (17.5 x 8.0 cm);
two flat jars, 3 x 4⅛ in. (7.5 x 10.5
cm); round jar including lid, 5¼ x
3⅝ in. (13.2 x 9.2 cm)

Sandvik Glassworks

Mrs. Agnes Hellner Collection,
Kungstenen Foundation, Stockholm
University
Inv. no. H259-264

Sandvik was a small, undistinguished glassworks purchased by Orrefors in 1917 and recognized for its inexpensive tablewares. Ekman and the other managers of Orrefors sought to elevate the prestige of this economically priced glassware by marketing it in three significant ways: the catalogues began to carry the prestigious name of Orrefors; they increasingly produced new designs by Edward Hald and Simon Gate; and finally, they marketed the Sandvik product line with the names of their new designers listed on the title page of each catalogue and elsewhere. Orrefors identified the vast numbers of individual designs in their catalogues with a "G" or an "H" to identify either Gate or Hald as the designer. Designer glassware had come to the everyday marketplace.

In a Sandvik catalogue of the early-mid 1920s, the firm offered hundreds of household items including candlesticks, carafes, pitchers, bowls, plates, stemware, tumblers, smoking implements, and dressing table items. Made from inexpensive glass, these thin-walled pieces came in a range of delicate colors. Decorated with optically blown details and cast-on ornament, the pieces were sold throughout the world, including the United States by the 1920s. The glass covered the aesthetic spectrum from severe pieces to those that were extravagantly decorated with cast-on work and painted decoration. Despite the fact that this work was inexpensive, the quality of glass was superb and the consistency of the thin walls of the vessels equal to that produced at other glassworks that served the upper levels of the market.
DEO

References: Edenheim and Reihnér, *Simon Gate, Edward Hald*, p. 41.

20. Tazza

ca. 1918
Simon Gate
Blown, cast-on elements; 9³⁄₈ x 9¹⁄₄ in.
(24 x 23.5 cm)

Sandvik Glassworks
Marks: "GS 557"

Orrefors Museum

The ceremonial design of this tazza indicates that its purpose was primarily decorative. Its basin reveals the purity of the "metal," and the articulation of the stem, the skills of the glassmaster who made this piece. Indebted to seventeenth-century *façon de Venise* designs, this footed bowl represents the early stages of Swedish modernism in the late 1910s and early 1920s. Emergent modernist aesthetics were frequently built on past traditions. DEO

References: Holmér and Reihnér, *Lyricism of Modern Design*, p. 59; Holmér and Ernstell, *Svenskt Glas*, p. 63; Ricke and Gronert, *Glas in Schweden*, p. 75.

21. Decanter and Pair of Liquor Glasses

1916
Simon Gate
Blown, cast-on elements; decanter, 11½ x 4⅝ in. (28.3 x 11.9 cm); glass, 3½ x 1⅜ in. (8.9 x 3.4 cm)

Orrefors Glassworks
Marks: "G KB" (decanter)

Orrefors Museum

The design of this set is indebted to the simple forms and applied decoration that had been popular in the eighteenth century. These earlier pieces were used in the late teens by many progressive Swedish designers who were seeking a new means of expression by building on past traditions. In many respects, this approach to the regeneration of the decorative arts had its roots in the work of British Arts and Crafts designers who were inspired by medieval English work.

The forms of this decanter and glasses were popular for many years; nearly identical pieces were still being retailed at the end of the 1930s in New York City, where they were identified in *House and Garden* as the "Baltic" pattern. The mark, "KB," identifies Knut Bergqvist as the glassblower. DEO

References: Hald and Wettergren, *Simon Gate, Edward Hald*, p. 34.

22. Footed Vase

1918
Simon Gate
Graal; 11 x 5¼ in. (28 x 13.8 cm)

Orrefors Glassworks
Marks: "SGraal Orrefors KB 18.HW No 711"

Mrs. Agnes Hellner Collection,
Kungstenen Foundation, Stockholm
University
Inv. no. H 31

The sophisticated colors of this vase impart a subtle quality to an otherwise fundamental form. Orange glass was flashed over the yellow core, and it is the minimal contrast between these two colors, as well as the interlocking pattern of the ornament, that lends this piece its greatest interest.

The word *graal* is taken from the medieval Latin for "platter" or "bowl." In the New Testament, the Grail was the chalice used at the Last Supper for the celebration of the first Mass. The marks on the underside of this piece indicate that it was made by the master-glassblower Knut Bergqvist ("KB") and decorated to Gate's designs by Heinrich Wollman ("HW"). DEO

References: Brunius et al., *Svenskt Glas*, p. 82.

23. Footed Bowl

ca. 1918
Simon Gate
Blown, engraved; 8³⁄₈ x 8¹⁄₄ in. (21.4 x 21.1 cm)

Orrefors Glassworks
Marks: "G 111/19 Orrefors"

Orrefors Museum

The powerful appearance of this footed bowl contrasts dramatically with the usually more graceful forms produced by Orrefors at the end of the First World War. The proportions of the articulated foot and the bowl are repeated to some degree in the almost kinetic design of the engraving. The closest parallel to this design would be progressive cubist-inspired Bohemian crystal that was being made around the same time.

Both the form and ornament of this piece are unlike Gate's general production; there are only a few similar examples in the serially numbered drawing books in the Orrefors archives. Produced just two years after

Gate joined the factory, this bowl may have been used to test different areas of the marketplace. DEO

References: Ricke and Thor, *Schwedische Glasmanufacturen*, p. 20.

24. Footed Covered Jar called "Negerhyddan" [The African Hut]

Designed 1918, this example 1923
Edward Hald
Blown, engraved, cast-on elements;
10³/₈ x 5 in. (26.5 x 12.7 cm)

Orrefors Glassworks
Marks: "Orrefors Hald 65.26.H."

Collection Birgitta Crafoord

By 1918 the manner of engraving that Hald requested from the engravers at Orrefors had changed considerably. From the loose, more expressive engraving on earlier designs (see cat. nos. 10 and 12), it had developed into meticulous, almost lavish depiction of detail. Hald rose to the challenge of producing glass that was both commercial and aesthetically significant. The technically flawless engraving also shows the dramatic improvement in the engraving rooms of the firm just after the First World War. Engraving had not been a common technique in the decoration of Swedish glass before the war. Instead, the industry had been dominated by wheel-cut faceted glass.

The precise, linear quality of the engraving of this jar, devoid of vigorous detailing and deep cuts, reveals the best precision engraving available at Orrefors in the 1920s and equals some of the finest work of Central European glass factories renowned for the technique. The absence of "chatter," or the concentric rings indicative of the movement of a copper wheel, around the clean lines of Hald's designs might suggest that a diamond-tipped stylus was used to produce this effect. There is no evidence, however, that a diamond was otherwise used to engrave the decorative elements of Orrefors's finest output, except to "sign" the bottom of the piece.

Although one of Hald's specialities was his series of humorous vases with engraved narrations, this piece is additionally significant in its remarkable symbiosis of form and engraving, a manner of design that Hald made his leitmotif in the 1920s. In this more specialized body of work, the anecdote told by engraved designs depends fully on the form of the vessel. Only Vicke Lindstrand in the interwar period would develop this idiom in his engraved designs. DEO

References: Ricke and Gronert, *Glas in Schweden,* p. 91.

25. Carafe and Assorted Glasses from the Service called "Wild Strawberries" or "Mimosa"

1918; carafe, 1917
Edward Hald
Blown, engraved; carafe [stopper missing], 12 ⅝ x 4 ¼ in. (32 x 10.8 cm); glasses, smallest, 3 x 2½ in. (7.6 x 6.4 cm); largest, 7⅛ x 3½ in. (18.2 x 8.9 cm)

Orrefors Glassworks
Marks: "Hd:KB" (carafe)

Orrefors Museum

In 1917 Orrefors had acquired the Sandvik Glassworks and began revising its product line. At the same time the factory was redesigning its own production. In addition to the new art glass made with the graal technique or decorated with virtuosic engraving, Orrefors also introduced new lines of stemware. These would play an increasingly important role both in elevating the reputation of the firm and in strengthening its finances. Because of the hand engraving on each piece, "Wild Strawberries," also known as "Mimosa," was among the most expensive functional glassware produced by Orrefors. According to the pattern book in the Orrefors archive, Hald's "Wild Strawberries" was an extensive line that included stemware, drinking glasses, vases, and plates. In 1920 Hald added several more forms

to the line, a possible indication of its continued popularity.

The pattern books in the Orrefors archives indicate that Gate's "Cloud" pattern (cat. no. 27) was introduced earlier than Hald's "Wild Strawberries." Although the flair of the bowls of Gate's glasses may not be as graceful as those used for "Wild Strawberries" and the articulation of Gate's stems may be less dynamic, the engraved designs for the "Cloud" pattern possess considerably more vigor. Hald's "Wild Strawber-ries" engravings are somewhat subservient to the blown forms of his pieces. DEO

References: cat. no. 26, Ricke and Gronert, *Glas in Schweden*, p. 96–97; cat. no. 27, Ricke and Gronert, *Glas in Schweden*, p. 79.

26. Dish and Underplate from the Service called "Wild Strawberries" or "Mimosa"
1918
Edward Hald
Blown, engraved; underplate, $10^{7}/_{8}$ in.(27.5 cm diam); dish, $2^{3}/_{4}$ x $10^{1}/_{2}$ in. (7 x 26.8 cm)

Orrefors Glassworks

Orrefors Museum

27. Glasses called "Molnet" (The Cloud)
1918
Simon Gate
Blown, engraved; smallest, 3 x $2^{3}/_{8}$ in. diam. (7.6 x 6.0 cm); largest, $7^{1}/_{2}$ x $3^{3}/_{4}$ in. (19.2 x 9.5 cm)

Orrefors Glassworks
Marks: "Of G 100"

Orrefors Museum

28. Footed Bowl

1918
Edward Hald
Graal; diam. 4³⁄₄ in. (12 cm)

Orrefors Glassworks
Marks: "SGraal Hd Orrefors 1918"

Knutsson Art & Antiques, Sweden

This simple bowl resting on a columnar foot represents a departure from the highly complex forms frequently used by Gate and Hald for the production of graal glass between the late 1910s and early 1920s. An examination of the drawings of graal pieces in the Orrefors archives and the considerable number of extant pieces made with this technique reveal that the designers often specified dynamic forms that would compliment the richly colored ornament of their graal work. Cast-on elements were also frequently used for the early graal pieces.

It is likely that this footed bowl was created by using an acid bath: the design was painted on with an acid resist material to protect the continuity of the deep blue tendrils, and the form was then repeatedly immersed in an acid bath to remove the deep blue outer glass and expose the underglass, which was lighter in color, providing the contrast necessary for

Hald's design. The more graceful, serpentine lines of the deep blue elements would have been very difficult and labor intensive to cut into the surface of the blank with copper wheels, which would have added considerably to the cost of this small piece. DEO

References: Knutsson, *Swedish Art in Glass*, p. 12.

29. Bowl

1919
Simon Gate, Knut Bergqvist, Heinrich Wollman
Graal; 2½ x 5½ in. (6.3 x 14 cm)

Orrefors Glassworks
Marks: "Graal Orrefors 19KB HW No 5/2"

Orrefors Museum

The complexities of the graal technique are easily understood by studying this simple bowl. The base glass was orange over which a darker, brown color was flashed. Once the blank had cooled, the engraver, in this case Heinrich Wollman, cut away the outer brown layers in an alternating, basketweave pattern according to Gate's design. When the form was reheated by Bergqvist so that it could be blown into its final shape, elements of the brown overlay overheated and became too fluid. This is apparent where elements of the brown basketwork run together. DEO

32. Vase

1920
Edward Hald
Graal; 7³/₄ x 6⁷/₈ in. (19.7 x 17.5 cm)

Orrefors Glassworks
Marks: "1920 HD Ofs"

Mrs. Agnes Hellner Collection,
Kungstenen Foundation, Stockholm
University
Inv. no. H 38

This vase is a deceptively simple example of graal glass produced to the designs of Hald. Although the form itself was easy to execute, the removal of the darker amethyst-colored overlay required a considerable amount of labor if this was achieved by engraving. It is more likely, however, that acid resist was used to paint the design on the vessel which was then dipped in an acid bath. DEO

References: Edenheim and Reihnér, *Simon Gate, Edward Hald,* p. 30.

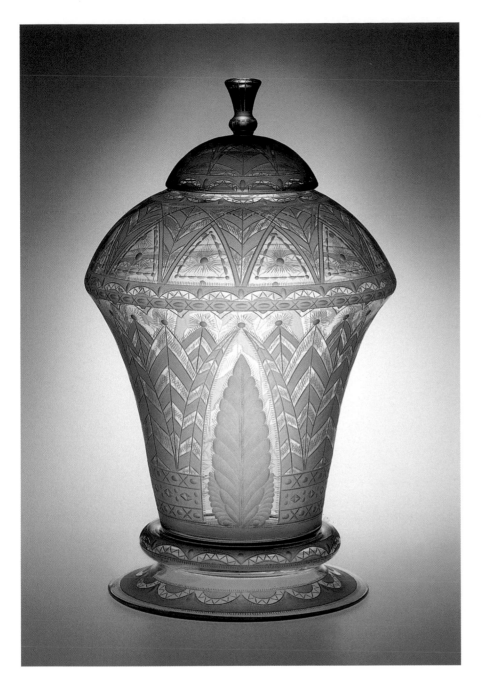

Fig. 33a. Detail of cat. no. 33.

33. Covered Footed Urn

Designed 1920, this example 1925
Edward Hald
Blown, engraved, cast-on element; 15
x 9¾ in. (38 x 24.7 cm)

Orrefors Glassworks
Marks: "Orrefors Hald 183.25
W.E."(1925)

Länsförsäkring Kronoberg, Växjö,
Sweden

The dense, ornamental motifs engraved on this piece are highly unusual both in Hald's decorative output and as an example of Swedish modernism. From the late teens until the late twenties, Swedish design, both in architectural circles and in the decorative arts, was characterized by neoclassicism. This is particularly evident in buildings and objects that were ceremonial in function. This neoclassicism was usually transformed by attenuated proportions and rich colors, and the ornament was frequently silhouetted against blank backgrounds. Hald's work at Orrefors was usually delicate and invariably graceful.

This urn by Hald contradicts the characteristics associated with his work of the 1920s, especially in the early part when he was developing his manner of decorating his pieces. The tight, aggressive ornament of the design of the engraving is reminiscent of work by the French master metalworker Edgar Brandt. His work was considered revolutionary when it was exhibited at the 1925 Paris exposition. A monumental screen called "L'Oasis," which was installed in Brandt's own pavilion at the fair, displayed similar motifs and the same density of ornament.

Another version of this urn in colorless, clear glass, with a crown for a finial and bearing a monogram, was presented to the Crown Prince of Japan by the Swedish Crown Prince (later King Gustav Adolf VI) during his honeymoon trip to Japan in December 1923. DEO

References: Ricke and Gronert, *Glas in Schweden*, p. 96; Holmér and Reihnér, *Lyricism in Modern Design*, p. 56.

34. Vase called "Girls Playing Ball" and Underplate

1920, this example 1960
Edward Hald
Blown, engraved; with underplate;
9¼ x 11⅝ in. (23.5 x 29.5 cm)

Orrefors Glassworks
Marks: "Orrefors Hald 176 C8 AR"

Orrefors Museum

Hald's training in the studio of Henri Matisse is revealed in his design for a vase called "Girls Playing Ball." Hald's early success as a designer for the ceramics and glass industries in the 1910s was dependent, in part, on the artistic sensibility that he brought to his work. His training in Paris had exposed him to the work of many of the most avant-garde designers. In some respects, his use of flattened, conventionalized ornament also echos Maurice Marinot's painting on glass in the 1910s in France. When Hald returned to Sweden before the First World War, he was not as encumbered

by provincialism as were many of his compatriots. The modernist sensibility that he brought to his design work made the Orrefors production distinctive.

The flat, representational ornament of Hald's vase, suitable to the flaired sides of this vessel, presents a densely packed frieze that initially appears to be abstract. This vase, an immediate critical success, was considered by many to be a leitmotif of Hald's early work. Many museums have added it to their permanent collections: The Metropolitan Museum of Art in New York; the Nationalmuseum in Stockholm; the Worcester Art Museum in Worcester, Massachusetts; the Rohsska Museum in Gothenburg, Sweden; and The Cleveland Museum of Art, where the piece was acquired in 1938. Even at the Golden Gate Exhibition in San Francisco in 1939, Orrefors chose to display this model in the Swedish decorative arts section, an indication that the firm felt that this twenty-year-old-design still represented one of their finest achievements. DEO

References: Ricke and Gronert, *Glas in Schweden*, p. 95; Wettergren, *The Modern Decorative Arts of Sweden*, p. 116; Brunius et al., *Svenskt Glas*, p. 93.

Fig. 34a. *Le Luxe* (II), by Henri Matisse, ca. 1908; casein on canvas. (Statens Museum fur Kunst, Copenhagen. J. Rump Collection)

35. Glass for Schnapps

1920
Simon Gate
Blown, engraved; 4½ x 2½ in. (11.5 x 6.3 cm)

Orrefors Glassworks

Smålands Museum, Swedish Glass Museum, Växjö
Inv. no. M 16793

It is likely that this design was a special commission. Small schnapps glasses, a novelty item in the firm's production, were designed to be fitted to the finger or worn from a ribbon around the neck. They do not appear in the Orrefors catalogues during the twenties and thirties. When filled with schnapps or another beverage, the design would have been shown in its proper upright position, and the engraving would have received a stronger definition from the liquid. Based on a principle similar to that of a rhyton (an ancient horn-shaped drinking vessel), this small glass is exceptional for the attention that was payed to its detailing. DEO

36. Plate called "The Broken Jetty"

Designed 1920
Edward Hald
Blown, engraved; ½ x 10¾ in. (1.5 x 27.3 cm)

Orrefors Glassworks
Marks: "Of/illeg./17"

Collection of The Newark Museum
Museum Purchase 1925, Inv. no. 25.35

Of Hald's designs produced by Orrefors in the early 1920s, "The Broken Jetty" is one of the most idiosyncratic. Setting aside the neoclassicism that characterized much of his early work, Hald investigated a more Japanesque idiom in this model. Arguably, the vortex of the whirlpool in the center of the plate relates to its circular shape, but the remainder of the composition cuts across the surface, providing it with the most important element of its design.

This model does not appear to have entered many museum collections during the twenties; its unusual design may have been considered at odds both with Orrefors's signature production at the time and with Swedish modern design in general.

"The Broken Jetty" was shown at the Paris exposition in 1925, the same year that this example was purchased for the Newark Museum. DEO

References: Ricke and Gronert, *Glas in Schweden,* p. 94; Erik Wettergren, "Orreforsglas," in Paulsson, ed., *Svenska Slöjdföreningens Specialnummer,* p. 15; idem, *The Modern Decorative Arts of Sweden,* p. 118; Dahlback-Lutteman, *Edward Hald,* p. 67, 106; idem, ed., *Svenskt Glas,* p. 33.

37. Hanging Light Fixture

1921
Edward Hald
Blown, engraved, metal fittings; $17^3/_4$ x $15^1/_2$ x $5^1/_4$ in. (45 x 39.5 x 13.2 cm), including mounting

Orrefors Glassworks

Smålands Museum, Swedish Glass Museum, Växjö
Inv. no. M 47887

This is one of the earliest lighting fixtures designed by Hald. It is more an engraved piece of art glass than a lighting fixture, and it was obviously designed to showcase the talents of the young Edward Hald, then in his fourth year at the factory. The use of acid etching produced the frosted effect on the bowl and highlighted the engraved designs.

Many of the first light fixtures produced by Orrefors in the 1920s were criticized because the harsh illumination of the electric lightbulbs obliterated the engraved designs, especially in a simple form like this one. It was felt that many of the pieces looked better with the lights turned off so that the meticulously detailed designs could be seen. Experimentation brought about thicker glass, frosted and col-

ored surfaces, and improved designs for the electric apparatus and placement of bulbs, which corrected this problem.

Many of the fixtures from the twenties were more sculptural in design than this model and were frequently monumental in scale. The more robust forms enabled those light fixtures to be used in large, ceremonial spaces and to show off the skills of Orrefors's accomplished glassblowers. This hanging fixture was intended for an intimate space where the delicate detail of the basin would have been readily seen. DEO

References: Wettergren, *The Modern Decorative Arts of Sweden*, p. 111; Ricke, *Schwedische Glasmanufakturen*, p. 60.

38. Vase called "Fireworks" and Underplate

Designed 1921, this example 1924
Edward Hald
Blown, engraved; vase,
8¹⁄₈ x 10¹⁄₂ in. (20.5 x 26.6 cm); plate,
³⁄₄ x 8 in. (2 x 20.2 cm)

Orrefors Glassworks
Marks: "Orrefors Hald 248.1924 TL"

Länsförsäkring Kronoberg, Växjö,
Sweden

The vase called "Fireworks" is perhaps the most memorable of all pieces
executed to Hald's design and possibly the most famous model made by
Orrefors. It was called "Hald's masterpiece" by Erik Wettergren, one of the
most powerful advocates of Swedish
arts and crafts in the twenties and thirties. The design received its first public exhibition at the 1923 Gothenburg
Jubilee Exhibition. It was also shown in
Paris (1925), New York (1926 and
1927), and many other American
venues in the late 1920s.

By the time this model was introduced in 1921, progressive art glass
had been produced for nearly half a
century. The ownership of this type of
glass was considered a "serious"
expression of one's intellectual and
aesthetic sophistication. The superlative pieces of glass with whimsical
designs were an innovation in international circles immediately after the
First World War. Abstraction and ambiguity in design, neoclassicism,
Japanism were all then accepted in art

glass, but the depiction of humor was
rare. The small dog standing among
people observing the display of fireworks and the young, overweight girl
by the tented bandstand were not part
of the standard repertoire of motifs
used on art glass.

Because this model was produced
for many years, many different engravers at Orrefors had the opportunity to execute the design, and as a
result there are numerous variations
both in the engraving and in the
design itself. The explosions of fireworks and the renderings of trees and
figures often vary dramatically from
piece to piece. "TL" identifies Thure
Löfgren as the engraver of this example.

Of all the progressive Swedish
glass produced in the twentieth century, Hald's "Fireworks" vase may be the
most frequently chosen model to enter
permanent collections of major museums. There are examples in the Nationalmuseum, Stockholm; the
Orrefors Museum, Orrefors, Sweden;

the Museum at Malmö, Sweden; The Metropolitan Museum of Art, New York; and The Art Institute of Chicago.

This example of the "Fireworks" vase (cat. no. 39), with its dramatic deep blue overlay, is one of the most spectacular versions of this often-reproduced design. Between the clear glass base of the vase and the outer blue flashing is a very thin intermediate layer of yellow flashing to depict the heat generated by the explosions of the fireworks. This is further evidence of the skill of the glassworkers at Orrefors. The absence of an underplate is not unusual; the vase was illustrated on several occasions without one. DEO

References: Wettergren, *The Modern Decorative Arts of Sweden*, p. 116; Erik Wettergren, "Orreforsglas," in Paulsson, ed., *Svenska Slöjdföreningens Specialnummer*, p. 1; Wollin, *Modern Swedish Decorative Arts*, p. 111; "Orrefors Bruk," *Decorative Kunst*, pp. 69–76; Paulsson, ed., *Modernt Svenskt Glas*, p. 82; Knutsson, *Swedish Art in Glass*, p. 35; Herlitz-Gezelius, *Orrefors Ett Svenskt Glasbruk*, pp. 38–39; Dahlback-Lutteman, *Edward Hald*, p. 79, 106; Duncan, *Orrefors Glass*, p. 24; Brunius et al., *Svenskt Glas*, p. 93.

39. Vase called "Fireworks"

1921
Edward Hald
Blown, overlay, engraved;
8¼ x 11⅛ in. (21 x 28.2 cm)

Orrefors Glassworks
Marks: "Of.H.248.F.H"

Länsförsäkring Kronoberg, Växjö, Sweden

Fig. 38a. Installation of Orrefors glass at the Gothenburg Jubilee Exhibition, 1923.

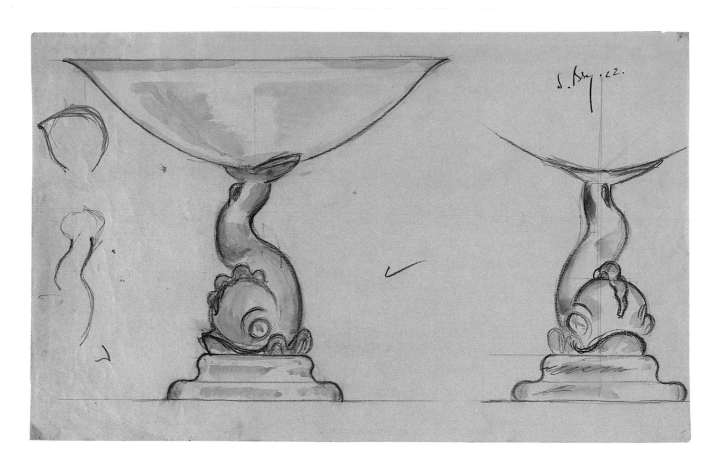

40. Drawing for Footed Bowl
1922
Sten Branzell
Watercolor, ink and pencil; 8$\frac{1}{8}$ x
14$\frac{1}{8}$ in. (20.7 x 36 cm)

Inscription: "S. Bra[?] 22"

Kosta Museum

During his tenure at Kosta (1922–29) Sten Branzell produced a remarkable body of work for the firm perhaps because he stayed longer than other principal artists at Kosta during the 1910s and 1920s: Edvin Ollers (1917–18, 1931–32), Karl Hultström (1917–19, 1927–28), and Ewald Dahlskog (1926–29). In contrast artists who worked at Kosta's chief rival, Orrefor—such as Edward Hald, Simon Gate, and Vicke Lindstrand—stayed with the factory for decades. Kosta, an older and more conservative company than Orrefors, may have had a more difficult internal, working environment. In seeking a share in a market that was rapidly becoming domi-

nated by Orrefors, Kosta and its directors may have had difficulty in working with the design department. DEO

41. Centerpiece

ca. 1930
Sten Branzell
Blown, engraved, cast-on elements;
13¾ x 11⅜ in. (35 x 29 cm)

Kosta Glassworks
Marks: "S.B. No 626"

Kosta Museum

By the First World War, Kosta was the oldest surviving Swedish glassworks; its name carried enormous prestige in Sweden. In 1923 architect Sten Branzell and painter Axel Törneman, working for Kosta, designed a 40-inch-high covered urn to commemorate the dedication of Stockholm's new City Hall. Surmounted by a dolphin, the City Hall urn was perhaps the only piece of Swedish presentation glass to equal the great "Paris Vase" which had been designed by Simon Gate.

This impressive centerpiece, which repeats the dolphin and other elements of the City Hall urn, was probably designed for a dining table. The working of the dolphin, the delicate engraving of the waves around the basin, and the ornament on the foot indicate an aesthetic at Kosta that was very different from new work then coming out of Orrefors. Kosta, an older and more conservative factory than Orrefors, was slower to change and had not yet embraced the new techniques and aesthetics that characterized its rival's production. DEO

References: Artéus, ed. Kosta 250 Years of Craftsmanship, p. 128; Paulsson, ed. Modernt Svenskt Glas, pp. 77, 149.

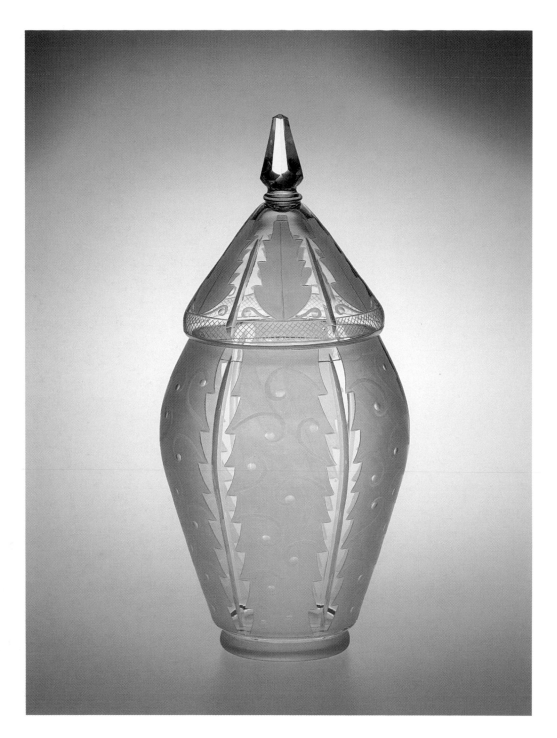

51. Covered Urn

1924
Edvin Ollers
Blown, engraved, cut with cast-on
element; 10¼ x 4⅝ in. (25.9 x
11.7 cm)

Elme Glassworks
Marks: "Edv. Ollers. 1924"

Smålands Museum, Swedish Glass
Museum, Växjö
Inv. no. M 15223

Edvin Ollers, who had worked at Kosta
for two years, was hired by Elme
Glassworks in 1926, nine years after
the firm had been started. Elme
became recognized for the quality of
its glass, and by the end of the 1920s,
it employed 300 workers. The firm
produced both pressed glass for the
middle range of the market and finer
art glass, such as this covered urn, for
the luxury market.

This piece reveals Ollers's own
deep awareness of the changes in the
Swedish glassmaking community that
had been initiated by Simon Gate and
Edward Hald at Orrefors. The richly
worked surface, expertly engraved,

recalls a covered jar Edward Hald had
completed at the beginning of the
1920s. Ollers was considered an artistic rebel for the shockingly new glass
that he had produced for Kosta to display in the 1917 Home Exhibition at
the Liljevalchs Konsthall in Stockholm.
He may have become more conservative in the years that had lapsed since
that seminal exhibition. It may be that
he also recognized the need to produce commercially viable glass if a
factory was to remain open and he
were to continue working as a designer. DEO

52. Footed Bowl called "The Turtle"

1924
Edward Hald
Blown, cast-on element, engraved, acid-etched; 4 x 7¾ in. (10.2 x 18.8 cm)

Orrefors Glassworks
Marks: "Orrefors [H]476.32.D"

Mrs. Agnes Hellner Collection, Kungstenen Foundation, Stockholm University
Inv. no. H 75

Most of Hald's pieces gain their decorative effect from the incision of lines into the walls of the vessels. Rarely did he design a truly sculptural piece such as this small bowl. Part of its charm is derived from the ambiguity of the four feet of the turtle, which are barely descernible from the creature's tail and head. DEO

References: Hald and Wettergren, *Simon Gate Edward Hald*, p. 86; Edenheim and Reihnér, *Simon Gate, Edward Hald*, p. 35; Brunius et al., *Svenskt Glas*, p. 117.

53. Assorted Glasses

Designed ca. 1922–30
Sten Branzell
Blown; smallest, 2¼ x 2⅜ in. (5.6 x
6.0 cm); largest, 5¾ x 4⅛ in. (14.5 x
10. 5 cm)

Kosta Glassworks
Marks: "S.B. No 1" (bottom of one
glass)

Kosta Museum

Trained as an architect and town planner, Sten Branzell succeeded Edvin Ollers as the leading designer at Kosta in 1922 and remained at the factory for eight years. There is a continuity in approach between the work of the two designers, seen in the formal simplicity of these glasses. Ollers received widespread acclaim at the 1917 Home Exhibition in Stockholm for his designs for domestic tableware. Since then this type of glassware has been associated with the Kosta product line.

This design is an early attempt at achieving the modernist ideal of simple, good design for everyday use that later became a slogan of Swedish design, especially at the 1930

Stockholm Exhibition. These glasses are notable for their lack of extraneous surface ornament; the handblown form is imbued with considerable elegance. Blue glass was a Branzell trademark through the 1920s. NS-L

References: Artéus ed., *Kosta 250 Years*, pp. 130–31; Ricke and Gronert, *Glas in Schweden*, p. 192.

54. Footed Bowl

ca. 1925
Edward Hald
Graal; 6¾ x 7⅞ in. (17.2 x 18.7 cm)

Orrefors Glassworks
Marks: "Graal Orrefors Hald 1920-talet"

Orrefors Museum

By the middle of the 1920s, the number of graal pieces produced by Orrefors had begun to decrease considerably, most likely the result of shifts in consumer taste as modernism began to have an impact in the marketplace. The rich colors and highly articulated forms used for graal glass of the late 1910s and early 1920s may no longer have appealed to consumers. Orrefors's own success with engraved glass may have overshadowed its production of graal glass.

This exquisite bowl, Japanesque in feeling, recalls Hald's 1920 engraved dish called "The Broken Jetty." The removal of the red flashing was most likely achieved by acid etching. DEO

References: Holmér and Reihnér, *Lyricism in Modern Design*, p. 64.

63. Drawing for Vase and Tray
1927
Ewald Dahlskog
Pencil and ink on paper; 14³⁄₈ x 17⁷⁄₈ in. (36.4 x 45.4 cm)

Inscription: "Skål med fat kallad vindarna Driven kant på skålen graveras med vågor i likhet med teckningen runt skålen Figurerna sättes in enligt kompassen ställningen enligt märken i lodlinje Väster blommor Öster frukt Västan Östan Nordan Norr Öster Söder Väster 16 Nov. 1927 Ewald Dahlskog" [Bowl with plate called the Winds / Flared edge on both bowl and plate; the foot on the bowl engraved with waves like the drawing around the bowl. The figures put according to the directions of the compass / according to marks in lines / West flowers / East fruits / West wind / East wind / North wind / North, east, south, west / Nov. 16 1927 / Ewald Dahlskog]

Kosta Museum

Having trained as a painter, Ewald Dahlskog brought a strong creative impulse to the production of art glass at Kosta during his tenure there from 1926 to 1929. His figurative style was consistent with the prevailing neoclassicism of engraved art glass. This preparatory sketch for an engraved vase and tray reveals an adept handling of the figure. It depicts the personification of the Four Winds as four classical-inspired figures, each with flowing drapery evoking the movement of the wind. The drawing also provides instructions to the craftsman for the placement of figures on the vase. NS-L

64. Footed Cup

ca. 1927
Knut Bergqvist
Optic blown, cast-on elements;
9 x 8⅝ in. (27.7 x 22 cm)

Orrefors Glassworks
Marks: "Orrefors K.B. 1927"

Collection Birgitta Crafoord

This is a generic design, similar to six-teenth- and seventeenth-century tazza produced in Venice. It was worked solely by Bergqvist and is a testament to his considerable skills as a glass-blower. The seamless application of cast-on decoration onto the stem and the striking regularity were difficult to achieve. Within the Orrefors factory, Bergqvist was usually entrusted with working out many of the new tech-niques and aesthetics developed by the design department. DEO

Fig. 64a. Master-blower Knut Bergqvist at Orrefors, 1920. (From Hald and Wettergren, *Simon Gate, Edward Hald*)

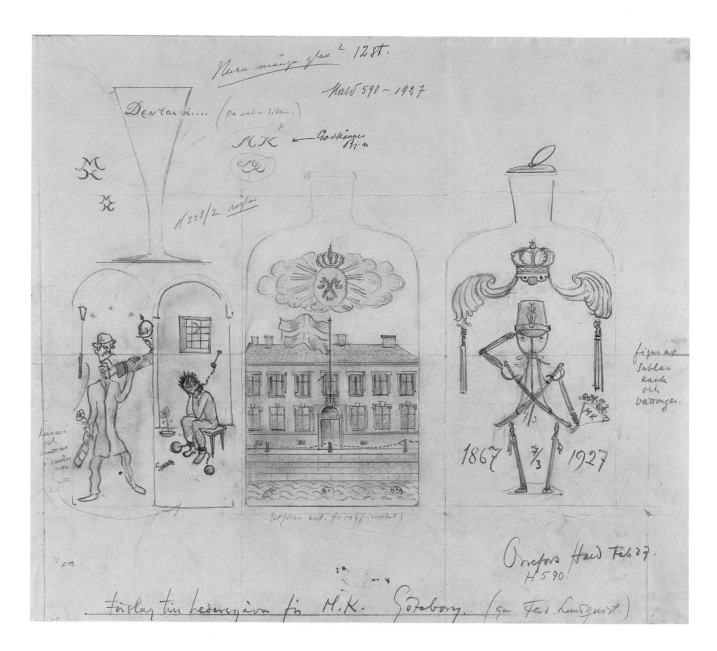

65. Drawing for Schnapps Bottle and Glass

ca. 1927
Edward Hald
Pencil on paper; 15¾ x 18⅛ in.
(40 x 46 cm)

Inscription: "Huru många glas? 12 st /
Hald 590 -1927 / Den tar vi... (på
andra sidan) / MK G[illegible] / MGK /
H 238/2 råglas / figur av sablar, kask
och batonger / MK / 1867 7/3 1927 /
Orrefors Hald Feb 27 / H 590 / Förslag
till hedersgåva för M. K. Göteborg /
(gm. Ferd. Lundquist) / Kasas och
mattas i kanten / Utföres enligt foto"
[How many glasses? 12 / Hald 590 -
1927 / We take it . . . (on other side) /
MKG[illegible] / MGK/ H238/2 rough
glass / figure of sabres, helmut and
batons / MK / 1867 7/3 / 1927 /
Orrefors Hald Feb 27 / H 590 /
Suggestion for commemorative gift M.
K. Gothenburg / (gm. Ferd. Lundquist)
/ Should be engraved and should be
done very matte at the edge / Should
be done according to photo]

Orrefors Museum

The archives at Orrefors contain a
large body of drawings for special
commissions. Many were for engravings to be applied to stock forms such
as this bottle and glass, but on occasion, individual pieces were designed
as well. The suggestion that the
humorous admonition "Not to Drink"
be engraved on this piece is paralleled by a proposed engraving of a
drunkard being pulled off the street
and then chained in a cell. It is not
known if this piece was ever executed.
DEO

66. Footed Vase

1928
Simon Gate
Graal; 7½ x 5⅜ in. (19.2 x 13.6 cm)

Orrefors Glassworks
Marks: "SGraal Orrefors 1928, KB
3197 SG"

Mrs. Agnes Hellner Collection,
Kungstenen Foundation, Stockholm
University
Inv. no. H 63

In 1928 glass made with the graal technique had been in production at Orrefors for twelve years. Although demand for it had diminished dramatically, Orrefors executed 173 pieces that year. In the previous year, for unknown reasons, only 8 pieces had been made, and in 1929/30, only 39. By the late 1920s, the graal technique had been greatly refined. The regularity of the wavelike scrolls that spiral around this bombe vase form and the consistency of the purple flashing even after the blank was blown into the form is remarkable. DEO

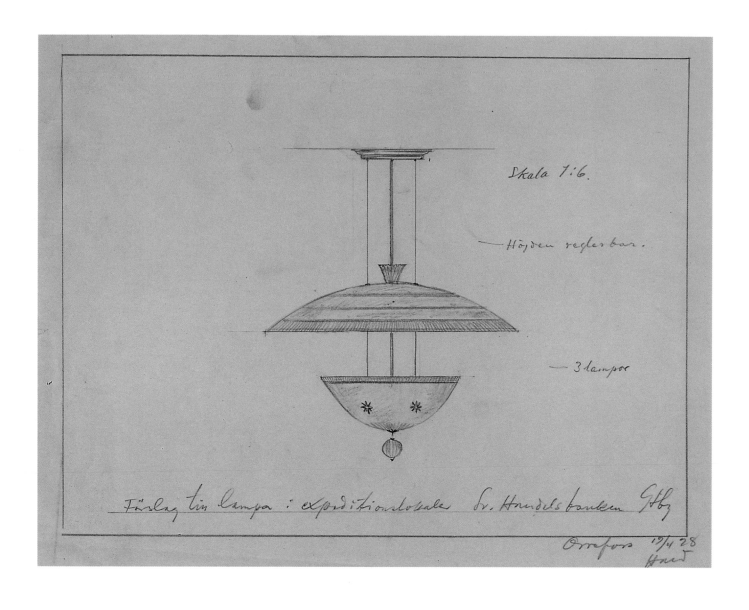

67. Drawing for Chandelier

1928

Edward Hald

Pen, ink, and charcoal on paper;
9½ x 12 in. (24.3 x 30.6 cm)

Inscription: "Skala 1:6 Höjden
reglerbar. Förslag till lampa i
expeditionslokaler. Gtbg Orrefors
19/4 28 Hald" [Scale 1:6. The height
adjustable. Suggestion for lamp in
offices. Gtbg Orrefors 29/4 Hald.]

Orrefors Museum

68. Vase

ca. 1929–30
Simon Gate
Blown and cut; 7$^{1}/_{8}$ x 9$^{1}/_{2}$ in. (18.0 x 24.0 cm)

Orrefors Glassworks

Marks: "Orrefors G A 270"

Mrs. Agnes Hellner Collection, Kungstenen Foundation, Stockholm University
Inv. no. H 323

The late 1920s represent a time of artistic reawakening for Simon Gate, during which he added considerably to his aesthetic vocabulary. A decade earlier he had helped develop the graal technique for Orrefors and had created a body of engraved designs that had garnered the firm international acclaim. Since then his work had

become relatively repetitious. In many reviews of the 1920s, it was the ingenuity of Edward Hald that received considerable praise, and it was Hald who was promoted to the position of artistic director at Orrefors in 1924. Gate, who had come to Orrefors in 1916, a year before Hald, might have felt somewhat rejected by the management.

By the late 1920s Gate may have been searching for some sort of liberation from his earlier style, or he may have been inspired by the talented young designer Vicke Lindstrand, who arrived at the factory in 1928. In any event Gate's manner of drawing would expand considerably in the early 1930s to include a more simplified means of expression for the engravings that he specified. He also explored freer forms for some vessels

and more architectural forms for others.

This powerful, unfooted form, unusual for Orrefors in the 1920s, recalls the "Triton" series Gate had created in 1917. The alternating concave and convex lobes cut from the thick walls of this vessel create a striped effect. Where the walls are thin, the green glass is lighter in color; where thick, it is darker.

There are similar models in the collections of the Museum of Applied Arts in Oslo, Norway, and the Orrefors Museum. DEO

References: Hald and Wettergren, *Simon Gate, Edward Hald*, p. 103; Edenheim and Reihnér. *Simon Gate, Edward Hald*, p. 37.

69. Footed Covered Urn called "Karusellskålen" (The Merry-Go-Round)

1929
Ewald Dahlskog
Blown, cast-on decoration, cut,
engraved; 15 x 10⅝ in. (38 x 27 cm)

Kosta Glassworks
Marks: "E. Dahlskog Kosta"

Nationalmuseum, Stockholm
Inv. no. NMK 262/1978

Ewald Dahlskog excelled in the design of art glass inspired by neo-classicism. He also brought a playful, expressive approach to his work at Kosta, comparable to the whimsical art glass Edward Hald designed for Orrefors, Kosta's main rival at the time.

Dahlskog's limited series of art glass were created in part to compete with Orrefors.

This is the most celebrated example of Dahlskog's designs for Kosta, and the lighthearted narrative it tells is filled with a wonderful sense of fantasy that is fairly typical of his work. Elegantly dressed, faceless men in tophats and tails, many waving outstretched arms, are shown riding different animals on a merry-go-round. One man sits on the back of a lion, another stands atop a charging elephant, a third is astride a galloping horse, and a fourth on a running ostrich, while a fifth figure summersaults on the back of a running pig. Trapezelike motifs swing from the top of the merry-go-round. The repetition of thin striations radiating atop the

lid reinforces the idea of movement. The cut decoration is of the finest quality, executed in low relief against the transparent surface of the glass. Dahlskog's robust figurative style is clearly revealed.

The earliest known example of this model is in the collection of the Kosta Museum; according to Helmut Ricke it was used to experiment with different decorative techniques (Ricke and Gronert, *Glas in Schweden*, pp. 194–95). NS-L

References: Artéus ed., *Kosta 250 Years of Craftsmanship*, pp. 138-39; Beard, *International Modern Glass*, p. 70; Dahlback-Lutteman, ed., *Svenskt Glas*, p. 103; Ricke and Gronert, *Glas in Schweden*, p. 194-95; Wollin, *Modern Swedish Decorative Arts*.

70. Footed Covered Urn

1929
Edward Askenberg
Blown and engraved; 12 x 11¾ in.
(30.5 x 30 cm)

Johansfors Glassworks

Marks: "Johansfors G 470 Askenberg"

Länsförsäkring Kronoberg, Växjö,
Sweden

Little is known about the designer of this impressive piece nor are there many examples of his work to study. The naive quality of the design contrasts with the superlative engraving technique with which it was applied, which is equal to that used at other Swedish glassworks by the end of the 1920s.

The expressions of delight on the faces of the fish and the stylization of the birds, clouds, and sea lend whimsy to this otherwise stately covered form. Askenberg divided the engraved design into three distinct sections that correspond to the form of this urn. The lid is engraved with the stars, clouds, and birds; the basin is decorated with leaping fish and cresting waves; the foot represents the floor of the sea with the shells and sand.

Johansfors was one of the many smaller glassworks that emerged in Sweden at the end of the nineteenth century during a period of rapid economic growth. Although cut glass was an important aspect of the company's line in the 1920s, the firm also produced superlative engraved glass during the interwar period. DEO

71. Carafe and Assorted Glasses from Service called "Östergyllen"

1929
Elis Bergh
Blown and cut; carafe, 14⅝ x 4½ in.
(37 x 11.5 cm); glasses: smallest,
3⅜ x 1⅞ in. (8.5 x 4.9 cm); largest,
4½ x 2½ in. (11.4 x 6.4 cm)

Kosta Glassworks

Kosta Glass Museum

Elis Bergh was considered one of the leading designers at Kosta during the 1930s. He made an unusually long-term commitment to the factory, staying on as artistic director from 1929 to 1950. Bergh designed art glass, but he excelled in the creation of domestic tableware. His stemware is recognized as his most important contribution to the Kosta product line. He tried to modernize glassware for everyday use by moving away from elaborate, traditional cut patterns that had been associated with the factory since the turn of the century.

Unlike Kosta's earlier cut glass, the "Östergyllen" and "Koh-i-noor" pat-terns are distiguished by the subtlety of their decoration and simplicity of the forms. The variety of engraved and cut patterns was extensive, including variations of the hanging-swag motif that embellishes the "Östergyllen" service. Bergh also achieved subtle differences in decorative effects by altering the proportions of the cut stem on the "Koh-i-noor" glasses and on a later design called "Thule" (see cat. no. 156). NS-L

References: cat. no. 71, Arteus, *Kosta 250 Years of Craftsmanship*, pp. 150–51; cat. no. 72, ibid., p. 148.

72. Assorted Glasses
from Service called
"Koh-i-noor"
1929
Elis Bergh
Blown and cut stems; smallest,
3½ x 2¼ in. (9.0 x 5.6 cm); largest,
6⅛ x 3¾ in. (15.4 x 9.6 cm)

Kosta Glassworks

Kosta Museum

85. Vase

1930
Vicke (Viktor) Lindstrand
Blown, cast-on elements, acid-etched,
painted; 5³⁄₄ x 4⁷⁄₈ in. (14.6 x 12.4 cm)

Orrefors Glassworks
Marks: "Of 30 Li.54"

Orrefors Museum

This is one of the finest examples of
the enameled and painted vases by
Lindstrand that were shown at the 1930
Stockholm Exhibition. The expressive
black lines used to render the facial
features are typical of Lindstrand's
handling of decorative figures on art
glass. Helena Dahlbäck Lutteman has
noted the similarities between the face
of the woman on this vase and
"Spanish Lady" on Edward Hald's covered cup (cat. no. 48). While the features are similar, Lindstrand's design is
more expressive, almost menacing, an
effect strengthened by the use of a
green and black palette. NS-L

References: Dahlback-Lutteman, ed.,
Svenskt Glas. p. 106; Herlitz-Gezelius,
Orrefors Ett Svenskt Glasbruk. p. 57.

86. Vase called "The Four Continents"

1930
Vicke (Viktor) Lindstrand
Blown, cast-on elements, acid-etched, painted; 6 x 5⅜ in. (15.2 x 13.7 cm)

Orrefors Glassworks
Marks: "OF 30 Li.64"

Collection Birgitta Crafoord

Among the vases with painted or enameled decoration designed by Lindstrand for the 1930 Stockholm Exhibition, the proportions of this round-footed form proved to be a particularly successful ground for the decoration. The personification of the "Four Continents" (Africa, Asia, Europe, and America) was well suited to Lindstrand's expressive figurative approach to decoration during this period. The same form was embellished with a mermaid executed in the black, white, and green palette and was also shown at the 1930 exhibition. NS-L

References: Holmér and Reihnér. *Lyricism in Modern Design*, p. 83.

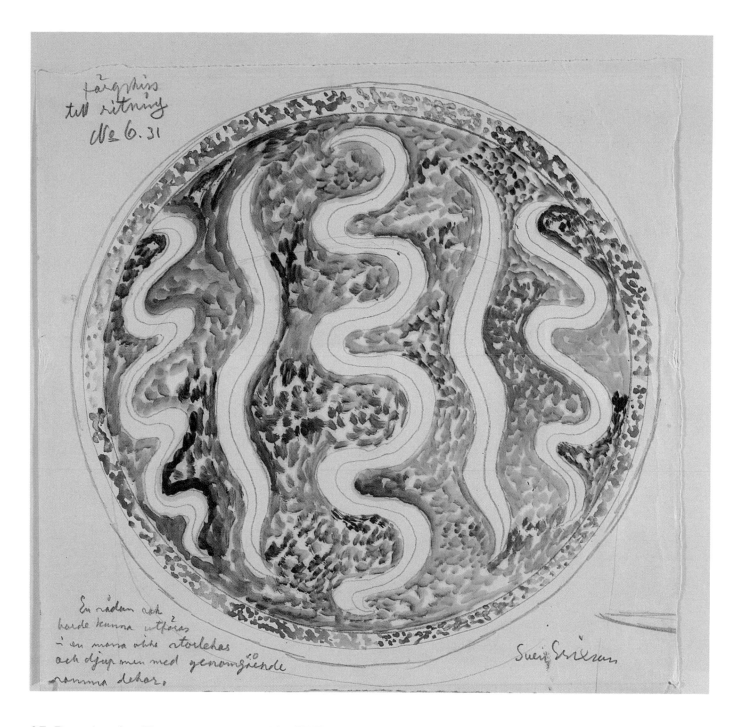

97. Drawing for Plate

Sven "the X" Erixson
1931
Watercolor, pencil on paper; 10⅞ x
11⅛ in. (27.6 x 28.4 cm)

Inscription: "Färgskiss / till ritning / No
6. 31 / En sådan sak / borde kunna
utföras / i en massa olika storlekar /
och djup men med genom- / gående
samma dekor. / Sven Erixson" [Color-
sketch / for drawing / Number 6. 31 /
A thing like this / ought to be done / in
many different sizes / and depths but
consistently / with the same décor. /
Sven Erixson]

Kosta Museum

This drawing for a glass plate by Sven

"the X" Erixson differs considerably
from the representational motifs that
characterized most of Erixson's work
at Kosta in the early 1930s. The organic design, composed of undulating
lines on a multicolored speckled
ground, is rendered in an abstract,
painterly manner.

Erixson provided very general
instructions for the execution of the
piece. While suggesting that the
design was appropriate for many different forms, he gave no indication of
the techniques or methods of production to be used, demonstrating his
greater interest in aesthetic details. It
seems that the design was never realized. NS-L

98. Sculpture "Pärlfiskare" ("The Pearlfisher")

1931
Vicke (Viktor) Lindstrand
Cast-on elements, optic blown,
engraved; 15¾ x 9½ in. (40 x 24 cm)

Orrefors Glassworks
Inscription: "Orrefors 1931 V.
Lindstrand 1012 EW (=Emil
Weidlich)"

Nationalmuseum, Stockholm
Inv. no. NMK 1/1971

This sculptural work represents a virtuosic feat of glassblowing and engraving. It is perhaps the best known of the so-called narrative pieces produced at Orrefors in the early 1930s. Unlike anecdotal work designed by Hald and Gate in the 1920s, which relied on the meticulous rendering of details to impart a charming story, this object is meant to shock the viewer. Despite a rather comic facial expression, there is menace in the figure of the octopus surmounting the orb. The engravings of the divers are produced with such simplicity that, size and complexity of the piece notwithstanding, the subject matter is readily grasped.

This piece is a closed form whose function was to serve as ocorporate propaganda. Orrefors lent it to several important exhibitions, including the Century of Progress exposition in Chicago in 1933/1934. DEO

References: Dahlback-Lutteman, ed., *Svenskt Glas*, p. 36; Duncan, *Orrefors Glass*, p. 51.

99. Footed Bowl

1931
Simon Gate; engraved by
Wilhelm Eisert
Blown, cast-on elements, engraved;
5³/₄ x 5⁷/₈ in. (14.5 x 15.0 cm)
Orrefors Glassworks

Marks: "Orrefors Gate 1161. 32 WE."
(1932)

Orrefors Museum

By the early 1930s, Simon Gate had expanded his repertoire of engraved work. Although he never altogether abandoned the rich, baroque idiom that he had developed in the late teens and early twenties, he began to create more conventionalized designs. His figures became flatter and simpler. This may have been the result of an aesthetic shift in Gate's approach or it may have been a response to the economic realities of the Depression. Sales of art glass had dropped, and Orrefors moved quickly to expand its line with lesser-priced art glass. The simple decoration on this bowl was not laborious to engrave, meaning a substantial reduction in production cost.

It was unusual for Gate to depict women in fashions of the day. This dated the piece and limited the longevity of the design. Gate's classical nudes were more timeless than the figures on this bowl and remained part of Orrefors's catalogue for decades. DEO

100. Assorted Glasses from
Service called "Byttan"
1933
Elis Bergh
Mold blown, cut; $3\frac{1}{4}$ x $3\frac{3}{8}$ in. (8.3 x
8.6 cm); $2\frac{1}{2}$ x $2\frac{7}{8}$ in. (6.5 x 7.4 cm);
$2\frac{3}{8}$ x $2\frac{5}{8}$ in. (5.9 x 6.8 cm); $2\frac{1}{8}$ x
$2\frac{3}{8}$ in. (5.4 x 6.1 cm); $1\frac{3}{8}$ x 2 in.
(4.5 x 5.1 cm); $1\frac{1}{4}$ x $1\frac{5}{8}$ in. (3.5 x
4.1 cm)

Kosta Glassworks

Smålands Museum, Swedish Glass
Museum, Växjö
Inv. no. M 13148 a-f

Fig. 101a. Back of decanter, cat. no. 101.

101. Decanter called "Suzanna and the Elders"

Designed 1933, this example 1979
Edward Hald
Blown, pressed, engraved, cut;
H. 9¼ in. (23.6 cm), diam. 5¼ x
2⅜ in. (13.2 x 5.9 cm)

Orrefors Glassworks
Marks: "Orrefors H. 1230-111. E9.
AS."

Collection Birgitta Crafoord

This decanter is remarkable for the approach taken by Hald in his depiction of the subject. Rather than treat the story in a sequential manner around the form, Hald has exploited the four-sided flask to show both the "front" and "back" of the same scene and to do so with a sense of humor. On the front of the bottle, the naked Suzanna is surprised by the two elderly men who peer over the edge of the pool where she is bathing. On the reverse is an unceremonious view of the backsides of these same men.

The decanter was designed in 1933, and this example was made in 1979, testimony to the enduring popularity of the design and the high level of the engraver's art that was maintained at the factory. Orrefors produced many engraved, square decanters during the 1920s; flat sides provided an ideal surface for engraved work. DEO

References: Paulsson, ed., *Modernt Svenskt Glas*, p. 128, fig. 63; Knutsson, *Swedish Art in Glass*, no. 36; Ricke and Gronert, *Glas in Schweden*, p. 111, no. 135.

102. Vase called "De Fyra elementen" (The Four Elements)

1934
Simon Gate; engraved by Ernst
Åberg and Gösta Elgström
Blown, engraved, acid-etched;
12⅝ x 10½ in. (32 x 26.7 cm)

Orrefors Glassworks

Marks: "DENNA BURK ÄR
TILLVERKARD VID ORREFORS 1934.
KOMPONERAD AV SIMON GATE,
GRAVERAD AV E. ÅBERG OCH G.
ELGSTRÖM." [This jar is made at
Orrefors 1934, designed by Simon
Gate, engraved by E. Åberg and
G. Elgström.]

Nationalmuseum, Stockholm
Inv. no. NMK 74/1934

Certain engravings, especially those
prized by the factory, were sometimes
applied to forms other than the model
for which the engraving had been
originally designed. "The Four
Elements" engraving had been introduced at the 1930 Stockholm
Exhibition on a square-sectioned footed urn (cat. no. 78). It was reused on
this simple vase form with the four
vignettes compressed into a continuous composition. The reworking imparts a liveliness lacking on the more
static original version. According to
the Orrefors catalogue of 1934, each
of the "Four Elements" vignettes was
available as a separate design and
could be applied to square-sectioned,
cylindrical, and octagonal bowls. DEO

References: Hald and Wettergren, *Simon
Gate, Edward Hald*, p. 120; Ricke and
Gronert, *Glas in Schweden*, p. 107;
Dahlback-Lutteman, ed., *Svenskt Glas*,
p, 118.

103. Cocktail Shaker

1934
Vicke (Viktor) Lindstrand
Blown, pressed, acid-etched;
10½ x 4⅝ in. (26.6 x 11.8 cm)

Orrefors Glassworks
Marks: "Of.LU 154/15"

Orrefors Museum

The production series that included this cocktail shaker was identified as "Iced" in the Orrefors catalogues, a reference to the frosted appearance of the glass. The surface texture may have been achieved by applying a weak, relatively unstable acid resist to the glass, causing an uneven erosion of the surface. The frosted effect was probably attained by immersing the piece in a bath of hydrofluoric acid mixed with ammonia.

The cocktail-shaker form was very new; it had been introduced in the 1920s. This pristine interpretation of the new form has a mechanistic appearance to it, despite the texturing of the surface. The same cocktail shaker was available in transparent glass for those who might not have appreciated the "iced" appearance. This product line also included ashtrays, bowls, hors d'oeurve trays, and cocktail glasses, reflecting the informality in certain circles in Sweden in the 1930s. DEO

References: Ricke and Thor, *Schwedische Glasmanufakturen*, p. 101; Ricke and Gronert, *Glas in Schweden*, p. 124.

104. Cocktail Trays and Glasses

1933–34
Vicke (Viktor) Lindstrand
Blown, pressed, acid-etched; tray,
3/8 x 47/8 x 61/4 in. (1.2 x 12.2 x
16 cm); glass, 21/2 x 3 in. (6.2 x
7.7 cm)

Orrefors Glassworks

Mrs. Agnes Hellner Collection,
Kungstenen Foundation, Stockholm
University
Inv. nos. H 391, H 392

These small trays and glasses are part of the "Iced" product line; the trays were intended to hold canapes. The concept reflects the shifting needs of Orrefors's clientele in the early thirties when many individuals began to change the manner in which they entertained. DEO

Reference: Ricke and Thor, *Schwedische Glasmanufakturen*, p. 101.

105. Bowl

ca. 1935–36
Vicke (Viktor) Lindstrand
Molded, acid-etched; 21/2 x 51/2 in.
(6.2 x 14.1 cm)

Orrefors Glassworks
Marks: "OF LU 154/22"

Orrefors Museum

This fully biomorphic bowl was included in Orrefors's 1936 catalogue as part of the "Iced" product line. In the same year, Finnish architect Alvar Aalto designed the first in his series of biomorphic forms that culminated in the "Savoye" bowl. When it was exhibited at the 1937 Paris Exposition Internationale des Arts et Techniques dans la Vie Moderne, the "Savoye" bowl was hailed as a triumph of a new, freer manner of design.

Orrefors produced several versions of this biomporphic bowl, varying the height and base size or including a small, individual candleholder. DEO

Reference: Ricke and Thor, Schwedische Glasmanufakturen, p. 114.

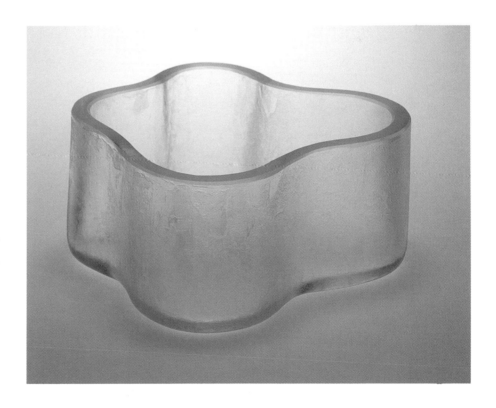

Fig. 105a. Bowl designed by Alvar Aalto; Kaarhula-Iittala, 1936. (Museum of Applied Arts, Helsinki)

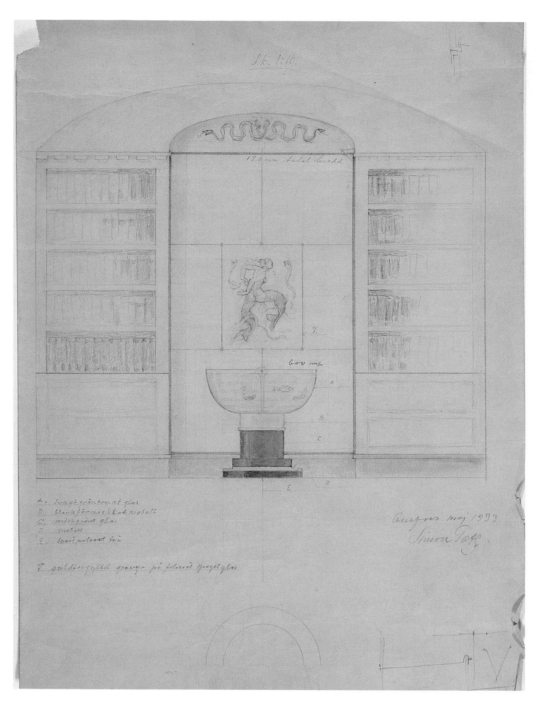

106. Drawing for Mirror and Fountain and Basin in Room Installation 1933

Simon Gate
Pencil, crayon on paper; 18 x 13³⁄₈ in. (45.8 x 34 cm)

Inscription: "S.k. 1:10 / 120 cm total bredd / 600 m/m / A. svagt gröntonat glas / B. blankförnicklad metall / C. mörkgrönt glas / D. metall / E. svartpolerat trä / F. guldförgylld gravyr på folierat spegelglas / Orrefors maj 1933 Simon Gate" [Scale 1:10 / 120 cm total width / 600 m/m/ A. faint green tone / B. shiny nickel-plated metal / C. dark green glass / D. metal / E. black-polished wood / F. gold-gilded engraving on foiled mirror glass / Orrefors May 1933 / Simon Gate]

Orrefors Museum

During the interwar years Orrefors received numerous commissions for large architectural installations, and Gate and Hald were the principal designers for many of these projects. Although the intended site for this impressive design is unknown, the drawing shows the kind of interior scheme that had become associated with Simon Gate's work. The placement of the fountain and basin in front of a mirrored wall exploits all the inherent expressive qualities of glass. The fish depicted on the fountain basin and the mermaid above it reinforce the aquatic theme.

Gate provided detailed instructions for the size of the different elements, the materials, and the decoration. NS-L

107. Bowl

1934
Simon Gate
Blown, cut, engraved; 6⅛ x 9½ in.
(15.4 x 23.9 cm)

Orrefors Glassworks
Marks: "Orrefors.G.1319.34"

Museum of Art, Rhode Island School
of Design
Gift of Mr. and Mrs. William E.
Brigham
Inv. no. 35.777

This bowl is decorated with three engraved female figures, presumably Javanese dancers, an oft-repeated motif in Gate's work at this time. A number of drawings by Gate in the Orrefors archive depict similar female figures, which the artist has labeled "Javanesisk danserska" (Javanese dancer). The different poses of the figures, their costumes, and features are stereotypical interpretations of Oriental dancers. The subject, despite its exploitative nature, was heavily charged with exoticism in the West and very popular in the commercial marketplace. Many variations of engraved decoration depicting Oriental female nudes appeared in the Orrefors trade catalogues, most notably in 1935 and 1939.

Although Gate produced numerous designs for figurative subjects, many featuring female nudes, his figurative style could be rather awkward, especially in the rendering of anatomical details. In this bowl, for example, the facial features and hands are somewhat unrefined. This bowl was part of a larger bequest of Orrefors glass given to the Museum of Art at the Rhode Island School of Design by William E. Brigham, head of the school's metalwork department. NS-L

References: Museum of Art, Rhode Island School of Design, *Glass From the Museum's Collection*, p. 204; Ricke and Thor, *Schwedische Glasmanufakturen*, p. 90.

108. Drawing for Desk Lamp

ca. 1932–34
Simon Gate
Pencil on paper; 11⅝ x 9 in. (29.4 x 23 cm)

Stamp: "Orrefors Bruks Aktiebolag / ORREFORS, SWEDEN / Simon Gate n:r..."

Orrefors Museum

109. Drawing for Bowl on
Wooden Base
1935
Simon Gate
Pencil on paper; 14³⁄₄ x 19³⁄₈ in.
(37.6 x 49.2 cm)

Inscription: "Orrefors 1935 Simon
Gate"

Orrefors Museum

110. Assorted Glasses from
Service called "Moiré"
ca. 1934
Elis Bergh
Blown and pantograph technique;
smallest, 2⅝ x 2 in. (6.7 x 5.1 cm);
largest, 4⅞ x 3⅜ in. (12.3 x 8.4 cm)

Kosta Glassworks

Kosta Museum
(Kosta 1932)

111. Assorted Glasses from Service called "Gulli"
ca. 1930s
Magni Magnusson
Blown and cut; 5½ x 3¾ in. (13.9 x
9.5 cm); 5½ x 3½ in. (13.9 x 9.0
cm); 3⅜ x 2⅞ in.(8.6 x 7.4 cm); 3¾
x 2½ in. (9.6 x 6.4 cm)

Skruf Glassworks

Smålands Museum, Swedish Glass
Museum, Växjö
Inv. nos. M 9260:1, M 44940,
M 9260:2, M 9260:3

Among the smaller glassworks that
existed during the interwar years, few
are thriving businesses in the late
1990s. Skruf is a notable exception.
Today it is considered one of the most
creative and innovative glassworks in
Sweden.

Magni Magnusson was both the
chief gaffer and principal designer at
Skruff during the interwar years when
the factory specialized in simple
domestic everyday glassware. The
"Gulli" pattern is one of the many simple, unornamented designs for
stemware produced during the 1930s.

A distinguishing feature of this design
is the molded decoration on the stem
which is consistent with the heavy,
dense nature of the form. NS-L.

112. Vase

1935
Elis Bergh
Blown; 6³⁄₈ x 6¹⁄₈ in. (16.2 x 15.5 cm)

Kosta Glassworks
Marks: "B 766"

Smålands Museum, Swedish Glass
Museum, Växjö
Inv. no. M 10290

This is one of the most visually expressive works created by Elis Bergh during his long tenure at Kosta. The swirling concentric circles of the vase create a highly mechanistic appearance. Bergh explored this type of circular form in a number of other designs, two of which were executed with blue glass as early as 1931. At Orrefors Edward Hald and Edvin Öhrström also created functional glassware in which the glass is blown in this configuration. The vigor and dynamism in Bergh's design, however, were unmatched by other Swedish glassworks and were not repeated in the rest of Bergh's extensive production at Kosta. NS-L

References: Artéus, ed., *Kosta 250 Years of Craftsmanship*, p. 164; Brunius et al., *Svenskt Glas*, p. 109; Dahlback-Lutteman, ed., *Svenskt glas*, p. 49; Ricke and Gronert, *Glas in Schweden*, p. 204.

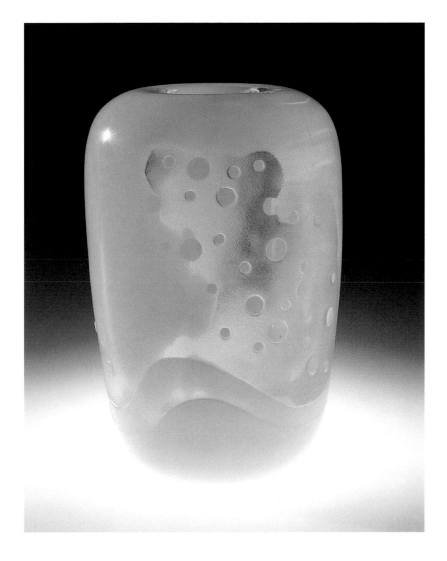

113. Vase

1934
Sven-Erik Skawonius
Blown, overlay, sandblasted,
etched(?); 7½ x 5 in. (19.1 x 12.7
cm)

Kosta Glassworks
Marks: "Skawonius 15/2 - 1934.
Kosta"

The Oslo Museum of Applied Art
Inv. no. OK. 10655

The art glass designs of Sven-Erik
Skawonius in the mid-1930s were
without equal in their exploration of
abstract imagery. Although the cre

ation of this vase required violent
manipulation of the vessel through
extensive wheel cutting and sandblasting, the results exhibit a remarkable
serenity. The delicate shading of the
outer edges of the white overlay may
have been achieved by immersing the
glass in baths of sulfuric acid. Despite
the vigorous working of the overlay to
expose the clear core, the actual handling of the glass has been quite sensitive, an indication that the artist himself may have supervised the process.
This vase was made during
Skawonius's first tenure at Kosta which
lasted from 1933 to 1935. His glass
was not especially popular in the
Depression market.

The Museum of Applied Art in Oslo
began collecting Orrefors art glass as
early as 1917 and may have been the
first museum to purchase work by
Hald and Gate (see cat. nos. 11 and
12). This piece was the first example
of Kosta's work that entered the museum's collection. It was purchased from
Nordiska Kompaniet in Stockholm on
November 30, 1934. Similar examples
are in the collection of the Kosta
Museum and the Nationalmuseum in
Stockholm. DEO

Reference: Paulsson, ed.,*Modernt Svenskt
Glass*, p. 154; Artéus, ed., *Kosta 250 Years of
Craftsmanship*, pp. 58–59, 174–75.

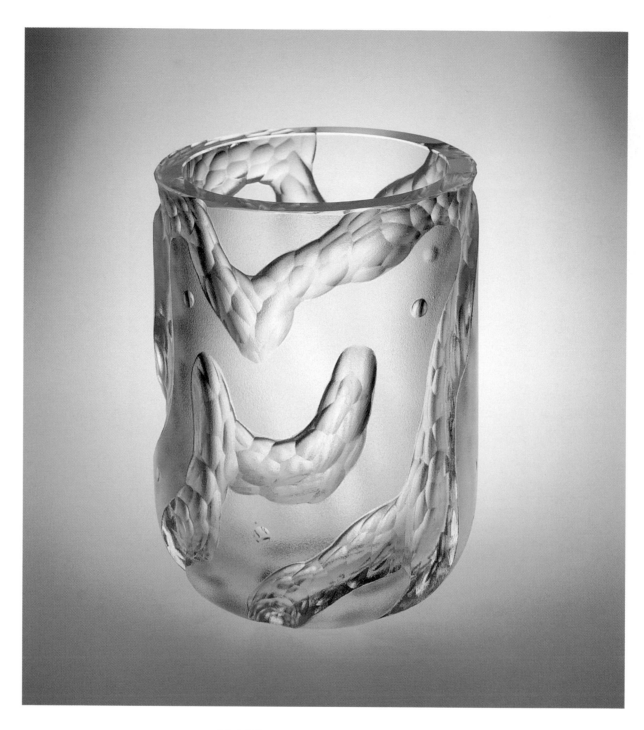

114. Vase

1935
Sven-Erik Skawonius
Blown, sandblasted, cut; 7$\frac{1}{2}$ x 5$\frac{1}{2}$
in. (19 x 14 cm)

Kosta Glassworks
Marks: "Kosta Skawonius 17"

Kosta Museum

115. Decanter and Assorted Glasses

1935
Sven-Erik Skawonius
Blown, sandblasted, cut; glasses:
3¹/₂ x 1³/₈ in. (8.8 x 3.5 cm), 4³/₈ x
2⁷/₈ in. (11.1 x 7.4 cm); decanter:
9 x 3³/₄ in. (23 x 9.4 cm)

Kosta Glassworks
Marks: "Skawonius 40/4 Kosta 1935"
(decanter)

Kosta Museum

Trained as an artist and set designer, Sven-Erik Skawonius came to Kosta in 1933 and emerged as one of the most dynamic experimenters in the design of art glass in the 1930s. The vase (cat. no. 114) and the decanter and glasses (cat. no. 115) demonstrate the sandblasted decoration he explored, a technique that he helped to revive at the factory. Skawonius introduced a unique interpretation of underwater and landscape scenes. He approached glass by laboriously working the surface to create contrasting effects of pattern and texture in sandblasted and transparent glass. Skawonius's sandblasted decoration makes an interesting comparison with the work of Tyra Lundgren (see cat. no. 120) who designed for Kosta in 1935.
NS-L

References: cat. no. 114, Artéus, ed., *Kosta 250 Years of Craftsmanship*, p. 170; Ricke and Gronert, *Glas in Schweden*, p. 208; cat. no. 115, Artéus, ed., *Kosta 250 Years of Craftsmanship*, p. 170; Ricke and Gronert, *Glas in Schweden*, p. 208.

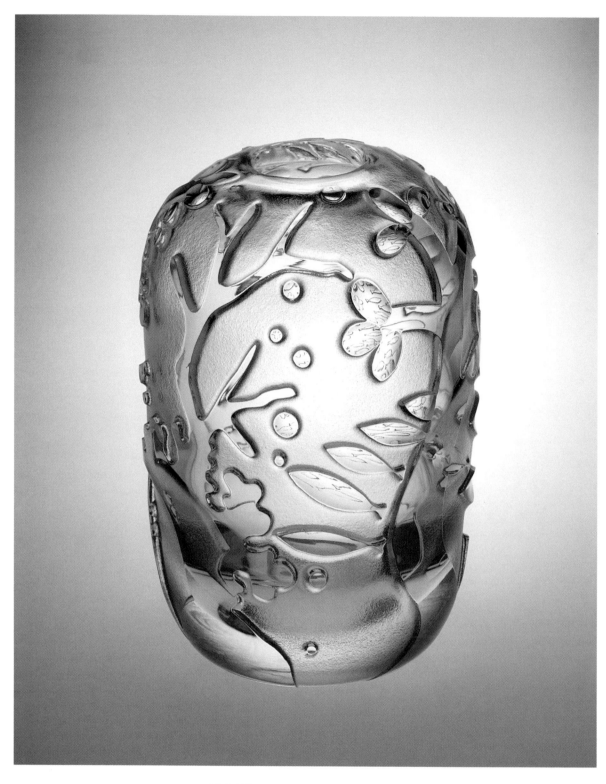

116. Vase
1935
Sven-Erik Skawonius
Blown, sandblasted, cut, etched;
7½ x 5⅛ in. (19 x 13 cm)

Kosta Glassworks
Marks: "Kosta 1935 Skawonius 14/7"

Kosta Museum

117. Drawing for Hanging Light Fixture

1935
Vicke (Viktor) Lindstrand
Watercolor, ink, pencil on paper;
22⅞ x 11⅜ in. (58.1 x 28.8 cm)

Inscription: "FÖRSLAG TILL
TAKBELYSNING I / SALONGEN
BIOGRAFEN PALLADIUM MALMÖ /
Längd c:a 2.4 meter / ORREFORS 34
/ Lindstrand" [Suggestion for ceiling
light fitting in the auditorium of The
Cinema Palladium Malmö / Length
ca. 2.4 meters / Orrefors 34 /
Lindstrand]

Orrefors Museum

Vicke Lindstrand was the most creative and prolific artist at Orrefors during the 1930s. Among his many contributions to the factory's product line was the transformation of its hanging light fixtures from the ornate crystal chandeliers designed by Gate and Hald in the 1920s to more modern fixtures that rivaled French art moderne lighting.

The two drawings (cat. nos. 117 and 118) reveal the stylistic changes that occurred. Both designs are composed of circular motifs reminiscent of the "Saturn" lamps produced by French companies such as D.I.M. The planetary form engenders a distinctly modern appearance. The hanging light in cat. no. 117 was intended for

the main auditorium of the Palladium Cinema in Malmö; the drawing conveys the quality of diffused yellow light that would have been achieved in the final design. Each of the three transparent glass balls enclosed a smaller opaque ball of yellow glass.

The other drawing (cat. no. 118) also uses circular shapes that suggest planetary forms. The relationship between the small circular form of the bowl, however, and the larger saucerlike shape is simplified. The design was conceived for the "Carolus Rex" bar in Gothenburg. NS-L

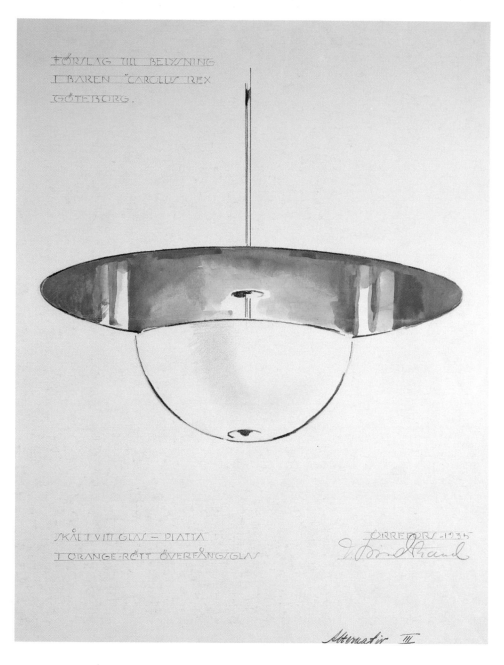

118. Drawing for Hanging Light Fixture

1935
Vicke (Viktor) Lindstrand
Watercolor, pencil on paper; 11⅝ x
9 in. (29.4 x 22.8 cm)

Inscription: "FÖRSLAG TILL
BELYSNING / I BAREN `CAROLUS
REX'/ GÖTEBORG / SKÅL I VITT
GLAS / PLATTA I ORANGE-RÖTT
ÖVERFÅNGSGLAS / ORREFORS
1935 / V. Lindstrand" [Suggestion for
light fixture in the bar 'Carolus Rex'/
Gothenburg / bowl in white glass /
plate in orange-red overlay glass / V.
Lindstrand]

Smålands Museum, Swedish Glass
Museum, Växjö

Fig. 119a. Alternate view of cat. no. 119.

119. Vase

1934
Simon Gate
Blown, sandblasted, engraved;
9 x 9¹/₄ in. (23 x 23.7 cm)

Orrefors Glassworks
Marks: "Orrefors. S Gate.1389: 1934
TL"

Länsförsäkring Kronoberg, Växjö,
Sweden

Orrefors built its reputation in the early years of the 1920s on its intaglio engravings based on designs by Edward Hald and Simon Gate. By the 1930s both designers began to explore cameo reliefs in their decorations. This raised effect could be achieved by acid etching, wheel cutting, sandblasting, or using a mold. Sandblasting—propelling sand or particles of crushed iron at high velocity through pressurized hoses—was especially important to the firm. It would be used in the "ariel" technique that furthered the factory's reputation for technical innovation and aesthetic excellence in the years before the Second World War.

The sandblasting used for this vase enabled the craftsmen to achieve depth in less time and less laboriously than by wheel cutting. A specially cut stencil protected areas from the sandblast, and the edges of the design are as crisply defined as in wheel-cut engraving. After sandblasting, the raised surfaces were polished and detailing engraved onto those areas. Sandblasting demanded fairly thick-walled vessels and most cameo vases from the mid-1930 were large in size.

This vase is also significant as stun-ning evidence of the new direction in Gate's engraving. The bold freize of women and fish, depicted primarily in silhouette, defy the formula that he had used in the 1920s when his work was defined by meticulous attention to detail. In several instances in this piece, Gate superimposed one figure over another so that they blended into single, raised forms, delineated only by simple engraving. The ambiguity created by these consolidations occurred only in Gate's sandblasted and engraved designs. DEO

Reference: Ricke and Thor, Schwedische Glasmanufakturen, p. 95.

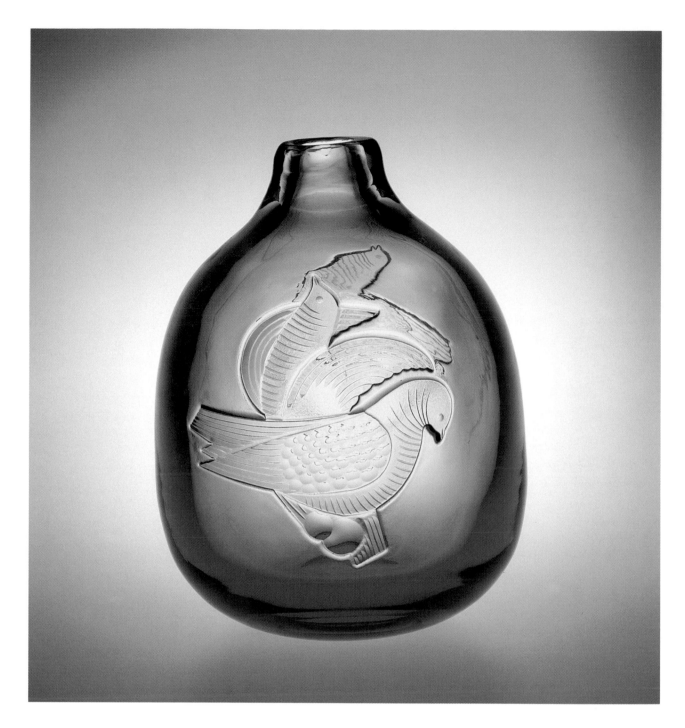

120. Vase

1935
Tyra Lundgren
Blown, sandblasted, cut; $9^7/_8$ x $7^1/_2$
in. (25 x 19 cm)

Kosta Glassworks
Marks: "Kosta 35 Camé 13"
Kosta Museum

Tyra Lundgren began her career in the 1920s as a designer of porcelain at the Rörstrand and Lidköping Porcelain factories in Sweden. She then studied painting in Paris under Andre Lhôte. Although she worked for Kosta for only one year, 1935, she is recognized as one of the most talented Kosta designers. While many of the other artists at Kosta collaborated directly with craftsmen in the factory, Lundgren preferred to send her drawings to the factory from Paris where she resided at this time.

This vase is one of the best-known examples of Lundgren's art glass production and was included in the Kosta "Camé" series which featured designs by different artists. The dove motif was favored by the artist and appeared in different manifestations on various glass forms. Lundgren's work often relied on sandblasting and cutting techniques to achieve nuances of texture and pattern as in the wings and neck of the doves. Sandblasting also allowed her to place the three doves back to back in a line on the surface. Two are shown in flight, adding to the rhythmic quality of the design. Lundgren experimented with different colored glass, including the distinctive green glass shown here as well as a rich blue glass. NS-L

References: Artéus ed.,, *Kosta 250 Years of Craftsmanship*, p. 177; Dahlback-Lutteman, ed,. *Svenskt Glas.* p. 121; Herlitz-Gezelius, *Orrefors Ett Svenskt Glasbruk*, p. 59; Ricke and Gronert, *Glas in Schweden*, p. 211.

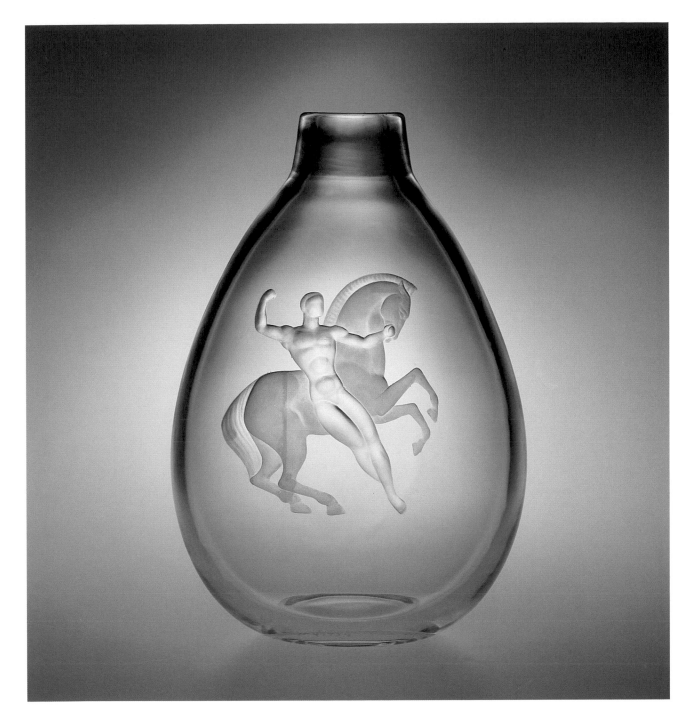

121. Vase

1936
Vicke (Viktor) Lindstrand;
engraved by Gösta Elgström
Blown, engraved; $9\frac{1}{2}$ x $6\frac{1}{2}$ in.
(24.1 x 16.5 cm)

Orrefors Glassworks
Marks: "Orrefors, Lindstrand
1557. A.5.G.E"

Smålands Museum, Swedish Glass
Museum, Växjö
Inv. no. M 47734

Engraving remained one of the principal methods of decorating art glass at Orrefors in the 1930s. Although the factory continued to produce meticulously detailed engravings like those of the 1920s, a new body of simpler designs was created. This shift was probably dictated as much by changing taste as by economic circumstances. Because simple designs required less time and labor, they were less costly to produce. The Orrefors catalogues after 1935 are filled with a wide array of simple engravings, many of which were repeated on various forms, including vases, bowls, decanters, and even ashtrays.

This design by Lindstrand, however, required a considerable amount of skill to execute. The subtle treatment of musculature represents an unusual merger of the real and the ideal in a more stylized way than the designs of the 1920s. The high polish given to the figure of the man causes it to stand out. By the mid-1930s, when this piece was made, Lindstrand was about to embark on the most significant period in his career when he would broaden his repertoire of glassworking techniques to include the new graal, mykene, and ariel glass. This vase, which was hand-blown, was produced in a limited series. DEO

Reference: Knutsson, *Swedish Art in Glass*, n.p.; Ricke and Thor, *Schwedische Glasmanufakturen,* p. 123.

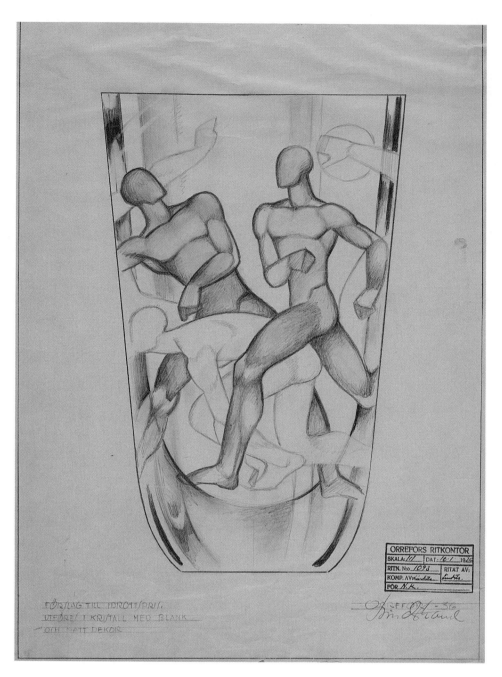

122. Drawing for a Trophy Vase

1936
Vicke (Viktor) Lindstrand
Pencil, ink on paper; 18³⁄₄ x 13¹⁄₂ in.
(47.5 x 34.2 cm)

Inscription: "FÖRSLAG TILL
IDROTTSPRIS / UTFÖRES I
KRISTALL MED BLANK OCH MATT
DEKOR / ORREFORS - 36 /
Lindstrand" [Suggestion for sports
prize to be made in crystal with
shiny and matte decor]
Stamp: "ORREFORS RITKONTOR /
SKALA 1:1 DAT: 16/1 1936 / RITN.
N.o 1093 / KOMP. av: Lindstr. RITAT
AV: Lindstr. FÖR N.K." [Orrefors
drawing office / Scale 1:1 Date 16/1
1936 / Drawing number 1093 /
Designed by: Lindstr. Drawn by:
Lindstr. For N.K]

Orrefors Museum
Inv. no. 1093

Lindstrand's skill as a draftsman is evident in this drawing for an athletic trophy which was commissioned through
Nordiska Kompaniet (NK), the leading
Stockholm department store. Nordiska
had been one of the earliest promoters of the new art glass produced by
Orrefors; in 1917 they had given the
firm a substantial showing of graal
glass by Hald and Gate. The feature-
less faces of the athletes resemble the
treatment of the horseman's face in
cat. no. 121. DEO

123. Urn

1936
Simon Gate
Blown, cut; 5⅛ x 8⅝ x 5¾ in.
(13.0 x 22.0 x 14.5 cm)
Orrefors Glassworks

Marks: "Orrefors bgA 276 1936"

Mrs. Agnes Hellner Collection,
Kungstenen Foundation, Stockholm
University
Inv. H 334

The radiant deep blue of this urn is unusual in the Orrefors production, and although angular forms were fairly frequent in the Orrefors line by the mid-1930s, the urn does not appear in the firm's catalogues. It may have been a special commission, or as a variant from the usual Orrefors aesthetics, it may have represented too great a financial risk to put it into production in the uncertain markets of the Depression. In any event, the urn was selected by Agnes Hellner whose family then controlled Orrefors.

This form does not function easily as a vase or as a display piece. Its heavy, low shape requires a relatively high position to ensure that the profile of the urn and not its large cavity is the focal point. Despite these reservations, this is still one of the most successful pieces designed by Gate. With its rich compilation of moldings, sheared off across its facade, Gate created a piece that exhibited a remarkable dichotomy when viewed from the front. The unadorned, planar surface of the urn intersects with the richly undulant, almost extravagantly profiled sides. These powerful neoclassical moldings were used in the 1920s by such designers as Gio Ponti in Italy and Josef Hoffmann in Vienna. DEO

124. Vase

1936
Edward Hald
Graal; 7⅛ x 7⅛ in. (18.0 x 18.0 cm)

Orrefors Glassworks
Marks: "Orrefors 18 sept 1936
Hald"

Mrs. Agnes Hellner Collection,
Kungstenen Foundation, Stockholm
University
Inv. no. H 85

By the early 1930s, Orrefors had abandoned the graal technique that Gate and Bergqvist introduced at Orrefors in the late teens. Such richly colored work had passed from fashion. In the mid-1930s, however, Hald returned to the overlay technique and revitalized it. Because this renewed technique was first used for marine motifs, it came to be known popularly as "fish graal."

This vase is one of the earliest executed in "fish graal." As in the earlier graal technique, a blank was flashed and then decorated by removing areas of the overlay. In the earlier work, when the blank was then reheated, its surface became the outer layer of the vessel (although this was sometimes flashed with a clear glass). In the revitalized version, Hald specified that a series of clear overlays be applied to the decorated blank. In this way the size and composition of the decoration were undisturbed during the finishing stages because the blank itself was barely worked by the glassblower. As a result, the finished piece had a decorated core that looked suspended, protected, in the middle of clear glass. This accounts for the precise detailing on many of these pieces.

This vase, like most of the other examples of late graal glass, is remarkably heavy. Its function as a vase is negated by the small size of its cavity. According to Agnes Hellner, this piece was the prototype for a series of heavy graal pieces that provided a basis for the "ariel" glass that was introduced the following year. Nine months after this vase was produced, the new technique was presented in an international showing at the 1937 Paris Exposition Internationale des Arts et Techniques dans la Vie Moderne. DEO

Reference: Agnes Hellner, manuscript (Stockholm University).

125. Blank for Graal with Birds
Edvin Öhrström
Blown, overlay (?), acid-etched (?);
6¹/₂ x 3³/₈ in. (16.6 x 8.7 cm)

Orrefors Glassworks

Orrefors Museum

This blank would have formed the core of a graal piece. It has probably been flashed with a darker glass and allowed to cool, after which the decoration was cut or made with an acid-wash to remove the dark glass. It has also been suggested that a resin-based paint was used to decorate some graal pieces. The resin served as a vehicle for applying ground-glass decoration to the cooled blank. When the blank was reheated, the resin would vaporize and the ground glass would melt into the surface of the blank. It would then be reshaped and finished by encasing with clear glass layers. DEO

References: Ricke and Gronert, *Glas in Schweden*, p. 295-96; Holmér and Reinhér, *Lyricism of Modern Design*, p. 236.

126. Vase

1936
Vicke (Viktor) Lindstrand
Mykene; 8³/₄ x 7⁵/₈ in. (22.2 x
19.4 cm)

Orrefors Glassworks
Marks: "Mykene No 4 ORREFORS
Lindstrand"

Orrefors Museum

The "mykene" technique was devised
by Vicke Lindstrand in 1936 and introduced in 1937 at the Paris Exposition
Internationale des Arts et Techniques
dans la Vie Moderne at which Orrefors
reestablished its reputation for technical innovation. Mykene was a revolutionary procedure, without precedent
in the glass industry, and serves as evidence that Lindstrand was more than
just a talented designer of forms and
ornament.

Developed on the same principle as
the late graal pieces, the mykene technique also required a decorated blank.
Carborundum, a chemical compound
of crystallized coke and sand, was
mixed with water and used to paint the
design on the cooled blank. Epoxy
may have been applied first to help the
mixture adhere to the blank. The blank
was then reheated, probably slowly so
that the design was not disturbed.
When the first sheet of molten glass
was blown over the blank, the cabo-
rundum vaporized and the gases that
were released were trapped, creating
the dense pattern of bubbles that char-
acterizes the mykene technique.
Invariably, these designs were grayish
in color.

Many of the early mykene designs
were based on animal or marine subjects. DEO

127. Blank for Mykene with Fish

Vicke (Viktor) Lindstrand
Blown, painted, sandblasted;
7¹/₄ x 3⁷/₈ in. (18.4 x 9.7 cm)

Orrefors Glassworks

Orrefors Museum

The grainy texture on the surface of
this blank is the powdered carborundum that had been mixed with water
into a thick paint. It may be that the
technician first painted Lindstrand's
design on the blank in an epoxy to
assure that the carborundum mixture
adhered to the glass. The color of the
epoxy would not interfere with that of
the carborundum. DEO

128. Footed Vase
1936
Vicke (Viktor) Lindstrand
Mykene; $9\frac{7}{8}$ x $7\frac{1}{8}$ in. (23 x 18.1 cm)

Orrefors Glassworks
Marks: "Orrefors Mykene, Nr 2 Lindstrand - 36"

Nationalmuseum, Stockholm
Inv. no. NMK 102/1936

One of the earliest mykene pieces produced by Orrefors, this piece was purchased from the Nordiska Kompaniet (Sweden's principal department store) in Stockholm by the Nationalmuseum in the year it was produced. According to its marks, it was the second piece made with the mykene process to survive the difficult process of experimentation. DEO

129. Footed Vase

1936
Vicke (Viktor) Lindstrand
Orrefors Glassworks
Mykene; 7$\frac{1}{2}$ x 7$\frac{3}{8}$ in. (19.0 x
18.7 cm)

Marks: "Mykene No 3 Orrefors
Lindstrand 1936"

Mrs. Agnes Hellner Collection,
Kungstenen Foundation, Stockholm
University
Inv. no. H 214

This piece was acquired by Agnes
Hellner soon after the mykene technique was introduced by Orrefors. The
degree of control that a painter could
exercise with the relatively fluid mixture of carborundum and water is evident in the small enclosed circles and
fins of the fish depicted on the basin.
DEO

130. Pitcher and Glass

ca. 1936
Edward Hald
Blown
Pitcher: 7¹/₂ x 7 in. (19.2 x 17.8 cm);
glass: 4¹/₄ x 2⁷/₈ in. (10.9 x 7.2 cm)

Orrefors Glassworks

Marks: Pitcher, "Of Hu 1598/6"

Smålands Museum, Swedish Glass
Museum, Växjö
Inv. nos. M 45397a (pitcher),
M45397b (glass)

This pitcher and glass are typical of the designs for everyday glassware produced by the leading Orrefors artists during the 1930s. Edward Hald, Simon Gate, and Vicke Lindstrand worked on designs for the tableware product line. The functionalist aesthetic of this pitcher and glass is more reminiscent of the production glassware that Hald and Gate created for Sandvik during the 1920s and 1930s. By using the mold-blown technique, designs could be mass produced and sold at relatively moderate prices. The Orrefors trade catalogues from the late 1930s featured numerous variations of these designs which were ostensibly a commercial success. NS-L

References: Ricke and Thor, *Schwedische Glasmanufakturen,* p. 159.

131. Vial and Stopper

1937
Edvin Öhrström
Blown, pressed; 4½ x 2½ in.
(11.5 x 6.5 cm)

Orrefors Glassworks
Marks: "Orrefors"

Orrefors Museum

Many designs for vials and stoppers were produced by Orrefors in the 1920s and 1930s. These two examples reveal the breadth of interpretation of modern design that existed at the Orrefors Glassworks during the 1930s. They also convey the more general conceptual and aesthetic dichotomies within modernism.

Both designs use the effect of encased glass but with very different results. The vial and stopper in cat. no. 131 demonstrate design dictates associated with functionalim in Swedish glass. An arresting double silhouette was created in which there is interplay between two stark geometric forms of translucent glass. It was more common at this time for Edvin Öhrström to use transparent glass to create different optical effects.

Edward Hald used the graal technique as a primary means of embellishment on the other vial and stopper (cat. no. 132). The diamond-shaped repeat pattern appears as though it was woven around the surface, rendering the glass opaque. A traditional surface treatment has been updated and given a more contemporary feeling.

Numerous variations of the vial-and-stopper design appear in the Orrefors trade catalogues during the late 1930s. NS-L.

References: Ricke and Gronert, *Glas in Schweden*.

132. Vial and Stopper

1937
Edward Hald
Graal, pressed; $5^7/_8$ x $2^5/_8$ in.
(15 x 6.8 cm)

Orrefors Glassworks

Marks: ''Hald Ofs 37'''

Collection Birgitta Crafoord

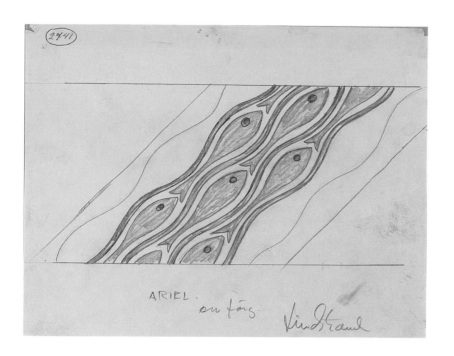

133. Drawing for Ariel Decoration
1938
Vicke (Viktor) Lindstrand
Pencil, crayon on paper; 9 x 11⅜ in.
(22.7 x 29.0 cm)

Orrefors Museum
Inv. no. 2741

This drawing of stylized fish was readily translated into the sandblasted blank
that would have formed the core of an
ariel vase. Given its rapid "repeat," it
was unnecessary to produce more
than a small portion of the pattern.
DEO

134. Blank for "Ariel"
Vicke (Viktor) Lindstrand
Blown, overlay(?); 6½ x 3⅜ in.
(15.9 x 8.7 cm)

Orrefors Museum

In some respects, the ariel pieces that
Orrefors produced were an outgrowth
of the slightly older graal and mykene
techniques devised at the factory in
1936. Using blanks as the basis for
these ariel vases may have been borrowed from the graal technique and
trapping air pockets between layers of
glass may have been inspired by
Lindstrand's mykene technique. The
technique was named "ariel" after the
spirit of the air from Shakespeare's
Tempest.

Sandblasting at Orrefors in the
middle 1930s (see cat. no. 119) must
have influenced the master-glassblower Gustaf Bergqvist in the development
of the ariel technique, which was introduced in 1937. By sandblasting decorative patterns into the blanks, Bergvist
was able to create the carefully controlled channels that would trap the
pockets of air when the first clear glass
sheet was flashed over the blank.
Bergqvist probably used a stencil to
protect areas of the design that were to
remain intact. DEO

Reference: Ricke and Gronert, *Glas in
Schweden*, p. 293

135. Vase called "Rabbits"
1937
Vicke (Viktor) Lindstrand
Ariel; 8¼ x 5¾ in. (21.0 x 14.6 cm)

Orrefors Glassworks

Mrs. Agnes Hellner Collection,
Kungstenen Foundation, Stockholm
University
Inv. no. H 213

Lindstrand's consummate skills as a
draftsman and observer of nature is
nowhere more evident than in this
remarkable vase, created soon after
the ariel technique was introduced. In
his minimal handling of form,
Lindstrand brilliantly exploited the
many poses adopted by rabbits while
playing, resting, and eating. In some
instances, his depiction approaches
abstraction but never neglects the distinct characteristics of the rabbit-
graceful, alert, and somehow always
humorous.

This was a particularly difficult vase
for Lindstrand to plan as a drawing.
The rabbits are of various sizes and
postures, and are scattered over the
complex curvature of the vase.
Lindstrand and the artisans had to
carefully plan the depth and size of the
sandblasted indentations to make certain that they would not collapse when
enveloped in the clear glass casing
that was applied over the heated
blank. The glassblowers had to be
particularly careful while they worked
the vase into its final shape so as not to
distort Lindstrand's fragile, but powerfully eloquent shapes.

Agnes Hellner, as a member of the
family that controlled Orrefors, had the
opportunity to select examples of the
firm's output before it was made available to the retail clientele. She was
also recognized as a connoisseur of
exceptional work from Orrefors. DEO

136. Vase called "Europa and the Bull"
1937
Vicke [Viktor] Lindstrand
Graal; $10^{1}/_{4}$ x $5^{7}/_{8}$ in. (26 x 15 cm)

Orrefors Glassworks
Marks: "Orrefors 1937 Graal No. 103 W. Lindstrand"

Collection Birgitta Crafoord

137. Vase called "Man and Horse"
1937
Edvin Öhrström
Ariel; 8¹/₂ x 5⁵/₈ in. (21.8 x 14.2 cm)

Orrefors Glassworks
Marks: "Orrefors 1937 Sweden Ariel No 51 Edvin Ohrstrom"

Orrefors Museum

The most important international event in the applied arts field at the end of the 1930s was the Exposition Internationale des Arts et Techniques dans la Vie Moderne, which was held in Paris in 1937. Orrefors used the exhibition to display the work of new artists and feature new aspects of its product line. The new designer featured in 1937 was the sculptor Edvin Öhrström who had come to Orrefors in 1936 specifically to prepare for the Paris exhibition. Working in collaboration with the craftsman Gustaf Bergqvist, Öhrström introduced the ariel technique, an extension of the graal method that exploited sandblasting to create rich decorative effects.

A comparison between these two vases illustrates the different decorative effects of the graal and ariel techniques. There are striking similarities between the colors and compositions: both use a palette of brown, white, and gold, and both incorporate human and animal figures. Lindstrand's vase (cat. no. 136) depicts the mythological story of Europa and the bull. The graal technique gives the decoration a flat, graphic appearance. Öhrström's vase (cat. no. 137) shows a man and rearing horse which was a common subject in his ariel work from the same period. The ariel technique produces a more sculptural effect, and the areas of colored glass are denser. NS-L

References: cat. no. 136, Dahlback-Lutteman, ed., *Svenskt glas,* p. 36; cat. no. 137, Holmér and Reihnér. *Lyricism in Modern Design,* p.108; László, *Svenskt Konstglas,* pp. 76-77.

Fig. 137a. Display of industrial design in the Swedish pavilion at the 1937 Paris Exposition Internationale des Arts et Techniques dans la Vie Moderne. (From Huldt, ed., *Konsthantverk Och Hemslojd I Sverige)*

138. Vase (Lettering in Ariel Orange)

Vicke (Viktor) Lindstrand
1937
Ariel; 8 1/8 x 5 1/2 in. (20.8 x 13.9 cm)

Orrefors Glassworks

Orrefors Museum

The use of overlay was an important aspect of the ariel technique. In light of the fact that this was not a production piece, but rather a special commission, it is likely that apart from the lettering, the vase was protected by a rubber resist that was impervious to the sandblasting. A specially made stencil that was created for pieces that were part of Orrefors's product line. DEO

139. Vase called "Tigers"

1937
Vicke (Viktor) Lindstrand
Graal; 7½ x 6⅜ in. (19.2 x 16.1 cm)

Orrefors Glassworks
Marks: "Orrefors. Lindstrand. Graal 1937/ no 15/ Sweden"

Mrs. Agnes Hellner Collection, Kungstenen Foundation, Stockholm University
Inv. no. H 72

His painterly qualities are evident in this vase for which no drawings are known to exist. It may be that many of the individual pieces of graal glass were created in the workroom, rather than planned in the studio. The "Tigers" vase is one of the first pieces produced by Lindstrand in the nw graal technique. DEO

Reference: "Exhibition of Swedish Pottery and Glass," p. 822, fig. 1.

140. Vase

1937
Vicke (Viktor) Lindstrand
Blown, engraved, etched; 13 x 8$\frac{1}{8}$ x
6$\frac{1}{4}$ in. (33 x 20.5 x 15.9 cm)

Orrefors Glassworks
Marks: "Orrefors LH 1756"

Collection Birgitta Crafoord

This large vase represents a forward step in Lindstrand's reduction of ornament in designs of the late 1930s. In comparison with his man-and-horse vase (cat. no. 121), this design eliminates most bodily details. In some respects, Lindstrand's spherical rendering of the woman's face and breast and articulation of her thighs recall Hald's work of the early 1920s, when he completed the vase called "Girls Playing Ball." This reductivism does not imply simplicity, however, or vacuousness. The figure of the man, a backdrop for the woman, has a powerful presence that belies the austerity used to depict him. The slightly larger outline of his body has been rendered with less polish than the woman's, making him appear darker, as though he is sulking in the shadows behind her. There is an implication in their postures that the man is moving to contain the woman, imparting an additional sinister quality to this piece.

The extensive use of cutting, polishing, and acid etching, all part of the technical battery of skills available at the firm in the twenties and before, have been used here to impart an emotional quality to the narrative rarely imparted at Orrefors. DEO

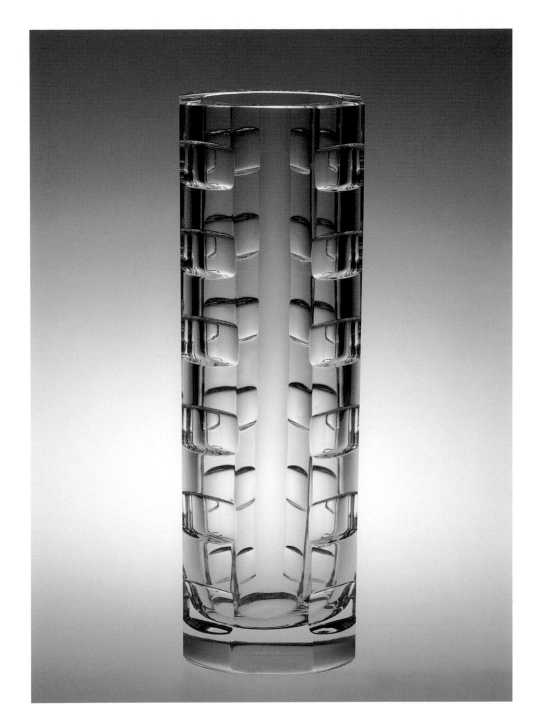

141. Vase

1938
Elis Bergh
Blown, cut; H. 10⅛ in. (25.7 cm)

Kosta Glassworks

The Metropolitan Museum of Art
Purchase, Edward C. Moore, Jr. Gift,
1939
Inv. no. 39.154.2

During the 1910s and 1920s, Kosta struggled to keep pace with the aesthetic, technical, and financial growth of Orrefors, its younger rival. In the midst of corporate turmoil, Kosta had difficulty keeping designers on staff and finding a niche in a rapidly changing market. Elis Bergh was an exception. During the twenty-one years he was on staff, he was known for the innovative glass that he designed for the firm, especially a wide array of cut glass.

This vase is reminiscent of a *ts'ung,* a tall, square-sectioned Chinese vessel made of jade and decorated with bold facets. The vase is one of the most contained pieces Bergh created for the factory in the 1930s when his work often exhibited a power rarely attained at other factories in Sweden.

The model was displayed the Brussel's fair in 1938, and this example was purchased by the Metropolitan Museum of Art in 1939 from the Sweden House outlet in the Swedish pavilion at the New York World's Fair. Until 1939, the majority of the purchases made of Swedish glass for the permanent collection of the Metropolitan Museum had been of Orrefors glass. This vase is one of the first official acquisitions of Kosta's production by an American museum. DEO

References: Artéus, ed., *Kosta 250 Years of Craftsmanship*, pp. 56–57; Paulsson, ed.,*Modernt Svenskt Glas*, p. 163, fig. 95; Remington, "Contemporary Swedish and Danish Decorative Arts," p. 104; Fong and Wyatt, *Possessing the Past*, pp. 42–43.

142. Vase

1938
Gerda Strömberg
Blown, cut; 6 ⁷⁄₈ x 7 in. (17.5 x
17.8 cm)

Strömbergshyttan Glassworks
Marks: "B 31"

Smålands Museum, Swedish Glass
Museum, Växjö
Inv. no. M 10298

In 1933 Edvard Strömberg, who had worked as managing director at the Orrefors and Eda glassworks, took over the Lindefors Glassworks and changed its name to Strömbergshyttan. The factory underwent a period of considerable economic difficulties at the beginning of the 1930s, but under Strömberg's direction it made a considerable comeback. Much of its newfound success derived from the contribution of Gerda Strömberg, Edvard's wife, who had established her reputation while designing glass at the Eda glassworks in the late 1920s. She joined Strömbergshyttan in 1933, applying her understanding of the technical and aesthetic qualities of glass to modernize the product line.

This vase, designed in 1934 and first produced in 1938, fully exploits the mechanical process of molding glass. It enabled the piece to be blown to an unusual thickness and imbued the simple design with a bold majestic quality. Despite its mass the vase is remarkable elegant, possessing a proportional grace.

Gerda Strömberg continued to explore this type of mold-blown vase form through the early 1940s, slightly altering the dimensions of the glass and embellishing it with cut decoration. These later manifestations, however, lacked the eloquence, balance, and harmony of this exemplary piece. NS-L

References: Dahlback-Lutteman, ed., *Svenskt Glas,* p. 122; Holmér and Ernstell, *Svenskt Glass Under Fem Sekler,* p. 106; Ricke and Gronert, *Glas in Schweden,* p .236.

143. Drawing for Vase

1938
Simon Gate
Pencil, ink on paper; 18¼ x 11 in.
(46.4 x 28 cm)

Inscription: "Til Axel Jonson" [on base of vase in drawing]; "1/2 8 onsdag [Wednesday] / S. Gate"

Orrefors Museum
Inv. no. G38II

Gate retained his considerable skills as a draftsman throughout his career. This design for a specially commissioned presentation piece, reveals an aesthetic judgment far different from the factory's standard offerings. The vase, with a sculptural treatment that is almost Art Nouveau, unfortunately does not appear to have been made.

The remarkable complexities of the vessel wall and the profile of the rim, without parallel in Sweden in the 1930s, would rarely be equaled until the 1960s. DEO

144. Drawing for "Zebra" Vase

1939
Vicke (Viktor) Lindstrand
Pencil, crayon on paper; 9 x 11⅝ in.
(22.7 x 29.4 cm)

Orrefors Museum
Inv. no. 2757

The preparatory work for Orrefors's art glass exists in a variety of forms, including drawings for decorations and forms as well as stencils for ariel and graal work. In this rendering of zebras for a 1939 vase, Lindstrand reveals his principal interest in form rather than detail (see cat. no. 88). The pink delineations around the zebra forms indicate areas that were to be sandblasted. In the finished piece the sandblasted areas would provide definition and would catch and reflect the light. This use of sandblasting introduced a dynamic quality to the glass that the late graal did not possess.

References: "Made in Europe," p. 33–37; Huldt, ed., *Konsthantwerk och Hemslöjd i Sverige*, p, 98, plate 2.

Fig. 145a. Alternate view of cat. no. 145.

145. Vase

1939
Vicke (Viktor) Lindstrand
Ariel; 9⅛ x 6½ (23.2 x 16.5 cm)

Orrefors Glassworks
Marks: "Orrefors Sweden Ariel 115
Lindstrom -39"

The Cleveland Museum of Art
Dudley P. Allen Fund
Inv. no. CMA 1939.676

Of the designers working at Orrefors
during the 1930s, Lindstrand may be
the finest draftsman and certainly the
most sympathetic observer of nature.
This piece, like his ariel vase depicting rabbits (see cat. no. 135), depicts

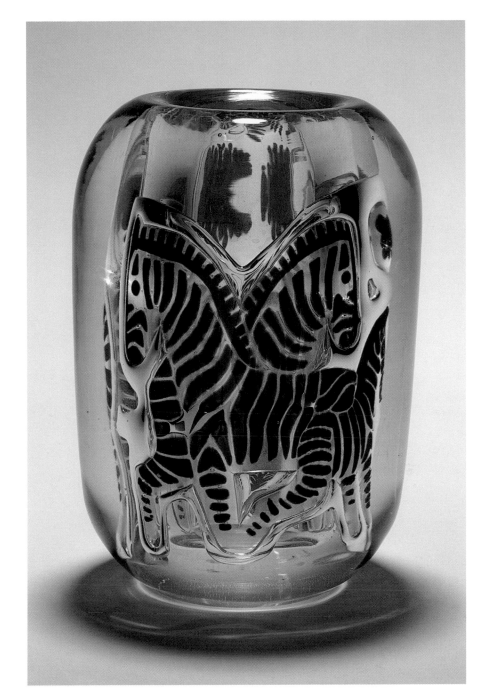

an animal subject, in this case a herd
of zebras. Lindstrand, a designer possessing a sense of humor, showed the
zebras from all angles, including an
unceremonius rear view. The use of an
amysthyst glass was somewhat rare in
the Orrefors production; it was also
used by Simon Gate for a decanter
(see cat. no. 31).

This design was shown in the
Swedish pavilion at the 1939 New York
World's Fair. It is not known if this
example was the piece on exhibit
there, but the Cleveland Museum of
Art purchased it from the Swedish
Royal Commission on December 12,
1939. In the previous year, the
Cleveland Museum had acquired an

example of Hald's "Girls Playing Ball"
(see cat. no. 34), an indication of the
museum's curatorial understanding of
the significance of Swedish glass,
especially for a design that was nearly
twenty years old at the time it was purchased. DEO

References: "Made in Europe," p. 33.

297

146. Blank for Ariel Vase
Edvin Öhrström
Blown, overlay and sandblasted;
6⅛ x 3⅜ in. (15.7 x 8.7 cm)

Orrefors Museum

This blank with its depiction of an octopus has been flashed with a colored overlay. It demonstrates the depth of bite necessary to keep the air pockets open in the ariel technique before the final application application of clear outer flashings. DEO

147. Drawing for Ariel Decoration
Attributed to Vicke (Viktor) Lindstrand
Pencil, crayon on paper; 9 x 11½ in. (22.7 x 29.2 cm)

Orrefors Museum
Inv. no. 2749

148. Vase called "Red Panther"
1938
Edvin Öhrström
Ariel; 8¼ x 5⅜ in. (21 x 13.8 cm)

Orrefors Glassworks
Marks: "Orrefors Suede Ariel No 81 E. Öhrström"

Orrefors Museum

This vase is characteristic of Öhrström's virtuoso work in the ariel technique. A vibrant red color, common in his art glass at this time, instills an element of exoticism in the design. It helps to create the effect of a fantasy landscape in which a panther walks amidst branches and leaves. NS-L

References: Holmér and Reihnér, *Lyricism in Modern Design*, p. 109.

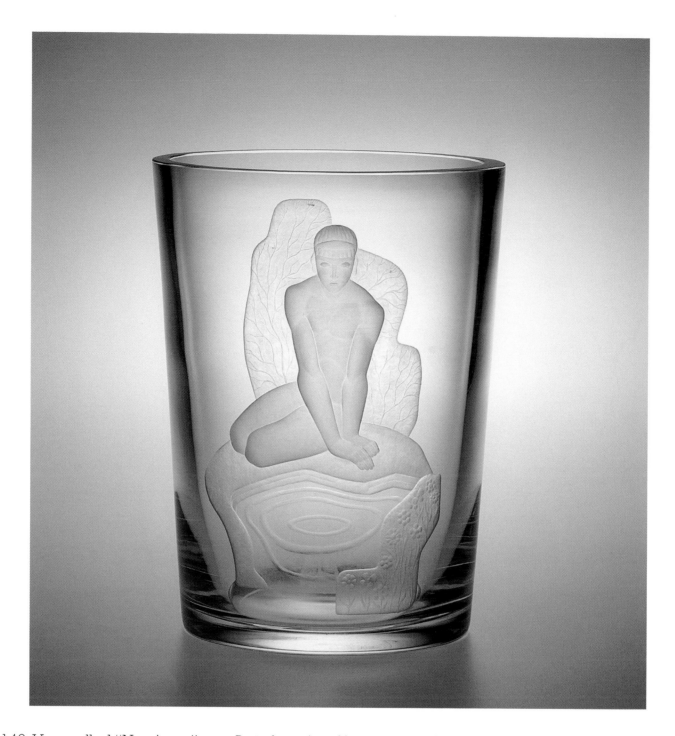

149. Vase called "Narcissus"

1939
Vicke (Viktor) Lindstrand
Blown, engraved, etched; 10⁷/₈ x
8¹/₈ in. (27.7 x 20.8 cm)

Orrefors Glassworks
Inscription: "Orrefors Lindstrand
2139 AG"

Collection Görander

Part of a series of large, engraved
vases that were produced to
Lindstrand's designs at the end of the
1930s, "Narcissus" is perhaps the
most subtle. The androgenous form of
the figure, silhouetted against a conventionalized pattern of vegetation, is
positioned so that his eyes engage
those of the observer. DEO

150. Vase called "African
Mask"
1939
Vicke (Viktor) Lindstrand
Ariel; 7⅝ x 6½ in. (19.5 x 16.5 cm)

Orrefors Glassworks
Marks: "Lindstrand/1939/Graal No.
406/Orrefors Sweden"

Collection Birgitta Crafoord

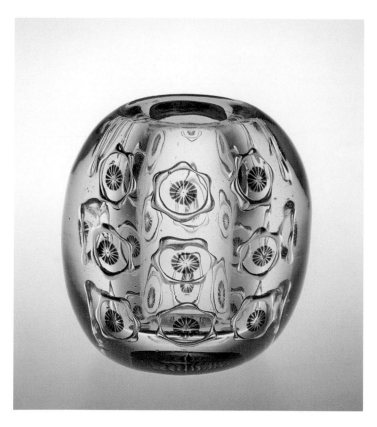

151. Vase called "Sea Urchin"

1939
Edvin Öhrström
Ariel; 6³/₄ x 7¹/₈ in. (17.3 x 18 cm)

Orrefors Glassworks
Marks: "ORREFORS SWEDEN ARIEL
No 153. E. Öhrström 1939"

Collection Birgitta Crafoord

The wealth of glass required to produce these large ariel pieces from the late 1930s is clearly evident in this vase with its minimal decoration. The discrete use of overlay, framed by the ariel decoration, creates a pattern that floats against the core of the piece. These motifs appear in the drawing for ariel decoration (cat. no. 152). DEO

152. Drawing for Ariel Decoration

Edvin Öhrström
Pencil on paper; 9⁵/₈ x 12¹/₈ in.
(24.5 x 30.9 cm)

Inscription: "2/8 / Även Rött och svart öfång / Färgen bort / djupt / I ansiktet allt utom ögat, ögonbryn och munnens och näsans linjer, luftblåsor / Färgen bort / E. Öhrström / ARIEL-GLAS dekor" [Also red and black overlay / The color away / deeply / In the face everything except the lines of the eye, eyebrow and of the mouth and the nose, air bubbles / The color away / E. Öhrström / Ariel-Glass décor]

Orrefors Museum
Inv. no. 4511

These motifs were combined in a number of ariel vases produced in the late 1930s. The sea urchin appeared on a vase (cat. no. 151) and the woman's face was interpreted on a variety of large pieces by Öhrström, including cat. no. 153.

Many of the drawings in the Orrefors archives were used as transfer drawings. The outlines of the forms were punctured with pins or other sharp instruments, after which the drawing would be secured to blanks and vessels, and powdered to transfer the outlines of the drawing. This centuries-old technique that had been used for the production of marquetry and ceramics. DEO

153. Vase

1939
Edvin Öhrström
Ariel; 7³⁄₈ x 4³⁄₄ x 4³⁄₈ in. (18.7 x
11.2 x 11.2 cm)
Orrefors Glassworks
Marks: "ORREFORS SWEDEN ARIEL
No. 144 E. Öhrström 1939"

Nationalmuseum, Stockholm
Inv. no. NMK 1076/1939

The richly colored and decorated
blank of this vessel appears to be suspended in a block of crystal. It is a
clear illustration of the use of a prelimi-
nary core to create the ariel pieces for
Orrefors. Only the purest glass produced by Orrefors would have permitted such an opulent effect without disturbing the central image. Close
examination reveals the wrappings of
clear outer glass that produced this
massive envelope. The vase was
shaped into its square-sectioned form
by a hand-held molds.

A ground metallic oxide must have
been mixed with pulverized green
glass before being cold painted on the
blank. This was probably then heated
again, allowing this mixture to fuse to
the blank. It appears as though, once

cooled, elements of the green flashing
were eliminated by wheel cutting and
sandblasting, using stencils to guide
the artisans.

Soon after this vase was made, it
was purchased by the Nationalmuseum. It is considered by many to be
Edvin Öhrström's prewar masterpiece
in a vase form. DEO

References: Ricke and Gronert, *Glas in
Schweden*, p 146; Duncan, *Orrefors Glass*,
pp. 142, 149; Dahlback-Lutteman, ed.,
Svenskt Glas, p. 116.

154. Vase called "Chameleon"

1939
Edvin Öhrström
Ariel; 9 x 7 in. (22.7 x 17.9 cm)

Orrefors Glassworks
Marks: "Orrefors Sweden Ariel
No. 125 E. Öhrström 1939"

Collection Birgitta Crafoord

One of the most massive of all the forms executed in this technique before the Second World War, this vase reveals the power of Öhrström's aesthetic vision. Öhrström did not rely on the basic traditions of elegance that had characterized much of the work produced by Orrefors from 1918 to 1939. His vessels are often ungainly, and his ornament unacademic. The compilation of these elements produced a body of work at the end of the decade that was recognizably different from that of his colleagues. His vision was fully explored in Orrefors architectural commissions, including enormous windows for churches, public halls, and exhibitions.

Öhrström also sought unusual subject matter for his pieces. Eschewing the subject matter of that lent itself to elegance such as the marine life, and horses that Hald and Lindstrand appear to have preferred, Öhrström appears to have gravitated to the eccentric on occasion, such as the comical chameleon on this vase. Rendered in a simple manner, it seems poised to snare a meal. The brilliantly colored blank has been exploited here as a backdrop for the applied ornament of reptiles and plant life. These components of the vase appear to be raised so significantly above the surface of the blank that they may have been applied to the blank separately, almost like *marqueterie de verre*, before the piece was enveloped in the outer layers of clear glass. Öhrström produced variations on this subject. DEO

References: Duncan, *Orrefors Glass*, pp. 141, 144.

155. Vase called "Adam and Eve"

1940–42
Vicke (Viktor) Lindstrand
Ariel; 9 x 5⅞ in. (23 x 15 cm)

Orrefors Glassworks
Marks: "Orrefors Sweden, Ariel nr. 228. V. Lindstrand"

Collection Birgitta Crafoord

This vase was completed after the beginning of the Second World War. The war soon cut Sweden off from the United States, its second largest market. The massive piece, executed with an ambitious, time-consuming, costly technique, might have been a special commission. A tour de force of Lindstrand's design capabilities, the ghostlike figures of Adam and Eve have been rendered with humor. Eve, who has the wisp of a satanic tail, tosses the proverbial apple of temptation seductively to Adam whose body has been rendered so that the indication of a spine bisects the form, perhaps a reference to the dichotomy of good and evil represented by the tempta-

tion. The curvilinear form of the snake, waiting behind the scene, is on the other side of the vase. The rich green color of the flashing suggests the verdant landscape of the Garden of Eden. DEO

156. Assorted Glasses from
a Service called
"Thule"
1942
Elis Bergh
Blown, cut; smallest, 4$\frac{1}{2}$ x 2$\frac{1}{4}$ in.
(11.6 x 5.9 cm); largest, 8$\frac{1}{4}$ x 2$\frac{1}{2}$
in. (21 x 6.3 cm)

Kosta Glassworks

Kosta Museum

157. Assorted Glasses from Service called "Charm"

1942
Elis Bergh
Blown; smallest, $4^3/8$ x $1^1/2$ in. (11.1 x 3.7); largest, $6^1/4$ x $2^7/8$ in. (16 x 7.2)

Kosta Glassworks

Kosta Museum

Beginning in 1929, Elis Bergh created numerous designs for stemware for Kosta. Some of his finest patterns were made during the Second World War when, despite the difficult economic situation, the factory survived by selling simple domestic wares for the home market. "Charm" represents both the culmination of a modern design aesthetic introduced by Edvin Ollers at the Home Exhibition in 1917 (see cat. no. 16) and the beginning of a new interpretation of modern design that emerged after the Second World War. In the postwar period, Swedish glass designers Vicke Lindstrand at Kosta and, in the 1960s, Nils Landberg at Orrefors continued the exploration of this form and aesthetic.

"Charm" was introduced in 1942. It represents the ultimate achievement of Sweden's twenty-five year effort to form a collaboration among artists, craftspeople, and industrialists in the creation of well-designed products for the home. In the design of everyday glassware, the aesthetic and technical quality achieved in this stemware series is unsurpassed in the twentieth century. NS-L

References: Artéus ed., *Kosta 250 Years of Craftsmanship*, pp. 162–63;Brunius et al., *Svenskt Glas*, p. 110; Herlitz-Gezelius, *Orrefors Ett Svenskt Glasbruk.* pp. 61–62; Holmér and Reihnér, *Lyricism in Modern Design*, p.114; Holmér and Ernstel, *Svenskt Glass Under Fem Sekler*, p.110; Dahlback-Lutteman, ed., *Svenskt glas*, p. 50; Ricke and Gronert, *Glas in Schweden*, p. 207.

APPENDIX

Swedish Glassworks and Designers, 1741 – 1996

Gunnel Holmér

This list is a compilation of the major glassworks in Sweden. It is by no means exhaustive; there were scores of other smaller factories, most of which were short lived. The information is based on interviews with owners and former owners, directors, and other personnel at the glassworks as well as on documents and archival materials in the Smålands Museum, Swedish Glass Museum, Växjö, and on a variety of published sources. Specific source references are given after each entry. Three general references were consulted: Olof Nordström, *Glasbruk och hyttor i Sverige, 1555 – 1985*, Smålands Museums skriftserie, no. 2. (Växjö, Sweden: Smålands Museum, 1986); Helmut Ricke and Ulrich Gronert, *Glas in Schweden, 1915 – 1960* (Munich: Prestel-Verlag, 1986); and Jarl Weidow, *Svenska glasbruk, 1555 – 1965* (Växjö, Sweden: Smålands Museum, 1969).

Åfors Glassworks
Founded 1876. Åfors Glassworks was founded by master-blowers C. A. Fagerlund, Oscar Fagerlund, Alfred Fagerlund and Carl J. Carlsson, three of whom came from Kosta and one from Johanstorp. The blowing room was destroyed by fire in 1876, the year the factory opened, but was soon rebuilt. In 1911 Åfors was reformed as a joint-stock company, and in 1916 it was purchased by Ernst Johansson, a wholesale merchant, and Oscar Johansson, the proprietor of Hjärtsjö glassworks. In 1917 Ernst Johansson became sole owner; after resolving financial difficulties he restarted the company. Modernization included new equipment and a new cutting shop. The glassworks soon passed into the hands of Eric Åfors (Ernst Johansson's son, who had changed his name to Åfors) and remained in the family until 1975, when, along with the other members of the Åfors Group (Kosta, Johansfors and Boda) it was sold to Upsala Ekeby. The Åfors Group was renamed Kosta Boda AB in 1976. The company's entire stock of shares was acquired by Investment AB Proventus in 1982, and since 1990 Åfors has been part of Orrefors Kosta Boda.

Åfors's early production comprised mainly household and domestic wares, but by 1910 it had expanded to include cut,

painted, and etched glass as well. Several glass painters came from Bohemia, and artists such as Karl Zenkert and Karl Diessner helped make Åfors a renowned glass-painting factory until painting was discontinued at the end of the 1940s. Around 1930 many glass cutters were laid off in the wake of the economic depression. About ten years later, cutting was resumed and continued until 1971. For a short period during the 1930s Astrid Rietz worked for Åfors, as did Edvin Ollers. Many pieces were also designed by Fritz Dahl (chief gaffer), Eric Strömberg (a civil engineer), Gunnar Håkansson (head of sales), and Ingvar Johnsson (a master-blower). In the mid-1950s the designer Ernest Gordon joined the company. In 1963 he was succeeded by Bertil Vallien, a representative of the bold young artists of the day, who experimented with hot-glass ornamentation and sandblasting. In the mid-1960s Vallien began casting glass sculptures in sand molds, a technique perfected over the next three decades, creating his well-known glass boats. He has also worked on glass designs for public spaces. As a designer for Åfors he has produced both ornamental glass and stemware such as "Chateau," one of the most successful of Sweden's stemware. In the 1970s Åfors launched its "Artist Collection" to introduce art glass manufactured in short series and falling somewhere between the company's unique pieces of art glass and its standard line of glassware. In 1971, Ulrica Hydman-Vallien, who was a ceramicist, began designing glass, primarily of limited-edition studio pieces. She is credited with reviving the practice of painting on glass at Åfors. Bertil Vallien and Ulrica Hydman-Vallien were for a long time the only designers at Åfors, although some glass was produced by Ken Done, an Australian, and Jerker Persson during the second half of the eighties. Persson was succeeded by Gunnel Sahlin, who, like the Valliens, has a studio close to the glassworks.

Reference: "I skenet från en glasugn, Åfors glasbruk och samhälle 1876 – 1978," in "I Glasriket — människan — miljön — framtidenm," a study project of the ABF och Svenska Fabriksarbetarenförbundet in Kalmar and Kronobergs län, 1982.

Alsterfors Glassworks

1885 – 1980. Originally an iron foundry, Alsterfors became a glassworks in 1885. Glass production commenced the following year. While still under construction, the plant and surrounding land were purchased by J. A. Gottwald Fogelberg, manager of Kosta. In 1903 Alsterfors joined the AB De Svenska Kristallglasbruken (Association of Swedish Crystal Manufacturers) and thereafter changed ownership on numerous occasions. It was leased to Orrefors in 1972, and in 1980 the furnaces were extinguished for good. Alsterfors's collection of samples, numbering some 10,000 objects, is now in the Smålands Museum in Växjö,.

During its early years Alsterfors made domestic wares and small items for everyday use, gradually expanding, however, to include tableware, restaurant and miscellaneous domestic wares, and ornamental glass. After 1958 Alsterfors began to make glass in a wide range of colors. Its designers included Edvin Ollers (1930 to 1934), Ingrid Atterberg (1958 to 1964), Fabian Lundkvist (beginning around 1960), and P. O. Ström (1968 to 1972).

Reference: "Ett glasrike i Glasriket: Älghults socken," in "I Glasriket — människan — miljön — framtidenm," a study project of the ABF och Svenska Fabriksarbetarenförbundet in Kalmar and Kronobergs län, 1982.

Björkshult Glassworks

1892 – 1978. This glassworks was originally called Björklunda. It was founded by three master-glassblowers — Carl M. Petersson, F. Oscar Johansson, and Oscar Carlström — and E. Robert Nyrena, a glass cutter. They directed the business until 1898 after which the company changed hands no less than four times until 1919 when it changed its name to Björkshult. The company was beset with economic problems through the 1920s, but in 1924 and 1925 two new partners, members of the Scheutz family, with many years of glassmaking experience, invested capital in the company so that improvements could be made. In 1934 Björkshult was sold by compulsory auction to three glassblowers, who initiated a modernization of the plant, including a new blowing room. In 1974 Björkshult became a member of the Krona-Bruken AB and in 1978 closed.

Björkshult initially manufactured domestic tableware and ornamental glass, but soon focused on cut crystal work. In the early 1930s Björkshult began manufacturing "stable glass," a toughened grade of glass used in particular for airport lights, although common drinking glasses were also made of it. "Stable glass" became one of Björkshult's largest exports.

During the 1940s Ragnar Johansson, a glassblower, began producing free-blown animals in glass. In the 1950s there were three primary designers: Hans-Christian Wagner (1957 to 1976), Margareta Schlyter-Stiernstedt (1953 to 1968) and Carl-Einar Borgström (into the 1970s). After 1973 a range of glasswares common to the entire Royal Krona Group was developed.

Reference: Tuva Bojstedt, "Björkshults glasbruks historia," manuscript in the archives of Smålands Museum, Swedish Glass Museum, Växjö.

Boda Glassworks

Founded in 1864. Boda Glassworks was established by two glassblowers from Kosta, R. Wictor Scheutz and Erik Widlund. In 1918 the factory changed hands and in 1947 was acquired by Eric Åfors. In 1964 Boda began collaborating with Kosta and Åfors, and in 1971 the three companies officially merged as AB Åforsgruppen. In 1975 the Åfors family sold out to Upsala Ekby, manufacturers of porcelain and ceramics, and a year later the group was reformed as Kosta Boda AB, which in 1990 merged with Orrefors AB to form Orrefors Kosta Boda.

Boda's early production consisted of blown and pressed domestic glassware and bottles. Crystal became an important part of the line around 1920. Gabriel Burmeister was hired to design art glass for a short period in the twenties. From 1925 to 1968 Fritz Kallenberg designed domestic glassware for mass production, as well as individual objects that followed a traditional aesthetic. During the Second World War Boda manufactured preserving jars, but at the end of the 1940s it resumed its standard production line. In 1953 sculptor Erik Höglund was hired to develop art glass that would be distinct to Boda and to design more sophisticated objects to supplement Boda's traditional glassware. Höglund remained at Boda until 1973. His robust, engraved crystal and colored, seedy potash glass with its imaginative, cast-on applications brought a new style to Swedish glass. Other artists worked sporadically at Boda: Elsa Fahlström Söderberg, whose glass was shown at the Nationalmuseum in 1954; Monica Backström (hired in 1965); Signe Persson-Melin (from 1967 to 1973); Lena Larsson (briefly in the 1960s); Rolf Sinnemark (from 1971 to 1985); and Kjell Engman (beginning in 1978).

References: "Generationers arbete på Boda Glasbruk," in "I Glasriket — människan — miljön — framtidenm," a study project of the ABF och Svenska Fabriksarbetarenförbundet in Kalmar and Kronobergs län, 1982; Gunnel Holmér, *Från Boda till New York: Knostnären Erik Höglund* (Borås, Sweden, 1976); Olof Nordström, *Boda, 1864 – 1964* (Malmö, Sweden, 1964).

Eda Glassworks

1833 – 1953. In 1833 a glassworks known as Emterud was set up by S. Lampa (a master-seaman), G. Ahlbom (a factory manager), A. L. Molin (a pharmacist), and A. Graff (a master-blower). Ten years later, it was sold, rebuilt, and renamed Eda. During the 1860s Eda was further reorganized, and in 1903 it joined the AB De Svenska Kristallglasbruken (Association of Swedish Crystal Manufacturers). From 1927 to 1933 the factory was run by Edvard Strömberg, former manager of Sandvik and Orrefors. After several changes of ownership and a continuous financial struggle through the 1930s and 1940s, Eda closed in 1953.

Until the early 1860s, Eda concentrated on window glass and a line of medicine bottles, vials, and small undecorated flasks. Pressed glass was introduced in 1845 and some mold-blown wares. During the late nineteenth century, Eda produced large quantities of glass for Swedish manufacturers of technical apparatus. The first cutter came to Eda in 1848, and by the 1890s a demand for cut glass, which had become Eda's specialty, outstripped the supply. In the 1920s functionalism reduced the popularity of traditional cut glass, and Edvard and Gerda Strömberg introduced a new range of more progressive models. The cut glass proved difficult to sell, however, perhaps because uncut surfaces were preferred at this time. Another designer, Bo Fjaestad, was employed in about 1950.

Reference: Torbjörn Fogelberg and Gunnar Lersjö, *Eda glasbruk*, Värmlands museums skriftserie, no. 13 (Karlstad, Sweden, Värmlands museum, 1977), p. 179.

Ekenäs Glassworks
1917 – 76. Hjalmar Stähl, a factory manager, and R. Stähl, a master-blower, both of whom came from Orrefors, started Ekenäs. The company went bankrupt in 1977 and was purchased by Sven Westberg the same year. After Westberg's death in 1962, Claes Tell and later his son ran Ekenäs until it closed in 1976.

Ekenäs manufactured an impressive range of wares including bottles and jars (also manufactured by automation), medical and laboratory glass, and ornamental glass and tableware. Production was highly flexible, allowing the company to avoid financial difficulties during the lean years of the 1930s. While other glassworks struggled to keep going, Ekenäs was able to increase its exports and hire or commission artists to design its wares. Tage Larsson was hired in 1930; Hildur Haggård in 1936; and Greta Runeborg-Tell in 1939, remaining until well into the 1950s. Astrid Rietz produced several pieces for Ekenäs in 1945, and Edvin Ollers also designed for Ekenäs in the late 1940s. From 1953 to 1976 John-Orwar Lake was in charge of design and development, and Michael Bang was affiliated with the factory during the 1960s.

References: C. G. Wictorin, *Ekenäs Bruks Aktiebolag, 1923 – 1948* (Vetlanda, Sweden, 1947); "Ekenäs: Vi som försvann; . . . Lindshammar: vi som är kvar," in "I Glasriket — människan — miljön — framtidenm," a study project of the ABF och Svenska Fabriksarbetarenförbundet in Kalmar and Kronobergs län, 1982.

Elme Glassworks
1917 – 70. In 1917 the Färe Glassworks in Sibbhult, which had been founded in 1896, transferred production to a newly built facility in Älmhult close to the railway and was renamed Elme Glassworks. The factory was owned by its manager and several others, including Gustaf Dahlén (a Nobel Prize laureate and developer of gaslit lighthouses). Their goal was to manufacture signal glass and lighthouse lenses. After the First World War, however, when Sweden resumed importing these and similar products, the factory concentrated on lighting fixtures instead.

In 1921 the company declared bankruptcy and was reorganized under new management to make pressed and blown domestic glassware, some of which was for export. From 1926 to 1930 Edvin Ollers designed for Elme, collaborating with the skilled glassworkers to make pressed wares

and art glass of high quality. At that time Elme had almost 300 employees, but in the early 1930s, as recession set in, much of the workforce was dismissed. Around 1935 the factory was sold to a consortium of businessmen, including Leonard Borgarp, a merchant. Under new management once more, the glassworks soon resumed normal production. A 1938 advertisement listed "pressed glass of excellent quality, cheap sets of tableware (plain or decorated with tasteful patterns), superior sets of stemware and tableware (cut and engraved), preserving jars, ornamental wares of all qualities and art glass of the very finest quality."

In 1940 the ownership structure changed yet again, and in 1962 the Borgarp family assumed control. Elme's designers during this period were Carl Olov Borgarp and his wife; Kjeld Jordan; and John Hall; beginning in 1967 Hjordis Olsson and Charlotte Rude also worked for the firm. Profits were small, however, and "Elme Nya Glashytta Aktiebolag" closed in 1970.

Reference: "Glas och sten i Linnébygden, Älmhult och Eneryda," in "I Glasriket — människan — miljön — framtidenm," a study project of the ABF och Svenska Fabriksarbetarenförbundet in Kalmar and Kronobergs län, 1982.

Flygsfors Glassworks
1888 – 1979. The village of Flygsfors was originally built around an iron foundry. When this closed in 1888, a window glass factory was constructed on the site by Ernst Wiktor Lundqvist and August Zeitz, who had been renting the factory at Gadderås for their production. Over the next few decades Flygsfors changed hands several times. The factory discontinued its hand-made window glass in 1920, unable to compete with machine-made imports. In 1930 a renamed AB Flygsfors Glasbruk began making tableware and preserving jars, later adding lighting fixtures to its production line in 1932. Prisms became a major item during the 1940s, as were domestic and ornamental wares, which were produced in long series. In 1959 the Gadderås Glassworks and in 1965 the Målerås Glassworks were acquired, and the three factories, known as the Flygsfors Group, came under a single management based in Flygsfors. Gadderås soon closed down, however, and Målerås became part of Krona-Bruken AB in 1974. Flygsfors was then taken over by Orrefors, but production at the factory ceased in 1979.

In 1949 the artist Paul Kedelv was employed to design light fixtures but, became best known for his art glass. He left Flygsfors in 1956 soon after Marie Bergkvist arrived for her brief tenure. Wiktor Berndt, who was hired in 1955, designed light fixtures and ornamental wares for the company until its takeover by Orrefors. Hans-Agne Jakobsson, who designed light fixtures beginning in 1957, was another long-term artist at Flygsfors. Ulla Nordenfeldt (around 1960), Sigvard Bernadotte, and the Finnish designer Helena Tynell (in 1968) also worked for the factory.

References: Olle Högström, ed., *Flygsfors, 1930 – 1955* (Kalmar, Sweden: AB Flygsfors glasbruk, 1955); "Järn. trä glas och sedan . . . Flygsfors Glasbruk, 1888 – 1979," in "I Glasriket — människan — miljön — framtidenm," a study project of the ABF och Svenska Fabriksarbetarenförbundet in

Gullaskruf Glassworks

1893 – 1921; 1927 – 83; 1990 – 95. The original glassworks at Gullaskruf was associated with Orrefors from 1900 to 1914. The factory made bottles but soon began to specialize in window glass. It could not compete with other Swedish makers of window glass or with machine-made imports of sheet glass, and production ceased in 1921. In 1927 the factory was reopened and modernized by William Stenberg, and in 1961 Lennart Andersson, Stenberg's son-in-law, took over as managing director. From 1974 to 1977 Gullaskruf was a member of the Krona-Bruken AB. In 1977 Gullaskruf was first leased and eventually sold to Orrefors; production again ceased in 1983, but started up in 1990. It was sold and resold several times in the 1990s before closing in 1995.

Gullaskruf is perhaps best known for its excellent pressed glass which ranged from automobile headlights to laboratory vessels and domestic tableware. William Stenberg, who came from a family of ironworkers, spent several years in his father's foundry, where among other things presses for the local glass factories were made. Stenberg learned to design and manufacture molds and gained practical experience of the craft in Germany. It was not surprising, therefore, that he concentrated on pressed glass after assuming control of Gullaskruf although the production included some blown and flared glass. Stenberg designed much of the line himself, with his daughter Marianne and son-in-law Lennart Andersson. Before the 1930 Stockholm Exhibition the factory employed Hugo Gehlin, a Swedish artist, who created pressed and blown household wares as well as enameled and free-blown art glass which gave Gullaskruf an identity of its own. By the time of Gehlin's death in 1953, Arthur Percy had been hired; he would stay with the company until 1965. Other artists of note were Kjell Blomberg (1955 to 1977) and Catharina Åselius-Lidbeck (1968 to 1970). In the early 1980s Orrefors manufactured a few of Lars Hellsten's series of pressed wares at Gullaskruf.

References: Jan Erik Anderbjörk, ed., *Gullaskrufs glasbruk, 1927 – 1952* (Gothenburg, Sweden: Gullaskrufs glasbruk, 1952); "Från fönsterglas till småglas: Gullaskrufs Glassbruk 1893 – ," in "I Glasriket — människan — miljön — framtidenm," a study project of the ABF och Svenska Fabriksarbetarenförbundet in Kalmar and Kronobergs län, 1982.

Johansfors Glassworks

1891 – 1991; reopened 1992. Among the founders were F. O. Israelsson, a churchwarden, and A. Ahrens, a glass painter, who had set up a glass-painting factory on the same site in 1889. From 1904 to 1911 Johansfors was leased to AB De Svenska Kristallglasbruken (Association of Swedish Crystal Manufacturers), after which it was run by Israelsson and, from 1950 to 1972, by Sixten Wennerstrand, who rebuilt and modernized extensively. In 1972 Johansfors was sold to the Åfors Group, (later known as Kosta Boda AB). In 1990 Kosta Boda was acquired by Orrefors, and in 1992 production at Johansfors was taken over by a group of former employees. The venture was short-lived, however, and the company is today under entirely new management.

During its early years, Johansfors concentrated on pressed and flared domestic glass and glass with painted decoration. The latter became something of a specialty, and during the first few decades of the twentieth century, many skilled glass painters from Bohemia were employed at the factory. Cut crystal was another specialty, and in about 1920 several cutters were brought in from Kosta and Bohemia. Four engravers were hired during the mid-1920s, one of whom, Folke Walwing, later became art director at Målerås. It was largely due to the success of its cut and engraved wares that Johansfors became known outside Sweden; it received several commendations for its products at the World Exhibition in Barcelona in 1929. Little is known about a Johansfors artist named Edward Askenberg except that he designed a magnificent footed covered urn (cat. no. 70). Around 1930 new models (such as cat. no. 76) were designed by Gunnar Håkansson (Grüno), and during the 1930s Johansfors thrived by concentrating on producing designs by its artists. From 1938 to 1947 much of the art glass produced at the factory was by Gustaf Hallberg, the chief gaffer. The artist and designer Bengt Orup, who was at Johansfors from 1952 to 1973, created a range of work, from popular sets of tableware and stemware to art glass. Other artists employed at Johansfors were Margareta and Erik Hennix (from 1965 to 1967) and Ingegerd Råman (from 1968 to 1971).

Beginning in 1972 the factory began to specialize in stemware, producing the work of several artists who were associated with the Kosta Boda group, such as Bertil Vallien and Ann Ehrner, who won international acclaim for their stemware, and Christopher Ramsey.

References: Jan Erik Anderbjörk, ed., *Johansfors, 1891 – 1951* (Karlskrona, Sweden: Johansfors glasbruk, 1951); "Liv och arbete under 90 år vid Johansfors," in "I Glasriket — människan — miljön — framtidenm," a study project of the ABF och Svenska Fabriksarbetarenförbundet in Kalmar and Kronobergs län, 1982.

Kosta Glassworks

Founded 1742. Kosta was founded by Anders Koskull and Bogislaus Staël von Holstein, two generals in Sweden's army and county governors. The name "Kosta" is formed from the first syllables — "Ko" and "Sta" — of their names. In 1756 Kosta was acquired by Johan Wickenberg, a magistrate, in whose family it remained, through marriage and inheritance, until 1893. Kosta thrived and expanded under the Wickenberg management; sales offices were opened in a number of towns in southern and central Sweden, including Stockholm, and Kosta glass found buyers from as far afield as Russia. Another Wickenberg manager, Uno Angerstein, modernized production to include cut glass and published the first printed price list in 1833. In 1887 a new manager, Axel F. Hummel, a forestry engineer, succeeded in putting Kosta's finances in order and thoroughly modernized the plant. Under his initiative the railway came to Kosta in 1890, and he participated in founding the AB De Svenska

Kristallglasbruken (Association of Swedish Crystal Manufacturers) in 1903 of which Kosta was a member until 1931. Later managers included C. Gottwald Fogelberg (from 1878 to 1886) and Sven Fogelberg, who was assistant to the director (1918 to 1922) and director (1927 to 1932). In 1936 Kosta was purchased by a consortium of Småland businessmen, which eventually came to be dominated by Eric Åfors and the members of his family. In 1971 Kosta was amalgamated with Åfors, Johansfors and Boda in the Åfors Group, which was purchased by Upsala Ekeby in 1975. In 1976 the trademark Kosta Boda AB was introduced, and in 1982 the company was acquired by Investment AB Proventus. Kosta Boda AB and Orrefors AB merged in 1990 to form Orrefors Kosta Boda.

During the first few years of its existence Kosta concentrated on the manufacture of sheet glass, having received an order for window glass for the royal palace which was under construction in Stockholm. Kosta also produced such sophisticated items as chandeliers as well as beer and schnapps bottles and simple household wares. In 1752 an engraver was employed to decorate glass. In the early nineteenth century the factory's production comprised ornamental objects and wares of both colorless and green glass, but in 1828 a range of cut glass was introduced and in 1839 a pressing machine was installed. In the 1880s stemware became one of Kosta's specialties. Cut glass was predominately decorated by miter grinding, but in the early twentieth century pantographs were also used. Much of Kosta's production was exported, making it Sweden's second largest glass producer after Reijmyre.

After the 1897 Stockholm Exhibition Kosta responded to critics by hiring an artist, Gunnar Wennerberg, to design a series of pieces with cut overlay designs for the Paris exposition of 1900. Alf Wallander, another celebrated artist, worked for Kosta in the early twentieth century. Although the combined production of Wennerberg and Wallander accounted for only a small part of Kosta's extensive offerings, their work attracted attention, and management recognized the importance of such collaborations. Edvin Ollers thus represented Kosta at the Hemutställningen (Home Exhibition) of 1917 where his functional designs met with an enthusiastic response. Most artists employed by Kosta, including Ollers, stayed for a very short time. Karl Hulstrom, who had worked alongside Ollers, left and returned during the 1920s. Other artists of note who designed glass for Kosta during the 1920s were Sten Branzell and Ewald Dahlskog. Sven Erixson was employed before the 1930 Stockholm Exhibition, and during the 1930s Sven-Erik Skawonius, Tyra Lundgren, Edvin Ollers (again), and several others were employer briefly at the factory. Elis Bergh was an exception in terms of the duration of his employment; he served as art director from 1929 to 1950. His earliest contributions were designs for light fixtures, but he was soon creating bowls, vases and, especially, stemware. During the 1940s he was rejoined by Skawonius, and Oskar Dahl and John Kandell also came to work at Kosta around this time. Bergh was succeeded by Vicke Lindstrand (1950 to 1973). Lindstrand was an extraordinarily versatile designer who experimented boldly with new shapes, colors, and techniques. In addition to unique pieces of art glass, he is also known for his stemware and glass for public spaces. Mona

Morales-Schildt, who was employed in 1958, is best known for her elegant designs using a cut overlay technique.

During the 1960s Kosta hired many young artists including Sigurd Persson, Lisa Bauer, and Rolf Sinnemark. Of special note, Ann and Göran Wärff were nontraditional glassmakers whose production included massive, sculptural pieces and sophisticated free-blown vases and bowls. Continuing the trend in the 1970s Kosta hired: Paul Hoff, who is chiefly remembered for his large sandblasted dishes decorated with animals; Anna Ehrner, whose stemware brought a new elegance to the dining table and whose "Line" is one of the most popular sets of modern Swedish stemware; Bengt Edenfalk, who is noted for his crystal utility wares and unique underlay pieces with marvered fields of color; and Klas-Göran Tinbäck, who produced a range of unique bowls and dishes with an etched and sandblasted decor.

Since the 1980s, Kosta has gradually adapted to changing times. New bowls, vases, and tableware, suitable for manufacture in long series, have been produced alongside art glass that has won acclaim in Sweden and abroad. Today eight designers are employed at Kosta Boda, three of whom — Göran Warff, Anna Ehrner, and Ann Wåhlström — have their studios in the village of Kosta. The others work mainly in Åfors and Boda but are frequent visitors to the blowing room at Kosta.

References: Jan Erik Anderbjörk, ed., *Kosta Glasbruk, 1742 – 1942*, Jubileumsskrift (Stockholm: Kosta glasbruk, 1942); Ann Marie Herlitz-Gezelius, *Kosta* (Lund, Sweden: Bokförlaget Signum, 1987); "Hanna på Kosta," in "I Glasriket — människan — miljön — framtidenm," a study project of the ABF och Svenska Fabriksarbetarenförbundet in Kalmar and Kronobergs län, 1982.

Artists at Kosta

Axel Enoch Boman	1895 – 1903
Gunnar G:son Wennerberg	1898 – 1902; 1908
Kai Nielsen	1903 – 1904
Ferdinand Boberg	1905
Karl Lindeberg	1907 – 31
Alf Wallander	1908 – 1909
Edvin Ollers	1917 – 18; 1931 – 32
Karl Hulström	1917 – 19; 1927 – 28
Lennart Nyblom	1919
Sten Branzell	1922 – 30
Sven Erixson and Arnold Karlström	1923
Sven Erixson	1929 – 31
Ewald Dahlskog	1926 – 29
Sven Philström	1926 – 69
Einar Nerman	ca. 1926
Elis Bergh	1929 – 50
Sven-Erik Skawonius	1933 – 35; 1944 – 50
Tyra Lundgren	1935
R.A. Hickman	1937
Oskar Dahl	1939 – 40; 1942 – 44
John Kandall	1946
Vicke Lindstrand	1950 – 73
Ernest Gordon	1953 – 55

Mona Morales-Schildt	1958 – 70
Ann Wärff	1964 – 78
Göran Wärff	1964 –
Stig Lindberg	1965
Rolf Sinnemark	1967 – 86
Sigurd Persson	1968 – 82
Lisa Bauer	1969 – 91
Paul Hoff	1972 – 82
Hertha Hillfon	1974
Anna Ehrner	1974 –
Bengt Endenfalk	1978 – 89
Klas-Göran Tinbäck	1976 – 81
Max Walter Svanberg	1980
Harald Wiberg	1980
Bengt Lindström	1982
Gun Lindblad	1982 – 87
Christian von Sydow	1984 – 89
Gunnel Sahlin	1986 –
Ann Wåhlström	1986 –

Limmared Glassworks

Founded 1741. Limmared was founded by Gustaf Ruthen-
sparre, an army officer whose large country estate offered a
plentiful supply of wood and some of the raw materials
needed for the manufacture of glass. The glassworks remained in the same family until 1778, after which it changed
hands many times. Fredrik Brusewitz, for example, bought
the factory in 1852, and his son Carl was manager until his
death in 1937. Since 1965 Limmared has been owned by
PLM, a large conglomerate whose chief business is the manufacture of glass, sheet metal, aluminum, and plastic packaging.

Limmared's early production consisted largely of blown-
glass goblets and drinking vessels of good-quality colorless
glass. Engraving was introduced in the 1740s, when a
German engraver was persuaded to transfer from
Kungsholm Glassworks in Stockholm to Limmared. In the
mid-eighteenth century, a series of chandeliers was manufactured at Limmared by a German master who had previously been employed by Kosta. In 1823 the company hired a
Swedish engraver who specialized in inscriptions, monograms, and scenes from everyday life rendered on schnapps
bottles. During the second half of the nineteenth century the
factory's output was adjusted to meet the rapidly increasing
demand for cut crystal. Production of cut glass at Limmared
reached a peak around 1910, after which it gradually
declined until it virtually disappeared, and by 1935 hollow
ware had almost entirely taken over. In addition to fine quality
glassware, Limmared also manufactured sheet glass and various articles of green and amber glass, including bottles, jars,
and pharmaceutical vessels. During the second half of the
nineteenth century, the factory began to specialize in glass
for chemical and medical uses. Large quantities of pressed
glass were manufactured after 1848.

In 1929, the year before the Stockholm Exhibition, Edvin
Ollers was employed to design glass for the cosmetics industry. The result was a series of vials manufactured both by
hand and partial automation. Ollers also designed a series of
covered jars. He left Limmared in 1940, and since that date

no designer has been employed by the glassworks.

References: *Limmared, 1740 – 1940* (Ulricehamn, Sweden: AB
Fredr. Brusewitz, 1940); *Limmared, Bygden — Bruket — Samhället, 1740 – 1990* (Gällstad, Sweden: Limmareds Hembygds
forening, 1990).

Lindefors. See Strömbergshyttan.

Lindshammar Glassworks

Founded 1905. Lindshammar was founded by Robert
Rentsch, a German glassblower who had previously worked
for both Kosta and Pukeberg. In 1916 the factory was
acquired by Anton Petersson who initiated a program of
modernization, including construction of a large new blowing
room. In 1949 Petersson's son Erik Hovhammar assumed
control and during the 1950s completely rebuilt the factory.
Lindshammar declared bankruptcy in 1981 and was sold
again in 1984 to Ulf Rosén. Since then it has been managed
by Rosén, whose father and uncle had both gained considerable experience of glassmaking at various other glassworks.

In its early years Lindshammar primarily produced cut-
glass tableware and colored ornamental wares, much of
which was for export. During the Second World War production also included preserving jars and bottles, and after 1949,
having previously manufactured utility wares for restaurant
and domestic use, the factory began producing art glass and
engaged the artist Gunnar Ander. Lindshammar also introduced what became known as "architectural glass" or glass
bricks that could be used in constructing walls and windows.
Other artists were hired after 1960, including Christer
Sjögren in 1963, Tom Möller (from 1967 to 1989), Gösta
Sigvard (from 1965 to ca. 1980), Sigvard Bernadotte (active in
the 1970s) and Catharina Åselius-Lidbeck (from 1970 to
1989).

Production of blown glass declined during the 1970s as
molded and centrifuged glass came to dominate production.
Objects in these techniques are still made, although after
1984 Ulf Rosén began reintroducing blown glass, both art
glass and everyday items. The new management also hired
Jonas Torstensson (from 1986 to 1990), Matz Borgstrom (from
1990 – 1992), Lars Sestervik, and Birgitta Watz. Sjögren has
worked uninterupted and Åselius-Lidbeck has been rehired.

Reference: "Ekenäs: Vi som försvann; . . . Lindshammar: vi
som är kvar," in "I Glasriket — människan — miljön —
framtidenm," a study project of the ABF och Svenska
Fabriksarbetarenförbundet in Kalmar and Kronobergs län,
1982.

Målerås Glassworks

Founded 1890. There have been several glassworks in the
village of Målerås. The first was founded in 1890, purchased
by AB De Svenska Kristallglasbruken (Association of
Swedish Crystal Manufacturers), and closed in 1904. Another
glassworks was active from 1916 to 1922. When it declared
bankruptcy, a third factory, AB Målerås Glasbruk, started pro-

duction in 1924. This was more successful than its predecessors and remained in independent operation until 1965, when it became part of the Flygsfors Group. In 1974 it joined the Royal Krona Group, where it remained until 1977, when it was taken over by Kosta Boda AB. In 1980 Målerås was purchased by its own employees and has been run by them since 1981.

Since its inception Målerås has produced both domestic glassware and art glass. During the 1930s Målerås survived by supplying glass to the Svenska Kooperativa förbundet (Swedish Cooperative Union and Wholesale Society). The designers affiliated with the factory at this time were architects employed by the union in Stockholm, including Kalle Lodén and Georg Scherman, who designed a set of tableware for the 1930 Stockholm Exhibition, Carl Horvik, Erik Ahlsén, J. Jansson, Sven Malm, and Olle Nyman. Folke Walwing, who trained at the Orrefors school of engraving, was Målerås's art director from 1924 to 1970. Hannelore Dreutler, Åke Röjgård, and Anette Sviberg-Krahner worked at the factory for short periods during the 1960s. Sviberg-Krahner rejoined the company during the 1970s at which time Lisa Larsson and Marianne Westman, who designed glass for the Royal Krona Group, produced designs for Målerås. In 1975 engraver Mats Jonasson began designing models of his own and became the factory's art director in 1981. Ingeborg Lundin, who had previously won acclaim for her designs at Orrefors, was at Målerås from 1989 to 1991, and in the 1990s Eva Englund and Rolf Sinnemark have worked as freelance designers for the company.

References: "Glasbruksliv i Målerås," in "I Glasriket — människan — miljön — framtidenm," a study project of the ABF och Svenska Fabriksarbetarenförbundet in Kalmar and Kronobergs län, 1982; *AB Målerås glasbruk, Nytryck av produktkatalog från 1930 – talet*, with a foreword by Torbjörn Fogelberg (Växjö, Sweden: Smålands Museum, 1990).

Orrefors Glassworks
Founded 1898. In 1726 Johan Silfversparre, an army officer, established an iron foundry on the grounds of the Orranäs estate. Bar iron was made there until 1883 and wrought-iron products until 1914. In 1875 a sawmill became associated with the factory, and in 1897 the entire complex was purchased by Johan August Samuelson, a merchant who established a glassworks on the property in 1898 as a way of using the waste from the sawmill. In 1913 the sawmill and glassworks were acquired by Johan Ekman, a consular officer. Although primarily interested in forestry and production of lumber, he maintained the glassworks from 1913 to 1919 and appointed Albert Ahlin as its managing director. In 1918 Ekman purchased the Sandvik glassworks and at his death in 1919 both companies were taken over by his children, Hedvig Piper, Carl Ekman, Agnes Hellner, Sigrid Beyer, and Birgit Ramström. Agnes was married to Chief Justice Johannes Hellner, who was appointed managing director and chairman of the board. In 1946 Orrefors was purchased by Henning Beyer and remained in his family until 1971, when a majority shareholding was acquired by Incentive, an investment trust company. A few years later Incentive purchased

the entire stock, but the relationship with Incentive ended in 1994. During the seventies Alsterfors, Flygsfors, Strömbergshyttan, and Gullaskruf were all acquired by Orrefors, and within a few years were closed down. In 1990 Orrefors also acquired Kosta Boda, and today Orrefors Kosta Boda comprises the following glassworks: Orrefors, Sandvik, Kosta, Boda, and Åfors, as well as SEA which is subsidiary. Since 1913, when Albert Ahlin joined the company, Orrefors has been run by nine other managing directors, including Edvard Strömberg (from 1918 to 1927), who later was owner of Eda and Strömbergshyttan; Edward Hald, (from 1933 to 1945), who was also one of the company's foremost designers; and Göran Bernhoff who has been managing director since 1981.

For its first few years Orrefors produced simple tableglass and hollow ware, although from 1898 to 1918 the factory also manufactured sheet glass. According to catalogues issued shortly after 1910 some cut and etched crystal tableware was also produced at this time. Ekman and Ahlin were both far-sighted, however, and recognized that the future of Orrefors pointed toward art glass. A master-blower, Knut Bergqvist, and chief gaffer, Oscar Landås, were recruited from Kosta; from Bohemia came Heinrich Wollman, a glass painter; and from the Teknologiska Institutet (Institute of Technology) in Stockholm came Fritz Blomqvist, who was to prepare the designs. In 1916 and 1917, respectively, artists Simon Gate and Edward Hald were hired to collaborate with the blowers, specifically in perfecting the graal technique. At the 1917 Hemutställningen (Home Exhibition) in Stockholm they presented a number of wares for everyday use. Around this time they also began experimenting with engraving, working primarily with the cutter and engraver Gustaf Abels. Hired in 1915 Abels played an important role at Orrefors during the 1920s, when the company's engraved pieces began to receive international recognition. Many patterns were duplicated by skilled engravers from Germany and Bohemia, and in 1922 Orrefors founded the first school for glass engraving in Sweden (it closed in 1951). Two of its most notable alumni were Sven Palmqvist and Nils Landberg, who went on to design glass at Orrefors and Sandvik for over forty years, including notable series of tableglass and other pieces for domestic use. A third designer, John Selbing, worked with Palmqvist and Landberg but may be best remembered for his photographs of glass.

In 1928, with the 1930 Stockholm Exhibition in mind, Orrefors hired Vicke Lindstrand, who designed a series of thick-walled, optic bowls with an engraved decor that were shown at the exhibition to great acclaim. Both Lindstrand and Edvin Öhrström, who joined the company in 1936, experimented freely with a variant of the graal technique known as ariel. Öhrström specialized in heavy, monumental pieces, which he designed in a wide variety of styles.

Glass for lamps and lighting fixtures had been designed at Orrefors — by Hald and Gate — as early as the 1920s. In 1946 Carl Fagerlund, a lighting specialist, was employed solely to design light fixtures.

In 1947 Ingeborg Lundin joined Orrefors. After a 1948 exhibition of her work, one critic wrote, "She ornaments her glass not only with a delicately drawn decor of figures and plants but also with a distinctively modern linear decoration, in contrast to the terse lines of the engraving we have seen hitherto." Gunnar Cyrén, hired in 1959, instilled a new vigor in painted and engraved glass.

In the early 1970s many prominent Orrefors designers retired, making way for emerging young artists. Among the newcomers were Olle Alberious, Lars Hellsten (who came from Skruf Glassworks), Eva Englund (who had previously worked for Pukeberg Glassworks), and, toward the end of the decade, Berit Johansson. They joined Jan Johansson, who had been employed in 1969. The new designers continued to develop the techniques and glassmaking skills for which Orrefors had become renowned. Several of them also turned their attention to sculpture, and, like their predecessors, accepted commissions to design glass for public spaces.

In the 1980s a new generation of designers arrived; after 1987 when Orrefors discontinued the practice of producing pieces by artists who were no longer active, bold, contemporary designs came to the fore. The celebrated Orrefors, so rich in glassmaking tradition, had become more progressive and more vigorous. Contemporary designers included Lena Bergström, Gunnar Cyrén, Lars Hellsten, Jan Johansson, Helén Krantz, Erika Lagerbielke, Anne Nilsson, Martti Rythönen, and Per B. Sundberg.

References: "Orresforsaren i Glasriket," in "I Glasriket — människan — miljön — framtidenm," a study project of the ABF och Svenska Fabriksarbetarenförbundet in Kalmar and Kronobergs län, 1982; Ann Marie Herlitz-Gezelius, *Orrefors ett Svenskt Glasbruk* (Stockholm: Atlantis, 1984).

Artists at Orrefors

Fritz Blomqvist	1914 – ca. 1917
Simon Gate	1916 – 45
Eva Jancke-Björck	ca. 1917
Edward Hald	1917 – 78
Nils Landberg	1927 – 72
John Selbing	1927 – 73
Vicke Lindstrand	1928 – 40
Sven Palmqvist	1928 – 71
Edvin Öhrström	1936 – 57
Fritz Kurz	1940s
Carl Fagerlund	1946 – 80
Ingeborg Lundin	1947 – 71
Gunnar Cyrén	1959 – 70; 1976 –
Jan Johansson	1969 –
Styrbjörn Engström	ca. 1970
Henning Koppel	1971 – 81
Rolf Nilsson	1971 – 72
Olle Alberius	1971 –
Lars Hellsten	1972 –
Eva Englund	1974 – 89
Wiktor Berndt	1975 – 79
Owe Elven	1975 – 78
Petr Mandl	1970s
Berit Johansson	1979 – 83
Börge Lindau	1970s
Bo Lindekrantz	1970s
Anette Krahner	1980 – 81
Arne Branzell	1980 – 82
Klas-Göran Tinbäck	1982 – 83
Erika Lagerbielke	1982 –
Anne Nilsson	1982 –
Matz Borgström	1984 – 90
Helén Krantz	1988 –
Vivianne Karlsson	1989 – 94
Lena Bergström	1994 –
Martti Rytkönen	1994 –
Per B. Sundberg	1994 –

Pukeberg Glassworks

Founded 1871. One of the founders of Pukeberg was C. W. Nyström, a master-blower from Kosta. In 1894 the glassworks was taken over by a Stockholm lamp factory (AB Arvid Böhlmarks Lampfabrik) and did not change hands again until 1978 (after bankruptcy). During the 1980s and early 1990s Pukeberg ran into serious economic difficulties and was sold and resold on several occasions.

Pukeberg's early production consisted primarily of domestic glassware, a large proportion of which was pressed. After its purchase by Böhlmarks, however, almost all its resources went to the manufacture of lampshades, globes, and other items for oil lamps. In the 1920s Pukeberg switched to the manufacture of fittings for electric lights and reintroduced domestic and table glassware. The factory specialized in large glass globes used as advertising signs by gas stations and garages.

In 1935 architect Uno Westerberg was hired by Böhlmarks to design light fixtures, and in the 1950s he began to design domestic and ornamental wares as well. In 1957 designer Göran Wärff joined the company, remaining until 1964, and Eva Englund also designed for Pukeberg (1964 to 1973; rehired in 1992). Wärff and Englund caused something of a design renaissance at Pukeberg during the 1960s. Erik Höglund was another Pukeberg designer (from 1978 to 1981), and Gunilla Lindahl, Ragnhild Alexandersson, Karin Johansson, and Lars Sestervik all worked freelance for the company during the 1980s. Other artists have included Margareta Hennix, Liselotte Henriksen, Börge Lindau, Rolf Sinnemark, and Birgitta Watz.

Reijmyre Glassworks

Founded 1810. Reijmyre Glassworks was founded by J. J. Graver, a forestry engineer, and lieutenant F. M. A. von Ungern-Steenberg. By 1900, under the astute leadership of Josua Kjellgren, the factory had become one of the leading glassworks in Sweden. In 1903 it became affiliated with the newly founded AB De Svenska Kristallglasbruken (Association of Swedish Crystal Manufacturers). In 1926 a reversal of fortune occurred: the company declared banckruptcy. It changed hands on several occasions until 1950, when Lennart Rosén, who had previously managed Kosta, assumed control. His tenure lasted until 1975, when the factory was taken over by the goldsmiths, G.A.B., and three years later, Reijmyre was sold to Upsala Ekeby, which also owned Kosta. Since 1981 the factory has been bought and sold several more times but has survived intact and is still producing fine glass under the ownership of Benny and Katharina Fihn.

During the first decade of its existence Reijmyre produced window glass, domestic glassware, pharmaceutical and technical vessels, and various wares of quality colorless glass, including a range of cut and engraved pieces. Reijmyre soon became Sweden's leading manufacturer of cut glass, especially miter cut, which became the dominant technique towards the end of the nineteenth century. Fixed molds were introduced in the 1820s, and pressed glass in the 1830s after which it was manufactured in great quantities for about a century. Reijmyre introduced many technical innovations in the glass industry. In 1872 it installed a gas-fired furnace, in 1877/78 a cracking-off plant, and in the 1880s the first etching machine, which was imported from Paris.

After the Stockholm Exhibition of 1897 Reijmyre was among the glassworks to respond positively to the critics by engaging artists to design its wares. The first at Reijmyre were Ferdinand Boberg (from 1907 to around 1909), Alf Wallander (1908 to 1914), Anna Boberg (1901 to 1902), and the engraver A. E. Boman, who arrived from Kosta in 1903. All four designed pieces in cut overlay (using the so-called Gallé technique). Betzy Ählstrom worked at Reijmyre from 1901 to 1902, designing Art Nouveau glass as did Greta Wellander (1913 to 1916) and Ellen Meyer (1913 to 1915). In addition to art glass, miter-cut and etched glass was manufactured at Reijmyre in large quantities during the first few decades of the twentieth century. During the First World War, production was adapted to the manufacture of light bulbs. Edvin Ollers designed glass for Reijmyre in 1918 and 1919. Axel Törneman and Sten Branzell designed glass for short periods during the 1920s. Production was halted by bankruptcy in the late 1920s, and only simple, everyday wares were produced for a time. Art glass was reintroduced around the mid-1930s, and since then many artists have designed glass for Reijmyre: Bjorn Trägårdh (1937), Monica Bratt-Wijkander (1938 – 58), Johnny Mattsson (1954 – 58), Paul Kedelv (1956 – 76), Tyra Lundgren (1960), Tom Möller (1960 – 67), Bert Kindåker (1956 –), Margareta Hennix (1993 –), Klas-Göran Tinbäck (1994 –), Filippa Reutersward (1996 –), John Larson (1996 –), Peter Gibson Lundberg (1996 –), and Gisela Montan (1996 –).

References: Åke Nisbeth and Torbjörn Fogelberg, *Reijmyre Glasbruk* (Linköping, Sweden: Ostergötlands/Linköping stads museum, 1960 – 61), p. 110; "Reimyre-urpost i glasriket," in "I Glasriket — människan — miljön — framtidenm," a study project of the ABF och Svenska Fabriksarbetarenförbundet in Kalmar and Kronobergs län, 1982.

Sandvik Glassworks
Founded 1889. Sandvik was started by four glassblowers from Lindefors, Kosta, Reijmyre, and Transjö, who were joined a few years later by a millowner from Transjö. By 1902 the factory was bankrupt, however, and passed into new hands. In 1905 it was bought by Axel F. Hummel, managing director of Kosta, and Edvard Strömberg who became the sole owner in 1906. In 1917 the factory was leased to Orrefors, who purchased the entire company a year later. In conjunction with the takeover Strömberg was made managing director of Orrefors. Sandvik is still owned by Orrefors and has been renovated and rebuilt several times, most recently in the 1980s when an extensive program of modernization was undertaken. In 1995 a glass-painting department was opened.

Sandvik's early production included both cut and painted domestic glasswares; bobeches for candlesticks and preserving jars were made in large quantities. When the company was taken over by Orrefors, however, Edward Hald and Simon Gate began to design glass for everyday use. These wares, which were often free-blown, were shown for the first time at the 1917 Hemutställningen (Home Exhibition) in Stockholm and at the much acclaimed 1925 Paris Exposition des Arts Décoratifs et Industriels Modernes. They remained a Sandvik trademark for many years. Several of Orrefors's best artists designed such glass, above all stemware, for production at Sandvik. The name most closely associated with Sandvik, however, is Nils Landberg, who was art consultant for the Sandvik/Orrefors constellation from 1936 to 1972. "Illusion," designed by Landberg in 1957, has been one of the factory's most successful sets of tableware. Other successful tableware of recent years includes two by Erika Lagerbielkes "Intermezzo" and "Merlot."

Reference: "Glas-Kultur-Samhällsdaning, 120 år i Hovmantorp," in "I Glasriket — människan — miljön — framtidenm," a study project of the ABF och Svenska Fabriksarbetarenförbundet in Kalmar and Kronobergs län, 1982; Anders Reihnér, *Sandviksglas, "Vackrare vardagsvara," 1918 – 1932*, exhib. cat. (Orrefors, Sweden: Orrefors Museum, 1987).

Skruf Glassworks
Founded 1897. Skruf was founded by Robert Celander, who had previously been manager of Johansfors. After initial success the factory was forced by bankruptcy to close in 1908. The furnaces were relit in 1910 and a new company formed. In 1946 the factory was completely destroyed by fire, but a year later glass was again being manufactured at Skruf. The factory was thoroughly modernized during the 1960s with new equipment such as a fully automated system for the cutting and polishing of domestic tableware. In 1974 Skruf and four other glassworks formed the Krona-Bruken AB, an enterprise which went bankrupt in 1977. Skruf itself was purchased by Kosta Boda AB, which closed the Skruf factory in 1980. However, an independent group of glassblowers, working on the former factory premises, has continued to produce glass there since 1981.

Skruf's original production consisted solely of simple drinking vessels, jam jars, and the like, but the inventory was soon expanded, and crystal glass was introduced some time after 1910. During the 1930s and 1940s Skruf enjoyed a period of considerable success, making an extensive range of table and domestic glassware including some for export. Many of the pieces made during this time were designed by Magni Magnusson, the chief gaffer. Beginning in 1953 Bengt Edenfalk designed plain and cut tableware as well as art glass, both colored and transparent. One of his specialties was known as Thalatta glass, in which designs of air bubbles are trapped inside the solid crystal. Edenfalk moved to Kosta

Boda in 1978.

The sculptor Lars Hellsten worked at Skruf from 1964 to 1972. Among his best-known pieces are sculptures of castles. Since 1981 another of Skruf's regular designers has been Ingegerd Råman, whose simple, functional wares have been very successful. Anetter Krahner also designed glass for Skruf (from 1982 to 1994).

Reference: "Skruf, En bygd — ett hantverk," in "I Glasriket — människan — miljön — framtidenm," a study project of the ABF och Svenska Fabriksarbetarenförbundet in Kalmar and Kronobergs län, 1982.

Strömbergshyttan (Lindefors)

1876 – 1979. Lindefors, as the glassworks was originally called, was founded by, among others, J. A. Sjö, a farmer, member of the Swedish Riksdag (Parliament), and glassblower. After a short break in production, the factory changed hands in 1919. Although Lindefors was modernized during the 1920s, the company, like so many other Småland glassworks, was forced to lay off workers in the economic depresion of the early 1930s. In 1933 Lindefors was taken over by Edvard Strömberg who had previously been at Kosta and had been the owner of Sandvik and managing director of Orrefors and Eda. The company name was changed Strömbergshyttan. In 1945 the factory was purchased by Strömberg's son Eric. After his death in 1960, his widow Asta continued to run the business, rebuilding and modernizing in 1962. A disastrous fire in 1973 caused serious economic difficulties, and in 1976 the company was purchased by Orrefors. In 1979 it closed for good.

The factory's early production consisted of plain, cut, engraved, painted, and pressed wares for domestic use and for restaurants. Bottles were also produced, and some tableware was exported. In the 1930s Edvard Strömberg combined innovation and tradition. Working with his son Eric, who was a trained chemist and technician, Strömberg experimented with new methods until he had produced a distinctive bluish silver hue, a color that was to become the factory's specialty. The first collection was designed in 1933 by Gerda Strömberg, who continued to work for the company until 1946. Asta Strömberg also designed many pieces for Strömbergshyttan from the late 1930 to 1976. The designer Gunnar Nylund joined the company from 1952 to 1975, and Rune Strand was added in the 1960s. During the 1970s Anders Solfors and Lars Wigell were also associated with Strömbergshyttan.

References: Helena Blom, "Lindefors-Strömbergshyttan, 1876 – 1979: The History of a Glassworks," Ph.D. diss., West Surrey [England] College of Art and Design, 1989; "Lindefors-Strömbergshyttan, 1876 – 1979," in "I Glasriket — människan — miljön — framtidenm," a study project of the ABF och Svenska Fabriksarbetarenförbundet in Kalmar and Kronobergs län, 1982.

GLOSSARY

Compiled by Vincent Plescia

annealing. The tempering process that glass objects must go through to relieve internal stress built up during production, which can cause the glass to crack as it cools. An annealing oven is used to allow the glass to cool slowly and evenly.

ariel. A technique for making glass whereby the a *blank* is *flashed* with one or more layers of colored glass. Once the blank has cooled, a frisket is used to mark the decoration, and the blank is sandblasted. The frisket protects areas of the design from the sandblasting which leaves deep impressions in the unprotected glass. A thin layer of glass is then applied to the blank trapping pockets of air in the impressions. Finally, another *gather* of molten glass is applied to the blank and the object is formed into its final shape. This technique was developed at Orrefors Glassworks by Gustaf Bergqvist in 1936, and the first ariel pieces were designed by Edvin Öhrström and Vicke Lindstrand who may have played a role in its development. Edward Hald named the process after the spirit of air from Shakespeare's *Tempest*.

blank. An unfinished glass object, representing a stage in the *ariel*, *graal*, and *mykene* techniques.

blow iron. A long metal pipe used to gather molten glass for blowing and enlarging. Also called a gathering iron or blowpipe.

cane. Colored glass rods that are solid or sometimes hollow and used for decorative effects.

casting. The process whereby a molten glass is blown or pressed into a mold and allowed to cool. Molds can be made from graphite, wood, metal, or damp sand.

cracking-off. The process of releasing a cooled glass object from the *pontil rod*. The blown-glass object is scored at the appropriate point with a diamond cutting tool and reheated locally so that tension breaks off the glass along the scratched line. (Also see *flaring.*)

cutting. Decorative technique whereby a grinding wheel is used to cut away the surface and thereby ornament it. Decorative cutting is done in stages. A pattern is drawn on the area to be cut and roughly ground out with an iron wheel, carborundum, and water, or with a carborundum wheel well-lubricated with water. This gives the surface a matte finish. In

the next step, a natural sandstone or artificial grindstone is used to smooth the area, producing a satinlike appearance. The glass is then buffed with finer polishing materials, such as a disk of felt or a cork coated with moist pumice, which gives the surface a glossy finish. Contemporary glassmakers may use a diamond wheel, which cuts more rapidly, instead of stone, especially for decorating fine crystal.

engraving. Decorative technique used to inscribe patterns in glass. Copper-wheel engraving is done with a lathe and as many as forty various-sized wheels depending on the intricacies of the pattern. The rotating copper wheels are lubricated with a grinding agent (emery powder) mixed with oil.

etching. A technique for applying patterns to the surface of glass by using hydrofluoric acid. The surface is coated with a layer of acid-resistant material (wax or varnish); a sharp tool is used to scratch the desired pattern through the acid-resist. The object is then immersed in an acid bath which eats away the exposed glass. The depth of etching depends on the length of exposure in the acid baths. This technique was developed in the nineteenth century to give glass a satin or frosted finish but was used more vigorously in the twentieth century.

flaring. The end of a heated iron rod, known as the *pontil rod* or punty, is gently placed against the bottom of a hot blown piece that is still attached to the *blow iron*. The glass adheres to the punty and is tapped off the blow iron by striking the iron sharply with another piece of metal, leaving an opening a   t the neck. This opening is softened by reheating the piece so that the edge can be cut roughly into shape with a pair of hand shears called "flaring shears." The glassmaker may repeat the process several times before using the flaring shears to give the opening its final shape. Flaring results in a soft, rounded rim.

flashing. The application of a thin layer of glass on the surface of an existing piece of glass or a blank, usually of a different color. This is also called overlay glass, or alternatively, underlay glass when it acts as an interlining between two layers.

free-blown glass. The process of blowing and shaping glass solely by with hand-held tools. (Also see *mold-blown glass* and *optic- blown glass.*)

gaffer. The master-worker who directs a team of glassmakers and performs the most skilled and detailed work. The gaffer controls production until the object begins its annealing process.

gather. A glob of molten glass attached to a blow iron preparatory to forming an object. The gather may be enlarged by collecting one or more layers of glass over it after blowing and shaping; adding glass in this way is often called *flashing.*

graal. A glassmaking technique whereby a gather of colorless glass, known as the *parison,* is collected on one blow iron while one or more other colors are collected on a second blow iron. The colored glass is drawn over the parison and allowed to cool. This blank is then decorated by cutting, etching, engraving, or, less frequently, sandblasting; it is then reheated and reattached to a blow iron. During this process, the blank softens and the applied decoration melts into the surface. A layer of colorless glass can then be applied over the blank, encasing the decoration until the piece is inflated to the desired shape. The graal technique was developed at Orrefors Glassworks in 1916 by Simon Gate and Knut Bergqvist. In the 1930s Edward Hald introduced a variation of graal work which is often called "fish graal." In this technique a decorated blank was essentially encased in several layers of clear glass. The name "graal" is said to have come from the story of the Holy Grail, the chalice used by Christ at the Last Supper, possibly inspired by the deep red color of the glass in the earliest graal production.

lead glass. A kind of glass that contains a high percentage of lead oxide to enhance its brilliance. It is less fragile than soda glass and lends itself to cutting and engraving.

marqueterie de verre. A glassmaking technique whereby pieces of hot glass of one color are set into an object of contrasting color. The inlaid pieces can be further cut and engraved to decorate the piece.

marver. A polished marble or iron table on which a gather of molten glass attached to a blow iron is rolled to form a cylinder prior to shaping. The process is known as marvering.

metallic oxides. Various chemical compounds that produce color in glass. Cobalt oxide, for example, produces a deep blue. Some oxides are used to neutralize trace impurities in sand thereby producing clear glass.

mold-blown glass. The process of using a blow iron to blow molten glass into a preformed mold. The blow iron is sometimes rotated to assist in the filling of the cavity. After the object has cooled and been removed from the mold, it can be reheated and further shaped. This process later was mechanized and used for making bottles and light bulbs.

mykene. A glassmaking technique, similar to graal, whereby the decorative pattern or design is painted on a cooled blank with a mixture of powdered carborundum and adhesive. When the blank is slowly reheated, the adhesive burns off and the carborundum fuses to the glass. And when a second layer of molten glass is applied to the blank, the heat causes the carborundum to vaporize and traps bubbles between the two layers of glass. This technique was developed by Vicke Lindstrand at Orrefors in 1936.

optic-blown glass. A glassmaking technique used to increase the size of an object by blowing it after it has been removed from a mold with a precast pattern. It is also used to modify or soften the lines of a pattern by blowing the existing object into a plain mold.

overlay. See *flashing.*

painting. In glassmaking, painting refers to a decorative technique whereby a flux (pulverized glass) and a coloring agent (such as a metallic oxide) that have been melted together are applied by hand to a piece. The glass is slowly and carefully reheated to a temperature of 500°C which fuses the paint to the surface.

parison. The first gather of glass on the end of a blow iron after it has been blown into a bubble. The parison serves as a base for additional layers of glass.

polishing. Producing an even finish on a piece of glass using rotating wheels, brushes, paper, cork, or felt, or reheating the piece in the furnace.

pressed glass. The process of shaping an object by placing molten glass into a metal mold. Molds are usually always made of cast-iron or high-grade steel.

pontil rod. Solid iron rod tipped with molten glass so that an object from the blow iron can be transferred to it, allowing the rim to be finished, handle applied, or final shaping carried out. The pontil rod is also called a punty.

sandblasting. A process used to decorate glass by projecting sand at a high rate of speed against the surface of the glass. A frisket impervious to sand serves as a mask to protect the areas of the pattern that are not be abraded.

soda glass. A kind of glass in which the main alkali ingredient is sodium carbonate, rather than potash, which serves as a flux to reduce the melting point of the silica in making glass. It is lighter in weight, easier to manipulate, and lacks the resonance of lead glass. Soda glass has a yellowish, green-gray, or brownish color.

underlay. See *flashing.*

BIBLIOGRAPHY

A Selected Collection of Objects from the International Exposition of Modern Decorative and Industrial Art at Paris 1925. New York: The American Association of Museums, 1926. Ahlberg, Hakon. "Framtidsmål." *Svenska Slöjdföreningens Tidskrift* 14 (1918).

Åhrén, Uno. "Brytningar." *Svenska Slöjdföreningen Tidskrift,* 1925, p. 1 *ff.*

———. "Betraktelse över enkelheten." *Svenska Slöjdföreningens Tidskrift,* 12 (1926).

———. "Standardization and personality." *Svenska Slöjdföreningens tidskrift* (1929).

Åmark, Klas. *Facklig makt och fackligt medlemskap: De svenska fackförbundens medlemsutveckling, 1890–1940.* Lund, Sweden: Arkiv Förlag, 1986.

Ambjörnsen, R. "En Skön, Ny Värld-Om Ellen Keys visioner och en senare tids verklighet." *Fataburen: Nordiska Museets och Skansens årsbok* (1991), pp. 260–96.

Ambrosiani, Sune. *Pukebergs glasbruk.* Stockholm: Nordisk, 1946.

American Federation of Arts. *International Exhibition of Ceramic Art.* Exhibition catalogue. Portland, Maine: The Southworth Press, 1928.

———. *International Exhibition: Contemporary Glass and Rugs.* Washington, D. C.: American Federation of Arts, 1929.

Anderbjörk, Jan Erik. *Kosta Glasbruk 1742–1942: Jubileumssktift.* Stockholm: Bröderna Lagerström, 1942.

———, ed. *Gullaskrufs glasbruk, 1927–1952.* Gothenburg, Sweden: Gullaskrufs glasbruk, 1952.

———, and Åke Nisbeth. *Gammalt glas.* Uppsala, Sweden: ICA- förlaget, 1968.

Andersson, B., and Tommy Svensson, eds. *Samhälle och idrott i Jonsered, 1830–1980.* Jonsered, Sweden: IF, 1985.

Andrén, Erik. *Aktiebolaget Arvid Böhlmarks Lampfabrik, 1872–1937.* Stockholm: Arvid Böhlmarks Lampfabrik, 1937.

"Applied Art in Sweden." *The Studio Yearbook* (1921), pp. 118–19.

Arnö-Berg, Inga. *Serviser från Gustavsberg.* 2nd ed. Stockholm: ICA bokförlag: 1985.

Artéus, Margareta, ed. *Kosta 250 Years of Craftsmanship: 1742–1992.* Jubileumsskrift. Malmö: Tryckeriteknik i Malmö AB, 1992.

Ashwin, Clive, "The Nordic Connection-Aspects of Interchange Between Britain and Scandinavia." *Studio International* 195 (November/December 1982), pp. 20–30.

"Aspects nouveaux des arts en suède." *Mobilier et Decoration,* no. 11 (November 1930).

Åström, Lars Erik, Folke Holmér, and Per Bjurström. *Sven erixsons konst.* Pulbication 75. Stockholm: Sveriges Allmänna Konstförening, 1967.

Äventyret Sverige: en ekonomisk och social historia. Stockholm: Utbildningsradlon, 1993.

Baeckström, Arvid. *Göteborgs Glasbruk, 1761–1808 och glashandel i Göteborg före 1820.* Meddelanden frän Industrimuséet i Göteborg, no. 5 (1962).

Baltiska utställningen, Malmö, 1914. Lund, Sweden: Signum, 1989.

Bang, Jacob E. "Glas-Orientering ved Begyndelsen af en ny Production." *Nyt Tidsskrift for Kunstindustri* 1 (October 1928).

———. "Glasset paa Stockholmsudstillingen." *Nyt Tidsskrift for Kunstindustri* 3 (September 1930).

Bauhaus Reassessed: Sources and Design Theory. London: Herbert Press, 1985), pp. 37 *ff.*

Bay, K. *Egne hjem.* Kristiania [Oslo]: Cammermeyer, 1903.

Geoffrey Beard, *International Modern Glass.* London: Barrie & Jenkins, 1976.

Berg, G. A. "Swedish Modern." *Form* (1938), p. 163.

Blaugrund, Annette, et al. *Paris 1889: American Artists at the Universal Exposition.* Exhibition catalogue. Philadelphia: Pennsylvania Academy of Fine Arts/Harry N. Abrams, 1989.

Blomberg, Erik. *Från Josephson till Picasso.* Stockholm: Tidens bokklubb, 1955

———. *Naivister och realister.* Stockholm: Aldus/Bonnier, 1962.

Böhn-Jullander, Ingrid. *Bruno Mathsson*. Lund, Sweden: Signum, 1992.

Breck, Joseph. "Swedish Contemporary Decorative Arts." *Bulletin of The Metropolitan Museum of Art* 22 (January 1927).

Bring, Maj. *Motsols: Memoarer*. Gothenburg, Bokförlaget Treangel, 1986.

Brugerolles, Emmanuelle, and David Guillet. *École Nationale Superieure des Beaux-arts*. Translated by Judith Schub. Exhibition catalogue. Cambridge, Mass.: Harvard University Art Museum/University of Washington Press, 1995.

Brunius, August. "Carl Larsson och en nationell möbelstil." *Svenska Slöjdföreningens Tidskrift*, no. 7 (1911), pp. 22–26.

———. "De åtta." *Svenska Dagbladet* (June 2, 1912).

———. "Konst," *Svenska Dagbladet* (October 3, 1916).

———. "Milles Triton till Valdemarsudde," *Svenska Dagbladet* (January 6, 1917), acquisition book, Kunstindustrimuseet, Oslo, Norway.

———. "Expressionisterna i Konsthallen." *Svenska Dagbladet* (May 15, 1918).

———. "Det konstindustriella samarbetet." *Göteborgs Handelstidning* (April 1, 1919).

———. "Den svenska konsthandeln." *Göteborgs Handelstidning* (January 3, 1919).

———. "Tiden och tidens konsthantverk: ett ord till försvar ochtill angrepp." *Svenska Dagbladet* (July 27, 1925).

Brunius, Jan, et al. *Svenskt Glas*. Stockholm: Wahlström & Widstrand, 1991.

Bukowskis Auction Catalogue (May 18–20, 1988), Lot 785.

Bull, Edvard, ed. *Norsk Biografisk Leksikon*. Vol. 3. Oslo: Aschehoug, 1927.

Caldenby, Claes, ed. *Göteborgs konserthus: ett album*. Gothenburg: White arkitekter, 1992.

Charney, Leo, and Vanessa R. Schwartz, eds. *Cinema and the Invention of Modern Life*. Berkeley: University of California Press, 1995.

Childs, Marquis W. *Sweden: The Middle Way*. New Haven: Yale University Press, 1936.

———. *Sweden, the Middle Way*. New Haven: Yale University Press, 1936.

Clark, Robert Judson. *Design in America: The Cranbrook Vision, 1925–1950*. Exhibition catalogue. New York: Detroit Institute of Arts/The Metropolitan Museum of Art/Harry N. Abrams, 1983.

Dahlbäck-Lutteman, Helena, ed. *Svenskt glas: 1915–1960*. Exhibition catalogue. Stockholm: Nationalmuseum, 1987.

———. *Edward Hald: Malare, Konstindustripionar*. Exhibition catalogue. Stockholm: Nationalmuseum, 1983.

Dahmén, Erik. *Svensk industriell företagarverksamhet: kausalanalys av den industriella utvecklingen, 1919–1939*. Stockholm: Industrins utredningsinstitut, 1950.

Danielsson, Märta Stina, ed., *Svenskt glas*. Contributions by Jan Brunius et al. Stockholm: Wahlström and Widstrand, 1991.

Darling, Sharon. *Chicago Ceramics and Glass: An Illustrated History from 1871–1933*. Chicago: Chicago Historical Society, 1979.

Davidson, A. *Two Models of Welfare: The Origins and Development of the Welfare State in Sweden and New Zealand, 1888–1988*. Publication of the Political Science Association in Uppsala, no. 108. Uppsala, Sweden: Scandinavian University Books, 1989.

Davies, Karen. *At Home in Manhattan: Modern Decorative Arts, 1925 to the Depression*. Exhibition catalogue. New Haven: Yale University Art Gallery, 1983.

de Geer, Hans. *Rationaliseringsrörelsen i Sverige*. Stockholm: SNS Förlag, 1978.

de Wolfe, Elsie. *The House in Good Taste*. New York: The Century Company, 1913.

Decorative Arts: Official Catalog, Department of Fine Arts, Division of Decorative Arts, Golden Gate International Exposition San Francisco. San Francisco San Francisco Bay Exposition Co., 1939.

"Dekorativa fönster och lampor." Orrefors sale catalogue (1944). Archives of Orrefors Glassworks.

Den svenska historien. Stockholm: Bonniers lexikon, 1967–1994.

Derkert, Carlo. *Nordisk målarkonst: Det moderna måleriets genombrott*. Stockholm: Ehlin, 1951.

Diarium Vadstenense. Copenhagen: Ernst Nygren, 1963.

Dietrichson, Lorentz. *Det skönas verld*. 2 vols. Stockholm, 1867–1879.

Drexler, Arthur, ed. *The Architecture of the Ecole des Beaux-arts*. New York: Museum of Modern Art, 1977.

Duncan, Alastair. *Orrefors Glass*. Woodbridge, Eng.: Antique Collectors' Club, 1995.

Edenheim, Katarina Hallin, and Anders Reihnér. *Simon Gate, Edward Hald: Glas 1916–1973*. Exhibition catalogue. Östergötlands, Sweden: Östergötlands Länsmuseum, 1983.

Eggum, Arne. "Lorentz Dietrichson som kunstpolitiker under naturalismens frembrudd." *Kunst og Kultur* 64, no. 3 (1981), pp. 133–59.

Ehrensvärd, Carl August. *De fria Konsters philosophi* (1786). Reprint. Stockholm: Sallskapet Bokvannerna, 1974.

Eidelber, Martin, ed. *Design 1935–1965: What Modern Was, Selections from the Liliane and David M. Stewart Collection.* Montreal and New York: Musée des arts décoratifs de Montreal/Harry N. Abrams, 1991.

Elsa Gullberg, textil pionjär. Catalogue 523. Stockholm: Nationalmuseum, 1989.

Endicott-Barnett, Vivian. *Kandinsky och Sverige.* Malmö and Stockholm: Malmö Museum/Moderna Museet, 1989.

Ericsson, Anne-Marie. *Arthur Percy: konstnär och formgivare.* Stockholm, 1980.

———. *Svenskt 1920–tal: Konstindustri och konsthantverk.* Lund: Bokförlaget, 1984.

Eriksson, Ulf. *Gruva och arbete: Kiirunavaara, 1890–1990.* Uppsala, Sweden: Ekonomisk-historiska institutionen, 1991.

Esping-Andersen, Gösta. *Politics Against Markets: The Social Democratic Road to Power.* Princeton: Princeton University Press, 1985.

"Exhibition of Swedish Pottery and Glass," *The Pottery Gazette and Glass Trade Reivew* (June 1, 1937).

Exposition internationale des arts décoratifs et industriels modernes à Paris 1925: Section de la Suède. Exhibition catalogue. Stockholm: Svenska Slöjdföreningen, 1925.

Fer, Briony, David Batchelor, and Paul Wood. *Realism, Rationalism, Surrealism: Art Between the Wars.* The Open University: Modern Art, Practices and Debates. New Haven and London: Yale University Press, 1993.

Fischer, E. "Vackra Vardagsvaror i Goteborg." *Svenska Slöjd-föreningens Tidskrift* 18 (1922).

Fogelberg, Torbjörn. "Om Kosta glasbruk och den småländs-ka glasbruksbygdens uppkomst." *Glasteknisk tidskrift,* no. 5 (1961), p. 151.

———. "Småglasindustriens lokalisering och struktur, 1870–1920." Parts 1 and 2. *Glasteknisk tidskrift,* no. 6 (1962) and no. 1 (1963).

———. *Sandö glasbruk, 1750–1928.* Sundsvall, Sweden: [T. Fogelberg], 1968.

———. *Den minderåriga arbetskraften inom glasindustrin under 1800–talet och tiden omkring sekelskiftet.* Växjö: Krono-bergs läns hembygdsförbund, 1973.

———. *Fackföreningsrörelsens genombrottsskede vid glas-bruken under perioden från och med omkring 1890 till och med år 1907.* Växjö, Sweden: Kronobergs läns hembygdsför-bund, 1973.

———. *Ettarps glasbruk, 1736–1756.* Årsbok för kulturhisto-ria och hembygdsvård i Hallands län, no. 66. Halmstad and Varberg: Hallands länsmuséer, 1983.

———. *Om glasförare tiden från omkring 1740 till 1820–talets början.* Smålands museums skriftserie, no. 1 (1985).

———. *Björknäs glasbruk: Nackas första främlingsholoni.* Stockholm: Nackaboken, 1989.

———. "Smältugnar och deras konstruktion vid de svenska glasbruken under tiden fram till första världskrigets slut." Part 2. *Glasteknisk Tidskrift,* no. 1 (1993).

———. *Ett sekel i belysningens tjänst: Rosdala glasbruk, 1895 –1995.* Växjö, Sweden: Rosdala glasbruk, 1994.

———. *Belysningenstjänst: Rosdala glasbruk 1895–1995.* Växjö, Sweden, 1995.

———, and Gunnar Lersjö. *Eda glasbruk, 1830–1953.* Arvika, Sweden: Varmlands Museum, 1977.

———, and Åke Nisbeth, *Liljedahls glasbruk,* Småskrifter utgivna av Värmlands museum, no. 14 (1979).

———, and Carl Ivar Scheutz. *Alsterbro glasbruk 1871–1961.* Kalmusserien no. 6. Kalmar: Kalmar länsmuseum, 1981.

Fogelberg, Torsten. [untitled]. *Dagens Nyheter* 21 no. 3 (1930).

Folcker, E. G. "Kosta och Orrefors." *Svenska Slöjdföreningen Tidskrift* (1917), p. 88.

———. "Ett hems möblering." *Idun* (1898).

———. "Konsthantverk." *Ord och Bild* 5 (1899).

———. "Ett modernt hem." *Idun* (1901).

Fong, Wen C., and James C. Y. Wyatt. *Possessing the Past: Treasures from the National Palace Museum, Taipei.* Exhibition catalogue. New York: The Metropolitan Museum of Art, 1996.

Frick, Gunilla. *Svenska Slöjdföreningen och konstindustrin före 1905.* Handlingar 91. Stockholm: Nordiska museet, 1978.

———. *Konstnär i industrin.* Handlingar 106. Stockholm: Nordiska museet, 1986.

———. "Furniture art or a machine to sit on? Swedish furni-ture design and radical reforms." *Scandinavian Journal of Design History,* 1 (1991).

Funktionalistiskt genombrott: Radikal miljödebatt i Sverige, 1825–31. English summary. Stockholm: Sveriges Arkitektur museum/PA Norstedt & Söner, 1970.

Furuhagen, Birgitta. *Äventyret Sverige: en ekonomisk och social historia.* Stockholm: Utbildningsradion/Bokförlaget Bra Böcker, 1993.

Garborg, Hulda. *Heimestell.* Kristiania [Oslo]: "Den 17de Mai," 1899.

Gårdlund, Torsten. *Industrialismens samhälle.* Stockholm: Tiden Förlag, 1942.

Gardner, Paul V. *The Glass of Frederick Carder.* New York: Crown Publishers, 1971.

Generationers arbete på Boda glasbruk. Nybro, Sweden: ABF Lessebo, 1982.

Glambek, Ingeborg. *Kunsten, Nytten og Moralen: Kunstindustri og husflid i Norge, 1800-1900.* Oslo: Solum, 1988.

———. "One of the age's noblest cultural movements." *Scandinavian Journal of Design History* 1 (1991), pp. 47–76.

———. "Arkitektur og ideologi." *Nytt Norsk Tidsskrift* 12, no. 3 (1995).

Glasindustrins Arbetsgivareförbund, 1908–1958. Växjö, Sweden: Glasindustrins Arbetsgivareförbund, 1958.

Glas-Kultur-Samhålle: 120 år i Hovmantorp. Nybro, Sweden: ABF Lessebo, 1980.

Glasvaror för elektrisk belysningsarmatur från Pukebergs glasbruk [sale catalogue] no. 119. Stockholm: Arvid Böhlmarks Lampfabrik, 1927.

Grandien, Bo. "Det skönas värld eller Venus i såskoppen." *Form* 82, nos. 2–3 (1985).

———. *Rönndruvans Glöd.* Handlingar no. 107. Stockholm: Nordiska museet, 1987.

———. *Den norrländska sågverksindustrins arbetare, 1890–1913.* Uppsala, Sweden: Scandinavian University Books, 1965.

———. "The Industrial Revolution in Sweden." manuscript, 1994.

Grünewald, Isaac. *Matisse och expressionismen* (1944). Stockholm: Prisma, 1964.

Hald, Arthur, and Erik Wettergren, *Simon Gate, Edward Hald: En Skildring av människorna och konstnärerna.* Stockholm: Svenska Slöjdföreningen/Norstedts, 1948.

Hald, Edward. "Glasmästaren blir målare: Konstnär och industri hör ihop säger Hald." *Dagens Nyheter* (December 18, 1944).

———. "Att balansera situationen." *Form* 41 (1945).

Halén, Gerhard. "Widar Munthe and 'The Movement that from Japan is Moving Across Europe Now'." *Scandinavian Journal of Design History,* no. 4 (1994), pp. 36-37.

Hanks, David A., et al. *High Styles: Twentieth-Century American Design.* Exhibition catalogue. New York: Whitney Museum of American Art/Summit Books, 1985.

Hansson, Sigfrid. *Den svenska fackföreningrörelsen.* Stockholm: Tiden Förlag, 1938.

Hård af Segerstad, Ulf. "Han stannade till festens slut." *Svenska Dagbladet* (September 24, 1983).

Hedin, Naboth. *Sweden at the New York World's Fair.* New York: The Royal Swedish Commission, New York World's Fair, 1939.

Hemma på Kosta: I Glasriket, människan-miljön-framtiden. Växjö, Sweden: ABF/Svenska Fabriksarbetareförbundet, 1982.

Henningsen, Poul. "Stockholms Udstillingen." *Nyt Tidsskrift for Kunstindustri* 3 (June 1930).

Herlitz-Gezelius, Ann Marie. *Orrefors ett Svenskt Glasbruk.* Stockholm: Atlantis, 1984.

———. *Kosta.* Lund: Bokförlaget Signum, 1987.

Hidemark, Elisabet, and Ove Hidemark. "Kontinenten och Sverige: influenser på arkitektur och konsthandverk omkring 1917." *Fataburen* (1968), pp. 71 ff.

Hirdman, Yvonne. *Att lägga livet till rätta: Studier i svensk, folkhemspolitik.* Stockholm: Carlssons förlag, 1989.

Hitchcock, Henry Russell. *The International Style: Architecture Since 1922.* New York: W. W. Norton and Company, 1932.

Hjertén, Sigrid. "Modern och österländsk konst." *Svenska Dagbladet* (February 24, 1911).

Holkers, Märta. *Edvin Öhrström: Skulptör i glas.* Stockholm: Carlsson Bokförlag, 1991.

Holmér, Gunnel, and Micael Ernstell. *Svenskt Glas Under fem Sekler.* Exhibition catalogue. Växjö: Kulturspridaren Förlag, 1996.

———, and Anders Reihnér. *Lyricism of Modern Design: Swedish Glass 1900–1970.* Exhibition catalogue. Sapporo, Japan: Hokkaido Museum of Modern Art, 1992.

Huldt, Åke, ed. *Konsthantwerk och Hemslöjd i Sverige, 1930–1940.* Gothenburg, Sweden: Förlag AB Bokförmedlingen, 1941.

"I Glasriket: människan - miljön - framtiden." A study project of the ABF and Svenska Fabriksarbetareförbundet in Kalmar and Kronobergs, Ian 1982.

Isacson, Maths. *Verkstadsarbete under 1900-talet: Hedemora Verkstäder före 1950.* Lund: Arkiv Förlag, 1987.

———, and Lars Magnusson. *Proto-industrialisation in Scandinavia: Craft Skills in the Industrial Revolution.* Leamington, England: Berg Publisher, 1987.

Iversen, Margaret. *Aloïs Riegl: Art History and Theory.* Cambridge: MIT Press, 1993.

Jakobsson, Bertil. "Företaget, kommunen och individen." *Uppsala Studies in Economic History* 15 (1976).

Janneau, Guillaume. *Modern Glass.* London: The Studio Ltd., 1931.

Johanneson, Lena. "Ellen Key, Mamah Bouton Borthwick and Frank Lloyd Wright: Notes on the historiography of non-existing history." *NORA: Nordic Journal of Women's Studies* 3, no. 2 (1995), pp. 126–36.

Johansson, Anders L. *Tillväxt och klassamarbete: en studie av den svenska modellens uppkomst*. Stockholm: Tiden Förlag, 1989.

Johansson, Christina. *Glasarbetarna, 1860–1910: Arbete, levnadsförhållanden och facklig verksamhet vid Kosta och andra glasbruk under industrialismens genombrottsskede*. Report from the Ekonomisk-historiska institutionen and Göteborgs universitet, no. 15 (1988).

Jörberg, Lennart. *Den svenska ekonomiska utvecklingen, 1861–1983*. Lund, Sweden: Ekonomisk-historiska institutionen, 1984.

Kardon, Janet, ed. *Craft in the Machine Age, 1920–1945: The History of Twentieth-Century American Craft*. Exhibition catalogue. New York: American Craft Museum/Harry N. Abrams, 1995.

Karleby, Nils. *Socialismen inför verkligheten*. Stockholm: Tiden Förlag, 1928.

Katalog å glasvaror för elektrisk belsnying. Norrhult, Sweden: Rosdala Glassworks, 1938.

Key, Ellen. *Barnets århundrade*. 2 vols. Stockholm, 1900.

———. "Folket och konsten." *Varia* 1 (1900).

———. *Folkbildningsarbetet, särskilt med hänsyn till skönhetsinnets odling*. Uppsala, Sweden: Tidens Förlag, 1906.

———. *Skönhet för alla* (1899). 4th ed. Stockholm: Bonniers, 1908.

———. *The Century of the Child*. Translated by Marie Franzos. Preface by Havelock Ellis. New York G. P. Putnam, 1909.

———. *Lyckan och Skönheten*. Liuslinjer 3. Stockholm: Bonniers, 1925.

Key-Åberg, K. *Arbetsstatistisk studie öfuer glasindustrin*. Stockholm, 1899.

Kilander, Svenbjörn. *Den gamla staten och den nya*. Uppsala, Sweden: Acta universitatis upsaliensis, 1991.

Knutsson, Bo. *Swedish Art in Glass, 1900–1990*. Vänersborg, Sweden: Knutsson Art and Antiques, 1991.

Konsten i focus. 2 volumes. Stockholm: Almqvist & Wiksell, 1971.

Kosta Glasbruk, 1742–1942, Jubileumsskrift utgiven av Kosta glasbruk med anledning av dess 200–åriga verksamhet. Stockholm: Kosta Glasbruk, 1942.

Landsorganisationens 15-mannakommitté, Fackföreningsrörelsen och näringslivet. Stockholm: LO, 1941.

Lärkner, Bengt. *Det internationella avantgardet och Sverige, 1914–1925*. Malmö: Stenvall, 1984.

Larsson, Carl. *Ett Hem*. Stockholm: Bonniers, 1899.

Larsson, Mats. *En svensk ekonomisk historia, 1850–1985*. Stockholm: SNS Förlag, 1991.

Laurin, Carl G. "Modern konstindustri på uställningen," *Ord och Bild*, (8:1897).

———. "Konsten i skolan och konsten i hemmet." *Föreningen Heimdals folkskrifter* 63 (1899).

———. *Minnen*. 4 volumes. Stockholm: Norstedt, 1929–32.

László, André. *Svenskt Konstglas*. Stockholm: Sellin & Blomquist, 1988.

Leach, William. *Land of Desire: Merchants, Power and the Rise of a New American Culture*. New York: Pantheon Books, 1993.

Lengefefeld, Cecilia. *Der Maler des glücklichen Heims: Zur Rezeption Carl Larssons im wilhelminischen Deutschland*. Heidelberg: Universitätsverlag C. Winter, 1993.

Lilja, Gösta, *Det Moderna måleriet i svensk kritik, 1905–1914*. Malmö, Sweden: Stenvall, 1955.

Limmared, 1740–1940. Ulricehamn, Sweden: AB Fredr. Brusewitz, 1940.

Lind, Sven-Ivar. "Vår Paviljong på Parisutställningen." *Form* (1937), p. 1 ff.

Lindstrand, Svea. "Glimtar från en världsutställnings tillblivelse." *Form* (1937), pp. 139–40.

Lindvall, Joran, ed. *The Swedish Art of Building*. Stockholm: The Swedish Institute and Swedish Museum of Architecture, 1992.

"Living Shipshape: The Lesson of the Stockholm Exhibition." *Creative Art* 7 (September 1930).

Loos, Adolf. *Trotzdem 1900–1930*. Innsbruck: Brenner Verlag, 1931.

———. *Spoken into the Void: Collected Essays, 1897–1900*. Translated by J. O. Newman and J. H. Smith. Cambridge, MA: MIT Press, 1982.

Looström, Lorentz. "Ludvig Dietrichson och Svenska Slöjdföreningen." *Svenska Slöjdföreningens Tidskrift* (1917), pp. 22–24.

Looström, Ludvig, *Stockholms Allmånna Konst- and Industriutställning 1897*. Stockholm, 1899–1900.

Lundberg, Bengt. *Arts and Crafts at the Swedish Chicago Exposition, 1933*. Stockholm: Centraltryckeriet, 1933.

Lundgren, Trya. "Vi är inte så bra som vi tror." *Stockholmstidningen* (April 4, 1936).

———. "Mitt liv i konst." *Julpost* 45 (1968).

"Made in Europe." *House and Garden* (July 1939), p. 33–37.

Madigan, Mary Jean. *Steuben Glass: An American Tradition in Crystal*. New York: Harry N. Abrams, 1982), p. 74.

Magnusson, Lars. *Arbetet vid en svensk verkstad: Munktells, 1900–1920*. Lund, Sweden: Arkiv Förlag, 1987.

———. *Sveriges ekonomiska historia*. Stockholm: Tiden Förlag, 1996.

Malmsten, Carl. "Om Svensk Karaktär inom Vår Konstkultur—Särskildt i Hemmets Utdaning." *Svenska Slöjdföreningens Tidskrift*, no. 10 (1915), pp. 163–74.

Merchandising Interior Design: Methods of Furniture Fabrication in America Between the World Wars. New Haven: Yale University School of Architecture, 1991.

Metropolitan Museum of Art. *Exhibition of Swedish Contemporary Decorative Arts*. Exhibition catalogue. New York: The Metropolitan Museum of Art, 1927.

———. *A Special Exhibition of Glass from the Museum Collections*. Exhibition catalogue. New York: The Metropolitan Museum, 1936.

Miller, R. Craig. *Modern Design in the Metropolitan Museum of Art, 1890–1990*. Exhibition catalogue. New York: The Metropolitan Museum of Art/Harry N. Abrams, 1990.

Moberg, Ulf Thomas, ed. *Nordisk konst i 1920-talets avantgarde: Uppbrott och gränsöverskridande*. Stockholm: Cinclus, 1995.

Modin, Maj. "Tyra Lundgrens självporträtt åren 1920–35," Ph.D. diss. Uppsala [Sweden] University, 1977.

Montgomery, Artur. *Industrialismens genombrott i Sverige*. Stockholm: Almqvist & Wiksell, 1947.

Munthe, Gustaf Lorentz. *Swedish Arts and Crafts on the M/S Kungsholm*. Sweden: Swedish American Line, [1935].

———. "Kvibergskapellet." *Form* (1936), pp. 22–23.

Münz, Ludwig, and Gustav Künstler. *Adolf Loos*. New York: Praeger, 1966.

Museum of Art, Rhode Island School of Design. *Selection IV: Glass From the Museum's Collection*. Exhibition catalogue. Providence: Rhode Island School of Design, 1974.

Muthesius, Hermann. *Das englische Haus: Entwicklung Bedingungen, Anlage, Aufbau, Einrichtung und Innenraum*. 3 vols. Berlin: Wasmuth, 1904–05.

———. *Stilarkitektur och byggnadskonst*. Translated by Axel Lindegren. Stockholm, 1910.

———. *Style-Architecture and Building-Art*. Translated by Stanford Anderson. Santa Monica, CA: The Getty Center, 1994.

Myrdal, Alva, and Gunnar Myrdal. *Kris i befolkningsfrågan*. Stockholm: Tiden Förlag, 1934.

Gillian Naylor. "Swedish Grace . . . or the Acceptable Face of Modernism?" *Modernism in Design*. Edited by Paul Greenhalgh. London: Reaktion Books, 1990.

Nervi, Elisabetta Margiotta, and Mirandolina Tasch-Fernandes, eds. *Autriche, Suède et Finlande les nouvelles frontières du verre européen*. Milan: Skira Editore, 1995.

Nicolaysen, Nicolay. *Kunsten i hus*. Kristiania [Oslo]: Cammermeyer, 1872.

Näslund, Erik. *Dardel*. Stockholm: Författarförlaget, 1988.

Niilonen, Kertuu. *Finskt glas*. Helsinki, Finland: Tammi, 1966.

Noever, Peter, ed. *Josef Hoffmann, 1870–1956: Ornament Zwischen Hoffnung und Verbrechen*. Exhibition catalogue. Vienna: Museum fur Angewandte Kunst, 1987.

Nordström, Olof. *Svensk glasindustri, 1550–1960*. Report no. 41. Lund, Sweden: Geografiska Institutionen/ Lunds Universitet, 1962.

———. *Glasbruk och hyttor i Sverige, 1955–1855*. Smålands museum skriftserie, no. 2. Växjö, Sweden: Smålands museum, 1986.

———. "Vadstena kloster—Sveriges första glashytta?" *Glasteknisk tidskrift*, no. 1 (1988).

———. "Glas och glastillverkning i Sverige från medeltid till 1800-talets början." *Glasteknisk tidskrift*, no. 2 (1990), p. 53.

———. "1700-talet—glasets användning vidgas." *Glasteknisk tidskrift*, no. 3 (1991), p. 115.

———. *Kosta: främling i järnbruksbygd / Kosta, 1742–1942: 250 Years of Craftsmanship*. Malmö, Sweden: Kosta Boda, 1992.

Noréen, Sven E., and Henrik Graebe. *Henrikstorp: Det skånska glasbruket, 1691–1760*. Gothenburg, Sweden: Skånska Ättiksfabriken AB, 1964.

Novak, Barbara. *American Painting of the Nineteenth Century; Realism, Idealism, and the American Experience*. New York: Praeger, 1989.

Obrestad, Tor. *Hulda*. Oslo: Gyldendal, 1992.

Officiell Berättelse över Baltiska utställningen. Exhibition catalogue. Malmö, Sweden: Fölagsaktrebolages Malmö Boktryckerier, 1914.

Ollers, Edvin. "Konstnärerna och depressionen." *Ares årg* 11 (December 12, 1922).

———. Statens Konstnärshjälp." *Ares årg* 11 (March 8, 1923).

Olson, Alma Luise. "Functionalism in Swedish Arts and Crafts." *Industrial Art* (June 1932).

Olson, Gösta, [and Kristina Jacobsson]. *Från Ling till Picasso: En konsthandlares minnen*. Stockholm: Bonniers, 1965.

Olsson, Lars. *Då barn var lönsomma*. Stockholm: Tiden Förlag, 1980.

Olsson, S. E. *Social Policy and Welfare State in Sweden*. Lund, Sweden: Arkiv Förlag, 1990.

Orrefors Belysningsarmatur [sale catalogue]. Orrefors glasbruk, 1937.

"Orrefors Bruk." *Dekorative Kunst* 34 (1925/26), pp. 69–76.

Östberg, Ragnar. *Ett hem: Dess byggnad och inredning.* Stockholm: Bonniers, 1905.

Österblom, Bengt O. *Arvid Fougstedt.* Stockholm: Wahlström & Widstrand, 1946.

Paulsson, Gregor. "Anarki eller tidsstil." *Svenska Slöjdföreningens Tidskrift,* no. 11 (1915), pp. 1–12.

———. *Den nya arkitekturen.* Stockholm: Norstedt, 1916.

———. "Konst och industri." *Svenska Slöjdföreningens Tidskrift,* no. 14 (1918), pp. 11–21.

———. *Vackrare Vardagsvara.* Stockholm: Svenska Slöjdföreningen, 1919.

———. "Drag ur Svenska Slöjdföreningens Historia och Nuvarande Verksamhet." *Svenska Slöjdföreningens Tidskrift.* 16 (1920).

———, ed. *Svenska Slöjdföreningens Specialnummer 1.* Stockholm: AB Gunnar Tisells Förlag, 1921.

———. "Sverige i Paris." *Svenska Slöjdföreningens tidskrift* (1925), p. 107.

———. "Stockholmsutställningens Program." *Svenska Slöjdföreningens Tidskrift* 24 (1928).

——— et al. *acceptera.* Stockholm: Tidens Förlag, 1931.

———. "Stockholmsudstillingen 1930 som led i Samfundsarbejdet." *Nyt Tidsskrift for Kunstindustri* 4 (February 1931).

———. "Saklig form i bruksförmål." *Nyt Tidsskrift for Kunstindustri* 4 (July 1931).

———, ed. *Modernt Svenskt Glas: Utveckling. Teknik. Form.* Stockholm: Jonson & Winter Förlagsaktiebolag, 1943.

———. "Stilepok utan morgondag." *Fataburen: Nordiska Museets och Skansens årsbok.* (1968).

———. *Upplevt.* Stockholm, 1974.

Rapp, Birgitta. *Richard Bergh-Konstnär och kulturpolitiker, 1890-1915.* Stockholm: Tryck Gotab, 1978.

Rasmussen, Steen Eiler. *Das Nordische Baukunst.* Berlin: Wasmuth, 1940.

"Rationaliseringsutredningens betänkande." 2 parts. *Statens offentliga utredningar* 14 (1939).

Reihnér, Anders. *Sandviksglas, "Vackrare vardagsvara," 1918-1932.* Exhibition catalogue. Orrefors, Sweden: Orrefors Museum, 1987.

Remington, Preston. "Contemporary Swedish and Danish Decorative Arts." *Metropolitan Museum of Art Bulletin* 35 (May 1940).

Reuterswärd, Hélène. "Inredningen i Stockholms Konserthus." Ph.D. diss., Stockholm University, 1983.

Ricke, Helmut, and Ulrich Gronert, *Glas in Schweden, 1915-1960.* Munich: Prestel-Verlag, 1986.

——— and Lars Thor. *Schwedische Glasmanufakturen, Produktionskataloge / Swedish Glass Factories Production, Catalogues: 1915-1960.* German, English, and Swedish. Munich: Prestel-Verlag, [1987].

Romdahl, Axel L. "Konstindustrihallen i Göteborg." *Svenska Slöjdföreningens tidskrift* (1923), p. 113.

———. "Konsthantverket i Stockholms Konserthus," *Svenska Slöjdföreningens tidskrift* (1926), p. 9.

———. "Hantverket i Göteborgs Konserthus." *Form* (1935), p. 204.

Rothstein, B. *Den korporative staten.* Stockholm: Norstedts, 1992.

Rudberg, Eva. *Sven Markelius, Architect.* Stockholm: Arkitektur Förlag, 1989.

Runbloom, Harald, and Hans Norman, eds. *From Sweden to America: A History of the Migration.* Studia historica Upsaliensia 74. Minneapolis: University of Minnesota Press, 1976.

Schiuller, Bernt. "Storstrejken 1909: Forhistoria och orsaker." *Studia historica Gothoburgensia* 9 (1967).

Schlüter, Mogens, et al. *Dansk glas, 1825-1925.* Copenhagen: Nyt Nordisk Forlag, 1979.

Schnitler, Carl W. *Kunsten og den gode form.* Oslo: Gyldendal, 1927.

Schön, Lennart. *Industrialismens förutsättningar.* Lund, Sweden: Liber Förlag, 1983.

Schulze, Franz. *Philip Johnson: Life and Work.* New York: A. A. Knopf, 1994.

Scott, Franklin D. *Sweden: The Nation's History.* Epilogue by Steven Koblik. Revised edition. Carbondale and Edwardsville, Ill.: Southern Illinois University Press, 1988.

Seela, Jacob. *Kring Finlands äldre glasindustri-Flaskor och buteljer under 200 år.* Annual report. Turku, Finland: Åbo stadshistoriska museum, 1970-71.

Seitz, Heribert. *Glaset förr och nu.* Stockholm: Albert Bonniers Förlag, 1933.

———. "Cedersbergs glasbruk och dess tillberkningar, 1781-1938." Offprint, *Meddelanden från Östergötlands Fornminnes—och Museiförening* (1933-34).

———. *Äldre svenska glas med graverad dekor—En undersökning av det bevarade 1700-talsbeståndet.* English summary. Nordiska Muséets handbook no. 5. Stockholm: Nordiska muséet, 1936.

Selkurt, Claire Elaine. "The Classical Influence in Early Twentieth Century Danish Furniture Design." Ph.D. diss. University of Minnesota, 1979.

Serota, Karen. "The Story of Cranbrook." Manuscript, The Cranbrook Academy of Art, Bloomfield, Michigan, 1950.

Shand, P. Morton. "Stockholm 1930." *Architectural Review* 68 (1930), pp. 67–72.

———. "Svenska paviljongen i Paris sedd genom engelska ögon / The Swedish Pavilion in Paris Through English Eyes." *Form* (1937), pp. 153 ff.

Sigrid Hjertén. Exhibition catalogue no 430. Stockholm: Liljevalchs Konsthall, 1995.

Silfverstolpe, Göran M. *Vera Nilsson.* Publication 95. Stockholm: Sveriges Allmänna Konstförening, 1986.

Skawonius, Sven-Erik, and Gregor Paulsson. "Glas från Kosta." *Form* (1934), p. 234.

Skedsmo, Tone. "Hos kunstnere, polarforskere og mesener." *Kunst og Kultur* 65 (1982), pp. 131–51.

Söderberg, Rolf. *Otte Sköld.* Stockholm: Sveriges Allmänna Konstföreningen, 1968.

———. *Den svenska konsten under 1900–talet.* Revised and updated. Stockholm: Aldus/Bonnier, 1970.

"Specimens of Modern Glassware in the Exhibition of Swedish Contemporary Decorative Arts on View Temporarily at the Metropolitan Museum of Art, New York." *The Glass Industry* (March 1927), p. 65 ff.

Stavenow, Åke. "Sverige i Paris." *Form* (1937), p. 126.

——— et al., eds. *Swedish Arts and Crafts: Swedish Modern, A Movement Towards Sanity in Design.* Translated by Gosta E. Sandström. New York: The Royal Swedish Commission, New York World's Fair, 1939.

———. "Världsutställningarna och New York World's Fair, 1939." *Form* (1939), p. 72.

Stavenow-Hidemark, Elisabet. "Hygienism kring sekelskiftet." *Fataburen: Nordiska Museets och Skansens årsbok* (1970), pp. 47–54.

———. "Hemmet som konstverk. Heminredning i teori och praktik på 1870-och 80-talen." *Fataburen: Nordiska museets och Skansens årsbok* (1984), pp. 129–48.

———. "Hur Svenskt Var Det Svenska?" *Fataburen: Nordiska Museets och Skansens årsbok* (1991), pp. 44–64.

Steenberg, Elisa. "Svenskt adertonhundratalsglas: en konsthistorisk studie." Ph.d. diss. Stockholm University, 1953.

Stella, Guido Balsamo. "Cristalli di Svezia." *Dedalo* (May 1921), pp. 822–30.

"Stockholmsutställningens Program." *Svenska Slöjdföreningens Tidskrift* (1928), pp. 109–116.

Stockholmsutställningen 1930 av konstindustri, konsthandverk och hemslöjd. Exhibition catalogue. Uppsala, Sweden: Almquist & Wiksells boktryckeri, 1930.

Stritzler-Levine, Nina, ed. *Josef Frank, Architect and Designer: An Alternate Vision of the Modern Home.* Contributions by Leon Botstein et al. New Haven and London: Bard Graduate Center for Studies in the Decorative Arts/Yale University Press, 1996.

Svenska Glasbruksföreningen SHF-SG, 1912–1962. Växjö, Sweden: Svenska Glasbruksföreningen, 1962.

Svenska Slödföreningens Hemutställning. Exhibition catalogue. Stockholm: Liljevalchs förlag, 1917.

Svenska Slöjdföreningen Konstindustriutställning. Exhibition catalogue. Gothenburg, Sweden: Svenska Slöjdföreningen, 1923.

Svenska textilier, 1890–1990 (Lund, Sweden: Signum, 1994.

Svenskt Industri. Stockholm: Industriförbundet, 1948.

Taylor, Arthur J., ed., *The Standard of Living in Britain in the Industrial Revolution* (London: Methuen, 1980).

Tenow, Elna. *Solidar.* 3 vols. Stockholm, 1905-07.

Thor, Lars. *Legend i Glas: En bok om Vicke Lindstrand.* Stockholm: Liber Förlag, 1982.

Thunholm, Lars-Erik. *Ivor Kreuger.* Stockholm: Fischer, 1995.

Topelius, Ann-Sofi. *Glas från Cedersbergs glasbruk.* Exhibition catalogue. Linköping, Sweden: Länsmuséet, 1981.

Vikström, Eva. *Industrimiljöer på landsbygden. Riksantikvarieämbetet.* Stockholm, 1995.

Wägner, Elin. "Revolution." *Svenska Slöjdföreningens Tidskrift* 25 (1929).

Wallander, Alf. "Om Smaken i Våra Svenska Hem." *Varia* 11 (1900), pp. 727–31.

Wängberg-Eriksson, Kristina. *Josef Frank, Livsträd i krigets skugga.* Lund, Sweden: Signum, 1994.

Weber, Nikolas Fox. *Patron Saints: Five Rebels Who Opened America to a New Art, 1928–1943.* New York: Alfred A. Knopf, 1992.

Weibull, Jörgen, *Swedish History in Outline.* Stockholm: The Swedish Institute, 1993.

Weinberg, Barbara, Doreen Bolger, and David Park Curry. *American Impressionism and Realism: the Painting of Modern Life, 1885–1915.* Exhibition catalogue. New York: Metropolitan Museum of Art/Harry N. Abrams, 1994.

Westberg, Bengt. "Casimirsborgs glasbruk, 1757–1811: En industri i Tjust för 175 år sedan." *Tjustbygden Kulturhistoriska Förenings Årsbok* (1961), pp. 5–6.

Westman, Carl. "Totalomdöme." *Svenska Slöjdföreningens Tidskrift*, no. 12 (1917), pp. 69–72.

Wettergren, Erik. "Varia." *Svenska Slöjdföreningens Tidskrift*, no. 10 (1914), pp. 132–43.

———. *L'Art décoratif moderne en Suède*. Malmö, Sweden: Malmö Museum, 1925.

———. *The Modern Decorative Arts of Sweden*. Translated by Tage Palm. Edited by Edward Russel. London: Country Life, 1927.

Wharton, Edith, and Ogden Codman. *The Decoration of Houses* (1902). Reprint. New York; Norton, 1978.

Widman, Dag. "Edvin Ollers—en av 1917 års män." *Form* 3/4 (1960).

———. *Konsthantverk, konstindustri, design 1895–1975.* Stockholm, 1975.

Wilson, Richard Guy, Dianne H. Pilgrim, and Dickran Tashjian. *The Machine Age in America, 1918–1941*. Exhibition catalogue. New York: The Brooklyn Museum/Harry N. Abrams, 1986.

"Wirkung und Asthetik in der Raumkunst." *Dekorative Kunst* 34 (1925/26).

Wittrock, Ulf. *Ellen Keys väg från kristendom till livstro.* Uppsala, Sweden: Appelbergs, 1953.

Wollin, Nils G. "Elektrisk belysningsarmatur." *Svenska Slöjdföreningens tidskrift* (1928).

———. *Modern Swedish Decorative Art*. London: The Architectural Press, 1931.

Wurts, Richard. *The New York World's Fair 1939/1940*. New York: Dover Publications, 1977.

Xet Sven Erixcon i Tumba och Stockholm: Lärling, gesäll, målare. Stockholm: Stadsmuseum, 1995.

Zickerman, Tage. "Nutida Glaskonst." *Svenska Slöjdföreningens Tidskrift* (1927), pp. 1–46.

INDEX

This index comprises references for chapters 1 through 10. Life dates for the principal figures mentioned in the text are included. The Catalogue of the Exhibition, beginning on page 156, is not indexed.

Photocredits

Photographs in chapters one through ten are courtesy of the collections, archives, or other sources listed in the captions; individual photographers or photograph services are listed below.

Cranbrook Archives, Nyholm: fig. 10-5; Florman & Halldin: figs. 4-7, 8-8, 8-9; Owe Hedman, fig. 6-8; Holmén: fig. 4-12; Per Larsson: fig. 7-1 to 7-5, 7-8; Ingvar Lindh: fig. 6-1, 7-6, 7-7, 7-9 to 7-13; Gunnar Lundh: figs. 2-4, 2-6, 2-7; Nordiska Museets arkiv, Stockholm: fig. 6-2; Bertil Olsson. figs. 6-3, 6-9; Photograph Studio, The Metropolitan Museum of Art: figs. 10-1, 10-2, 10-3, 10-8, 10-12; Max Plunger: figs. 9-5, 9-10; John Selbing: figs. 9-3, 9-4, 9-6 to 9-8, 9-12, 9-15, 9-16; Småland museums arkiv: figs. 6-6, 6-7, 6-10 to 6-14; Stockholm Information Service: fig. 1-1; Svensk Form, Bildarkivet, Stockholm: figs. 4-4, 4-6, 4-11, 8-10; Bruce White: fig. 4-10

Catalogue of the Exhibition: Jan Alanco: fig. 103a' Per Bergström: cat. nos. 4, 5, 9, 17, 18, 19, 22, 30, 32, 44, 52, 66, 68, 78, 87, 123, 124, 135; Per Larsson: cat. nos. 1, 2, 3, 6, 7, 8, 10, 14, 15, 16, 20, 21, 23, 24, 25, 26, 27, 28, 29, 34, 35, 37, 40, 41, 45, 46, 47, 48, 50, 51, 53, 54, 57, 59, 60, 61, 62, 63, 64, 65, 67, 71, 72, 73, 74, 75, 76, 80, 81, 82, 83, 84, 85, 86, 88, 89, 90, 91, 92, 93, 94, 95, 96, 97, 99, 100, 101, 103, 104, 105, 106, 108, 109, 110, 111, 112, 114, 115, 116, 117, 120, 121, 122, 125, 126, 127, 128, 129, 130, 131, 132, 133, 134, 137, 138, 139, 140, 142, 143, 144, 145, 147, 148, 149, 150, 151, 152, 154, 155, 156, 157.; Musée d'Art Moderne de la Ville de Paris: cat. no. 42; Museum of Art, Rhode Island School of Design: cat. no. 107; Nationalmuseum, Stockholm: cat. nos. 13, 69, 79, 98, 102, 153; Bertil Olsson: cat. nos. 33, 38, 39, 49, 70, 78, 119; Royal Ontario Museum: cat. no. 55; The Art Institute of Chicago: cat. no. 31; The Cleveland Museum of Art: cat. no. 146; The Detroit Institute of Arts: cat. no. 56; The Metropolitan Museum of Art: cat. nos. 58, 141; The Oslo Museum of Applied Arts: cat. nos. 11, 12, 113; Bruce White: cat. no. 36